AN
# ASSAULT
ON
# POVERTY

RELATED PUBLICATIONS

Gender Working Group, United Nations Commission on Science and Technology for Development. 1995. Missing links: gender equity in science and technology for development. International Development Research Centre, Ottawa, ON, Canada. (ISBN 0-88936-765-5)

Panel on Integrated Land Management, United Nations Commission on Science and Technology for Development. 1997. On solid ground: science, technology, and integrated land management. International Development Research Centre, Ottawa, ON, Canada. (ISBN 0-88936-820-1)

# AN
# ASSAULT
## ON
# POVERTY

BASIC HUMAN NEEDS,
SCIENCE, AND
TECHNOLOGY

*Panel on Technology for Basic Needs*

*United Nations Commission on
Science and Technology for Development*

INTERNATIONAL DEVELOPMENT RESEARCH CENTRE
UNITED NATIONS CONFERENCE ON TRADE AND DEVELOPMENT

*Published jointly by the*

International Development Research Centre
PO Box 8500, Ottawa, ON, Canada K1G 3H9

*and the*

United Nations Conference on Trade and Development
Palais des Nations, CH-1211 Geneva 10, Switzerland

**Canadian Cataloguing in Publication Data**

United Nations. Commission on Science and Technology for Development.
Panel on Technology for Basic Needs

An assault on poverty: basic human needs, science, and technology

Co-published by United Nations Conference on Trade and Development.

Includes bibliographical references.
ISBN 0-88936-800-7

1. Basic needs — Planning.
2. Sustainable development — Planning.
3. Technology — Planning.
I. International Development Research Centre (Canada).
II. United Nations Conference on Trade and Development.
III. Title.

HC79.B38U54 1997          338.91          C97-900030-0


A microfiche edition is available.

# Contents

# Foreword

After 2 years of intense and innovative efforts, the Panel on Technology for Small-scale Economic Activities to Address the Basic Needs of Low-income Populations (the "Panel on Technology for Basic Needs") of the new United Nations Commission on Science and Technology for Development (CSTD) is presenting its findings. After recent international summits and decisions, CSTD was entrusted with debating and laying down guidelines for one of the most complex and delicate problems of contemporary life: the role of science and technology (S&T) in development.

The CSTD benefited from the presence of dozens of experts from the member states; the advice of specialists of the highest calibre; the contributions of multilateral, governmental, and nongovernmental organizations (NGOs); the support of the United Nations, the Secretariat, and its finest professionals; the guidance of the Friends of the Chair (see Appendix II); the efficiency of an active bureau; and unprecedented preparatory activity.

Barely 50 years have gone by since the United Nations was created, and during this time the world has made great headway in acquiring the instruments needed to pursue fraternal solidarity. Thanks to technology, cultures are communicating with each other, learning about each other, interacting day to day, and conveying invaluable information to each other via electromagnetic waves across the air and through outer space. Nevertheless, everyone must recognize that in this surge of modernity, we have left by the wayside profound problems related to equity and justice. Here is where the CSTD sees the challenge to be met in the next 50 years — or, we hope, much sooner, because despair and hopelessness are already all too prevalent in many parts of the world. Today, one fifth of the people in the world are literally starving, one fourth do not even have potable water, and one third live in a state of extreme poverty — all this amid the greatest accumulation of knowledge and productivity in history. Three decades ago, the income of the most affluent fifth of the population was greater than that of the poorest fifth by a factor of 30 to 1. Today, this factor has reached 60 to 1. Is that reality sustainable?

Everyone knows that S&T is present in one way or another behind the bright and dark spots of the new world reality. The evolution of productive forces has broken down old structures and built, or sometimes destroyed, strategies for living throughout broad areas of our social geography. Thus, the major issues CSTD faced were poverty, gender, and land. What a challenge it had, at a time when the state, the market, and science were in crisis. And yet, although the problems may be great, what is greater than the United Nations? Although everyone may feel humbled by the dimensions of the issues, no one is humbler than those in the S&T community, who, despite their ability to discover the big bang and to probe the core of the atom, are the first to acknowledge that S&T is still in its infancy.

A complete vision of the whole can perhaps be achieved by a renewed science, one that places the human being at the centre of the universe so that humans can become the active builders and shapers of a universe that is also evolving and that many cultures view as transcending the purely material. This should be a simple science that recognizes complexity and draws nourishment from all sources and creates a capacity for doing so. The complex present-day panorama prompts us to seek a globalizing science that will include not only the know-how of instruments but also the know-what of the researcher, the know-who of the actors, and the know-why of the values. We must now break down the walls separating praxis and the holistic approach, the barriers separating science and art, and the gaps between rich and poor, man and woman, technology and ethics. We are all dwellers in a common home. We are all strands in that tightly knit web of fate, woven of reciprocal links and responsibilities so deeply shared that where there is no justice for some, there is no justice for all.

The universe is not linear; nor is a human being. But science, in an act of faith, can re-embark on an inquiry concerning the lost wholeness of its origins and aims. Science emerged to give people the opportunity to find opportunities, and it has always cultivated the ethic of sharing the options of the present with the people of the future — what is now known as sustainability. Therefore, the two directions of change should be toward being and toward the universe, which means moving ahead along parallel tracks using the principles of anthropocentrism and ecosystems. These are the complementary lines of endeavour that constitute what is now called sustainable human development. This means investing in the debate between cultural heritage and instrumental reason. In the field of instrumental reason, scientists and technologists have a great deal to offer toward the building of bridges raised by agents of change. Agents of change are organizing networks of unexpected energy among indigenous peoples, generational or gender groups, local communities, and NGOs to help close the gaps. We can support their quest to acquire a greater understanding of their fellows and their environment and to interact better with them, not only to satisfy their basic needs but also to find their place again in a changing world, reaffirming their own sense of identity. What force, if not knowledge, can strengthen individual and collective values and reverse the present trends?

History teaches us that something can always be done, that human beings can always find answers to problems in their stubborn struggle for survival. The findings of the CSTD can be of service to all.

*Oscar Serrate*
Chair, United Nations Commission on
Science and Technology for Development

# Preface

Poverty has been a bane of humanity for all of recorded history, so much so that it has been accepted as a permanent feature of human existence without attracting the moral indignation and practical revulsion that it should. The globalization of prosperity and overconsumption has produced the globalization of poverty and despair. This, in turn, has created a growing awareness of the human, material, and environmental waste that accompanies poverty. Poverty has grown and spread to such an extent that it now threatens social and political stability and is a serious block to the attainment of sustainable development. Fortunately, with the worldwide recognition of the extent and depth of the problem have come the knowledge, skill, and capital to eradicate this blight of human insensitivity.

In 1993, the Economic and Social Council of the United Nations, in recognition of these facts, instructed the Commission on Science and Technology for Development (CSTD) to examine the use of technology for small-scale economic activities to address the basic needs of low-income populations. Subsequently, CSTD established the Panel on Technology for Basic Needs (PTBN), from CSTD's members, to conduct an in-depth study of this issue and to report to the second session of the CSTD, held in May 1995.

PTBN adopted a new working style: its members not only reviewed existing data but also conducted studies and provided information on the topic from experiences in their own countries during the intersessional period. The United Nations Conference on Trade and Development (UNCTAD) Secretariat was accordingly called on to review the work conducted by the United Nations on this subject and to support, in general, the activities of PTBN. PTBN, therefore, took full responsibility for the results of and inferences drawn from this endeavour. This departure from the customary Secretariat-designed and Secretariat-written reports introduced a new vigour, dedication, and cohesion among PTBN members and the single-mindedness to ensure that the agreed recommendations would be implemented in a timely fashion. A reflection of the new working style was the involvement of the prime minister of Jamaica, who, at the March 1995 Social Summit held in Copenhagen, devoted a substantial portion of his speech to the findings of the PTBN.

This publication is a compilation of the more important findings of the intersessional exercise, embodying all the consultants' reports, all the contributions from countries and the United Nations agencies, and the overall report of the UNCTAD Secretariat on the United Nations activities. From this extensive review and contemporary studies, a picture has emerged of the intricate complexity of the poverty problem. This work clearly indicates the magnitude, ubiquitousness, and incisiveness of the problem and places it squarely at the front of the international agenda. These efforts must not be seen as the end but rather as the beginning of a process to tackle one of the most reprehensible and intractable problems of humanity.

The most compelling of the facts emerging from this compilation is that the resources exist to relieve both absolute and relative poverty and that a major reason for the failed attempts of the past was in mistaken notions about the causes of poverty and the fact that science and technology (S&T) was not considered a vital factor in their eradication. Perhaps for the first time, S&T has provided a range of options for seriously tackling the global poverty problem. The factors needed in the quest for a solution are social and political will, sufficient moral purpose, enlightened self-interest, and acceptance of the unity of all members of the human family and its precarious position on this planet.

Rather than subscribing to the notion that the issue of poverty is a mere distraction from issues of economic well-being, political disenchantment, and environmental rescue, this work makes poverty central to these issues. Furthermore, there is mounting evidence that the general breakdown of human security and hopes for the future have much to do with poverty and injustice. It is hoped that the facts and ideas in these pages will convince leaders and functionaries in the S&T community that banishing poverty is an urgent and worthwhile objective of research, experimental development, and technological investment. S&T that serves only the interests of a small fraction of humanity is S&T that has betrayed its promise and limited its options.

*Arnoldo K. Ventura*
Chair, Panel on Technology for Basic Needs

# Acknowledgments

### United Nations Economic and Social Council

### Friends of the Chair
F. Antezana, M.R. Bhagavaan,
A. Bhalla, C. Brundenius,
T. Salazar de Buckle, M.S. Swaminathan,
M.S. Zehni, C.M.Correa,
M. Simai, S. Lanfranco

### United Nations Conference on Trade and Development Secretariat

**Deputy to the Secretary-General**
Carlos Fortin

**Division for Science and Technology**
Pedro Roffe, Gloria-Veronica Koch,
Vladimir Pankov, Dieter Koenig,
Taffere Tesfachew, Maurizio Dal Ferro

**Secretarial Support**
Dominique Borvo, Estela Erb-Paniagua

### Government of the Netherlands

### International Development Research Centre

**President:** Keith Bezanson
**Assistant:** Geoffrey Oldham
**Administration:** Louise Brouzes
**Publications:** Bill Carman
and all the staff

### This book

### United Nations Commission on Science and Technology for Development

**Chair:**
Oscar Serrate (Bolivia)

**Bureau:**
Vladimir A. Labounov (Belarus),
Mohamed M. El Halwagi (Egypt),
Jawaharlal Dhar (India),
J. George Waardenburg (Netherlands)

### Panel on Technology for Basic Needs

**Chair:** Arnoldo Ventura (Jamaica)
Oscar Serrate (Bolivia),
Geoffrey Oldham (Canada),
Niels E. Busch (Denmark),
Getaneh Yiemene (Ethiopia),
Mikoto Usui (Japan),
Fauzi El Mugassabi (Lybia),
George M. Mhango (Malawi),
J. George Waardenburg (Netherlands),
Messanvi Gbeassor (Togo),
Stephen P. Kagoda (Uganda),
Serguei Yampolsky (Ukraine)

### Initiative 2000

**Members of the Board**
Alfred Matter, Antonieta Matter, Jesus Schabib,
Mabel Schabib, Sergio Palacios,
Jose Luis Martin, Jackeline Serrate

**Consultants**
Gustavo Fernandez (Bolivia),
Dilmus James (United States),
Martin E.D. Henry (Jamaica),
Francisco R. Sagasti (Peru)

**Secretarial Support**
Paola Dugue, Evelyn Villagomez

### Thanks to all

Part I

# The Panel on
# Technology for Basic Needs

Chapter 1[1]

# Science and Technology for Basic Needs: A Bridge

*The Panel on Technology for Basic Needs*

Technological progress has been responsible for vast improvements in the physical conditions and living standards of the majority of the world's population. Although technologically the world has never been in a better position to improve the conditions of the very poor, roughly 20% of the world's population have not benefited materially from advances in technology. The basic needs of this portion of the population remain a critical problem.

The Panel on Technology for Basic Needs (PTBN) seeks to refocus the world's attention on this grave question. PTBN has defined basic needs as the minimal requirements to sustain life — adequate nutrition, health care, water, and sanitary facilities — as well as access to education and information that enable individuals and communities to be productive and to make rational use of the available basic goods and services. The members of PTBN agreed that priority should be given to technology strategies, approaches, and policies, rather than to specific technologies, and that a pragmatic and pluralistic approach should be taken to investigate the potential of diverse technologies. In reviewing experience with basic-needs programs as well as relevant work on technology and basic needs carried out by the United Nations, PTBN found

---

[1] This chapter is an edited version of the report of the Panel on Technology for Small-scale Economic Activities to Address the Basic Needs of Low-income Populations, which was submitted to the second session of the Commission on Science and Technology for Development in May 1995 (document E/CN.16/1995/2).

that scant attention had been given to the role of technology in alleviating poverty. One problem was the failure to replicate successful programs; another was the failure to make a systematic effort to apply technology to basic needs. Nevertheless, PTBN found that nations that had launched determined and protracted campaigns to provide for basic needs were, in a number of cases, able to demonstrate progress.

PTBN defined the fundamental objective of technology for basic needs as creating conditions in which the poor can generate, understand, have access to, and creatively use technologies to satisfy their basic needs. The panel emphasized the importance of six bridging elements or "pillars" linking technology to basic-needs satisfaction: education, access to information, participation, health, basic infrastructure, and small-scale economic activities. Special recommendations for action were formulated for these elements and for a science and technology (S&T) policy for basic needs.

Among the recommendations were the following:

▼ The promotion of a conference to sensitize the S&T community and policy- and decision-makers to the issue of using S&T for basic needs;

▼ Periodic reviews of basic-needs programs;

▼ The monitoring of basic-needs indicators;

▼ A mechanism to evaluate different countries' S&T policies to determine how adequately issues of basic-needs satisfaction are being addressed;

▼ A one-stop service to refer people to information networks;

▼ The strengthening of networking of S&T institutions and enterprises of both private and public sectors at the national and international levels;

▼ Programs to deliver credit to micro-, small-, and medium-scale enterprises (MSMEs);

▼ A pilot program, involving countries from different regions, to report to the Commission on Science and Technology for Development (CSTD); and

▼ A series of sessions involving CSTD, as well as a joint session of CSTD and the Commission on Human Rights, at which to address technology for basic needs.

The concern with technology for basic needs is motivated by the grave and widening fissure between the very poor, representing approximately 20% of the world's population, and the remaining majority. Closely associated with this growing gulf is the serious discontinuity between the day-to-day existence of those living with basic-needs deficiencies and the corpus of knowledge concerning S&T. The predominant theme throughout this book is devising bridging mechanisms to give the very poor the access to technology enjoyed by most of the planet's population.

The problem of unmet basic needs is intimately connected with other worrisome facets of the human condition, one of which is the fact that the majority of the world's very poor are women and the children and elderly who ordinarily depend on them. This is a telling symptom of fissures along gender lines. The disconnection between humanity and nature is leading to mounting ecological and environmental problems, some of which affect regions far beyond the countries in which the problems originate. Once again the question of basic needs is relevant, because some of the most egregious ecological degradation is in regions of extreme poverty. Sustainable human development is patently incompatible with these widening gulfs. Fashioning, maintaining, and improving an adequate bridge is a prerequisite to the long-term improvement of the human condition. The bridge emphasized in this report, namely that between S&T and basic needs, is closely associated with and complementary to measures designed to resolve gender and environmental difficulties.

## The Panel on Technology for Basic Needs

### Its origin

At its first session, in April 1993, CSTD identified as one of the themes for its intersessional work the issue of technology for small-scale economic activities to address the basic needs of low-income populations. In accord with Economic and Social Council (ECOSOC) resolution 1993/320, CSTD established a panel of its own members (the PTBN) to prepare a draft report on this issue for consideration by CSTD as a whole at its next session. Additionally, ECOSOC resolution 1993/74, on the future work plan of CSTD, indicated that PTBN should build on relevant studies from inside and outside the United Nations, including studies by the regional commissions, the United Nations Conference on Trade and Development (UNCTAD), the United Nations Industrial Development Organization (UNIDO), the International Labour Organization (ILO), the Food and Agriculture Organization of the United Nations, the World Bank, and the regional development banks.

## Its focus

At its first meeting, PTBN defined its task as a review of technology as it pertained to basic needs and discussed how fresh approaches to S&T could ensure that the basic needs of low-income populations were met. Following up on CSTD suggestions, PTBN decided to focus on food production and processing; education, especially technical and vocational training; and health care. The panel decided to give priority to technology strategies, approaches, and policies rather than to specific technologies and to emphasize, in accordance with ECOSOC resolution 1993/74, dissemination mechanisms (including training and regional and international cooperation), as well as capacity-building and research and development (R&D) activities.

## Its methods

PTBN held sessions on 2–3 June and 17–18 October 1994 and 18–20 January 1995. PTBN consists of interested representatives from CSTD member countries. Arnoldo Ventura, a member of CSTD and special S&T adviser to the prime minister of Jamaica, was elected chair of PTBN. Representatives of a number of international organizations also participated in the panel's deliberations (see Appendix I). PTBN's work has been based on input from its members and international organizations and on issue papers prepared by international consultants. At PTBN's request, the UNCTAD Secretariat reviewed the work of the United Nations and selected organizations dealing with technologies for basic needs (see Chapter 9). This material, together with deliberations and the exchange of views at PTBN meetings, has served as the basis for the present report. PTBN wishes to record its gratitude for the generous contribution of the Government of the Netherlands to this work and for the valuable support of the experts among the Friends of the Chair (see Appendix II).

# Basic needs in a changing landscape

## The concept of basic needs

Basic needs have been defined in different ways. Stewart (1985, p. 1) sees the best approach to basic needs as

> one which gives priority to meeting the basic needs of all of the people. The actual content of basic needs have [sic] been variously defined: they always include the fulfilment of certain standards of nutrition (food and water) and the

*universal provision of health and education services. They sometimes also cover other material needs, such as shelter and clothing, and non-material needs, such as employment, participation and political liberty.*

A review of the literature and case studies has shown that a considerable amount of work has been devoted to the basic-needs issue, predominantly attempts to identify and quantify features of basic needs and evaluate programs designed to meet them. Studies have concentrated on methodological and statistical aspects of basic needs, such as elaborating on specific country, regional, or sectoral data; identifying population segments lacking goods and services; outlining the characteristics of basic needs; searching for indicators to measure the extent of those needs; attempting to define common ground and understanding that could help in formulating targeted policies; and evaluating countries' performance in meeting basic needs. The role of technology in meeting basic needs — its application and diffusion and its policy-related aspects — scarcely appeared in this material.

## Current developments

The planet has experienced sweeping technological, economic, political, and social change over the past two decades. This has affected the fundamental nature of the problem of poverty and, to a great extent, impinged on the possibility of realizing sustainable human development. The distribution of power shifts both within and among nations. Countries in transition to a market economy are seeking to redirect resources for S&T (Yampolsky 1994). Although potent interactions and feedback mechanisms operate among these facets of the new landscape, technological change is the primary driving force. Technology is changing the structure of production all over the world and, in consequence, affecting such economic variables as comparative advantages, international division of labour, income levels, productivity, employment, skill profiles, and patterns of international commerce. With microelectronic innovations in the vanguard and modern biotechnology and new materials science rapidly coming on stream, newly emerging technologies are affecting the human condition and prospects profoundly. These emerging technologies are more mobile, flexible, and knowledge intensive than ever but less energy and resource intensive. Also, although technology transfer remains important, it is now subordinated to the desire to accumulate more domestic technological capabilities, an aspect that did not carry quite the same weight in earlier basic-needs programs.

The ability to become competitive domestically and internationally is all-compelling: in the new global economy, virtually every

country has made some move toward deregulating its domestic economy and liberalizing its trade regime. Many nations have accomplished
drastic shifts toward more market-oriented, outward-looking economic
systems. On the world political scene, a significant movement toward
democratization and the assertion of human rights is taking place, and
this presents new avenues and opportunities for formulating policies
directed toward satisfying basic needs. Democracy tends to decentral-
ize political control; it also signals a more propitious atmosphere for
widening and deepening involvement with poor populations. Moreover, democracy has created a more favourable climate for linking
basic-needs satisfaction with human rights. Taken together, economic
liberalization and political democratization point to reduced reliance
on paternalistic, top-down approaches in favour of policies encouraging
the broader participation of key actors, including the poor. Closely
related to this is the current trend to encourage decentralized decision-
making and problem-solving, a trend laden with both challenges and
opportunities for effectively broaching the subject of deficiencies in
basic-needs satisfaction.

## Poverty, income polarization, and technological progress

Over the past several decades, technological progress, supported by the
new economic and political arrangements, has been responsible for
vast improvements in the physical conditions and living standards of
most of the world's population. This trend is substantiated by indicators
such as rising per capita income and life expectancy and declining
infant mortality. For millions of people, technological progress has satisfactorily resolved the basic-needs problem. Although technologically
the world has never been in a better position to improve the conditions
of very poor populations, roughly 20% of the world's population have
not benefited materially from advances in technology.

In many parts of the world the poor, especially poor women,
are losing ground in income and amenities relative to the remainder of
the population. During 1980–91, the least-developed countries experienced a rate of growth in per capita income of 0.7%, in contrast to a
rate of 2.1% in developed market economies. Meanwhile, the per
capita food production in least-developed countries actually declined
between 1980 and 1992 at an annual rate of 1.2% (UNCTAD 1994). The
World Food Council estimated that 550 million people in the world
were hungry in 1992, a number that jumps to around 1 billion when
those vulnerable during periods of hunger each year are included
(United Nations 1993). In 1981, the average per capita output in
developed countries was about 20 times greater than that in developing countries; by 1991 it was 22 times greater (United Nations 1993).

Looking at the polarization problem somewhat differently, the Economic Commission for Latin America and the Caribbean (ECLAC) estimated that in 1960 the world's highest income quintile received an average income 30 times higher than that of the lowest income quintile; in 1990 the disparity had grown to twice that much. ECLAC also estimated that 45.9% of Latin America's population lives below the poverty line, an increase of 2.5% since 1986, and 22% lives in extreme poverty (IDB and UNDP 1993). The World Bank (1993a) estimated that the number of people living on less than $1 per day (1985 prices)[2] rose from 1.051 billion in 1985 to 1.133 billion in 1990. In a news release following the recent International Monetary Fund–World Bank Summit in Madrid, the World Bank's president, Lewis Preston, pointed out that in the next generation 3 billion more people will be in desperate need of clean water, sanitation, electricity, and other basics. By no means is income polarization confined to the South. The United States Congressional Budget Office reported that between 1949 and 1989 the lowest income quintile saw a decrease of 10% in real income, whereas in the highest income percentile income increased by 105%. According to *The Economist* (4 June 1994), "since 1979 real income of the poorest 10 per cent has fallen in real terms while average income of the whole population rose by 25 per cent and that for the top 10 per cent of the population expanded by 50 per cent."

These conditions have contributed to a greater marginalization of poor populations and a feeling of alienation and hopelessness among them. The term *marginalization* is intended to convey that the poor are excluded and have no way to influence the distribution of power or resources to their benefit. It does not imply that they have no visibility or influence on the lives of those who are not poor. The basic-needs problem means that directly or indirectly, people who are not impoverished are open to a variety of detrimental impacts. They suffer a heightened sense of insecurity, run greater health risks, incur increasing expenses for personal protection, and pay higher taxes. Partly owing to technological advances (coupled with a greater emphasis on competitiveness) the middle class and elites of many nations already suffer from less job security and growing anxieties, augmented by the increasing violence and criminality of those with basic-needs deficiencies.

In the experiences of three least-developed countries — Ethiopia, Togo, and Uganda — the problem of extreme poverty is a dramatic feature (Gbeassor 1994; Kagoda 1994; Yiemene 1994). In Ethiopia, for example, almost 51% of the population lives below the absolute poverty line. Other salient aspects of these countries were the

---

[2] Unless otherwise indicated, all monetary values are expressed in US currency.

predominantly rural population and the extremely high proportion of youth under 15 years of age, resulting in a high level of dependency in the total population. The overwhelming majority of the economically active people in the rural areas and a great portion of those in the urban sector are self-employed. Health coverage and sanitary conditions are poor, and, accordingly, life expectancy is low, as is the number of educational facilities. Consideration of these aspects is fundamental to formulating a strategy for directing technology at the satisfaction of basic needs, which is almost synonymous with formulating national economic-development objectives.

Previous models for addressing the basic-needs problem have become inadequate. A sea change is occurring in important facets of the human condition, and this renders earlier models at least partially obsolete. People who are denied the opportunity to meet their basic needs are fiercely expressing their discontent. Increasingly, their situation presents the greatest challenge for socioeconomic development and has acquired environmental and national security dimensions. The Jamaican case (Chapter 4) demonstrates clearly that

> an assertive attack on the basic-needs problem needs to go far beyond the traditional poverty-alleviation strategies tried unsuccessfully in the past. A local basic-needs approach calls for a greater emphasis on domestic technological management, a greater absorptive capacity among the poor for the benefits of S&T, and a wider spread of the fruits of growth through decentralized production and consumption planning, as well as popular participation ....

Deleterious poverty-related effects are no longer compartmentalized in poor countries, and extreme poverty is adversely affecting the quality of life of all the world's people. The spirals of less security and more expenses, fractures along cultural, ethnic, religious, and social lines, and North-to-South interventions are unsustainable. This is primarily why a fresh strategy is sought for solving basic-needs deficiencies that is consonant with the new technological, economic, political, and social realities. Several other factors of great importance also figure in this context. First (and absolutely central to the discussion), market forces can and should be constructively and imaginatively employed in ameliorating abject poverty; however, to improve the conditions of the very poorest segments of society, extramarket interventions are a prerequisite. To achieve the goal of technology for basic needs, a fundamental condition is the fashioning of avenues, bridges, or linkages through which poor populations can breach the expanding knowledge and technology gap that perpetuates their economic, political, and sociocultural marginalization. Second, the focus must be squarely on human beings. Things, such as technology and knowledge, are important but only insofar as they relate to human beings and only to the extent that they are deployed and manipulated for the betterment of the human condition and further sustainable human development. Third, the process of combating basic-needs deficits is value laden: ethics and attitudes influence the chances and extent of success. A primary ethical element is the challenge to the global S&T community to recognize that with the capacity to make significant contributions to resolving basic-needs problems comes an associated responsibility and a moral obligation. The battle concerning attitudes will entail moving from passivity, a sense of inferiority, and a feeling of helplessness to active participation, with confidence based on collective and individual achievements and justifiable hope. These and perhaps other matters of value will interact powerfully with access to and deployment of S&T for the alleviation of poverty (see Chapters 3 and 7).

# Technology-related approaches to satisfying basic needs

This section briefly examines three technology-related approaches to solving basic-needs shortfalls. First, a review of experience in the informal sector indicates that a substantial number of micro- and small-scale enterprises (MSEs) could undertake technical innovations. Second, two alternative levels of technological sophistication — appropriate technology and technology blends — are singled out for review because they are explicitly dedicated to improving the living conditions of the poor. Third, an appeal is made for the use of technological pragmatism, an approach that does not automatically exclude any level of technological sophistication that might contribute to the cause of reducing basic-needs deficiencies. Finally, case studies are presented to illustrate a variety of experiences with the application of technology for basic needs.

## The informal sector

Traditionally, the informal sector has been associated with strategies for meeting basic needs because of three important factors:

> ▼ The role of this sector as producer and supplier of basic goods and services at prices affordable to the poorer section of the population;

▼ The capacity of the informal sector to absorb the rapidly growing urban labour force and generate income to enable the urban poor to satisfy their basic needs; and

▼ The informal sector's application of technologies appropriate to local factors.

These characteristics, together with easy entry into this sector and its size, structure, and adaptability, render the informal sector one of the most important components of any basic-needs strategy. This sector has recently been expanding and proliferating, particularly in urban areas. In some cases, especially where major trade and industrial-policy reforms have resulted in the contraction of the formal sector, the informal sector is providing most of the urban jobs and supplying goods and services essential to the poor. In African countries in particular, informal-sector activities now employ more people than the formal sector and provide higher incomes than do rural-sector activities.

The key questions are whether the technologies used in the informal sector are conducive to basic-needs satisfaction and, more important, whether this sector has the potential to undertake techno-logical upgrading. A collection of studies on the technological capabili-ties of Third World informal-sector enterprises in metal-engineering activities reveals that some firms are capable of accumulating capital, upgrading equipment to successively more sophisticated levels, con-structing hand-operated equipment or tools, developing new product designs, improving product quality, making inputs of new materials, investing in human capital, and, in some cases, producing the capital goods required by other informal-sector enterprises (Maldonado and Sethuraman 1992). A review of the literature has uncovered consider-able corroborative evidence of the innovative abilities of MSEs, enter-prises, many of which are in the formal sector (see Chapter 5). Despite some major handicaps, the informal sector can also exhibit innovative behaviour, which implies that under more favourable conditions tech-nological progress in the sector could be more robust and that the rate of graduation to the formal sector, which is now quite low, could be accelerated.

## Alternative technologies

Several levels of technological sophistication can be distinguished, although they cannot be defined in watertight compartments. Tradi-tional technologies are technologies employed over an extensive period and tend to be well adapted to local culture and habits. Con-ventional technologies are commercially viable technologies whose progress rests mainly on engineering innovations and scaling up for larger markets. Emerging technologies are relatively new and primarily science driven. In addition to these levels of technological sophistication, two others can be named: intermediate (or appropriate) technology and technology blends.

Intermediate technology, later designated *appropriate technology*, was popularized in the early 1970s as a level of technological sophistication somewhere between traditional and modern (conventional and emerging) technologies. The work that gave intermediate technology a strong following was that of Schumacher (1973). For early reviews of appropriate technology see Singer (1972), Bhagavan (1979), UNIDO (1979), and Jequier and Blanc (1983); for a later critique see Willoughby (1990).

There is no universally accepted definition of appropriate technology, but compared with modern technologies it usually has all or most of the following attributes: it is more labour intensive; its productivity is on a smaller scale; it is more ecologically friendly; it requires less demanding worker and managerial skills; it uses more local inputs; and it requires a lower investment per job created. Appropriate technology has been criticized for not accomplishing enough to benefit the poor. It had a checkered record in the early days, and all too often its successes were geographically very circumscribed or confined to a single application; the spread to alternative uses and the development of complementary innovations were not always evident. Yet, appropriate technology might well be a valuable tool for combating extreme poverty. High-impact appropriate technologies include systems for delivering micro loans, like those inspired by Bangladesh's Grameen Bank; bamboo-tube wells in southern Asia; and improved cook stoves in China. Furthermore, appropriate technology was once hampered by a disinclination to commercialize innovations and a tendency to connect such technology with a subjective vision of a proper lifestyle rather than with its effectiveness. Organizations promoting technological development in developing countries — such as the Intermediate Technology Development Group, Volunteers for International Technical Assistance, and scores of other agencies — appear to have largely overcome these shortcomings. The sizeable and growing arsenal of appropriate technologies should be taken seriously in any process of screening and selecting technologies for poverty-related projects.

Another approach, technology blends, began to be investigated about a decade later than appropriate technologies. Technology blending, as it is now customarily known, entails the constructive integration of emerging technology into low-income, small-scale economic activities in developing countries, with the important proviso that, as the word *blending* implies, the introduction of the emerging technology should blend with and preserve at least some of the prevailing traditional production techniques (Usui 1994). The original impetus for investigating technology blending came from the former United Nations Advisory Committee on Science and Technology, and a small but growing literature has resulted (von Weizsacker et al. 1983; Bhalla et al. 1984; Bhalla and James 1988; Colombo and Oshima 1989). The literature includes cases in which modern biotechnology, laser technology, new materials sciences, microelectronics innovations, satellite communications, and photovoltaic power have been blended with such traditional economic activities as smallholder agriculture, agribusiness, service delivery systems for the poor, informal urban enterprises, and small- and medium-scale manufacturing (see Chapter 5).

Current technology-blending efforts include the application of microelectronic innovations in traditional small-scale manufacturing in Latin America, "biovillage" and "information-village" projects in India, a variety of projects being implemented in Malaysia, and the development of artificial intelligence software suitable for solving problems in developing countries. As expected, some technology-blending efforts have run into difficulties, and some involve trade-offs to meet various goals; however, the incidence of clear successes appears to warrant more vigorous experimentation and increased efforts to alert the S&T community and the decision-makers in developing countries to the potential benefits of a marriage of indigenous and high technology.

## Technological pragmatism

Although appropriate technology and technology blending have been singled out for discussion because they are expressly geared to bettering the lot of the poor, it should be stressed that the application of conventional and emerging technologies can, under the proper conditions, provide the goods and services to satisfy basic needs: advanced technologies were involved in developing oral rehydration salts (ORS); sophisticated computer techniques were used to develop wind-powered generators for developing countries and to get the correct degree of porosity for small dams in India; frontier technology was applied in developing an environmentally friendly brick-firing kiln for small-scale brick producers in Mexico. Whether these and similar technological advances constitute examples of appropriate technology, technology blends, or emerging technology is considerably less important than the fact that they work effectively. What seems called for is a multilayered technological approach, that is, technological pluralism. This rests on the more fundamental principle of technological pragmatism — an eclectic search for the best technological means to satisfy basic needs given the prevailing set of constraints and opportunities inherent in each situation.

## Recent experiences

A few selected cases are summarized in this section to illustrate some of the efforts undertaken by developing countries to tackle basic-needs satisfaction. There is an emphasis on the dissemination and commercialization of technology and on the correlations between education and nutrition and between human-resources development and technology adaptation, innovation, and R&D.

With the advent of the green revolution during the 1960s and 1970s, an interesting situation occurred in the Punjab, an Indian agrarian state (Singh and BNDP 1983). The green revolution increased yields and brought overall prosperity to rural workers. Despite their limited land base, marginal and small farms of the Punjab were able to record almost as much total crop output and income per acre as their larger counterparts, primarily because of a much higher cropping intensity accomplished through a rational year-round use of family labour, which implies a highly skilled use of techniques and resources. The Punjab case shows that agricultural and industrial development and the application of technology are best viewed as interlinked and supportive. The growth of agricultural productivity was based on the application of science and the introduction of modern industrial inputs (for example, fertilizers and capital goods) and irrigation facilities. In this case, the Government of India played a major role in organizing the necessary agricultural inputs for the individual farmers through the credit facilities of state-supported cooperative societies. The government also financed the infrastructural framework: the roads and markets, the agricultural university, and the agricultural extension services.

The commercialization and diffusion of technology are taken up in detail in a recent study on transforming the Indian rural economy (Bhalla and Reddy 1994). An overview of cases reveals that in developing countries the people living below the poverty line do not have the purchasing power to express their demands through the market, nor can the market alone channel goods and services to people basically engaged in subsistence production. In these case studies it is recognized that markets and competition will increasingly provide a framework for more effectively organizing the production and distribution of goods and services. A synthesis is required to fully harness the advantages of the market and overcome its limitations — for example, its equity blindness, its environmental externalities, and its preoccupation with the short term. This recent study also stresses the magnitude of the technology gap between rural and urban sectors and the low levels of agricultural productivity, which reflect low levels of technology. Technology diffusion in the Indian rural sector has also been hindered by a lack of skills, largely owing to the so-called rural skill drain, and by a lack of adequate R&D projects designed to improve rural technology. However, some of the limitations suffered by small-scale producers in the rural sector — such as limited access to credit, information, services, and infrastructure — have been overcome by combining traditional and modern elements of technology through the technology-blending process. This includes initiatives for down-scaling modern technology to suit different levels of scale and energy and modes of production.

Although a battery of policy measures had been in operation for nearly 40 years in India, Bhalla and Reddy (1994) affirmed that this did not lead to rapid growth and technological transformation of the rural sector. A number of factors explain this, including the fact that various measures took the form of hidden subsidies, which may have discouraged innovation. One of the primary objectives of the policy measures was social welfare and employment; thus, governmental policies had been much less development oriented than desirable. Finally, Bhalla and Reddy also stressed the importance of a suitable macroeconomic policy environment. Such a policy is essential to generating demands for improved technologies to respond to rural-sector requirements.

Other experiences are reflected in case studies of Mexico (Szretter 1985) and Ecuador (Teekens 1988). In Mexico the strong correlation between educational level and undernourishment and the differences between the urban and the rural sectors are clear. For example, 41% of the heads of households in the malnourished groups had no formal education, and about half of them were economically active in agricultural tasks. The case study of Ecuador provides elements for analyzing that country's performance in meeting basic needs during 1970–82. The study includes recommendations for improved backward and forward linkages between agriculture and industry and for specialized industrial development to provide fertilizers and appropriate machinery to foster agricultural development. Such development is critical to overcoming the input-supply bottlenecks of agro-industries and food-processing industries, which also suffer from a general lack of interindustry integration. Rural industry is recognized as an important employer but lacks major technological development and faces infrastructural and marketing problems.

The case study of Ecuador also shows that in many consumer industries, linking up with various technological levels will be

necessary if the objectives of employment creation, income generation, and reduction of overall production deficits are to be met simultaneously. Too much emphasis on small-scale, labour-intensive
industry may lead to a sacrifice in growth objectives. It is further stated
(Teekens 1988, pp. 334–335) that

> in the case of milk and dairy products, small-scale rural
> industries may play an important role in rural income and
> employment generation, but modern small-scale and large-
> scale industries would be needed to provide adequate sup-
> plies of dairy products to satisfy a target level of domestic
> demand ... . In other sectors, modern small-scale industry
> could function at an intermediate technology level where
> growth and employment objectives are reconciled. Such
> options exist in both basic consumer goods (for example,
> processed meat, milking products, dairy products, clothing
> and shoes) and in intermediate goods industries (for exam-
> ple, textiles, leather, wood, metal products).

A selective type of import-substitution policy, based on a criterion of
meeting basic needs, is proposed. Such a selective policy must not discriminate against potential export industries. Finally, Teekens stressed
the role of an income-redistribution policy for low-income groups, particularly its importance in expanding the domestic market.

An analysis of the educational characteristics of technology
innovators in the small metalworks industry in Peru showed the importance of training for technology adaptation and innovation (Villarán de
la Puente 1989). Of a group of 13 successful entrepreneurs engaged in
activities connected with adaptation and innovation, nearly two thirds
(61%) had followed university studies for an average of about 5 years.
Seven had followed courses or technical careers for an average of
2 years. Only one of the entrepreneurs had not benefited from university or technical studies, although this entrepreneur had attended a secondary school that offered technical components in its curriculum.
Most of the entrepreneurs had had previous working experience in the
same field, which the author considered a form of training.

With regard to R&D and technological dissemination, an
important case study is that of the transfer and adaptation of a technology for milk substitution in the Andean Group. In the context of the
Technology Policy Group of the Junta del Acuerdo de Cartagena and
under the responsibility of Salazar de Buckle of the Andean Technological Development Projects, the final products were commercialized
under the name *Chicolac* (Guevara 1985). On the basis of multidiscipli-
nary and multinational teamwork, several technological alternatives
could be developed to solve critical nutritional problems in these developing regions. The experience reflected in this study proved that R&D

of new, inexpensive products for meeting the pressing needs of the majority of the population should be directed to solving clearly identified problems, should include studies of the characteristics of the economic sector and the consumers to be served, and should be supplemented by activities aimed at promoting the market for the resulting products.

## Conclusions

The cases reviewed in the previous section show a diversity in technology choice, economic policy orientation, and interaction among the parties involved. The evidence from successful initiatives suggests that meeting basic needs is intrinsically related, among other things, to making significant investment in education and health and to having clear priorities, including the targeting of the appropriate groups. Other contributing factors are the promotion of technology generation and R&D; diffusion and wider application of R&D results; development of infrastructure, support services, and adequate delivery systems; and a favourable macroeconomic environment.

The cases reviewed also indicate that satisfying the basic needs of the bulk of the population holds a key position in the development agendas of many developing countries, although it is far from being accomplished; indeed, in some cases efforts have deteriorated. However, the role that technologies play in satisfying basic needs has so far received only limited attention. To look forward, therefore, it is vital to examine the satisfaction of basic needs together with the role of technologies in production and services, including the contribution that new technologies can make to upgrading production processes and the knowledge base of skills. This appears to favour pluralistic and pragmatic approaches to technology. The case studies in this report call for not only the improvement of technology development and diffusion but also new "institutional blends" that will satisfy basic needs. These blends include diverse forms of partnerships among nongovernmental organizations (NGOs) and governmental and private-sector entities, such as the S&T research and teaching institutions. The studies stress the importance of a suitable macroeconomic policy environment embracing industrial and trade policies, investment approaches, and price policies to ensure favourable terms of trade for rural sectors. Specific technology policies are needed to improve the competitiveness of small enterprises, promote technological improvements, upgrade the quality of products, and ensure adequate quality control. In these efforts, human-development programs are considered crucial.

# Pillars linking technology to basic-needs satisfaction

Six integrating themes are identified in this report as a focus for the recommendations. These were the main pillars in the effort to tackle basic-needs fulfilment resting on a sound S&T-policy foundation. The pillars are education, access to information, participation, health, basic infrastructure, and small-scale economic activities.

## Education

The economic gains to be made from meeting basic needs are most distinct in education. Investment in primary education in developing countries has very high rates of monetary return, both for society and for the individual (UNCTAD 1994). As well, there are mutually reinforcing nonmonetary returns, especially from the education of women and the resulting reduced child mortality, altered fertility patterns, and improved human development (UNCTAD 1994). Differences in education are extremely important in explaining differences in income. For example, about 40% of personal-income inequality in Brazil is related to education (Behrman 1993). Donors and nations suffering serious deprivation could make high-quality education a cornerstone of their basic-needs strategies.

The concept of education used here goes beyond the traditional meaning (that is, almost exclusively the process of formal education). Education intended to enable the poor to gain access to and understand technology must create the necessary instruments for this end. The following objectives are suggested:

▼ Education about ways to increase production and productivity of small-scale economic activities;

▼ Education enabling the poor to participate effectively and constructively in community life;

▼ Education enabling the poor to practice policies and programs of preventive medicine, indispensable for improving levels of health and nutrition; and

▼ Education for the poor that gives impetus to a process of sustainable development, to preserve and protect the environment.

Education expenditures and curricula should be carefully reviewed and evaluated for their ability to meet these objectives. Nations with significant shortfalls in meeting basic needs would benefit from a review of the composition of their education expenditures in terms of primary, secondary, and higher education and the geographic distribution of these expenditures. These nations could thus determine whether the composition and pattern of their investment in education are consonant with optimal social returns and basic-needs objectives. Such nations should make sure that students are taught science in a manner that is meaningful and are exposed to production techniques relevant to future income-generating activities. There should also be awareness of the new, effective technologies used in education, such as computer networking and other microelectronics-based tools for learning.

Technical assistance and extension services for MSEs can reach the poor through delivery systems that function well. For an example of a successful urban delivery system in Ghana, see ILO (1993). For a description of a more ambitious, experimental biovillage in India, see M.S. Swaminathan Foundation (1993). Careful, comprehensive surveys could be made of existing programs for the technical improvement of small enterprises, and the programs that seem best suited to the circumstances could be adopted. International agencies can furnish the raw material, for example, through evaluative case studies. Such surveys have been initiated by specialized United Nations agencies, for example, the ILO in the case of the delivery system for Ghana. International financial institutions and NGOs can also play an important role.

Clearly, overall responsibility for providing education to the very poor rests with national governments, although at regional and local levels there could be valuable contributions, not least of which would be to make suitable adjustments for local circumstances. For training, private- and public-sector partnerships may well be practicable. Donors and education administrators should possibly give first priority to teaching teachers and training trainers, rather than to building new schools. Decision-makers in countries with a large low-income population, as well as the entire global scientific community, must become more aware of and sensitive to the potential contributions that S&T can make to improving the income, productivity, and quality of life of the very poor. This is of the utmost importance. Sufficient international prestige and publicity should be vested in an effort to galvanize further actions aimed at rechanneling, to some extent, the world's S&T undertakings.

## Access to information

Information is an essential pillar in technologies for basic needs. Students and teachers in low-income communities, striving to keep abreast of the changing economic, political, social, and technical configurations affecting their lives, require access to information. Information is basic to participatory action and movements to empower poor populations. Information is extremely useful for smaller enterprises that need to know how to apply for credit or to learn about possibilities for product diversification, market conditions for their products, product specifications established by state regulations or buyers, price, availability of inputs, transportation alternatives and schedules, and alternative techniques of production. Decision-makers must also know to what extent resources to meet basic-needs deficiencies are hijacked by people in higher income strata who are not really in dire need: programs designed to alleviate poverty could be periodically reviewed to determine whether the targeted group is actually benefiting. Although this is a national matter, NGOs are strategically placed to provide information on how much benefit is being reaped by the very poor.

Information can come through a rich variety of media, including printed matter, telephones, radios, personal contact, and computers. The central idea is to use all practical information avenues to increase the exposure of the poor to comprehensible and useful information. The S&T community can be of great value in consultations with targeted groups to identify and facilitate access to such information. The information should be structured and made intelligible to poor populations, and the flow of information should not be unidirectional. The international community, donors, NGOs, and state agencies all need to receive, process, analyze, and share locally collected data on quality-of-life indicators, the progress of development programs, and new opportunities for and challenges to achieving further technical learning and improvement in regions with low-income populations. Furthermore, the international community must be the leader in monitoring technological progress in those areas likely to yield benefits to poor communities. A great deal of the necessary information routinely appears in the United Nations Development Programmes's annual *Human Development Report* (for example, UNDP 1991b, 1992, 1993, 1994). UNCTAD's *ATAS Bulletin* could devote an issue entirely to monitoring S&T undertakings or outputs that hold significant promise for satisfying basic needs.

## Participation

When poor populations are introduced to technologies, the chances for successful outcomes are improved markedly if the prospective users are directly involved in selecting adequate technologies, properly adapting them to prevailing economic activities and conditions, disseminating the technologies among themselves, and mastering and improving on them. Agents responsible for upgrading technologies and skills in poor communities should build a strong participatory dimension into such programs (see UNCTAD 1990, section B of chap. 3).

Participation in a more general sense could have equally important beneficial effects on innovativeness, incentive to risk experiments with new technologies, and ability to recognize opportunities inherent in market-oriented national and international economies. When poor populations are politically impotent and socially marginalized, these attributes are severely diminished. The keys to participation are political empowerment and greater social integration of poor populations. Closely associated with these objectives is more decentralization of government to increase local decision-making. As one report on human development observed, "Greater people's participation has become an imperative, a condition of survival" (UNDP 1993, p. 99). One of the most effective avenues for fostering participation is the decentralization of state functions, which frees and, indeed, obliges local communities to solve problems and to formulate and execute development policies. Governments should recognize the political, economic, and social benefits of both decentralized governance and the empowerment and social integration of poor populations and should implement actions supporting these objectives. Special effort should be devoted to encouraging the participation of both men and women. Although all levels are involved in achieving these objectives, the linchpin is the engagement of intermediate and fundamental NGOs to help local organizations solve their own problems. This fits comfortably with the World Summit for Social Development emphasis on the goal of social integration, which was on the agenda of its session in Copenhagen in March 1995.

## Health

Health is basic to becoming independent, productive, and fully responsible for one's own development. Health, sanitary conditions, and, accordingly, life expectancy are fundamental indicators of basic-needs satisfaction. Health, together with education, housing, and food, is a determining factor in the social position of low-income populations. Health problems in these populations show a specific pattern related to deficiencies and hazards originating in poverty. About 1 billion people live without adequate water and sanitation, which causes the spread of many of the most prevalent diseases in developing countries. Many health problems can be prevented, diagnosed, and treated with available and relatively simple and affordable equipment. Work in the field of sanitation and waste management is proving critical through its promotion of technologies affordable to low-income communities, as is work promoting technology in vaccines and diagnostics. The United Nations Centre for Human Settlements (Habitat) and UNIDO have been active in these fields (see Chapter 9). Also, recent technology based on physical and engineering sciences has provided new health-care devices and techniques. However, many of these technologies are complex, costly, and technically demanding, particularly for developing countries. Their effective introduction, use, and maintenance require sophisticated managerial, medical, and engineering talent, which points to the need to evaluate health priorities in allocating scarce resources. Of particular importance in the context of basic needs are the World Health Organization's efforts to provide guidance on essential equipment for health facilities and to strengthen national capacities for the use of health technology as integrated components of overall health-system development. Such efforts require sustained support from the whole international community.

## Basic infrastructure

Basic physical infrastructure is another critical pillar supporting the bridge between basic-needs deficiency and prosperity. Infrastructure provides an environment in which innovative behaviour can be meaningful and facilitates the necessary inputs and the marketing of products. Many of the methods for providing basic infrastructure are already on the technology shelf; it is mainly a question of giving the priority and commitment to infrastructure that it deserves. Special attention should be directed to ease of obtaining water and fuel. This could, for example, reduce or eliminate the burdens falling disproportionately on women. Clearly, the responsibility for infrastructure often rests with the state, but donors, especially those supporting the least-developed countries, can be extremely helpful in influencing priorities. Because infrastructure projects are almost always construction intensive, they may use local resources and generate work and income for unemployed or underemployed members of the local labour force. In this respect, local and regional agencies can serve a useful function. In addition, long-term efforts might focus on studies investigating the feasibility of large-scale science and engineering projects. The more ambitious of these projects have included water-diversion schemes.

## Small-scale economic activities

Small-scale economic activities will, for the foreseeable future, be the primary source of employment and income for poor populations. As such they are one of the critical pillars of the bridge between unmet basic needs and prosperity. There is ample evidence that small loans to low-income entrepreneurs starting or operating a micro- or small-scale enterprise can be made available on commercial terms or with a very modest subsidy. Governments without adequate methods for delivering credit to these enterprises could investigate the experiences of countries with such mechanisms in place before initiating their own program. The primary impetus must be national, but international agents can be instrumental in conducting evaluative case studies of credit delivery to low-income entrepreneurs in developing countries. NGOs might be useful as screening agencies and conduits between the centrally provided credit and the borrowers.

However unintentionally, certain macroeconomic policies frequently affect both labour-intensive production techniques and smaller enterprises adversely (Stewart 1987; Stewart et al. 1990). Because of the importance of the informal sector, governments should consider ways to reduce antagonism between players in the informal sector, the formal sector, and the state. Monetary and fiscal policies, as well as policies affecting trade, exchange rates, pricing, labour, and wage regulations, can be biased against MSMEs. Because of this it may benefit nations with poor populations to systematically examine their macroeconomic policy and remove any unwarranted disincentives to the promotion of these enterprises. Other aspects are also critical, particularly technical assistance. This can include help with the identification of promising projects, feasibility studies, organization and management of an enterprise, the process of selecting technologies and using them efficiently, quality control, transportation, and marketing. Regulatory provisions that hamper the technical progress of enterprises in the informal sector should be under scrutiny. Although the nation is the prime mover, international agencies could provide technical assistance when it is needed.

Although all such measures could be implemented in fairly short order, in the long run technological progress is necessary, especially in emerging technologies that could usefully be blended with traditional production methods. Particularly promising in this respect are new biotechnological innovations that tend to be scale neutral; new materials that can be used as inputs for small-scale manufacturers; nutritional enhancement of ORS; new methods for direct casting and thin films for photovoltaics; long-range meteorological predictions of drought conditions; and information technologies suitable for poor communities. The international community could encourage R&D to promote such emerging technologies and conduct experiments leading to their integration with traditional, low-income, small-scale activities. Replication of programs that effectively support MSMEs could do a great deal to satisfy basic needs.

# Recommendations

The complete picture of poverty alleviation is complex, and alleviating poverty is a serious challenge, but the fundamental objective of technology for basic needs can be formulated very succinctly: to create participatory conditions that enable the poor to generate, have access to, comprehend, and creatively use technology to satisfy their basic needs. Clearly, considerable interaction and complementarity occur among the six bridging elements. These elements should be introduced in concert rather than in isolation. The following is a list of recommendations for addressing basic needs, according to each of these elements, and for formulating fundamental S&T policy.

## Education

1. Considerable evidence attests to high rates of return, in both monetary and indirect social benefits, accruing from expenditures in education. This is especially so for women and for those benefiting from primary basic education. It is therefore recommended that S&T-based education be considered a cornerstone of a strategy to meet basic needs.

2. Although an entire range of curricula, topics, and emphases can be part of education, the following should be considered essential for alleviating basic-needs shortfalls:

   ▼ Education that increases the production and productivity of small-scale economic activities;

   ▼ Education that enables the poor to relate to their environment and to participate effectively and constructively in community life;

   ▼ Education that enables the poor to practice preventive medicine, which is indispensable for improving their levels of health and nutrition; and

   ▼ Education that provides impetus to a process of sustainable development, one that will preserve and protect the environment.

3. State-of-the-art technology-assisted education and vocational training should be seriously considered.

4. Countries should be encouraged to review the allocation of their expenditures on primary, secondary, and higher education, their geographic configuration, and their gender equity to determine whether the investment brings optimal social returns and meets basic-needs requirements.

5. The United Nations should promote and sponsor a conference to sensitize the S&T community and policy- and decision-makers to the contribution S&T can make to the satisfaction of basic needs.

## Access to information

1. Information must be accessible to poor populations for general education purposes, to further participatory action leading to empowerment, and to inform small-scale enterprises about applications for credit, product diversification, market conditions, product specification, price and availability of inputs, transportation alternatives and schedules, and alternative production techniques. The poor should have help in gaining access to existing information sources in structured and intelligible forms useful for basic-needs satisfaction.

2. The S&T community should be encouraged to consult with targeted low-income groups to identify their important information needs and facilitate access to such information.

3. Through periodic review, decision-makers must get information on the extent to which less needy groups are benefiting from basic-needs programs while the objectives of these programs are left unmet.

4. The international community can make major contributions by collecting and disseminating information in the following ways:

   ▼ Monitoring the most significant basic-needs indicators for the world's poor populations;

   ▼ Offering a one-stop service to refer people to information networks; and

   ▼ Monitoring new technologies for those that are particularly promising for satisfying basic needs.

## Participation

1. It is recommended that technology-related projects geared toward bettering the lot of poor populations fully involve the target group at every stage.

2. Support for participatory actions to empower the very poor to affect the political, economic, and social aspects of their lives is recommended for intrinsic reasons and because participatory-driven empowerment can create an atmosphere more conducive to innovative behaviour.

## Health

1. Countries should be encouraged to give greater emphasis to preventive medicine and less to curative health measures.

2. Countries should review the geographic configuration and gender equity of their health programs to determine whether the investment brings optimal social returns and meets basic needs.

## Basic infrastructure

1. Basic physical infrastructure is needed to support the other pillars of the bridge leading from poverty to prosperity. The state has primary responsibility, but donors can provide adequate supplies of safe water, energy, sewage-treatment and other sanitation facilities, transportation grids, and the means of communication.

2. Because work on such basic infrastructure is often construction intensive, every effort should be made to mobilize local resources and provide income-generating employment.

## Small-scale economic activities

1. Governments without adequate methods for delivery of credit to MSMEs should seriously consider starting a program after observing the experiences of countries with such mechanisms in place.

2. However unintentionally, macroeconomic policies often adversely affect labour-intensive production techniques, smaller enterprises, or both. Therefore, it is recommended that nations meticulously and systematically review each major component of their macroeconomic policy and remove any unwarranted disincentives to the promotion of vital and progressive MSMEs.

3. Governments should recognize the informal sector as a source of employment, income, and innovation. Means should be explored for technically upgrading informal-sector activities, increasing rates of graduation to the formal sector, and reducing friction between the informal sector, the formal sector, and the state.

4. The S&T community should be encouraged to take the initiative in linking (in a participatory fashion) its technologies and smaller scale entrepreneurs.

## Science and technology policy

1. Because of the inadequate antipoverty programs, the new technological means for addressing basic needs, and the sweeping economic, political, and social transformations in the global landscape,
it is proposed that the United Nations adopt the issue of technology
for basic needs as an agenda of concern. The United Nations should
implement a mechanism to evaluate national S&T policies with the
aim of determining how adequately basic-needs satisfaction is being
addressed. Countries should be exhorted to build into their S&T
strategies a major component addressing basic needs.

2. It is recommended that nations carefully and comprehensively survey technical assistance, extension services, and other programs
that support technological upgrading of small- and medium-scale
enterprises and adopt those that seem suitable for use in their own
circumstances.

3. The networking of S&T institutions and enterprises of both the private and the public sectors at the national and international levels
should be strengthened.

4. A pilot program, involving countries from different regions, should
be developed for S&T for basic needs. If this recommendation is
accepted, CSTD should establish a Board on Technology and Basic
Needs. The functions of this institution would be to

▼ Examine the overall approach and feasibility of the program;

▼ Select participating countries, formulate an operational program
and budget, and find the necessary financial resources for its
implementation; and

▼ Report on these activities to CSTD at its third session.

5. Technology for basic needs should be addressed in a series of sessions involving CSTD. It is also recommended that CSTD hold a joint
session with the Commission on Human Rights.

Chapter 2[1]

# Science and Technology for Development: An Overview

*The Panel on Technology for Basic Needs*

As we make the transition to the 21st century, we are witnessing the emergence of a new world order that is global but not integrated, an order that puts most of the world's populations in contact with one another but simultaneously maintains deep fissures between different groups of countries and between peoples within countries (see Chapter 6). The new world order concentrates "global" activities in certain countries, regions, cities, and even neighbourhoods while increasingly marginalizing many production and service activities and the people engaged in them. The multiplicity of changes and trends that can be observed indicates that an accelerated, segmented, and uneven process of globalization is under way. The range and diversity of changes in many aspects of the international economy appear much greater at this juncture than at any other time in the last four decades.

At the root of this global transformation lie scientific advances and technological innovation, which act as enabling factors and exert pressure toward further globalization. At the same time, however, political, economic, social, and environmental changes have stimulated and supported the growth of science and technology (S&T) and have

[1] This overview deals with recent changes in the global order that have a direct bearing on science and technology for development and sets out the background against which the issues identified by the Commission on Science and Technology for Development (CSTD) are examined. The overview was prepared by the chair of the CSTD and CSTD bureau members, with the assistance of the UNCTAD Secretariat and on the basis of a background paper prepared by F.R. Sagasti. This chapter represents an edited version of document E/CN.16/1995/5 ("Overview of the Reports of Panels"), which was submitted to the second session of CSTD. Financial contributions from a number of governments, foundations, institutions, and individual donors are gratefully acknowledged.

shaped their evolution. A brief examination of the main changes that are taking place may help us to appreciate the extent and depth of the transformation in the global order; establish the background against which the Commission on Science and Technology for Development (CSTD) has selected the substantive themes for its intersessional work; and reveal the common threads running through those themes.

The major transformations taking place in the patterns of world economic interdependence include the rapid growth and globalization of financial markets, fundamental changes in trade patterns, and deepening inequalities between rich and poor countries and between men and women. Growing interdependence and globalization — to some extent a consequence of advances in communication and information technologies (ITs) — have created not only opportunities, but also challenges.

As Sagasti (in Chapter 6) puts it,

> International financial markets now constitute a tight web of transactions involving global securities trading, arbitrage in multiple markets and currencies, portfolio investments through a bewildering array of international funds, and massive transborder capital movements .... Changes have also occurred in the direction and content of international trade, as exemplified by the ... rise of regional trading blocks, such as the European Union and that of the North American Free Trade Agreement; and the shift in the content of international trade away from primary commodities (exported primarily by developing countries) and toward high-technology services and products (exported by industrialized nations).

With the increasing interdependence of the world economy, movements toward political pluralism, popular participation, and democratic processes are rapidly becoming a fact of life. However, as indicated by persistent conflicts in countries with vastly different political and economic backgrounds, advances toward democracy, respect for human rights, and peaceful coexistence are by no means guaranteed. Be that as it may, the new international political context is altering the balance in favour of democratic forms of governance.

In this connection, the issue of governance has become a concern in recent years in both industrialized and developing countries, albeit for different reasons. In industrialized countries, the causes of this may be traced to the changing norms of political and economic life; in developing countries, the problems have been intensified by the sharp contrast between the growth in social demands and the capacity of the institutional framework — including the institutions of the state, the private sector, and civil society — to satisfy them. Governance and appropriate systems of government have also emerged as an area of concern for international development organizations in the wake of the realization that many projects supported with external financial and technical resources yielded less than their expected rates of return (see Chapter 6). One reason for this was that investments were made in highly distorted policy environments, which prevented the benefits from materializing.

The most worrisome feature of the current globalization process is the widening fissure between the very poor — representing about 20% of the world's population — and the remaining majority of people. Despite improvements in life expectancy and standards of living in many parts of the world in the past several decades, enormous economic differences between regions and countries and particularly between the industrialized and developing nations persist. The absolute number of poor people in the world has continued to increase, and disparities between the rich and the poor have widened. In developing countries, the growth in social demands has been triggered largely by population increases in the last four decades. Coupled with a significant slowdown in population growth in the industrialized nations, this has led to a highly skewed worldwide distribution of social needs and capacities to satisfy them. The dynamics of population growth strongly affect the demand for food, education, employment, housing, and other social benefits. Demands for food have multiplied many times over, particularly in the poorest countries; demands for basic health care and elementary education have expanded at a rapid pace; and unemployment has emerged as perhaps the most troublesome and persistent problem (see Chapter 6).

Another prominent and disturbing feature of the global social situation is the difference between the socioeconomic situations of men and women. Despite continued efforts on behalf of women, gender discrimination remains widespread. In industrialized countries gender discrimination is evident in employment and wages; and in developing countries the greatest disparities, other than those in the job market, are to be found in education, health care, and nutritional support. These disparities persist, despite clear acknowledgment of the pivotal role that women play in education, health, and the household.

Environmental concerns have also found a place at the top of the international public-policy agenda in the past two decades (see Chapter 6):

> We are now aware of the limits that the regenerative capacity
> of natural ecosystems imposes on human activities, of the
> dangers of uncontrolled exploitation of natural resources
> (fisheries, forests, land, and rivers), and of the overload of the
> Earth's capacity to absorb waste (air and water pollution,

*acid rain, and toxic and nuclear wastes). The 1980s and early 1990s witnessed the emergence of truly global environmental problems, such as global warming and the depletion of the ozone layer, which underscored the danger that ecological instabilities could cause irreversible environmental damage.*

The problems of environmental sustainability and resource use are closely related to population growth and poverty in developing countries and to the often wasteful consumption habits of the rich nations. Major changes in lifestyle will be essential in both groups of countries to address the problem of environmental sustainability in the transition to the 21st century. The Earth Summit, in Rio de Janeiro in 1992, endorsed Agenda 21, a wide-ranging world program of action to promote sustainable development, although further negotiations on its implementation have brought to the fore the fact that industrialized and developing nations disagree about the best approach. Nevertheless, a consensus has emerged on the need to tackle the immediate environmental problems facing developing countries through cooperative actions and the application of S&T.

Sagasti (in Chapter 6) says the following:

*Since World War II the products of scientific research and technological innovation have become more and more deeply enmeshed in all aspects of human activity, and there have been profound modifications in the way knowledge is generated and used. A problem — which could also be seen as an opportunity — is that too little of the great power of modern S&T has been directed at development. ... the S&T capabilities of developing countries are far too limited to deal adequately with the enormous problems of development .... Only about 4% of the world expenditure on R&D [research and development] and about 14% of the world's supply of scientists and engineers are in developing countries, where more than 80% of the world's people live (CCSTG 1992; UNESCO 1993; Annerstedt 1994). Discrepancies like these, which have persisted for a long time, are a distinguishing feature of the emerging fractured global order. The role that knowledge now plays in the process of development is so critical that development could be redefined in terms of the capacity to generate, acquire, disseminate, and use knowledge, both modern and traditional. The presence or absence of this capacity marks a crucial division between the developed and developing nations .... Two aspects of S&T merit further attention during the transition to the 21st century: the changes in the way scientists are conducting research; and the increasingly systematic character of technological innovation (Salomon et al. 1994).*

# Scientific research

As noted by Sagasti (in Chapter 6), significant cross-fertilization has taken place between scientific research, technological innovation, and the commercial exploitation of research results. Moreover,

> the institutional settings for basic research, for applied research, and for the development of new products and processes are changing, particularly as a result of shifts in the sources of funding and a more prominent role for the private sector. Links between universities and industries are being strengthened; industrial research and technological alliances have become imperative in certain fields; and venture-capital firms and some specialized government agencies are playing a greater role in funding the commercialization of new technology.

However, these very mechanisms have also become the Achilles heel of developing countries. Sagasti (in Chapter 6) goes on to say that

> the closer links between scientific capabilities, developments in technology, and economic growth, as well as the increasing costs of scientific research, ... the emergence of new transdisciplinary fields, and the growing complexity of the institutional setting for research all make it more difficult for most developing countries to push quickly toward the frontiers of knowledge and take advantage of advance in S&T. At the same time, the slowdown in the rates of economic growth, severe resource constraints, and growing social demands undermine any long-term efforts to build S&T capabilities in developing countries.

# Technological innovation

The innovation process has changed significantly, particularly in science-intensive industries (see Chapter 6):

> [It] has become more complex: it is more expensive; it requires more sophisticated management techniques; it has intensified international collaboration and competition; and it has expanded the government's role in the support of innovation. ... The costs of incorporating research results into goods and services and of bringing new products to the market have been steadily increasing in the past few decades. ... In addition, innovation requires the support of a well-developed infrastructure, including a good network of roads,

> *transportation facilities, telecommunication and data-transmission networks, a reliable supply of electricity, waste-disposal facilities, and clean water supplies. … The higher costs of innovation and the greater risks faced by firms in a more competitive environment have in effect increased barriers to many fields of industry (Ernst and O'Connor 1989).*

These impediments aside, the building of an appropriate level of S&T capacity will continue to be essential for development. Without this capacity no country will be able to formulate policies and strategies for achieving sustainable human development; absorb, adapt, and improve imported technology; or expect to develop its production potential, even in those areas where it has competitive advantages.

## The new challenge: sustainable human development

Although S&T progress during the past century has freed much of humanity from dire poverty, the very poorest have not shared in the benefits. Indeed, the globalization of the world economy has broadened even further the gap between the poor and the nonpoor. Wide disparities between countries' abilities to use modern technology and innovate have led to disparities in their degree of integration into the new global system. Consequently, the benefits of globalization are shared unevenly among and within nations, thereby increasing marginalization both internationally and domestically. The deepening economic stagnation in the low-income countries — more specifically the plight of the very poor and women — is a cause for concern to governments and international organizations alike. The issues identified by CSTD at its first session reflect these concerns.

The challenge to the international community is to find ways to effectively support the most underprivileged groups, particularly women and the rural poor, and achieve sustainable human development. Efforts to meet this challenge will involve a commitment to provide all human beings, individually and collectively, with the opportunity to realize their full potential. Above all, this implies a determination to embrace and put into practice a new conception of sustainable human development.

However, two aspects should be emphasized (see Chapter 6): sustainable human development is applicable not just to developing countries but also to industrialized nations; and although S&T can contribute a great deal to sustainable human development, it does not offer a ready-made solution to the problem of values that is raised by the clash between tradition and modernity. Therefore, sustainable human development has to be considered an uncertain quest in which the seekers use the knowledge and innovations offered by modern S&T as well as the wisdom and experience offered by traditional, local knowledge systems.

Against this background and with the objective of tackling these pressing issues, CSTD decided its intersessional work would address the role of S&T in the following areas: basic needs, gender issues, and land management. To this end it set up three panels: one to analyze technology for basic needs; one to analyze the gender dimension of S&T for sustainable human development; and one to analyze integrated land management (ILM). In addition, as a follow-up to an earlier report of the United Nations Secretary-General on the contributions of technology to industrialization and regional integration (E/CN.16/1993/2), a panel of experts was established to examine ways of strengthening linkages between the national research and development (R&D) systems and industrial sectors of developing countries.

These four panels, together with working groups, functioned according to the new style adopted by CSTD for carrying out its intersessional work. Directors of study were appointed to design and coordinate the work plans of some of the panels. This new style encourages debate among CSTD members, who are responsible for preparing inputs, drafting reports, and following up on recommendations. The United Nations Secretariat acted as facilitator and assisted in the finalization of the panels' reports.

The following sections contain an overview of the salient conclusions reached by these four panels.

## Technology for basic needs

The Panel on Technology for Basic Needs (PTBN) discussed how a fresh approach to S&T could ensure that the basic needs of low-income populations are met. Basic needs were defined as the minimal requirements for sustaining life: adequate nutrition, health services, water, and sanitary facilities. Also implied is access to elementary education and information to enable individuals and communities to be productive and make rational use of the basic goods and services available. In the course of its work, PTBN looked at food production and processing; education, especially technical and vocational training; and health care. PTBN agreed that technology strategies, approaches, and policies (rather than specific technologies) and a pragmatic and pluralistic approach (rather than a doctrinaire stance) should be given priority.

The rapidly evolving global order has fundamentally affected the problem of poverty and, to a great extent, the possibility of realizing

sustainable human development. The concern with technology transfer has now been superseded by a preoccupation with technological
capacity-building. Moreover, with the trend toward decentralization
and democracy, more of the poor populations are becoming involved
in finding a solution to their own problems. This trend is thus creating
a better climate for linking the satisfaction of basic needs with human
rights.

The fundamental objective of the mobilization of S&T to meet
basic needs should be to create conditions that enable the poor to gain
access to, comprehend, and creatively use knowledge and technology
to satisfy their basic needs. The PTBN report placed its recommendations under six integrating themes: education, health, participation,
small-scale economic activity, basic infrastructure, and access to information. PTBN also made recommendations for S&T policy for basic
needs.

The role of the United Nations in the implementation of the
basic-needs objective is crucial. The United Nations could

▼ Promote and sponsor activities that will sensitize the S&T
community and policy- and decision-makers to the contributions S&T can make to the satisfaction of basic needs;
and

▼ Implement a mechanism to evaluate countries' S&T policies
to determine how adequately basic needs are addressed.

## The gender dimension of S&T

The analysis of the panel on the gender dimension of S&T for sustainable human development was underpinned by the explicit recognition
that development is gender specific and that S&T for development
must respond appropriately and equitably to the concerns, needs, and
interests of both women and men.

Unfortunately, the impact of S&T on society has not been uniformly beneficial. Even at the close of the 20th century, women in
developing countries, especially in the rural areas, are still finding it
very difficult to meet their own basic needs and those of their households. S&T interventions have improved many aspects of women's
lives, leading to important declines in both maternal and infant mortality. However, in the last three decades women in developing countries have become disproportionately poor in relation to the men in
their communities. This difference between men and women cannot
be understood without explicit reference to the gender-specific nature

of development, including S&T contributions to the development process.

There is also significant gender inequality in education and career prospects for girls and women, which is by no means confined to developing countries: in most industrialized countries, girls and women face similar obstacles, particularly in obtaining a science education and in pursuing S&T careers. The available data clearly demonstrate that women are underrepresented in scientific careers and decision-making bodies in both the developing and the industrialized countries.

The panel on the gender dimension of S&T identified many areas in which the needs and aspirations of women are relatively neglected: S&T decision-making processes, S&T training, S&T career prospects, the manner in which statistics are collected, ethical issues in S&T, and the S&T activities of the United Nations. As well, there has been a lack of recognition of women's local knowledge systems.

The differential impact of new technologies, particularly ITs on women's and men's employment received particular attention. A commissioned study suggested that new technologies have made many jobs in manufacturing redundant or obsolete (see Gender Working Group–UNCSTD 1995). These changes have affected men and women differently, but, overall, female labour has been displaced more than male labour. New jobs are more skill intensive than old jobs, and women have been at a disadvantage because training opportunities are more limited for women than for men.

The role of the United Nations in addressing gender issues and promoting better awareness of relationships between gender and S&T is crucial. The United Nations could

▼ Initiate, monitor, and evaluate activities in the field;

▼ Encourage the recruitment of women into S&T-sensitive positions;

▼ Incorporate gender analysis in the design of S&T programs; and

▼ Strengthen informal interagency networking in this area.

Finally, the panel formulated seven "transformative actions" and a declaration of intent with six goals for equity in S&T. All governments are invited to subscribe to this declaration and to establish ad hoc committees to formulate national action plans to achieve these goals.

# Integrated land management

The essential role of land resources in supporting all current and future human activities makes land management one of the primary tools in sustainable human development (see Chapter 6). The ILM panel agreed that managing land requires a holistic and integrated approach. An integrated approach to land management is not fixed; rather, it is a continuous and iterative process of planning, implementing, monitoring, and evaluating. The basic techniques for carrying out each of these steps are already available, but their application in many parts of the world is limited by training, financial, and institutional constraints. Failure to manage land resources in an integrated manner could lead to permanent destruction or degradation of the land's capacity to provide economic and environmental benefits; inefficient use or waste of resources; and cumulative effects that lead to transboundary problems.

Diverse social, economic, and environmental considerations influence current and future land uses because land has multiple functions in society. "Systematically examining the potential uses of land makes it possible to improve social and economic development while protecting and enhancing the environment" (see Chapter 6). "A fundamental goal of ILM is to use S&T to prevent the degradation of the land's capacity to support human activities, particularly the production of food."

Four major barriers to the effective global application of ILM methods were identified:

▼ Limited access to appropriate technology and information;

▼ Lack of appropriate infrastructure to use S&T effectively;

▼ Problems emanating from unsustainable land-use practices; and

▼ Conflicting land-use goals.

Elimination of these barriers requires approaches specific to each country.

The panel identified four approaches to the effective implementation of ILM:

▼ Intra- and intergovernmental cooperation to pool resources among countries with common interests;

▼ Private–public partnerships to provide credit and undertake R&D;

▼ Programs to provide targeted training and technology support; and

▼ Direct public investment to protect resources, for example, by building dykes to prevent water erosion and planting trees to prevent wind erosion and desertification.

# R&D–industry linkages

CSTD also considered the issue of linkages between national R&D systems and the industrial sectors of developing countries and countries in transition. The panel analyzing this theme confirmed the view that the R&D systems in these groups of countries were not up to the task of promoting industrial development. These R&D systems in these countries are characterized by a number of common weaknesses:

▼ Rates of R&D expenditure are extremely low, compared with those in industrialized countries.

▼ Little or no R&D is undertaken by the enterprise sector, the main agent in the innovation process.

▼ Public-sector R&D is fragmented and insufficiently oriented to the needs of the industrial sector.

▼ The R&D institutes (RDIs) are not generating a sufficient volume of commercially applicable innovations.

▼ The RDIs emphasize basic research at the expense of applied research.

▼ The scientists at RDIs tend to be more concerned with career prospects than with the needs of industry.

▼ There is a lack of appropriate incentives for undertaking R&D.

Although most of these weaknesses are common to publicly funded RDIs in both developing countries and countries in transition, the two groups of countries are, nevertheless, different. Developing countries in general have a more articulated market mechanism that favours commercialization of R&D results, but countries in transition are better endowed with scientists and engineers who can carry out R&D.

Recognizing that the issue of how, when, and whether to intervene in favour of technological capacity-building is contentious, the panel singled out three measures to strengthen linkages between national R&D systems and production sectors:

▼ An environment conducive to R&D and technological innovation should be created. This would involve establishing a stable economy and a competitive market environment.

▼ Some of the existing public RDIs should be transformed, through increased commercialization and refocusing of their activities, to become more responsive to the needs of industry.

▼ R&D should be stimulated in the enterprise sector through the use of general measures (for example, tax and credit incentives, levies, subsidies, and duty exemptions) and selective measures (for example, targeting).

# Information technologies

Finally, as part of its intersessional work, CSTD also considered the effect of ITs on the development process. ITs are widely believed to have a generic influence on the development of modern technologies, thereby determining the pace of social and economic progress. However, their effects on the development process in general and the technological advancement of developing countries in particular are not yet fully understood. Because of its increasing importance to the progress of S&T, IT is a subject CSTD might wish to consider in its future work.

# Part II

# Individual
# Contributions

# Introduction

The Panel viewed basic needs as a dynamic concept, changing over time and varying from society to society. The many contributions made by individual members of the Panel reflect this diversity.

The experiences presented by members of the Panel from Ethiopia, Togo, and Uganda merit particular attention. In these three countries, the problem of extreme poverty is most dramatic. In Ethiopia, for example, over half of the population lives in "absolute poverty." As well, the populations of these countries were predominantly rural and quite young, with an extremely large segment under the age of 15. Of the economically active population, self-employed workers account for the overwhelming majority in the rural areas and for a great portion in the urban sector, as well. Health coverage, sanitary conditions, and, accordingly, life expectancy are at low levels, and educational facilities are scarce. All of these characteristics are fundamental in formulating a "technology strategy" aimed at the satisfaction of basic needs, as they are in formulating national economic development objectives in general. Thus, Ethiopia, Togo, and Uganda are enhancing their technological capabilities through projects aimed at meeting the interests of low-income populations — particularly through increased agricultural productivity, stronger educational systems, and improved health facilities, water supplies, sanitation systems, and housing conditions.

The case study from Togo, presented to the Panel by Messanvi Gbeassor, described six major research programs vital to the country's socioeconomic development. Selected by Togo's National Council for Scientific Research, the programs included projects for improving food crops and cash crops, soil enhancement and management, agronomic upgrading of phosphates and peats, investigating the dynamics of social and economic change, and raising rural health standards. Through these projects, a variety of science and technology inputs has been made available and adapted to various rural population

From Uganda, S.P. Kagoda provided the Panel with a presentation of similar ongoing projects designed to improve the standard of living of low-income populations. They addressed issues including improved housing, rural development, water supplies, and sanitation. Designating responsibility to local residents, as well as regular consultations with them, contributed to the success of the projects.

The Panel also considered some recent experiences from technologically advanced economies in transition. From Ukraine, Serguei L. Yampolsky, of the Ukraine State Committee on Science and Technologies, outlined directions for preserving and developing scientific and technological potential. He suggested that technology policy should combine self-management with state planning and involve both producers and consumers in the process of developing national capacities. Linkages with the international scientific and technological community were also seen as important. According to the Ukrainian experience, particular emphasis should be given to vocational training as an element of a basic-needs strategy.

From Japan, Mikoto Usui, in his contribution to the Panel, established the necessary linkages between local projects and global action in areas such as energy and water. He described previous endeavours in "blending" traditional and newly emerging technologies and their lessons, and he provided a list of existing technologies with high potential for blending that could be applied as part of a basic-needs strategy in areas such as electronics, biotechnology, and energy.

The many individual presentations to the Panel reflected a diversity of approaches. This section includes some of the full-length articles that were submitted.

# Chapter 3

# Policy Guidelines

*Gustavo Fernández*

This paper examines the policy context for the appropriate use of technology to satisfy the basic needs of people living in extreme poverty in Latin American countries. I will point out the main tendencies of the democratic systems and economic policies in place in most of Latin America and suggest the main lines of responsibility in meeting basic social and familial needs.

A nation's economic policy defines the way basic social needs in its territory must be met and the instruments to be used to reach this objective. An economic policy is the result of the interaction of international and local factors, which regulate economic performance. For this reason, I will begin with a summary of the external and internal tendencies that have had a decisive influence on the orientation and mechanisms of national development.

## The framework of contemporary development

During the last decade of this century, two tendencies have caused a deep transformation in the objectives, functions, and structure of the state in Latin America and, in consequence, of national development strategies. One, an external tendency, is a product of accelerated and unexpected change in the international economic and political systems. The other, an internal tendency, is a consequence of the crisis of the 1980s, the structural adjustment programs, and the reestablishment of democracy.

Internationally, the collapse of socialist regimes in Eastern Europe, the end of the Cold War, and the triumph of democracy as a paradigm of political organization in modern society changed both the ideological debate and the perspectives on political development in Latin America. Meanwhile, the process of globalization and internationalization of the market economy, affecting mainly the flow of information, knowledge, and money, strongly modified the conditions of economic operation in the region. A technological revolution at the root of this change has corroded the values of traditional comparative advantages, creating new, dynamic competitive advantages; this has led to a new international division of work and has set the conditions for building a system based on the production and distribution of knowledge. However, changes in the international system, which are incomplete and fragmented, have not yet had their full effect. In consequence, it is difficult to predict with any certainty the future forms of political and productive organizations.

At the national level in most of Latin America, the rebuilding of democracy revealed enormous faults in institutional structure that had been hidden or promoted by authoritarian governments; it also revealed the prevalence of ideological conflicts. When issues such as the legitimacy of political representation, citizen participation, decentralization, and relations among state branches — to mention a few of the most important ones — reached the surface, they were greatly magnified in the mass media.

In turn, the collapse of raw-materials prices and the external debt crisis at the beginning of the 1980s led to public bankruptcy and revealed deep faults in the economic systems of Latin American countries, forcing governments to establish monetary stabilization programs and, furthermore, far-reaching structural adjustment plans that relied on external trade, liberalization of international finance, and a more important role for private enterprise in the productive and service sectors.

Different forms of market economy greatly increased the capacity for economic growth and accelerated the transformation of modern society. However, as experience has shown, when a capitalist economy becomes the dominant system it reinforces its secular inclination toward the concentration and unequal distribution of wealth, as much in the industrialized nations as in the developing world. Recent studies by international, specialized organizations show that the incidence and intensity of poverty have increased by almost 40% among Latin American people. As both a cause and a result of poverty, marginalization has grown, excluding large sectors of populations from activity in the economic and democratic systems. The social confrontation and fragmentation brought about by this situation have been demonstrated in social protest in different countries and the growth of common delinquency in practically all major Latin American cities.

# Dual society in Latin America

These external and internal tendencies have reopened the old problem of a dual society in Latin America. At the end of this century, there is more conflict about the issue than at the beginning. Even though events in this century have significantly improved the living standards of the majority of people — as evidenced by longer life expectancies, reduced mother and child mortality, and higher literacy rates — they have also widened the gap separating the high- and low-income groups. This situation has been seen before and is characteristic of the market economy, but it was worsened by the structural adjustment measures taken at the beginning of the 1980s.

The phenomenon of a dual society does not necessarily mean an absolute polarization of the rich and the poor. The middle class remains an important part of society, representing 40–60% of the total population. The conflict arises between the richest group in society (about 15–20% of the population), with its growing concentration of wealth, and the group in extreme poverty (almost 20% of the population), for whom living conditions constantly worsen and basic needs for survival are difficult to meet.

In the groups suffering extreme poverty, the backwardness accumulates and promotes a structure that leads to even greater backwardness; this is a result of geographic and historical factors or shortages of resources, information, and knowledge. This is why, in most communities, poverty can almost be described as inherited: the children of the poor are born with a legacy of accumulated backwardness. The effort needed to break the barrier of extreme poverty is much greater for these underprivileged groups than for impoverished communities that have no history of marginalization.

Moreover, the poor are less and less involved in the process of cumulative production, because in practice they are outside the market. Whether they are unemployed in the cities or surviving on their little rural plots, they have no contact with the national economy at all. In this sense, the poor can be distinguished from the exploited, because the poor are unable to generate surpluses for others to appropriate. The rich and the rest of society do not depend on the work of or production by indigent workers and are consequently not worried about them.

The risk of social fragmentation resulting from the resurgence of the dual society and from worsening problems of extreme poverty is grave, and it is greater than in the past. The poor are now aware of their poverty and marginalization. Until recently, poverty seemed to be part of the human condition and divine dispensation; things had always been that way, and it seemed they always would be. Nowadays, the poor know that their poverty is not part of the natural order and can be overcome, as it has been overcome by others.

On the other hand, violence is the natural language of communication between the poor and the rest of society, for the poor live under constant pressure of brutality and abuse. The end of the Cold War weakened or wiped out the hope of a socialist utopia, and the poor no longer join political organizations to change society by force. Some are seeking salvation in religious fundamentalism; others have no other option than delinquency, which is prevalent in almost all the marginalized belts around the major Latin American cities. The traditional guerrilla has been replaced by this chaotic and unpredictable one, who has created unbearable conditions for citizen security.

## Priorities and instruments of the national development strategy

The risk of Latin American countries' being marginalized in the international economy is still worse than the threat of social fragmentation taking place in these countries, as international marginalization increases internal imbalances. Consequently, national development strategies, especially those resulting from the structural adjustment programs, give priority to the export-oriented modern sector. The whole system — money and interest rates, commercial offerings, technology policy, and investment — is defined by this orientation. The main objective is to achieve a competitive reintegration of Latin America into the international economic system, even though this strategy has not yet developed beyond the opening, passive phase of policy implementation.

Another element in this plan is the significant reduction of the state's role in the production of goods and services (including the so-called strategic sectors) and in those areas designated as public services and thus deemed to be the exclusive domain of the public sector. Privatization efforts in Latin America and in a good part of the developing world differ in their objectives and rate of application but have the same goals of removing the state from any direct economic activity and of transferring or closing down public enterprise.

This is a unidirectional strategy, the success of which depends on the behaviour of the export sector and the ability of Latin American business people to meet the challenge. The fault in the strategy is that it intentionally or unintentionally ignores the problem of social disequilibrium. Instead, the strategy is formulated on the assumption that the economic growth produced in an open and competitive economy will reach the whole of society sooner or later and create the conditions of stability and development needed to overcome poverty. However, experience has extensively shown that there will be no such "trickling down" of growth but that prosperity will concentrate even more in higher income sectors. The risks of social breakdown and citizen insecurity will grow to the point at which social coexistence becomes intolerable. This is why the strategy of a competitive and open economy, designed to reintegrate Latin American countries in the dynamic flow of contemporary society, requires a complementary, clearly defined strategy to eliminate extreme poverty and reestablish the feeling of solidarity essential to successful national projects.

## Basic needs in an open-market economy

Many of the instruments used to combat poverty and meet basic needs are incompatible or difficult to use with the new development strategy. For example, price-support mechanisms, state subsidies, tariff protection, and subventioned interest rates would conflict with the basic principles of this strategy or the conditions imposed by international financial organizations. This difficulty also applies to public enterprise or state-owned agencies involved in the production of goods and services or technology.

These considerations reveal the need to objectively identify the elements of a strategy to combat extreme poverty and meet the basic needs of the poorest sectors of the population. The strategy should not be in conflict with an open and competitive market economy. It will require direct action and constant support from the state. It will require financial and technical cooperation from international organizations, help that should be motivated by a real interest in the problem rather than by a desire to merely ease the donor's conscience. Such a strategy will have to achieve social legitimacy.

Moreover, in my view, a national development strategy that also helps the poor should focus on three central priorities: democratic participation, education, and small-scale enterprise.

### Democratic participation

The concepts of poverty and marginalization are often confused because of their connotations, but they are distinct concepts. Poverty is the lack of resources or services necessary to survival; it is an economic concept. Marginalization, on the other hand, is the exclusion or isolation of certain groups from the economic, social, and political life of their communities; it is thus a political concept.

Poverty does not necessarily create marginalization, but marginalization almost always deepens poverty, even though it does not always create it. Marginalization can take many forms because exclusion can be on economic, ethnic, or class grounds. In nearly all cases, marginalization is very closely associated with indigence. This is why the fight against poverty has to begin with the eradication of marginalization. Nonetheless, the intention of the strategy is not to "include the excluded," which has a paternalistic connotation that clouds the issue, but to promote the "participation of the marginalized." Nothing from the outside would be useful without their active and conscious participation.

Democratic participation is essential because it has a decisive influence on political power and consequently on the objectives and priorities of any national development strategy. The postulate of participatory democracy can no longer be regarded as unrealistic. Access to education and the revolution in communications media have greatly increased the potential for the whole of society to shape political power and community administration. Marginalized populations should start to use these instruments, not only to enjoy the freedom guaranteed by the welfare state but also to assume responsibility for changing their role in society.

Unlike traditional political participation, exercised individually at elections or through political parties, the participation of the poor in Latin America should be exercised collectively through traditional base organizations: communities, unions, and neighbourhood associations. The participation of the poor should have the wider and more concrete objectives of contributing to the solutions to their communities' problems, defining their priorities, discussing procedures, helping with the work, overseeing public works, and reporting corruption.

The democratic participation of marginalized people, essential to reducing or eliminating their poverty, coincides with another great movement in today's society: decentralization. There is an unstoppable social demand for participation in economic and political activity. The citizen — that is, the central protagonist in democratic society — is determined to recover this source of power and sovereignty. This is essentially in contradiction to the objectives of the Latin American authoritarian and centralist political system. This is why the postulate of decentralization implies a horizontal and vertical redistribution of power and why the task of promoting participation is such a complex one.

Other advantages of decentralization are efficiency in the assignment and use of resources, support for regional entrepreneurial spirit, and growth in local economic activity resulting from the growth in expenditures at the local level.

Usually, it is argued that the decentralization process will be hampered by a lack of technical and administrative experience at the regional level or by poor planning and execution of development projects at the local level. Decentralization means than certain sectors would clearly lose their benefits from economies of scale. With decentralization, central governments might try to distance themselves from local problems, arguing that this responsibility has been transferred to local levels of government. There are two possible results: growth in the gap between rich and poor regions and a risk of national fragmentation. The risk of national fragmentation is the worst of these, without doubt.

The risks of decentralization are greatest for the poor. The rest of society will be greatly tempted to forget the marginalized people and use decentralization as a way of evading the problem, particularly in the case of rural marginalization, distant from the urban centres. To combat this, there must be an effective transfer of responsibilities to the base organizations of the marginalized peoples to foster local participation. At the same time, there will be a need for national society, the government, and international organizations to cooperate with these base organizations and supply the essential technological and financial resources.

## Education

Education is without a doubt the most important of the basic social needs. It is defined by experts as a prerequisite for the productive and economic labour needed for survival. Education affects all groups living in a common territory. Attending to this basic need for all children, youths, and adults in a way that guarantees free access, equity, sustained participation, and effective achievements in learning improves both the individual and society. Such education is a fundamental dimension of any social, cultural, or economic national project. The effects of an educational policy go beyond those of any other human activity, including activities intended to promote health, the environment, productivity, employment, or competitiveness. Moreover, learning to learn is a critical requirement for development in a knowledge-based society.

The exceptional growth of accumulated experience in contemporary society and the expansion of the communications media have greatly improved the capacity to offer basic education to everyone and have placed this objective within reach. The World Declaration on Education for All of March 1990 states that this central objective must be reached through multisectorial plans, which may fix concrete goals in a set time, determine the priority of population categories, and establish indicators to measure the outcome. These plans must

▼ Identify traditional systems of apprenticeship in society and the real demand for basic formal and informal education;

▼ Take into account the different needs for basic apprenticeship; and

▼ Take advantage of the potential of electronic and traditional information media.

The main technological requirements of the plans include

▼ Strongly developed planning and groundwork capabilities at the regional and local levels;

▼ Training programs for special personnel, particularly techniques for groundwork, supervision, and administrative reform;

▼ Technical services and mechanisms to collect, process, analyze, and transmit data;

▼ Efficient and elaborate systems to evaluate the performance of teachers and their methods; and

▼ Improved educational technologies.

Basic education is the responsibility of the whole of society. Apprenticeship is not produced in isolation. The government must provide basic education for all, but it cannot be expected to do all the work; the community has a binding responsibility, along with the state.

With the proclamation of the failure of the state and the absolute and relative reduction of its role in society, it is particularly important to underline the state's protagonistic role in any war on poverty, especially in providing basic education for less favoured groups. Certainly, the reduction or elimination of poverty and the satisfaction of basic needs cannot rely on the philanthropy of a few private agencies. In Latin American countries and in most developing nations, poverty is a problem that affects the structure of society, its cohesion, and its future, and for this reason it must occupy first place in strategic state affairs. Furthermore, the state function in satisfying basic needs goes beyond the defensive attitude of trying to avoid social fragmentation and its consequences and becomes an important element in the training and administration of human resources, which are the main factors in production and growth in a knowledge-based society.

In its national budget the state should assign the resources necessary to meet this responsibility. Tax policy takes on or reclaims an important role because it becomes the central mechanism for redistributing wealth and providing equal opportunity. This role for a tax policy will become clear once a reduction has been made in funds to the state-owned enterprises engaged in the production of goods or services. International development organizations may play a critical role in social investment, education, and health, not only because of the volume of the development funds but also because of the capacity of these organizations to contribute knowledge as well.

In addition to collecting and assigning resources to meet basic needs, particularly the need for education, the state has to ensure that these funds reach their goals. In other words, it has to focus on investment and social spending. The administration of investment and social spending is one of the conditions of success for the fight against poverty and should be under constant supervision, which is mainly the task of the potential benefactors, who must organize to demand their rights.

Basic social needs — such as education, health, basic infrastructure, and environmental protection — have common characteristics in Latin America but also involve specific problems, depending on different local characteristics and different levels of priority. Decentralization has a very important place in this strategy: it allows civilians to participate directly in the definition of political priorities and operative mechanisms and in the efficient and constant supervision of public-sector entities. Among the different options for decentralization, the municipality is the most efficient venue for achieving participation and effective supervision.

## Small-scale enterprise

Direct participation of society — especially the poor — in economic activity is another necessity in the successful fight against poverty. We all know the limits of assistance policy. It offers food and essential services to the most vulnerable sectors and saves people in emergency situations, but it does not attack the root of their problems, which is a lack of education and employment.

Employment is required to generate family income to meet the basic familial needs: food, housing, and clothing. Unlike the case of basic social needs (like education), the responsibility for employment generally rests with the private sector. State employment policy will have to change, gradually reducing its generation of direct employment, at least in the case of public enterprises. The responsibility for creating jobs should then be taken up by the private sector, which is responsible for creating small- and medium-scale enterprises (SMEs) to meet the big demand for new jobs. The state, in turn, would then be responsible for devising and implementing policies to promote the creation of jobs in the private sector. Close cooperation between the state and the private sector is essential to success.

At this point, it is useful to look at the role of private national and foreign investment in job generation. In theory, formal private enterprise is responsible for competitive integration into the world economy. In reality, the activity of this sector is generally more intensive in information and knowledge than in labour, which is why its effects on employment are not as strong as we wish.

Thus it is necessary to design policies to promote SMEs, to bring the informal sector into the nucleus of economic activity, and to stimulate agriculture — industry and agriculture being the main sectors in which jobs will be created. Industrial and agricultural development policies are not incompatible with the open-market economy, as they do not necessarily imply direct state intervention or contradict either commercial expansion or macroeconomic equilibrium. The rational use of such policies permitted growth, first, in the industrialized countries and then, later, in the Asian economies.

Public policies should be designed to encourage the rural and urban poor to set up SMEs to create jobs, generate family income, and meet the basic needs of food, clothing, and housing. At the beginning, these policies would relate to credit, technical assistance, and commercial and distribution services. Financial assistance would be appropriately provided through international development funds and the mobilization of national institutional savings. Technical-assistance programs would have to include imaginative, local contributions and be applicable to the most economically depressed areas. University students and young professionals could participate in technical-assistance programs, rather than leaving this responsibility to youngsters from industrialized countries. Business people and local universities could share their experience and resources with these programs.

The state and the international development agencies have an important role as catalytic agents and as supporters of this national mobilization of the marginalized sectors of society. Although the state and these organizations cannot by themselves assume this responsibility in a direct way, it would be unjustifiable for them to neglect it or limit themselves to purely philanthropic assistance.

In sum, technology — whether this is simple technology capable of general application and diffusion or high technology applied to simple procedures — is needed to satisfy the basic needs of the people living in extreme poverty by helping them set up small enterprises. The use of patent-protected technologies would probably be required in only a few cases, and in those cases licencing agreements would be needed to facilitate and control their use. We have to assume that among people who live below the poverty line, managers are inexperienced or nonexistent and workers are poorly trained if they are trained at all. Technical performance in this sector will likely be inefficient. These are the first issues we must address in developing technology for the basic needs of the very poor.

# Chapter 4

# The Forgotten Strategy

*Arnoldo K. Ventura and Martin E.D. Henry*

The concern with the basic needs of large sections of the population of the developing countries originated about two decades ago in a debate about the new international economic order (NIEO). This was caused by the failure of the trickle-down economic strategy to stem the increase in worldwide poverty (UNCTAD 1976; Soedjatmoko 1980). The call for an NIEO came soon after the oil embargo staged by oil-exporting countries toward the end of 1973 (United Nations 1973). It was reasoned then that the economic position of developing countries could be substantially improved only with significant changes in international arrangements in trade, finance (Ramphal 1978), and technology transfer (Goulet 1976). This later led to two resolutions of the United Nations General Assembly to establish an NIEO (Savant and Hasenpflug 1977; Streeten 1979).

## The new international economic order

The NIEO was seen as an alteration in the global power structure needed to bring about, at the local level, self-reliance, rural development, and the satisfaction of basic needs. The ultimate objective was to provide a basis for economic independence and wider local participation in socioeconomic development in developing countries. In essence, the NIEO was intended to reduce the developing countries' economic dependence on the developed countries: widespread poverty could be alleviated by allowing the developing nations to better manage their resources.

The NIEO was conceived as a dynamic and evolving process that would eliminate economic injustice and equalize economic opportunity. Productive capacities would then be unleashed, thereby making it possible to respond to the basic needs of people in all parts of the world (Hope 1983). In practical terms, the developing countries were hoping during the 1960s and 1970s to convince the developed countries to allow fairer and more stable prices for raw materials; open access to Northern markets for industrial products; and give more aid, in line with the United Nation's target of 0.7% of gross national product, to help reduce poverty (some of which, it was argued, was a legacy of colonialism). As one might imagine, this idea of an NIEO fell immediately into disfavour among the rich capitalist countries, and a drawn-out international debate ensued. Finally, the view of developed countries prevailed, and the crucial resources for the implementation of any NIEO strategy were withheld.

# Global economic policies

## The International Monetary Fund and the World Bank revisited

Because of the adjustment programs of the International Monetary Fund (IMF) and the activities of the World Bank, the NIEO gradually gave way to the ideology of the supremacy of the market. During this period, many developing countries were seduced by massive foreign loans, with escalating interest rates, which they were later forced to repay under onerous conditions. Even after many initiatives and debt-forgiveness programs, the total debt of the developing countries still amounts to more than $1.7 trillion. In this new atmosphere, the cry for self-reliance and for the fulfilment of basic needs gradually fell from the international agenda. This has since proven to be a serious regression in attempts at international development. Indeed, widespread criticism and opposition to the IMF and World Bank programs today are directly due to the growing poverty and despair that resulted from the neglect of basic needs in countries where these programs were implemented.

In addition to the many food riots in places like Brazil and Sudan, crime and lawlessness increased on a global scale because both the developed and the developing countries abandoned the basic needs of large sections of their populations. The prevailing situation is also marked by growing squalor and disease in the poorer developing countries. The reemergence of cholera in Latin America, after an absence of more than a century, has been attributed to this blatant neglect. The squalid environments in many Latin American cities have been responsible for waterborne diseases, including the spread of cholera. Moreover, diseases formerly contained, such as malaria and tuberculosis, began a comeback in some cities of the United States and Latin America.

The visible failure of purist economic policies to stem the rise of poverty and the rapid decline in the quality of life for many in the developing countries, together with the added attention paid to the Bretton Woods institutions (occasioned by the celebration of their 50th anniversary), prompted a reevaluation of the effect of these on the world economy. There has been a general dissatisfaction with the influence of the Bretton Woods institutions on the sociodevelopment of developing countries, and lately calls have been heard for their complete restructuring. The operations of the Bretton Woods institutions have been under serious criticism from progressive thinkers for some time (see, for example, Killick et al. 1986). Today the outcry also comes from governments, nongovernmental organizations (NGOs), and research institutions in the developed countries.

The multilateral lending agencies recently insisted that the Jamaican government increase lending rates to the agricultural sector to commercial levels, which in effect meant doubling interest rates. Government policy had deliberately provided preferential interest rates to farmers to encourage the development of agro-industry, the principal employer of low-skilled and unskilled labour and a traditional cornerstone of the Jamaican economy, in which 50% of the population is rural and a large proportion is small-scale farmers. The lower margins of profit and the unattractiveness of the sector for new investments also justify lower interest rates.

These lending agencies are now insisting that the mortgage interest rates of the National Housing Trust (NHT) also be raised to commercial levels. The government has so far resisted. NHT is a quasi-governmental institution that provides housing and, therefore, also supports the construction industry, doing so through a pool of funds deducted from the salaries of Jamaican workers.

## Neglect of basic needs

The basic strategy of the Bretton Woods institutions is to enlarge the economic cake, hoping that crumbs will fall to the base of society, but this strategy has failed. Its failure was quite visible in the so-called lost decade of the 1980s. In that decade, poverty increased: by the end of the decade, about 1.3 billion people in the developing world lived in dire poverty.

Studies have shown that the pursuit of export- or industry-led strategies at the expense of agriculture aggravated the spread of poverty. This problem showed signs of abatement when sectoral policies centring on agriculture, health, education, and transportation were deployed. The success of the International Funds for Agricultural Development confirms the validity of the agricultural approach. In contrast, other poverty-alleviation strategies failed because they lacked a clear focus on poverty and tended to place too little emphasis on agriculture. The studies have also revealed that redistribution measures, such as lease reform, often stumbled on legal loopholes and the narrow interests of the elites in society.

In many countries, along with economic growth came increases in prices for land, skilled labour, and capital. Unfortunately, the poor had none of these assets but had to face the ensuing inflation. In this situation, which was common in the 1980s, the poor often neglected to provide parental care, the result of which was greater poverty and desperation among the next generation. The street children, visible in many of the capitals of the so-called rapidly developing countries, are testimony to this fact. Furthermore, the patterns of growth often added to poverty and the neglect of basic needs. Biases, such as urban concentration of growth, displaced unskilled labour, altered prices to the disadvantage of the poor, created gender gaps, undermined child welfare, and eroded tradition, social protection, and entitlements. Additionally, in capitalist countries, economic fortunes fluctuated widely, the poor were left out when resources were limited and were only grudgingly considered when growth rates were high and the poor appeared to be a nuisance.

Of even greater importance is the fact that the industrialization model fostered by the Bretton Woods institutions and pursued by most developing countries failed to satisfy even the minimum needs of large sections of their populations. Resources for social programs were literally choked off by the international structural adjustment programs, further increasing the numbers in dire poverty and creating a new working poor. This group, including women, the elderly, and workers with education and skills, was more vocal and socially connected than the rural and urban poor and mounted great opposition to the World Bank and IMF. Those in the silent majority, who were historically denied the opportunity to meet their basic needs, began to openly express their dissatisfaction. Fierce challenges to the current political and social power structures have surfaced, acquiring serious environmental and national security dimensions.

In this climate of discontent, the old questions of the interdependence of nations and the wisdom of tackling basic needs in a systematic manner have once more surfaced. There is now fresh support for making the satisfaction of basic needs a central strategy in global development. The direct relationship of poverty to environmental stress and decay has also added to the concern with basic needs. The focus on the satisfaction of basic needs must also be seen as part of a new global development assessment, prompted by recent economic and political changes throughout the world that have generated significant economic growth for a few and crushing poverty for many (Streeten 1979; UNDP 1991b–94). At this juncture, the old suspicion harboured by the developing countries that the basic-needs strategy is a paternalistic ploy by the industrialized countries to cop out of development assistance (Streeten 1979) can no longer be a major deterrent.

## Concepts and orientation

A basic-needs approach can be defined as a type of development that attaches special weight to the satisfaction of the fundamental material and nonmaterial requirements of a particular society to enable it in the shortest time to empower all of its citizens to participate in its chosen objectives. Because the basic needs of the poorest people are less likely to be fulfilled in the normal course of development, the poor are, accordingly, identified as a priority target group.

The primary objective, then, of a basic-needs approach to socioeconomic development is to provide opportunities for the physical, psychological, and social uplift of all individuals, especially those who are deemed deficient in these resources. This strategy calls for a greater emphasis on domestic technological competence and management, a greater absorptive capacity for the benefits of science and technology (S&T), and a wider spread of the benefits of growth through decentralized production and consumption planning — in essence, a more comprehensive pattern of development (Bhalla 1979).

A basic-needs objective entails improved access to goods and services through appropriate institutions and technologies. Information technologies (ITs) and technologies for marketing, distribution, transport, and production become extremely important. The idea is to mobilize essential resources for groups identified as lacking these resources. The focus is on the resources to be provided, rather than on the mere provision of income. An income approach may fail to ensure the fulfilment of basic needs; for example, income generation alone will not ensure the provision of essential services, and additional income could be spent on products that do not satisfy basic needs, such as food items with low nutritional value but advertisement appeal (Ventura 1992b).

This strategy calls for changes in the composition of production and in the rates of growth of different goods and services in a society, as well as the better distribution of purchasing power among diverse groups. The basic-needs strategy is premised on the fact that poverty is widespread in most developing populations, and therefore action should target the population as a whole, rather than isolated groups. This is a fundamental conceptual difference between contemporary poverty-oriented development strategies and a basic-needs approach (Streeten and Burki 1978).

The way we visualize poverty will determine our approach to basic needs. If poverty is viewed as the result of inadequate growth rates in national incomes, the prescription for relief is to remove the economic constraints and replace them with stimulants for growth, such as increased local savings, earned foreign exchange, heightened agricultural and industrial productivity, better education, and improved skills. The theory is that the benefits from total-factor productivity will eventually trickle down to the poor. Empirical evidence now shows that this is seldom the case, and poverty often increases in the face of economic growth. Sen (1987) considered poverty as individuals' lack of entitlements and absence of capabilities. So poverty in developing countries is seen as "reduced lives," rather than merely as reduced incomes. However, if poverty is seen as a lack of individual entitlements and capabilities, the prescription for poverty becomes the improvement in the ability of individuals to meet their basic needs. In other words, as Marx (1968 [1867]) surmised, the prescription is "replacing the domination of circumstances and chance over individuals by the domination of individuals over chance and circumstances." Improving people's ability to live and to become productive, according to this vision, is more important than giving them an income.

The basic-needs strategy is not only to significantly raise the level of aggregate demand but also to increase the supply of basic goods and services, as opposed to merely raising the income of the poor to a minimum subsistence level. The satisfaction of basic needs is intended to eliminate absolute poverty, as well as to mitigate relative poverty, by a continuous process of economic development and social improvement. Mass participation is, therefore, a prominent feature in the formulation, implementation, and evaluation of measures to attain basic needs.

It must also be noted that the old basic-needs approach has serious difficulties in reaching the absolute poor. The simple provision of basic-needs services will not automatically lead to their use by the poor. The sense of powerlessness and dependency experienced by the poor will have to be removed for this to happen. This will depend on the willingness of the absolute poor to participate in the planning and organized use of new resources. Even community participation by poor populations will not ensure the participation of the poorest of the poor. Often, relevant information fails to reach them. They are fully occupied with survival and have no time for taking care of illnesses. They cannot risk leaving their low-paying, often unproductive work to take up initiatives that may not redound to their interest. This means that much more information is required to deal with this group. The pattern of dependency and powerlessness and the social structure of absolute poverty resulting from exploitation, permanent indebtedness, and hopelessness are not clearly understood. The same is true of the geography of poverty and the ways it is distributed in special circumstances (for example, the situation of those without land, women, and those who sleep on sidewalks, under bridges, and in garbage dumps). The absolute poor, therefore, cannot be helped by the old basic-needs approach. Any strategy to reach them must probe the depths of society and be given special support and attention. The most vulnerable must not be overlooked in efforts to overcome rural and urban poverty and backwardness.

The satisfaction of basic needs must be seen as more than a moral appendage to national industrial policy. A concern with basic needs must become an explicit component of industrial and macroeconomic policies. Fundamental institutional and strategic changes are required to put the improvement of society on solid, sustainable foundations.

In most countries, the satisfaction of basic needs cannot be achieved without systemic economic growth and social enhancement. However, changes in the pattern of growth needed to ensure the lowest income groups have more access to productive resources and more influence on decision-making are the centrepiece of this strategy. The poor, instead of being considered liabilities on the state, must become net contributors to development. The unemployed, underemployed, seasonally employed, and the general mass of the working poor in the informal sector have to be mobilized to become involved in the overall productive process. Higher levels of output and proper distribution of resources will then ensure that basic needs can be met (ILO 1976). The association of basic needs with low-level, labour-intensive methods has to be dispelled, although labour-intensive activities in countries with high unemployment seems a reasonable strategy. The emphasis should be on the ends, rather than the means. In other words, technology should be selected to ensure the most efficient use of resources and distribution of wealth.

A basic-needs strategy will tend to make more use of local resources because of the inherent linkages, complementarities, and interdependencies among diverse sectors. For example, attacks on malnutrition, disease, and illiteracy will not only satisfy the basic needs in these areas and improve the quality of life but also improve the work force. A basic-needs approach is, therefore, a more efficient harvester, mobilizer, and user of resources than a purely income-oriented approach. In a sense, the basic-needs approach allows the resource gap between the rich and the poor to be closed from both ends of the economic spectrum, that is, from the supply and demand ends.

Nonmaterial basic needs are a vital component of the basic-needs package. Respect, participation in decision-making, self-determination, self-reliance, political and economic freedom, security, and national and cultural identity are vital aspects of the basic-needs strategy. A sense of purpose in life and occupation becomes the pivot for action. The nonmaterial basic needs are often the prerequisite for meeting the material basic needs. Nevertheless, trade-offs and sacrifices are to be expected because of the dynamic relationship between material and nonmaterial needs.

This study will not extend the concept of basic needs to encompass those of roughly the 20% of people in most populations who are destitute, sick, disabled, aged, or orphaned, but it must be remembered that they have specific basic-needs requirements, which generally are not being satisfactorily met in either the developed or the developing countries. Certain minimum physiological conditions for life can be established for all human beings, but other basic needs that allow for a humane quality of life vary among geographical areas, cultures, states, and strategies for development. Each society, therefore, will have to identify its own basket of basic goods and services. "The concept of basic needs is a country specific and dynamic concept and it should be placed within a context of a nation's over-all economic and social development" (ILO 1977). This declaration was made in 1976 as part of the principles and program of action of the World Employment Conference and is as relevant today as it was then.

## State of the planet

### Global poverty

The relevance and urgency of the imperative to address the basic needs of vast numbers of people worldwide can best be appreciated by reviewing human development in the recent past. The United Nations Development Programme *Human Development Report, 1994* (UNDP 1994) stated that there had been "breathtaking globalization of prosperity side by side with a depressing globalization of poverty." The report went on to mention that "despite all our technological breakthroughs, we still live in a world where a fifth of the developing world's population goes hungry every night, a quarter lacks access to even the basic necessities, like safe drinking water, and a third live in abject poverty." The report bemoaned the fact that, although so many go hungry, so much food goes to waste, and the richest billion people command 60 times the income of the poorest billion. The report called for a new "paradigm of sustainable development," with a "new framework for development cooperation." In essence, an NIEO, involving a major restructuring of the world's income-distribution, production, and consumption patterns, is considered a precondition for any feasible strategy for sustainable human development. The highest priorities are poverty reduction, productive employment, social integration, and environmental regeneration. Clearly, the satisfaction of basic needs fits directly in with the new vision of world development held by the United Nations Development Programme (UNDP), although this is not explicitly stated.

## Impact of multilateral and bilateral interventions

George (1987), in her introduction to the book, *The Hunger Machine*, wrote "charity, however necessary it may be to alleviate distress, is not the relevant virtue for fighting hunger. The virtue is justice, because charity can never be more than a stop-gap." Massive amounts of capital have been poured into the developing countries as aid in the form of grants and soft loans. These aid packages, however, lack specific S&T components to ensure a relevant impact on development problems (UNDP and GOJ 1992b). About $75 billion a year is spent on aid of all kinds; the ultimate effect, however, is the net outflow of resources from the developing to the developed countries, to the tune of about $37 billion net a year. The total debt of the developing countries amounts to more than $1.7 trillion, and servicing these debts costs more than $175 billion annually.

Aid in some quarters is called the poison gift (George 1987), but increasingly many countries stake their hopes on aid to correct decades of exploitation and underdevelopment. To understand this dilemma, we must realize that *aid* in its current usage refers to the transfer of resources from the developed countries to the developing ones. Bilateral aid is the transfer of goods and services from one government to another, which accounts for more than three quarters of all aid to developing countries. Multilateral aid consists of the contributions of several countries, channeled through an international institution, such as the World Bank, IMF, and European Economic Community. Private aid comes from private organizations or NGOs and goes directly to those countries in need. Private aid represents only a very small fraction of total aid. The prevailing attitude throughout the world is that it is foolhardy to expect aid to reach the powerless when channeled through the powerful. The most efficient method is to have the people in need become the direct beneficiaries and to have programs designed specifically with their welfare in mind.

Often, official aid is simply an extension of foreign policy and a means to gain political advantage. Aid is often given to countries not in need and for areas that are not priorities for the recipient countries. Food aid grew since World War II out of the desire to stop the march of communism and started as surpluses of food sent to Europe to consolidate the Atlantic Alliance. Food aid in the form of dumped subsidized commodities has a devastating effect on domestic production. Many staples have been forced from local production and have become a source of deep dependency. So entrenched have the dependencies become that sudden removal of this form of aid would be catastrophic for recipient governments. Food aid also has been used as a political weapon against communist countries or their sympathizers. Therefore, it may not be the best means to satisfy basic needs.

In some instances, aid is simply the transfer of capital from the taxpayers in the developed countries, via the aid recipient, to the same developed countries' private companies. These funds are often spent in donor countries on equipment and expatriate salaries, as a condition for the aid.

Although, on the surface, aid always appears attractive in the short term, it must be realized that it could become quite destructive. For example, in Jamaica, the PL480 program, under which rice and other staples are provided at concessional prices, has served to strangle rice and other staple production on the island and discourage investments in these areas of agriculture. The Jamaican people have become dependent on these imports for their food. These cheap stocks will not last for much longer, and when they are finished, the cost of these commodities will revert to world prices, making them unaffordable for the average person if the Jamaican economy does not significantly improve. Basic foods will then be curtailed even further.

The satisfaction of basic needs is seldom on the agenda of aid agencies, and when it is, the agencies tend to undermine local production and reduce incomes in the communities in need. International-aid patterns have benefited the well-off urbanites more than the rural or urban poor. This is confirmed by the fact that after decades of aid, the basic needs of most of the Jamaican people are barely being met, and for about 40%, basic needs for adequate food, water, health, and housing are simply out of reach.

The World Bank and IMF have, for the last decade, insisted on structural adjustment programs, which have imposed severe hardships

on the poor working classes. The macroeconomic changes the World
Bank and IMF have increased poverty and despair. These strategies are
proving to be blatantly counterproductive, and society is rebelling
against their consequences. The World Bank and the IMF seem to have
found religion and have now targeted the poor for special attention.
This is a window of opportunity for reinstituting the concept of basic-
needs satisfaction as a fundamental pillar of socioeconomic development. No country can expect to prosper economically or, indeed, have
the ability to repay loans if that country suffers constant strife, crime,
and general dislocation of normal life, which seem to have been the
primary achievements of the multilateral banking institutions. The
"small" person has been neglected in the shuffle to satisfy the dictates
of these institutions.

Many people are now forced into the informal sector of petty
trading, services, crafts, and light manufacturing, without the technological assistance to become truly efficient and competitive. Manufacturing has stagnated, and trading has suffered from the opening up of
Jamaican markets and the devaluation of the Jamaican dollar. Tourism
and financial services are still vibrant, and these have kept the economy going. The total result of all this is that the gap between the rich
and the poor has widened, and consumerism has literally exploded.
Jamaica's annual trade deficit is now about $1 billion. The poor and
those at the lower end of the income scale are literally outside this
economy and benefit little from these activities, although these people
have to bear the brunt of the high prices caused by inflation.

## Growth is not enough

It is difficult to conceive of how global order and integrity can be maintained without ensuring that most of the citizens of the world are in a
physical and psychological state to contribute to these aspirations. The
benefits of increased production do not automatically trickle down to all
sections of society, especially to those who are most in need. Therefore,
growth is not enough, a point exemplified by the United States, which
has had sustained growth for more than 200 years yet has about 20 million people who are without enough to eat (United Nations 1989).

The poorest people are either scattered, isolated in remote
places, or crowded into ghettoes, in so-called inner cities. These people
are the least skilled, have the fewest productive resources, and have
the least access to technology or capital. Special measures are necessary if the lot of these people is to improve (United Nations 1989). Furthermore, although roughly 50% of the absolute poor live in the rural
areas, the basic needs of the rural poor are met less adequately today
than they were a decade ago (FAO 1988). All projections indicate that

the number of people living in poverty will increase unless direct and drastic measures are taken. The International Labour Office has estimated that the number of people in the Third World who were living in extreme poverty increased from 819 million in 1980 to 881 million in 1985. The projection was that 913 million would be living in poverty in 1995. All evidence suggests that this may have been an underestimate (Cornia et al. 1991; UNDP 1991b).

The alleviation of poverty should be seen, not as charity but as an investment in the future of all people. There has been a call to have reduction of severe poverty and deprivation become the central objective of the next decade of global development. The United Nations (1989) stated quite clearly that "the minimum objective for a new international development strategy should be to reduce the absolute number of people living in poverty by the year 2000." This is a laudable goal. If we attempt to meet it, we must have a proper monitoring and reporting system. At present, the data on poverty and basic needs are grossly out of date. To make sound decisions, we require new, more accurate indicators and new social theoretical constructs. So, up-to-date initial data are required if proper monitoring and evaluation are to take place.

The World Bank (1990), using a poverty line of $1 per person per day at 1985 values, estimated that one third of developing countries suffered in a state of poverty and that poverty increased by 8% during the period between 1985 and 1990. About 1.1 billion people were living in poverty. Clearly, the income-growth strategy prevailing during that period had failed to contain poverty. Growth does not help the poor unless the poor are participants in creating growth, and the poor will have to be the direct beneficiaries of public policy for this to happen, that is, with a direct attack on their basic needs. The Jamaican case has also revealed that transfer of wealth is a complex and difficult issue and does not really cure poverty. The strategy of enabling the poor to generate their own wealth must now be considered.

## Strategies to reduce poverty

UNDP (1994) gave the most comprehensive account of the steps needed to reduce poverty. Poverty was described as "the greatest threat to political stability, social cohesion and the environmental health of the planet." "Strategies for poverty reduction," the report said (p. 20),

*will embrace:*

▼ *Basic social services* — *The state must help ensure a widespread distribution of basic social services to the poor, particularly basic education and primary health care.*

▼ *Agrarian reform* — *Since a large part of poverty in developing countries is concentrated in the rural areas, poverty reduction strategies often require a more equitable distribution of land and agricultural resources.*

▼ *Credit for all* — *One of the most powerful ways of opening markets to the poor is to ensure more equal access to credit. The criteria of creditworthiness must change, and credit institutions must be decentralized.*

▼ *Employment* — *The best way to extend the benefits of growth to the poor and to involve them in the expansion of output is to rapidly expand productive employment opportunities and to create a framework for ensuring a sustainable livelihood for everyone.*

▼ *Participation* — *Any viable strategy for poverty reduction must be decentralized and participatory. The poor cannot benefit from economic development if they do not even participate in its design.*

▼ *A social safety net* — *Every country needs an adequate social safety net to catch those whom markets exclude.*

▼ *Economic growth* — *The focus of development efforts, in addition to increasing overall productivity, must be to increase the productivity of the poor. This will help ensure that the poor not only benefit from, but also contribute to, economic growth.*

▼ *Sustainability* — *Poverty reduces people's capacity to use resources in a sustainable manner, intensifying pressures on the ecosystem. To ensure sustainability, the content of growth must change — becoming less material-intensive and energy-intensive and more equitable in its distribution.*

### Employment creation

The report (UNDP 1994) then outlined a set of strategies for employment creation:

▼ *Education and skills* — *To compete in a fast-changing global economy, every country has to invest heavily in the education, training and skill formation of its people.*

▼ *An enabling environment* — *Most new employment opportunities are likely to be generated by the private sector. But markets cannot work effectively unless governments create an enabling environment — including fair and stable macro-economic policies, an equitable legal*

*framework, sufficient physical infrastructure and an ade-
quate system of incentives for private investment.*

▼ *Access to assets — A more equitable distribution of physical assets (land) and better access to means of production
(credit and information) are often essential to ensure sustainable livelihoods.*

▼ *Labour-intensive technologies — Developing countries
have to be able to make the most efficient use of their factors of production and to exploit their comparative advantage of abundant labour. Tax and price policies should,
where appropriate, try to encourage labour-intensive
employment.*

▼ *Public works programmes — Where private markets consistently fail to produce sufficient jobs, in certain regions or
at certain times of the year, it may be necessary for the
state to offer employment through public works programmes to enable people to survive.*

▼ *Disadvantaged groups — Where markets tend to discriminate against particular groups, such as women or certain
ethnic groups, the state may need to consider targeted
interventions or programmes of affirmative action.*

▼ *Job-sharing — With the growing phenomenon of "jobless
growth," it has become necessary to rethink the concept of
work and to consider more innovative and flexible working
arrangements — including job-sharing.*

## Basic needs and security

Clearly connected with the concept of basic needs is the concept of
security — freedom from fear and freedom from want — which has
been recognized from the time the United Nations was set up. To tilt
the balance toward freedom from want, "the concept of security," the
UNDP (1994) report said,

*must ... change in two basic ways:*

▼ *an exclusive stress on territorial security to a much greater
stress on people's security.*

▼ *From security through armaments to security through sustainable human development.*

*Threats to human security have been identified in seven
principal categories:*

▼ *Economic security*

▼ *Food security*

▼ *Health security*

▼ *Environmental security*

▼ *Personal security*

▼ *Community security*

▼ *Political security.*

The first three in particular directly relate to income generation and the alleviation of poverty. "Economic security requires an
assured basic income," according to the report, and "food security
means that all people at all times have both physical and economic
access to basic food." Most of the deaths in developing countries are
linked with "poor nutrition and an unsafe environment particularly
polluted water."

**Access to credit**

The importance of access to credit for the economic elevation of the
poor was underscored by the UNDP (1994) report. "Study after study on
credit schemes for the poor," UNDP observed,

> *confirms that the poor are creditworthy:*
>
> ▼ *The poor can save, even if only a little.*
>
> ▼ *The poor have profitable investment opportunities to
> choose from, and they invest their money wisely.*
>
> ▼ *The poor are very reliable borrowers and hence a very
> good risk. Repayment rates of 90% and more are not rare.*
>
> ▼ *The poor are able and willing to pay market interest rates,
> so that credit schemes for the poor stand a good chance of
> becoming viable, self-financing undertakings.*

An abundance of statistical evidence shows that even quite
modest levels of credit make significant differences in income generation and job creation.

**Crisis and social integration**

The UNDP (1994) profiles of countries in crisis present a recurring picture of oppressive regimes, human-rights violations, internal conflicts,
and high military spending. In contrast, the case studies of "successes
in social integration" are of countries that have preferentially invested
in human development, following policies designed to address specific
areas of inequity and injustice within their mixed populations.

**Investment in human development**

UNDP (1994) proposed a 20 : 20 compact for investment development. "Experience shows," the report said, "that countries can achieve decent levels of human development if their governments allocate, on average, 20% of public spending to human development priorities." This, matched by an allocation of 20% of external aid budgets to human-development priorities, could allow the following targets to be realized in a decade:

> ▼ *Everyone has access to basic education.*

> ▼ *Everyone has access to primary health care, clean drinking water and sanitation.*

> ▼ *All children are immunized.*

> ▼ *Maternal mortality is halved.*

> ▼ *All willing couples have access to family planning services.*

> ▼ *Adult illiteracy is reduced to half the current figure. Female illiteracy is no higher than male illiteracy, and girls' education is on a par with that of boys.*

> ▼ *Severe malnutrition is eliminated, and moderate malnutrition halved.*

> ▼ *World population moves towards stabilization at 7.3 billion by 2015.*

> ▼ *Credit schemes are extended to the poor to enable them to seek self-employment and a sustainable livelihood.*

As things now stand, "aid is not focused on the priority areas of human development. Bilateral donors direct only 7% of their aid to such priorities as basic education, primary health care, rural water supplies, nutrition programs and family planning services," whereas multilateral agencies average around 16%.

**Technical assistance**

The original objective of technical assistance was to narrow the gap between industrialized and developing countries by accelerating the transfer of knowledge, skills, and expertise, but the aim of building national capacity has hardly ever been realized. In fact, as UNDP (1994) put it, technical assistance has often had "precisely the opposite effect — reining in national capacity rather than unleashing it." How can technical assistance be improved, taking advantage of the successes of the past and avoiding the many known pitfalls?

> *One simple and direct solution would be to give the technical assistance funds directly to developing countries — and let them decide how to spend the money. Offering the resources as budgetary support would enable the receiving governments to employ national experts where available or international ones where not. This would have several advantages: the experts would be more appropriate to the country's real needs, and they would probably cost less since their salaries would be determined by international market forces rather than by living costs in the sending country. The result would be a more efficient, effective and equitable allocation of development funds. Technical assistance could also be improved through regional development cooperation. This may even open up new funding sources and encourage self-financing.*

This overview of the UNDP (1994) report indicates that basic-needs thinking is again very much on the agenda of the United Nations and that strategies for tackling the issue are being developed. Indeed, the whole concept of *Human Development Report, 1994* centres on the vision that

> *Sustainable human development is development that not only generates economic growth but distributes its benefits equitably; that regenerates the environment rather than destroying it; that empowers people rather than marginalizing them. It is development that gives priority to the poor, enlarging their choices and opportunities and providing for their participation in decisions that affect their lives. It is development that is pro-people, pro-nature, pro-jobs and pro-women.*

# International S&T and basic needs

## S&T for the rich

The work of scientists and technologists has in the main been geared to satisfying the perceived needs and wants of the dominant economic power centres (Ventura 1994). The few so-called intermediate, or appropriate, technology institutions are today no more than relics of the past, and even then their activities were of a token character. The majority of investments in the past three decades have been in developed-country technologies (UNESCO 1993), which have been introduced into developing countries without adaptation and have failed to deal adequately with the problems of poverty and unemployment.

The developed-country technologies demand more capital than labour and often meet the needs of a very small, affluent portion of the population of developing countries. Patterns of production, investment, and consumption are therefore distorted in the developing countries that have followed strategies and used technologies from developed countries without modification. Unemployment, under-employment, and low productivity are seen throughout most parts of developing countries. The large-scale technologies imported from the developed countries do not often fit with the small, weak markets of the developing countries. In addition, most of the technology transfers are made in the urban centres. This overlooks the fact that most people in the weak economies make their living in the rural areas, where the bulk of the natural resources of comparative advantage are to be found.

The products of these technologies have a relatively high sophistication and price, too. These products are outside the reach of those who cannot meet their basic needs. If the poor and the rich are going to be partners in socioeconomic development, the international S&T community will have to spend time and, indeed, a good deal of resources on adapting large-scale, capital-intensive technologies to make them more appropriate for satisfying the basic needs of econom-ically weaker societies. To achieve more efficient diffusion and use of these technologies in developing countries, the stronger S&T institu-tions and developed countries should help domestic S&T establishments acquire the capabilities to adapt these technologies. Also needed are technologies more suited to small enterprises in developing countries.

The skewed distribution of technology is patently displayed in the case of biotechnology (UNESCO 1993): "While the [poor] struggle to keep their young alive and reduce the fertility of those who want no more children, developed world biotechnology is helping the rich keep the old alive and improving the infertility of couples." People who need clean water and tropical-disease vaccines are being offered new cos-metics and organ transplants. More effort in biotechnology goes into making plants tolerant to chemicals than to increasing the quality of tropical agriculture. The spirit of what is happening is eloquently con-densed in the following statement (UNESCO 1993): "While the poor search for solutions to malaria and diarrhoea, bio-business pumps the Yuppie market with genetic screening and human growth hormones, so that every girl can be a Barbie doll and every boy can look like Ken." Farmers seek lower input costs and hardier, pest-resistant plants; biotechnology provides encapsulated embryos and pesticide-resistant plants. Farmers in the developing countries look for market security; biotechnology provides low-priced commodity substitution for their products and enables their comparative advantages to be undermined by factory farms.

The poor require reliable high-calorie, high-protein food stocks to establish nutritional diversity. A good way to meet this requirement is through self-reliant production of local commodities. However, biobusinesses deliver frivolous, brandname food fads and information to gain control of the natural-resource base of the developing countries. The biotechnology power brokers, with their strategies for genetic modification and sell-back schemes, have their sights on the wealth of biodiversity in tropical regions.

Other S&T developments exemplify the world's neglect of the basic needs of the poor. This is true of other scientific technologies, such as electronics, telecommunications, and "smart" materials. The developed world is busy constructing information superhighways while most of the poor do not even possess the telephone that is needed to access the system or, for that matter, the education to fully understand the centrality of this industry. Computers are seldom used to assess or monitor the degradation of the poor and the dispossessed, but images of the rich and famous and their entertainment proclivities flood the world. These technologies could improve training and skills, but, instead of providing more jobs, IT threatens to take jobs away from people who are insufficiently skilled. The poor still have to hustle up lodging from discarded boxes, old car bodies, and other refuse at a time when technologies can provide adequate building materials for housing at affordable rates. A major reason for this skewed distribution of global S&T efforts is the fact that S&T specialists in the developing countries spend more time on problems that are relevant mostly to developed countries and less time on problems that are relevant to their own productive sectors, thus re-enforcing the neglect of the poor in their own societies.

Although the applied science practiced by many of the world's foremost institutions is directed to solving their own problems and those of the wealthy, if the results of these efforts were judiciously followed, selected, and adapted, they could be harnessed for the satisfaction of basic needs. The challenge, then, is to apply these technological developments to basic needs, in other words, to blend traditional and modern technologies (von Weizsacker et al. 1983). The enterprise of dedicating developed country's technology to basic needs will remain a forlorn hope for some time unless this concern receives special attention.

## Basic needs and technology

The basic needs of the poor of the planet can only be met in the long run by increasing the productive capacity of the poor themselves. Productivity is a function of technological competence, and technological competence can be increased in small, affordable increments.

The starting point for linking technology to basic needs must be the UNDP's (1994) recognition that the poor know best their opportunities for productive and remunerative work. What the poor really need is modest assistance for their own microenterprises.

The Vienna Programme of Action, which came out of a United Nations Conference on Science and Technology for Development held in 1979, has not had the desired impact on the application of S&T to development. The conference addressed three major issues in S&T for development. The most fundamental issue was endogenous capacity in S&T. Endogenous capacity, as it came to be defined, is "the extent of internal national capability to exercise independent informed judgement and actions regarding the generating, acquisition and use of technologies for economic and social development, including the fulfilment of basic human needs." The end-of-decade review of the Vienna Programme of Action sought to clarify the concept of endogenous capacity and to initiate a pilot project to field-test the concept in some developing countries with the objective of developing an approach other developing countries could use to build their endogenous capacity in S&T.

Jamaica has been one of six countries participating in the current phase of the experiment, part of the United Nations interregional project, Strengthening Endogenous Capacity in Science and Technology Through Stakeholders' Policy Dialogues. Other participating countries are Cape Verde, Pakistan, Togo, Uganda, and Vietnam. Central to the design of this endogenous capacity-building (ECB) project is the concept of stakeholders' dialogues: people who make decisions about S&T and development, who generate or use technology, or who are involved in education, training, financial support for S&T, aid, and so on are brought together in a series of dialogues. These dialogues are supported by diagnostic studies to elucidate S&T needs, options, and priorities. The results of these dialogues and studies provide the raw material for a Portfolio of Initiatives for strengthening endogenous capacity in S&T for development. Initiatives are specified for policy-makers in the public sector, for the productive sector, for the educational sector, for the donor community, and even for consumer advocacy groups. Financial support for the program of initiatives is then sought from government, the national private sector, and external donors.

The ECB project involves much more than a narrow concern with S&T per se. The project encompasses economic, social, cultural, and political considerations insofar as these affect the productive capacity of the country. The ECB project is best described, then, as a development project with emphasis on enhancing the endogenous capacity in S&T that makes development possible. The project has generated many insights into the old problem of linking S&T to development in an organic and synergistic manner. One such critical insight, derived from the Jamaican experience, is that national stakeholders' dialogues can and should be broken down into regional, sectoral, and even community stakeholders' dialogues on ECB. Engaging stakeholders in dialogue at or near the place of actual production or consumption will provide the best information on technological interventions needed for increasing productive capacity.

The need to integrate S&T policy with economic and social policy has been reemphasized in the ECB project. In the Jamaican context the ECB project has contributed to the emergence of a functional integrator, the National Commission for Science and Technology (NCST), an independent body drawn from government, industry, education, and technical and professional organizations. The importance of communicating S&T to the general population as a condition for absorption and greater use of S&T has been strongly underscored in stakeholders' dialogues, and a number of initiatives have already been launched to meet this need. The Government of Jamaica's information service, for example, now broadcasts S&T material specific to people's everyday needs, and an S&T Communications Centre is at the design stage.

External donors are very receptive to the idea of supporting a coherent portfolio of technical projects that has clear development objectives and to the idea of including ECB as a component of their programs for aid to the developing countries.

## Appropriate technology and basic needs

The notion that basic-needs satisfaction always requires labour-intensive, small-scale, low-level technology is inaccurate, as is the converse notion that goods and services for the rich always require capital-intensive, highly modern technology (Singer 1982). The poor gain considerably from many chemical products, such as fertilizers, plastics, and bicycles, that require large-scale, capital-intensive technology. The rich buy handicrafts and hand-made products that require small-scale, traditional technology. Technology for basic-needs satisfaction, therefore, cannot be standardized in any one model but will have to respond to the factor proportions, as well as to other sociopolitical and economic factors, in the local environment. Technology will determine factor use, and the main objective should be to ensure the most efficient deployment of the factors that affect the production of goods and services for the poor and needy. The efficiency of an activity cannot be determined simply by its being either capital or labour intensive.

Below certain minimum subsistence levels, people will find it difficult to embrace new technologies. Such people will depend heavily on local S&T systems to assist with technology transfer and improvements. The idea is to create employment opportunities, assets, and knowledge for the poor and neglected. The selection of more appropriate technology will depend on local S&T personnel's capacity to conduct research and development (R&D), to locate and use global knowledge, and to generate and apply local information. To make proper choices, local personnel will have to be able to deal with a range of functions and issues, including patent information, tenders and licences, and, of course, negotiations with investors and transnational enterprises. Another requirement will be the ability to seek, obtain, analyze, and use technoeconomic, business, and social information. Imported technologies will often have to be adapted to local conditions. This is true in most instances for agriculture, but it is also true for small-scale enterprises in the rural and urban informal sectors. Appropriate technology will probably be built on existing traditional or other indigenous technologies, rather than from scratch. In the final analysis appropriate technology is technology that gets the job done. What that job is should be defined in public policy and human-development strategy as a basic first step in applying technology to basic needs.

The innovative capacities of S&T communities seeking to satisfy basic needs will, therefore, have to be honed and actively asserted. Not all developing-country technologies will be appropriate, and not all developed-country technologies will be inappropriate. Careful selection is the key to success in these endeavours. Irrespective of what technologies are initially used to enable poor people to satisfy their basic needs, it ought to be realized that these technologies are transitional and will have to be improved as the situation changes.

The goal is to use the most appropriate technology to provide the most appropriate products. If the market is to work, then the income levels of the prospective consumers of these products must be adequate. Some argue that policies for improved income distribution must be in place before policies for enhanced technology and products can have a beneficial effect (Singer 1982). It cannot be denied that these factors have a reciprocal relationship. A change to more appropriate basic-needs products means more local control and management of technology, which is related to more equitable distribution of incomes and, in turn, to more local innovations, R&D, and social intelligence.

Technologies for basic needs will not be automatically promoted in most circumstances. The dualism in society will favour technologies for the upper income classes, technologies akin to those in use in the developed countries. Foreign investors will also tend to use capital-intensive technologies to circumvent labour and administrative problems. Furthermore, technological progress in the modern sector does not mean technological enhancement in the rest of society. Therefore, government policies will have to directly address the satisfaction of basic needs if these needs are to be effectively met. When a developing country aggressively takes the lead in addressing its own S&T needs and has clearly defined development objectives, after consultation with the people and the external aid agencies, positive results can generally be expected, even if they emerge slowly.

## Environmental decay — a rationale for basic needs

Underdevelopment is as damaging to the environment as overdevelopment and its concomitant waste. Overdevelopment problems, such as global warming, radioactive waste, acid rain, and depletion of the ozone layer, are clearly on the international agenda, but the effects of poverty and deprivation are scarcely mentioned. The argument for this is that environmental problems caused by poverty and despair are local, but the other problems are more amenable to international intervention. However, poverty is widespread, especially in developing countries, and these countries are inhabited by nearly 80% of the world's people, so it is just a matter of time before these local problems add up to a major degradation of the planet's forests, watersheds, and soil cover.

To avoid overexploitation of natural resources by the poor, leading to deforestation, desertification, and degradation of land, the distribution of productive resources has to be made more equitable. Without this, the poor will have no alternative but to earn a living by extracting as much as possible from the little available to them. People who are in dire straits have very little time or energy to contemplate the protection of the environment. Under these conditions, growth will surely be unsustainable in developing countries, and incomes for the poor will be on a path of steady decline, putting more pressure on the environment. It makes good sense, therefore, to provide for the basic needs of the poorest people in society. This means that development strategies have to be redesigned to favour the full participation of the poor and to give high priority to ensuring that growth directly benefits those most in need. Such policies must work on the assumption that investment in the poor can have great rewards, not only in environmental protection but also in bringing productive occupations and a better quality of life to all citizens.

# Jamaica and its basic-needs history

## Population and poverty

Jamaica is a small (10 940 km$^2$) island with a population of about 2.4 million and a rapid rate of growth in the urban areas. The estimates of poverty on the island vary from the optimistic figure of around 33% (World Bank 1994a) to more than 40% (Witter 1994). According to most estimates, however, more than 50% of the rural population is poor by any standard.

## Economy and dualism

Jamaica, like nearly all other developing countries, is a recent ex-colony of a European power (in this case, England), becoming independent in 1962. For 250 years, Jamaica had essentially a monoculture plantation economy, producing cane sugar with African slave labour and, later, Asian indentured labour. At the turn of the 20th century, bananas became the second most important export crop. A bauxite industry emerged after the discovery of deposits in the 1950s. Tourism has become, in recent years, the most vital component of the Jamaican economy. Light manufacturing has been encouraged under industrialization and modernization programs running back to the end of World War II. However, the Jamaican economy remains essentially a producer of primary products and low-value-added secondary products, the demand and prices for which fluctuate with the vagaries of world markets, over which the country has no control.

Most Jamaican people struggle outside the formal economy as small farmers, traders, artisans, and crafts people to satisfy their basic needs, without adequate access to either credit or technology. Many production processes are the same as they were in the 19th century. For example, people rely on pack animals to transport agricultural products (in only small quantities) in deep rural areas, and human energy is the only source of energy for cultivating land on most small farms. However, the numerous innovations generated by trial and error in the informal economy could be used as starting points for generating more efficient appropriate technologies.

## Debt burden

Jamaica, like most developing countries, fell into an international debt trap in the 1970s. Jamaica's current obligation to the multilateral institutions and commercial banks of the developed countries runs in excess of $4 billion. To service these debts, the island uses more than

40% of its total foreign-exchange earnings and about 50% of the national budget. Because of this heavy outflow of capital, not much is left for social-infrastructure maintenance, much less development. Health, education, security, and other social services have, therefore, been in steady decline. Malnutrition has begun to increase, and crime has become a serious national problem. Housing is out of the reach for most Jamaicans, and transportation has become a nightmare. The political and financial leadership has become totally distracted by fiscal and monetary problems, ignoring the promotion of the goods and services sectors.

Jamaica has one of the world's worst income disparities between the rich and the poor (Davis and Witter 1986), despite a lot of talk about Jamaica's improving macroeconomic position. Jamaica was recently lauded by the multilateral institutions for meeting set macroeconomic targets, having a relatively stable currency, reducing inflation, and building up exchange-currency reserves. The World Bank (1994a, p. 1) declared that since independence Jamaica has had three problems with growth:

> First, growth has been too slow on average and too often negative. Second, it was achieved very inefficiently in the sense that Jamaica borrowed and invested a lot, forgoing welfare in the past and future, without the commensurate results. Third, growth has only recently started to break down the economic dualism that Jamaica shares with many other developing countries. Growth in the enclaves of the formal sector still does not draw enough labour and material inputs from the informal sector.

## S&T programs until 1960

Jamaica's introduction of technology was very impressive in its early history, from the establishment of the botanical gardens in the 17th century to the installation of a hydroelectric power system and railways in the early 19th century. Jamaica was the first country in the Western world to construct a railway, even before the United States. A telephone system was erected in the early 20th century. The University of the West Indies was established in Jamaica in 1948. The natural science faculty was among the first three faculties established at the university. This was followed by the College of Arts, Science and Technology (CAST) in 1958 and the Jamaica Industrial Development Corporation in 1952. Jamaica had a very impressive record in agricultural research by the mid-1950s. The policy, however, was to import technologies to exploit the resources and export raw materials to England. Science was simply encouraged as part of the training program for the Civil Service and people in professions, but an adequate local, complementary technological and engineering contingent was not encouraged.

## Contemporary S&T policies and plans

### Management
The first explicit S&T policy was the law establishing the Scientific Research Council (SRC) in June 1960. The law gave SRC the power to promote research on the use of indigenous raw materials, to undertake the management of S&T information, and to coordinate scientific research in the public sector.

After 1960, a number of other institutions were deemed necessary to the island's development, including the Jamaica Bureau of Standards, the Jamaica Bauxite Institute, the Petroleum Corporation of Jamaica, and seven agricultural commodity boards and research stations. Unfortunately, in 1960 these rapid institutional developments were not anticipated, so the law failed to specify the relationship between SRC as the coordinator and these other bodies. Consequently, no real national coordination of R&D took place on the island after the emergence of these other S&T bodies. The result was fragmentation, duplication, and confusion of effort.

This problem received national attention in the 1990s, and NCST was formed in 1992 to ensure better national management of S&T. The prime minister was made the chair of NCST, and members were drawn from a wide cross section of the public and private sectors, as well as academia.

The SRC policy was updated in 1990 (SRC 1990): the principal aims of the island's S&T system were delineated; priority areas were identified; and measures and courses of action were stipulated in an S&T plan. The island by then had an estimated 98 S&T institutions. The figure varies according to the definition of an S&T institution, but none was specifically designed with the mandate to address the basic needs of the population. This is not to discount the work of the Rural Agricultural Development Agency (RADA), which is responsible for conducting extension work for small-scale farmers. Unfortunately, this agency is without an assertive R&D backup. RADA, therefore, depends solely on raw outside results to discharge its duties, and some of these results may not be directly applicable to Jamaican circumstances. In the late 1950s to 1970s, Jamaica boasted one of the best agricultural research stations in the region. This establishment, however, was simply allowed to deteriorate during the 1980s, a result of the IMF and World Bank edicts.

The latest S&T policy (SRC 1990), which was a decade in the making, does not feature, implicitly or explicitly, the satisfaction of basic needs, despite the fact that it promoted "appropriate management of the nations' resources and S&T developments" to improve the welfare of citizens. The policy also mentioned that S&T should enhance the cultural, social, and economic development of the country and contribute programs for attaining self-reliance.

### New vision

Jamaica has made substantial S&T investments in training, institution building, and recurrent operational expenditures. Nevertheless, a critical lack of connection remains between the S&T system and the formal and informal economy. However, a new vision of S&T for development for all the people is now emerging. Policies, plans, and institutional mechanisms are being put in place to link S&T to the economy and to the satisfaction of basic needs. For example, for financial year 1994/95, the government mandated "extension services in S&T especially to small businesses and small farmers" (GOJ 1994, p. 5). The constraints of debt payment and budget limitations, on the supply side, and the lack of a technoculture, on the demand side, are real obstacles to linking S&T and production.

As mentioned in an earlier section, Jamaica has been participating in the United Nations ECB project. The ECB project has systematically examined the status of S&T for development and has advanced recommendations for bringing S&T to further bear on the development problems of the country. If handled correctly, the explicit connection between endogenous capacity in S&T and satisfaction of basic needs will prove a fruitful paradigm. The solution to the problem of poverty is to make the poor more productive through access to resources, technology, and information.

## Impact of research

In the last three decades, S&T projects were propelled more by the personal inclinations of research workers and ad hoc management directives than by any logical plans for national development. The consequence has been a surfeit of unapplied research results and the perception that R&D has little to do with local business or national development. This gap between S&T and development has been further widened by recent heavy reliance on foreign aid for R&D projects. The aid agencies have their own policy directives, often at variance with local development imperatives, and their programs are subject to sudden changes in client groups and emphases.

Scientific thinking and action have never really taken root because most of the island's inhabitants have never seen S&T as an indispensable element of socioeconomic progress. Most of Jamaica's people, including educated professionals, are still scientifically illiterate, and science therefore receives only token verbal support from the nation's leaders. Technical skills still lack the status of white-collar employment. In many firms and institutions, scientists and technologists are forced to relinquish their chosen professions for so-called management streams if they wish to advance their careers. The pay for scientists and technologists is lower than that for administrators and managers, and in times of economic hardship, scientists and technologists are the first to be laid off (UNDP and GOJ 1992c). So although research has produced exciting results, which have been supported at great national expense (especially if the work at the University of the West Indies is included), the results are left unused and have no significant impact on the society. Meanwhile, a number of entrepreneurs, especially in the informal sector, are crying out for technical assistance (Ventura 1992a). Although local innovations could make a difference in local production and management, the local S&T community yearns more for the respect of the international S&T community than for the practical usefulness of producing results for local application (Ventura 1992a). Because of local S&T investments, there have been some inventions in Jamaica, but much less innovation and wealth creation.

An argument that has been advocated for some time (Ventura 1992c, 1994) is that the capabilities of the island's research establishments, especially the industrial extension services, are more capable of responding to the needs of the micro-, small-, and medium-scale enterprises than to the sophisticated demands of large-scale modern firms. However, it is understandable that the beleaguered and weak domestic S&T community should save itself for firms that offer financial and political support. Unfortunately, the large industries have not yet taken the local R&D institutions into their confidence or provided significant support for these institutions' endeavours, preferring instead to use foreign technology and foreign consultants to meet their needs (UNDP and GOJ 1992a).

The basic needs of people in places like Jamaica will apparently not be taken seriously by the local S&T fraternity unless attractive incentives are provided to meet government objectives. Some basic-needs work has begun. SRC and CAST recently joined forces to upgrade small-scale enterprises; support comes from a Dutch grant to foster small businesses (GOJ and GON 1993). SRC has assembled technological packages for small rural entrepreneurs on the basis of work done some time before. The message here is that it took outside intervention and funding to trigger this type of response to basic needs, and one wonders what will happen when the funds are exhausted.

Jamaica, like many other developing countries, has an inadequate endogenous base of S&T to make proper use of the various forms of aid it receives. S&T decision-making capabilities are not only weak but essentially faulty; consequently, S&T decisions are left up to industrialists, engineers, scientists, and business people of the industrialized nations.

## The gap between policy and budget

The Government of Jamaica has fashioned a succession of development policies and plans since the Five-Year Independence Plan, 1963 to 1968 (Jamaican Ministry of Development and Welfare 1963) and is currently formulating an industrial policy. In all these initiatives, poverty alleviation, basic needs, growth, equity, social justice, and development have figured prominently, although the results have been much less than expected. Resources are scarce, and the implementation of policies has been impeded by a competing array of uncoordinated government ministries and departments. Budget allocations have never been programmatic or long range. Each fiscal year there is an interministerial and interdepartmental scramble for slices of the pie, and this tends to obstruct policy implementation.

The current range and diversity of programs related to basic needs do not constitute the elements of a single composite strategy but represent the semiautonomous prescriptions of particular portfolios of public administration. With such an operating method, it is clearly very difficult to achieve a sustained attack on the problem of basic needs. In the current formulation of industrial policy, the same tactical error is being repeated by combining the recommendations of competing interest groups without an organizational theme or centre.

However, efforts have been made to provide coherent policy leadership in government. In the early years of independence, there was a Ministry of Development and Welfare (which prepared the Five-Year Independence Plan, 1963 to 1968). A more recent attempt was the creation of the short-lived (1989–91) Ministry of Development, Planning and Production. None of these initiatives led to a significant curbing of the fragmentation and competition that have been derailing the implementation of policy. In this respect, Jamaica is typical of developing countries. But what is common in the case studies in "Successes in Social Integration," presented in the UNDP (1994) report, is the systematic and sustained field implementation of a widely supported master plan, with clear, specific objectives and quantifiable output, that drives the national budget and gives thematic coherence to public administration. The policy-coordination approach and the program budget are made more attractive by the obvious counterproductive nature and exhaustion of the old ways of doing things in Jamaica.

# Jamaica today

## Policies, plans, and programs for basic needs

Every country has economic and social policies, plans, and programs related to basic needs, but usually these are not specifically labeled as such or coordinated in a single scheme. The welfare programs in the developed Western countries are well-known interventions, but they have had limited success in curbing residual poverty and deprivation. If we have learned any lesson from decades of aid to the poor, it is that unless people are helped to become more productive and independent and to take direct responsibility for their own development, aid neither cures poverty nor addresses the long-term satisfaction of basic needs.

In Jamaica, as early as the Five-Year Independence Plan, 1963 to 1968 (Jamaican Ministry of Development and Welfare 1963, p. 57), the government of the newly independent nation took the stance that

> *a program of economic development requires comprehensive concurrent attention to the alleviation of social problems, if the program is to prove effective in achieving perceptible betterment of the living conditions of the majority of the population. Without effective social policy, measures for economic development may fail to attract the degree of interest and co-operation of the people which is necessary to attain economic growth for the nation, and even if such growth is achieved, new and more complex social problems may be created while attempting to alleviate others.*

The Second Five-Year Plan, 1970–1975 (Jamaican Ministry of Development and Welfare 1970, p. 1), proclaimed that

> *Jamaica's social policy is intended to achieve lasting social well-being, accompanied by sustained economic development. The latter is regarded as a pre-requisite for raising the capacity of this society to attain its social goals. One major social goal is human development, which will enable the people of Jamaica to attain and maintain a reasonably adequate level of living. ... Unemployment is one of the social ills requiring more urgent attention. Unemployment is at once a cause and a consequence of insufficient work.*

Among the basic assumptions of the Government of Jamaica's philosophy are that

> *it is the responsibility of the Government and people to work towards:*
>
> ▼ *Creating the environment which will enable all citizens to obtain their basic needs for food, shelter, knowledge, and employment*
>
> ▼ *Distributing more equitably the national product in order to create social justice; permit the protection of the aged and handicapped; and promote the mental and physical development of young people*
>
> ▼ *Improving the quality of life for all citizens by placing people first in the development process.*

"Policies and Programs will be implemented," the document said, "to ensure that all persons have access to goods and services which are essential to their survival and development. These basic needs relate primarily to the areas of housing, health, nutrition and education."

For the first time in Jamaica, a plan for S&T was explicitly incorporated in a Five-Year Development Plan. Among the stated major objectives of the S&T plan were "provision of the socio-economic infrastructure which will bring more disadvantaged individuals into the process of development and reduce poverty, ... spreading income-earning opportunities by making technical information available to small entrepreneurs in rural and urban Jamaica." Practical mechanisms and the requisite budgetary support to achieve these basic-needs objectives have yet to be adequately provided. Here, as in other developing countries, programs for the least-privileged members of society and for long-term investments, such as in S&T, are the first to be sacrificed in the face of budgetary constraints.

Some recent or current programs related to the satisfaction of basic needs in Jamaica include the following:

▼ Food Stamp Program;

▼ Social and Economic Support Program;

▼ Micro Investment Development Agency;

▼ Hillside Agricultural Project;

▼ Self-Start Fund;

▼ Social Development Commission;

▼ Human Employment and Resource Training;

▼ School Feeding Program (primary level);

▼ Members of Parliament Local Development Fund;

▼ Squatter Settlement Program; and

▼ Women in Development Program.

These programs are scattered across ministries without any apparent coordination or measurement of impact. The application of technology as a tool for production for human development does not specifically enter into program design or implementation.

The 1994/95 Throne Speech, the government's statement of intent for the fiscal year, declared that "the time has now come for an assault on poverty itself" (GOJ 1994, p. 7). Previous assaults on poverty in other countries seldom yielded the expected results, and now a great deal of effort, perhaps led by the United Nations system, must be poured into answering the question "Why not?" and devising strategies that will work.

## Conclusions

The satisfaction of the basic needs of the poor and disfranchised in developing countries is an essential condition for the economic and social progress of these nations, but it is also an end in itself for giving the poor a decent standard of living, to which they have a right. The information available indicates that an income trickle-down approach to the alleviation of poverty cannot significantly mitigate poverty or despair in these nations.

The Jamaican case demonstrates clearly that an assertive attack on the basic-needs problem needs to go far beyond the traditional poverty-alleviation strategies tried unsuccessfully in the past. A local basic-needs approach calls for a greater emphasis on domestic technological management, a greater absorptive capacity among the poor for the benefits of S&T, and a wider spread of the fruits of growth through decentralized production and consumption planning, as well as popular participation to ensure redistribution of income, other assets, and social entitlements.

The complex problem of satisfying basic needs, especially among the poorest people in society, demands up-to-date information to allow effective use of resources through better decision-making and implementing mechanisms. Reforms are necessary in a variety of areas: incentives, credit, technology flow, access to markets, and so on. It will be extremely difficult, if not impossible, for developing countries on their own to satisfy the basic needs of their populations in a timely fashion without multilateral and bilateral assistance. The United Nations agencies, therefore, will have a vital role to play in placing this matter squarely on the international agenda.

## Recommendations

The global problem of basic needs must be tackled at several levels, and recommendations for each are given below.

### The United Nations

1. Keep the issue on the international agenda for at least the rest of the century.

2. Operate a think tank to provide analysis, case studies, and the circulation of information on the issue.

3. Provide strategic seed funding for policy development and field models in a variety of country settings.

4. Operate a technology bank to collect and disseminate small-scale technologies suitable for microenterprises among the poor.

Already, a commitment to action is clearly articulated in the United Nations system. In the foreword to *Human Development Report, 1994* (UNDP 1994, p. iv), for example, the director of UNDP, J.S. Speth, wrote the following:

> *There is an urgent need today to establish a more integrated, effective and efficient UN development system to promote the worldwide movement towards sustainable human development. For this purpose, the UN system requires a clearer mandate, integrated policy frameworks and additional resources. ... It is our principal goal to restructure and strengthen UNDP so that it can make a critical contribution to these new imperatives of sustainable human development — from assisting countries in the formulation of their own development strategies to helping donor nations reflect this new development perspective in their aid allocations, to launching global policy initiatives for new designs of development cooperation, to working closely with other UN development programmes and agencies in identifying common missions and complementary approaches so as to help our member countries realize their sustainable human development goals. In other words, we are now poised in UNDP to move from the basic messages of the* Human Development Reports *to their concrete operationalization.*

## Donors

1. Fulfill the 20 : 20 compact on human development proposed by UNDP, whereby donors would allocate at least 20% of their aid to human-development priorities.

2. Allow governments to decide priorities for funding support, using criteria sensitive to development and human rights.

3. Channel a higher proportion of assistance to the poor through NGOs, which tend to deliver benefits more efficiently than governments.

4. Provide credit, with mandatory technical assistance, for micro-enterprises.

5. Support S&T and R&D projects specifically for human development.

## World trade

1. Offer preferential treatment for selected low-technology, value-added products on the world market.

2. Control the dumping of subsidized products on weak open economies.

## Countries

1. Adopt stakeholders' policy dialogues (the methodology of the ECB project) to clarify and build support for national development objectives and strategies.

2. Develop a coordinated master plan for satisfying the basic needs of the entire population.

3. Mobilize and use resources to meet specific development objectives.

4. Develop and support institutional mechanisms (such as the NCST in Jamaica) to build endogenous capacity in S&T for development and cultivate an S&T-friendly technoculture.

5. Facilitate technology transfer for human development.

6. Facilitate external and internal aid flows for sustainable satisfaction of basic needs, that is, to raise the productive capacity of the poor.

7. Help make external and internal credit available to the poor for capitalizing microenterprises.

8. Provide incentives for innovating, increasing productivity, and providing credit.

9. Provide basic S&T education and help to popularize S&T.

10. Invest preferentially in primary and skills education.

11. Work forward from indigenous traditional technologies in R&D for basic needs (Jamaica has an inventory of endogenous traditional technologies, under the United Nations ECB project).

It goes without saying that for governments to seriously target the basic needs of their citizens, the maintenance of a stable civil society in which human rights are respected is a nonnegotiable requirement. Peace, security of person and property, equality before just laws, and the maintenance of public institutions are basic requirements for effectively addressing basic needs.

Chapter 5

# Old Imperatives, Fresh Approaches

*Dilmus D. James*

It is widely known that the need for basic-needs satisfaction was popularized by the International Labour Office's World Employment Conference, held in 1976 (ILO 1976). The idea spawned a sizeable literature in the ensuing decade (Ghosh 1984), but more recently, discussions of a basic-needs approach have become less fashionable. I welcome this opportunity to participate in a reexamination of the concept.

Basic needs are those minimal requirements for sustaining life at a decent level. Basic needs encompass adequate nutrition, health services, water, and sanitary facilities. The concept of basic needs also implies access to education and information that will enable individuals and communities to participate in productive activities and intelligently use available basic goods and services. Some reasonably adequate level of psychological tranquility would also seem a requisite condition. Although wealthy countries are not exempt from basic-needs deficits — witness, for instance, the large homeless population in my own country, the United States — this paper will concentrate on very poor populations in developing countries.

One can take many avenues in attempting to satisfy the basic needs of the abjectly poor. Macroeconomic policies for redistributing income is one such avenue; the instigation of entitlement programs might be another (Sen 1987). Top-down, general economic development has done the trick, but in this century this has worked for a mere handful of nations. Many people fervently believe that slowing population growth in poor regions is the key. Reducing political and military

tensions could also help, especially if some of the savings were channeled to basic-needs satisfaction (internal conflicts in approximately 60
developing countries [UNDP 1993], of course, increase the ranks of
those with basic-needs deprivation).

My emphasis here will be on the technological perspective.
Furthermore, I am concerned with sustained technological progress
that can in some ways alleviate the plight of the very poor. Technological progress can be stifled at the outset or curtailed after a successful
run by any number of causes at every conceivable level. Individual
enterprises often choose a low-tech route; those firms that are technologically competent can fail because of inept management, a dearth of
marketing acumen, or poor accounting practices. Research and development institutes (RDIs) may never get off the ground because of a failure to attain a minimum threshold of resources to do productive work;
or, after some initial triumphs, an RDI may grow moribund. Technological gains at the national level can be interrupted by stop-and-go
macroeconomic polices or by complete political breakdown accompanied by severe ethnic violence. Toynbee's (1934) 12-volume *A Study in
History* is strewn with civilizations that after dazzling progress some-
how hit the skids. Thus, sustaining technological progress involves
many cultural, ecological, social, political, and economic elements that
are not technological per se. Although my focus will be on technology
for basic needs, I will have to occasionally remark on some of these
extratechnological matters, which impinge significantly on the sustainability of technological advance.

Is there justification for the revitalization of a basic-needs
approach? I could easily cite a long catalogue of shocking and daunting
evidence that poor populations suffer a lack of adequate housing, sanitation, water, education, nutrition, and medical care, but perhaps one
figure is most telling: almost one third of the total population in developing countries, or 1.3 billion people, live in absolute poverty (UNDP
1993).

Clearly, if there is a renewed determination to ameliorate the
harsh conditions of extremely poor populations through technology-
related programs, then new realities must be taken into account. In the
interest of brevity, I have selected six new realities that I believe will
have a direct and palpable bearing on how technologies for basic needs
can be generated, disseminated, and mastered on a sustainable basis.
During the past two decades, perhaps the most striking alteration in
the world's economy is the degree of liberalization that has taken place.
This has taken the forms of privatization, deregulation, and a relaxation
or elimination of impediments to the international flow of goods, services, technologies, and investment. The second new reality is the
international debt crisis, which came to a head in the early 1980s; this

debt still lingers as a significant financial burden for the majority of Third World countries.

The remaining four new realities likely have as much to do with the evolution of our perceptions as they do with changes in actual conditions. The third, for example, is the rather sudden "discovery" of nongovernmental organizations (NGOs). The NGOs were, of course, active all along, but recently they have been seen as a major player in achieving socioeconomic progress in the South. The fourth new reality is similar in this regard. Twenty years ago, no one thought that small-scale enterprises could do much more than offer job havens for large segments of the labour force; today, one is considerably more opti-mistic about small-scale producers' ability to make dynamic contribu-tions to a nation's accumulation of technological capacity. The fifth new reality is the global environmental movement, which was widely seen as a futile, fragmented, and radical undertaking but is at present a potent political force, with environmental concerns much more visi-ble in mainstream development institutions. Virtually the same can be said about the sixth new reality: concern about the condition of women in developing countries. The issue has gone from being a marginal con-sideration to being a mainstay in the portfolio of concerns of develop-ment agencies.

Two questions have been very fleetingly addressed: What is the extent of the basic-needs problem? What are some of the current conditions that will dictate or influence the way a basic-needs approach is conceived and implemented? This paper will proceed by addressing three others: What are some elements of our current understanding of the role of technology in achieving socioeconomic development that can contribute to a meaningful basic-needs approach? What are some contemporary technology-related experiences that offer guidance for more effectively ameliorating dire poverty? What are some concrete actions for satisfying the basic needs of very poor populations?

I am very aware of what is not given sufficient attention in the paper. I think many lessons can be learned from some of China's expe-riences, but you will not find them here. The extremely important issues of the environment and women in development receive scant consideration, and the treatment is in a political context, rather than being addressed substantively. International trade is slighted. The possible negative impact on the satisfaction of basic needs from technology-driven shifts in comparative advantage is neglected. The serious trade-off between resources devoted to generating new knowl-edge at universities and RDIs and efforts redirected to basic education is not seriously broached in the paper. The catalogue of deficiencies could be extended, but one cannot adequately cover all the issues (however pressingly important they may be) in one paper, even one of this length.

# Technology and development:
# a 20- to 30-year retrospective

Why choose the period 1965–75 as a base for comparing current and past views on the nature of technology and the role of technology in the development of the Third World? Several reasons apply. First, in this period, some heterodox economists, such as Charles Cooper, Christopher Freeman, Amilcar Herrera, Francisco Sercovich, Frances Stewart, Constantine Vaitsos, and Miguel Wionczek, became dissatisfied with the treatment of technology in orthodox, neoclassical economics and began to develop alternative theories. They rebelled against the notion that technological change should be seen as a factor exogenous to the economy and against the idea that past experience does not matter when technology is adopted by enterprises or nations. Second, during the late 1960s and early 1970s, many larger developing countries established or significantly strengthened national councils for science and technology (S&T) and drew up legislation to regulate the importation of technology, all strong indications of dissatisfaction with the existing institutional mechanisms by which developing countries acquire technology. Third, and most apropos to my deliberations, this period ended shortly before the first global interest was shown in a basic-needs approach to development. Thus we can ask, What did we think we knew about technology and Third World development between 1965 and 1975? What do we think we know now?

Although technology transfer to developing countries dominated earlier thought and effort, the emphasis today has shifted to fostering internal technological capacity. The importation of technology remains important, but it is now subsumed under the ultimate objective of technological capacity-building. An important corollary of this tendency is that most heterodox economists routinely treat technology as an endogenous factor at all levels of analysis. This is illustrated by the work of Fransman and King (1984), Enos and Park (1987), Segal et al. (1987), Sercovich (1988), James (1989), Bhagavaan (1990), Forsyth (1990), Enos (1991), Shahidullah (1991), and Lall (1992), who stressed technological capacity-building and either implicitly or explicitly incorporated technology as an endogenous element in their analyses.

In the past, economists tended to think of technological capabilities in terms of large regions, nations, or, occasionally, industries but focused very little on individual enterprises. Currently, economists recognize that a lot of technology is generated at the enterprise level and that enterprises as receptacles and absorbers of technology are central to technological capacity-building. One typical stance is that of

Enos (1991, p. 85): "The evidence for a few rapidly industrializing countries is overwhelming: the producing firm is the most important creator of technological capacity. If technological capacity resides anywhere, it is within the producing firm." Another such stance is that of Cimoli and Dosi (1990, p. 52): "at a micro level, 'technologies' are to a fair extent incorporated in institutions, the firms, whose characteristics, decision rules, capabilities, and behaviors are fundamental in shaping the rates and directions of technological change."

At an earlier time, a widespread belief surfaced that the international market for technology was marred by substantial imperfections. Powerful multinational enterprises were viewed as the primary sources of commercial technology. Because the technology had already been developed, it was alleged that the selling entity incurred no, or only trivial, costs and thus that any positive price entailed monopoly profits (Vaitsos 1970; Stewart 1977). Equally prevalent was the idea that technology conceived in mature industrial countries was ill suited to factor endowments, market sizes, and income distributions in developing countries.

Today, attitudes are considerably different, partly because of changing conditions and partly because of changing perceptions. Alternative sources of technology have proliferated substantially. Smaller multinationals are active in technology markets (Bell and Scott-Kemmis 1985; TCMD 1992). Small- and medium-scale enterprises (SMEs) in developed countries transfer technologies to countries of the South (Herbolzheimer and Ouane 1985; Noisi and Rivard 1990). Centrally planned economies in Eastern Europe are sources for technology (Monkiewicz and Maciejewicz 1986; Monkiewicz 1989). Technology can now be secured from some developing countries (Whitmore et al. 1989; Tolintino 1993).

Teece (1977) firmly established that in many instances technology transfer entails a substantial cost to the seller. His work is substantiated by studies such as that by Bell and Scott-Kemmis (1985, p. 1978), who surveyed 93 technology-transfer agreements between British suppliers and Indian receiving firms and found that "few of the supplier firms incurred trivial or zero costs — for most firms they were of considerable significance." For example, lengthy bargaining over petrochemical technology sought by South Korea, which began with 13 multinational enterprises and ended up with Dow Chemical securing the contract, was not a costless exercise for any of the prospective suppliers (Enos 1982).

The earlier preoccupation with monopolistic imperfections in international technology markets and the associated calls for technology importation have waned. Because of the proliferation of sources of technology, the improved bargaining skills of purchasing entities, and the marked trend toward trade liberalization, the current focus is on complementing local technological capacity-building with technology obtained through investment flows, licences, consulting contracts, technical-assistance arrangements, and other conduits for acquiring technology from abroad.

Economists now know that focusing exclusively on commercial markets for technology and treating technology as discrete bits of hardware or specific bits of technical information leaves out some extremely interesting parts of the story. Although commodity-like characteristics can be ascribed to many technology transactions, if technology is a commodity, it is for at least two reasons somewhat fuzzy around the edges:

1. Even with the best of intentions and full cooperation of suppliers, some technologies are difficult to codify; and some, impossible. This attribute of "tacitness" means that mastery over these technologies cannot be purchased like commodities. Mastery requires experience, often accumulated through experimentation and trial and error. First mentioned by Polanyi (1965) and later popularized by Nelson and Winter (1982), the concept of the tacitness (or "firm specificity") of technology has become a mainstay of the analytical toolbox of Neo-Schumpeterian economists (Pavitt 1987; Rosemberg 1990; Arora 1991). Nelson (1990) used the analogy of purchasing a tennis racket (a commodity) and mastering the game of tennis.

2. The pure commodity thesis ignores the richness and diversity of the network of linkages for transmitting and receiving technical information. Such linkages include the circulation of workers and key personnel, subcontracting arrangements, spin-offs, user–producer interactions, and information supplied by sales representatives. For this reason, Bell (1991) reminded us that we must guard against overstating the importance of the individual firm, in isolation. The individual firm works in a complex nexus. As Bell (1991, p. 9) stated, "technical change is generated out of complex structures of interaction between firms, and sometimes between firms and supporting infrastructural institutions." Very often, these relationships have varying degrees of social, as well as commercial, content. Other important linkages for technical learning are associations with family, friends, and old schoolmates.

One final point: most development economists are convinced that past experience matters a great deal. Heterodox economists were never comfortable with the analysis of conventional economics. In this vein, a consensus has been growing among development economists that nations attract more robust flows of technology and can better internalize and extract benefits from imported technology if these nations have already upgraded their domestic S&T base by establishing incentives and an economic atmosphere conducive to innovation; by developing adequate levels and categories of human resources; and by providing appropriate institutional, infrastructural, and real-services support (Lall 1992).

The situation is similar for individual enterprises. Nelson and Winter (1982) — as well as later writers like Bell (1984), who emphasized the differences between passive and active pursuit of enterprise-level technological capacity-building in developing countries — indicated that past efforts to improve technical competence significantly influence (some would say determine) the current capacity to search for, acquire, and absorb technology, as well as the extent and direction of intrafirm generation and exploitation of new technologies. Benefits from passive absorption of technology and routine, relatively risk-free learning by doing will ordinarily be quickly exhausted. Thus, history matters at both the national and enterprise levels, and this fact provides a powerful imperative for active learning at both levels.

# Technology-related experiences: innovation systems, with an African emphasis

One can find examples of extremely high quality R&D activities in developing countries, but these are the exceptions. On the whole, R&D undertakings in the South suffer from a whole constellation of difficulties and shortcomings. This section begins with a very brief overview of these deficiencies in Third World R&D. The discussion then broadens to include R&D and other aspects of innovation, although the situation in Africa is emphasized. The regional stress is explained by the fact that the great majority of least-developed countries are found in that continent.

## Problems with R&D in the South

R&D in developing countries very often suffers from a variety of inefficiencies at research institutes, including overly hierarchical managerial structures; equipment chosen by administrators rather than by users; severe neglect of equipment maintenance; a low ratio of supporting technicians to scientists; almost no interinstitutional sharing of expensive equipment; a biased incentive structure that leads scientists to abandon research in favour of careers in administration — the list could go on (Gaillard and Ouattar 1988; Gaillard 1991).

An additional problem is in the selection of research projects. It is often alleged that the typical R&D portfolio in developing countries is too heavily skewed toward pure or basic research, at the expense of applied research; too heavily influenced by what is in vogue in the international scientific community, at the expense of locally pressing development problems; and too heavily laden with intrinsically promising projects that are not backed by a critical minimum threshold of resources, human and otherwise, to have much chance of success. An obstacle is presented by volatile fluctuations in government financing for public R&D, a practice especially detrimental to S&T endeavours that by their nature require lengthy gestation. Further frustrations are due to premature withdrawal of external financial aid to RDIs in the South by funding bodies that are short-sighted in their assessment of the time it takes to launch an R&D project or RDI. Finally, there is a considerable discrepancy between the R&D activities that are being carried out and the R&D results sought by producing enterprises (Williams Silveira 1985; Alvarez and Gomez 1994).

## The crisis in Africa's system for innovation

An almost universal dissatisfaction is felt with the old African model, which emphasized large-scale industrial manufacturing and featured the importation of complex systems of capital-intensive technology to produce items for export or for the urban domestic market. The old African model represents technological relocation rather than transfer. Before attempting to identify a few building blocks for African development and by extension for that of poor populations anywhere in the developing world, I will examine some current realities.

### National S&T bodies

In the 1970s, African countries established, in accordance with recommendations by the United Nations Educational, Scientific and Cultural Organization, national S&T entities called councils, centres, commissions, or occasionally ministries (Vitta 1990, 1992a, b, 1993). These national institutions have had very few resources but great responsibilities, which has led to their having the unspoken goal of perpetuating themselves and their lobbying activities (the salaries for which constitute the largest item of their budgets). Technology policy requires considerable horizontal coordination across many ministerial boundaries, yet ministers tend to be rigidly vertical in their organization and very guarded about intrusions on their turf. Despite formal positioning, national S&T entities do not in fact have the political clout to challenge the system. As Vitta (1992a, p. 33) put it, "in practice, the formality does not stop heads of state from consigning them [S&T entities] to the big scrap heap of other institutions, also directly under the head of state, whose activities they oversee remotely through the normal layers of bureaucracy." According to Eisemon and Davis (1992, p. 86), "few [S&T entities] are presently involved in analysis, coordination and direction of scientific activities."

## S&T and African universities

The university system in Africa, which is host to a significant proportion of the regional scientists and technicians and does most of the S&T training, is caught in the triple pincers of high cost, falling funding, and rising enrollment. In Africa's public universities, real expenditures per student fell from $6 300 in 1980 to $1500 in 1988 (Eisemon and Davis, unpublished).[1] Rising enrollments have led to overcrowding, course repetition by those not making the grade, and strained institutional resources. At Kenyatta University, some students have had to sit outside classrooms to listen to lectures. Double-occupancy rooms in dormitories have as many as six occupants, and the student enrollment far exceeds the capacity of the library to serve them (Eisemon and Davis, unpublished).[1] Evidently, a considerable amount of "crowding out" of R&D effort has been the result. Some faculty have to repeat lectures many times because of the shortage of large classrooms, and the number of classes taught by faculty has increased. Because of reduced salaries, many faculty members spend time on second jobs, or moonlighting as it is called in the United States — figures on time spent on second jobs by researchers in a sample of RDIs in developing countries can be found in Gaillard (1991). As a result, scientific output, in terms of scientific papers and articles, has declined since the mid-1980s (Eisemon and Davis 1991).

## Lack of commercialization

Given the development needs, it appears that too much emphasis is placed on basic research as a proportion of total effort, and hence mammoth problems have arisen with seeing even feasible innovations through to actual use. Sub-Saharan Africa spends a higher proportion of its research budget on basic research than the United States (Vitta 1993). As noted, however, the monumental shortcoming of Africa's innovation system is the chasm between research and actual use. Ogbimi (1990) used the word "negligible" to describe the amount of commercialization. He went on to say that a good deal of the reason for this is the contempt that many scientists have for "technician's work," which translates into the considerable effort, time, and expense

---

[1] Eisemon, T.O.; Davis, C.H. Kenya: crisis in the scientific community. Unpublished manuscript.

required to even attempt to see an innovation through the experimental, pilot, and marketing stages.

Only a tiny fraction of African research results prove commercially feasible — about one in a hundred in Vitta's (1993) estimation. Tiffin and Osotimehin (1988) reported on a study of 15 agricultural tools in Nigeria, all of which had already gone through field testing: 3 went beyond this stage, and of those, 2 were eventually widely diffused, but no attempt was made to market the remaining 12. I have already noted two of the main problems: the disdain with which researchers typically view practical activities necessary to prepare innovations for the market; and the lack of funding, which precludes such undertakings even if the will is present. Researchers are rarely exposed to the viewpoints of final users, whether entrepreneurs or the consuming public. The innovation system is not geared to useful end-products: the whole incentive structure is inverted, rewarding beginnings rather than completions. The International Development Research Centre (IDRC) instituted a program in 1988 whereby grants would be based on final results, but so far there is no evidence that the emphasis has paid off (Vitta 1993).

## Funding problems

The shortage and unpredictability of financing for R&D exacerbate and sometimes cause inefficiencies. Africa devotes less than 0.4% of its gross national product to expenditures on R&D; the annual budget of a typical RDI is a scant $50 000 (Vitta 1993). This endemic shortage of funds leads RDIs to "take shortcuts, skip essential stages, rush products to the market and, predictably, fail to achieve commercial success" (Vitta 1992b, p. 224). When a feasible product results from research, it is almost always licenced or forgotten. Financial constraints prohibit the RDI from taking part in the process of commercialization, which could afford learning and insights about the needs of final users and what it takes to bring a product to market. The RDIs continue to house dreamers, and from an economic standpoint, a lot of research more nearly resembles consumption activity than investment (Vitta 1990, 1992a, b, 1993). Irregularity of funding leads to "outages," meaning that promising projects are abandoned and forgotten (Gaillard and Waast 1992).

## External dependence

Herbert-Copley's (1992) survey of African enterprises revealed an extremely high dependence on foreign technology, both in the areas of machinery, equipment, and components and in terms of technical assistance and expatriate engineers and managers (the firms had received IDRC support; the industries represented were iron and steel, textiles, food processing, petroleum and petrochemicals, metalwork-ing, building materials, vehicle assembly, and a "multisector and other" category). Quite often, the choice of technology is controlled by the source of external financing. The reduction in public funds has led to reductions in training programs, leading to the "prolonged infancy" of firms (Oyeyinka and Adeloye 1988). Technology tends to be imported in modern packages, and because of the available skills, these packages provide little room for experimentation and incremental improve-ments. Even international R&D centres in Africa, which are clearly designed to contribute to technological capacity-building, frequently encourage pure imitation rather than approaches more suited to endogenous technological exigencies (Eisemon 1986). About 50% of African R&D is externally funded (Vitta 1993), a dependency that also affects African universities (Eisemon 1986; Eisemon and Davis 1992). In addition, negotiations for foreign funds are usually highly central-ized at the national level, with little or no involvement of the entity that is to receive the funds, a procedure that cannot contribute much to technological capacity-building at the university, RDI, or enterprise level (Gaillard and Waast 1992).

**Miscellaneous shortcomings**
Other worrisome conditions in the African innovation system abound. Typically, RDIs give available salary increases across the board, rather than rewarding productive research, and salaries are so insufficient that key researchers and administrators leave for alternative employ-ment. Of course, some leave Africa altogether, and the irony is that the brain drain from sub-Saharan Africa, at least the proportion going to the United States, has been significantly higher than from Africa as a whole (Logan 1987). (The increases were 9 and 28% in 1980, 5 and 12% in 1983, and 10 and 15% in 1985, from Africa and sub-Saharan Africa, respectively.) I noted earlier that the ratio of technicians to scientists is low in developing-country RDIs, but if one includes all support person-nel, these institutes have about 10 typists, lab assistants, gardeners, messengers, security personnel, and drivers for every scientist, which is an auxiliary–scientist ratio that appears higher than necessary (Gaillard and Waast 1992).

Agricultural research stations are kept going, even though they have become inaccessible because of a lack of roads or vehicles (Gaillard and Waast 1992). During 1988, virtually all experimental work ceased in the Faculty of Science at the University of Ibadan because of a shortage of glassware and other imported scientific supplies and equipment. Stubborn regulators do not help. Gaillard and Waast (1992) wrote of a leading hematologist who needed to import specific reagents. Because these reagents are rarely used, customs agents could not identify them in their manuals and put a value on them that was 100 times higher than the values for other common laboratory products. Neither the institute accountants nor import licence-issuing authorities were sympathetic. Some institutes have to battle continually for supplies of water and electricity, cannot purchase or repair equipment, and are short of even the most common reagents. "In these conditions, no serious research is possible" (Irle 1989, p. 132).

In the use of industrial technology in the productive sector, excess capacity occasionally coincides with excess demand because of the inability to get foreign exchange to import parts (Herbert-Copley 1992). In the productive sector, firm-level studies are sparse, but those that we have indicate that the accumulation of technological capacity through learning is very limited. There is an especially acute deficiency in Africa of the type of capital-stretching innovations detected in Latin America and Asia.

## Toward a new model

Virtually all development economists agree that the old model for low-income nations and regions, which rests on large-scale industrialization and imported technology and advice, has not worked (World Bank 1989; Mytelka 1990; Herbert-Copley 1992). Suggesting a complete, alternative model is too ambitious for a paper such as this; rather, I will focus on a few building blocks.

It will be convenient to distinguish five levels of technology on the basis of technological sophistication:

▼ Traditional technologies;

▼ Conventional technologies;

▼ Emerging technologies;

▼ Intermediate, or appropriate, technologies; and

▼ Blended technologies.

(The definitions will follow closely those in Bhalla and James [1991].) These categories are not intended to be airtight; borderline examples notwithstanding, however, they should be sufficiently distinct for our discussion. Because intermediate and blended technologies are the only ones expressly intended to benefit the low-income strata of society in developing countries, they are treated at length.

## Traditional technologies

Usually, traditional technologies have been used for a very long time and tend to be well rooted in local culture and tradition. Reddy (1979, p. 35) put it well when he said that traditional technologies are "the evolutionary product of a long process of natural selection of innovations often stretching over several centuries." Ordinarily, traditional technologies fit comfortably with local skills profiles, socioeconomic conditions, and value systems. Although traditional technologies can be ingenious (Reddy mentioned the navigational techniques of the South Sea Islanders and the intercropping practices of prehistoric civilizations in Latin America), most of them are routine.

## Conventional technologies

The commercial feasibility of conventional technologies, having been firmly established, is not in doubt. They constitute the core production techniques for the bulk of production in developed countries and in the modern sectors of the South. Conventional technologies are likely to offer little incentive for major research; any R&D that is conducted tends to be engineering based rather than science based. Improving designs and scaling up for increased capacity are two major R&D objectives for conventional technologies.

## Emerging technologies

Four characteristics distinguish emerging technologies from other levels of technology: first, emerging technologies are products of recent scientific research and to a significant extent remain driven by scientific R&D; second, the rates of development and application of emerging technologies exceed those of most other types of technology; third, emerging technologies show every indication of maintaining their dynamism in the near future; and fourth, extensive application of emerging technologies can lead to considerable social and economic change. Laser applications, modern biotechnology, new-materials science, photovoltaics, space technology, and microelectronics are cases in point.

## Intermediate, or appropriate, technologies

Intermediate technology is inextricably bound up with its champion, E.F. Schumacher, who was the protagonist of the movement to promote its use among the poorer strata of developing countries. An intermediate technology represents, in terms of technological sophistication, something between the indigenous, traditional production methods and those used by the modern sectors of both the South and the North. In 1965, Schumacher was involved with the establishment of the Inter-mediate Technology Development Group, an organization that remains extremely active in promoting technological progress in the Third World and is considered the flagship institution for promoting the use of intermediate technology. The publication of Schumacher's (1973) seminal work, *Small Is Beautiful: Economics As If People Mattered,* attracted an enormous amount of attention and spawned a large and fervent group of followers from across the disciplinary spectrum.

The term *intermediate technology* caused some confusion; later the term *appropriate technology* came into vogue, and even greater semantic turmoil ensued. The trouble is that a literal interpretation of appropriate technology becomes so broad that it becomes vacuous. Who will take a stand for inappropriate technology? In an attempt to sidestep the definitional minefields, I will use *appropriate technology* and *intermediate technology* interchangeably, although others distin-guish the terms and have perfectly legitimate reasons for doing so. (For an exhaustive survey and analysis of the definitions of intermediate and appropriate technology, as well as related items, see Willoughby [1990].)

Given the origin of the concept and its post-Schumacher evo-lution, I might say that an intermediate, or appropriate, technology should have all or, at least, many of the following characteristics:

▼ The use of this technology is associated with a low cost per job created.

▼ This technology is more labour intensive than conventional technology.

▼ The demands this technology places on locally available worker and managerial skills are modest.

▼ The bulk of the inputs needed for this technology are avail-able locally.

▼ When this technology is used circumspectly, it is environ-mentally friendly.

Intermediate technologies can be developed by introducing improve-ments on existing traditional technologies, scaling down or otherwise adjusting conventional technologies, or coming up with new ideas.

A mystery surrounds appropriate technology. On the one hand, there is an astonishing — one might even say bewildering — array of alternative technologies pertaining to agriculture, livestock, fishing, forestry, food and fibre processing, farm equipment, water availability and purity, sanitation, energy, construction, transportation, and service delivery. These appropriate technologies, among many others, have been described by Een and Joste (1988, 1991) and IDRC (1992a). Dozens of organizations publish information on appropriate technology; scores of organizations actively promote and supervise its adoption and use. On the other hand, the attention given to appropriate technology and choice of technique for Third World production, so profuse two decades ago, has slowed to a trickle in today's economics literature and virtually dropped out of the more orthodox, neoclassical economics journals. I first suspected this when I was preparing a review essay for *Latin American Research Review*: I looked at seven works on technology and development and found only one serious mention of appropriate technology. My suspicion was reinforced recently while I was working on a review and analysis of the literature on technological capacity-building in developing countries. The mystery, then, is how this can be so in light of feverishly ongoing appropriate-technology activities. To broaden the question, one may ask why the visible benefits flowing from appropriate technologies have not been commensurate with their generation and availability.

Many explanations are possible, not all of which apply exclusively to appropriate technologies. Sometimes effective technologies are underused. For example, oral rehydration therapy is underused in Pakistan because doctors excessively prescribe antibiotics and antidiarrheal drugs (Saunders 1991). Sometimes effective technologies are misused, with disastrous results. Dudley (1993) tells how the ventilated, improved pit latrine, which has been promoted for two decades, can become a disease factory if the fly screen is not placed properly over the chimney. Not infrequently, the technology thought to be appropriate turns out to be something else entirely. A good example is China's unsuccessful attempt to transplant its rice-production techniques to Liberia, where massive differences in terrain, factor proportions, and worker skills were ignored (Brautigam 1993). Geographic or cultural specificity make some technologies difficult to disseminate.

In the past, too much ideological baggage was carried by practitioners, who saw appropriate technology as part of an alternative life style. A director of a large NGO that promotes technologies in developing countries confided, in correspondence, that the benefits of appropriate technology were oversold, which inevitably led to disappointment and discouragement. Small-scale technologies or the products they produce often compete with large-scale conventional industries and thus confront powerful entrenched interests.

The introduction of appropriate technologies rarely leads to sustained dynamic trajectories, spreads to alternative uses, or inspires complementary innovations. Perhaps most appropriate technologies fit so comfortably with prevailing institutions and cultural values that attitudes toward innovation remain guarded. In the past, people were preoccupied with the technologies themselves and insufficiently appreciated the detailed, imaginative, costly, and time-consuming effort needed to get the technologies functioning satisfactorily in the field. Until recently, commercialization as a means for promoting appropriate technology received inadequate attention. Macroeconomic or technology policies that discriminate against micro- and small-scale enterprises (MSEs) or labour-intensive production are a large part of the explanation for this (Stewart 1987; Stewart et al. 1990). On the other hand, many appropriate-technology projects that were feasible only with policy-related economic distortions became unfeasible when economies were deregulated.

Despite these obstacles, I think it is premature to give up on appropriate technology. We seem to have learned our lesson about becoming overly preoccupied with things, eschewing commercial promotion, and being excessively optimistic about the appropriate-technology movement. Perhaps, in an economic atmosphere where market forces are allowed freer sway, we will see a reduced tendency for policy interventions to discourage MSEs from using alternative technologies. Furthermore, we should avoid allowing the catalogue of difficulties to divert our attention from the successes. The microloans of the Grameen Bank in Bangladesh have inspired many countries to fashion similar systems to deliver financing. (For a thorough evaluation of the Grameen Bank, see Wahid [1994].) Oral rehydration salts (ORS) have saved millions of lives (Fricke 1984; Hirschhorn and Greenough 1991). Now more than 100 million improved cook stoves can be found in China (Smith et al. 1993). One could easily extend the list of what Appropriate Technology International has referred to as high-impact appropriate technologies. (See Fricke [1984], who described seven other high-impact appropriate technologies.)

## Blended technologies

In the early 1980s, people became concerned that the impressive advances in emerging technologies were not palpably improving the standard and quality of life of the extremely poor in developing nations. M.S. Swaminathan and U. Colombo, who were consecutive chairs of the United Nations Advisory Committee on Science and Technology for Development, nurtured an investigation to see whether emerging technologies could be constructively integrated into traditional economic activities of developing countries. What was intended was blending, as opposed to completely replacing. An essential ingredient in the whole enterprise was to investigate situations in which modern technology complemented low-income and small-scale activities or in which larger scale production of goods or services satisfied the basic needs of the very poor while retaining a significant proportion of the traditional modes of production.

After a panel on technology blending was hosted by the International Rice Research Institute at Los Banos, Laguna, the Philippines, in December 1982, the idea was considered sufficiently promising for further exploration. The Technology and Employment Branch of the International Labour Office agreed to spearhead the effort. The resulting literature, although not voluminous (von Weizsacker et al. 1983; Bhalla et al. 1984; Bhalla and James 1986, 1988, 1991; Colombo and Oshima 1989; Colombo 1991; Swaminathan 1991, 1993), constitutes a solid foundation, and several major efforts in the area are under way.

Technology blending might involve the application of modern biotechnology, new-materials sciences, microelectronics, satellite technology, photovoltaic power, or laser techniques to smallholder agriculture, agribusiness, urban informal activities, micro- or small-scale manufacturing enterprises, and delivery of services such as health, nutrition, sanitation, and education. The objectives might be to increase productivity, per capita income, and quality of life of the poorer strata of society in Third World nations. Technology blending differs from intermediate technology in at least three respects: blending will almost always involve a greater investment per workplace created than intermediate technology; blending will ordinarily entail a larger leap in skills and technological sophistication; and a greater proportion of the requisite inputs must, typically, be imported.

What about the comparison of technology blending with the straightforward application of conventional or emerging technology without blending (with traditional economic activities), in short, the virtually total replacement of prevailing traditional production techniques? With this, I am speculating because the following comparative hypotheses have been only partially tested and the evidence is fragmentary and indicative at best. The working hypothesis is that technology blends could have the following advantages over technology replacements:

1. Blending will entail some adjustment to social institutions in traditional societies, but the cost in social adjustments to changes in work organization, employment opportunities, and general community values are likely to be less severe.

2. The leap in demand for technical skills and managerial capabilities is likely to be less acute.

3. With emerging technology being intentionally melded to fit in with traditional activities, the benefits are more likely to be shared more equitably.

4. The chance for successfully stimulating further innovation and creative use of technological blends is greater than in instances in which completely alien technology supplants prevailing methods of production.

5. With respect to emerging technologies like microelectronics innovations, for example, it is likely that in many applications, the technology will be compatible with efficient MSEs.

As might be expected, technology-blending activities differ in their economic impact. Two triumphs are the use of electronic load-controllers for mini-hydroelectric projects in Colombia, Sri Lanka, and Thailand and the use of laser-guided land-leveling techniques in Egypt. The trade-offs are illustrated by the cloning of oil palms in Costa Rica that threaten to reduce employment but promise to increase efficiency and export earnings. Photovoltaic lighting in Fiji for dwellings with shops proved practical but only because users were willing to accept some limitations on the number of hours during which light was available. In situations with diverse consumer preferences, the results could well be different. Village street lighting in the Indian village Achheja, in Uttar Pradesh, was cost effective but probably would not have been if the village had already been connected to a power-grid extension. Some cases reveal severe difficulties. It took years for a project by the Faiyum Governate of Egypt to get the bugs out of a microcomputer system designed to gather health information from villages, although eventually it operated effectively. India's use of satellite technology for dissemination of information on farming techniques has been disappointing.

Several current blending efforts are noteworthy. (A great deal of the information on new blending initiatives was kindly furnished by A.S. Bhalla.) The first of these was inspired by U. Colombo, former director of the Italian National Commission on Environment, Energy and New Technologies (ENEA). It involves two Latin American projects that stem from experience with ENEA-inspired Italian blending projects (Colombo 1991). The Italian Ministry of Foreign Affairs, using technical support from ENEA, is promoting the use of robotics, irradiation technology, and separation technology for SMEs in Argentina's textiles and garments, leather and footwear, and furniture industries. Also, the Commission of the European Communities is funding a project (once again, with ENEA technical support) that is to investigate advanced technologies for the leather-goods sector. This project covers Argentina, Brazil, Paraguay, and Uruguay.

M.S. Swaminathan, formerly the director of the International Rice Research Institute and currently the director of the M.S. Swaminathan Research Foundation (Madras), has been the catalyst for initiatives involving information villages in India and biovillages in India and China. Both ideas were spawned by two meetings sponsored by the foundation: a Dialogue on Biotechnology, held in 1991, and a Dialogue on Information Technology, held the following year (Swaminathan 1991, 1993). On the east coast of India, three villages were selected in the Union Territory of Pondicherry. In China, the Chinese Academy of Sciences initiated the biovillage project, selecting six villages in Herbei province, Qinxian township, and Yuanshi county. The Indian foundation collaborates closely with the Chinese Academy of Sciences: for example, Swaminathan serves as chief adviser for the biovillage project in China. The biovillage effort seeks both technological and institutional blending through participatory meetings attended by scientists, local extension workers, and target beneficiaries, such as small-scale farmers, landless workers, women, and youth. A consortium of scientific institutions and research agencies in India provides technical assistance to the project through the Chinese Academy of Sciences, and a committee of regional research establishments in China is charged with managing the Chinese biovillage undertaking. The project in India targets women in landless households, women on small farms, and small-scale farmers generally. A consortium of supporting institutions includes the Government of India Department of Biotechnology, Tamil Nadu Agricultural University, and the National Bank for Agriculture and Rural Development.

The information-village project entails a combination of traditional village information channels, such as folk media and demonstrations, and new-technology information networks and computer-aided extension systems geared to farm- and off-farm-related activities. Data on sanitation, water, primary health care, primary education, and other quality-of-life indicators in rural areas will be simultaneously collected and processed. Feasibility studies are proceeding in six administrative districts in different states. The intent is to establish information shops, which will be managed by unemployed graduates, school teachers, or both, from the village, with the objective of making information available in a form directly usable by poor and often semiliterate or illiterate farmers. The project will eventually meld into a larger endeavour, the Small Farmers' Agri-business Consortium, an autonomous corporate entity funded by the Reserve Bank of India and the National Bank for Agricultural and Rural Development. This more comprehensive undertaking is also geared to furthering development that benefits the extremely poor in rural areas.

A third new technology-blending initiative, begun by the Government of Malaysia, is the use of information technology for SMEs. The Bumiputera Congress, held in Kuala Lumpur in 1992, endorsed the concept of technology blending, and then A.S. Bhalla, who has been involved in technology-blending studies for more than a decade, was asked to act as an adviser and resource person for a national seminar organized by the Malaysian Agricultural Research and Development Institute. As a result, feasibility studies on technology options in the food-processing sector are under way. Activities in other areas, such as textiles, garments, and furniture, are expected to be included.

A fourth example of new blending initiatives encompasses numerous independent projects, rather than involving a unified research effort. These projects apply expert systems to the problems in developing countries, especially those in agriculture, forestry, and village health care. Expert systems are computer programs that use information and reasoning techniques to simulate those employed by human experts. Expert-systems applications in developing countries are in the early planning or pilot stages, but some of those currently functioning in the North appear to be feasible in the South, for example, the AGASSISTANT system, designed to assist in diagnosing soybean diseases in Illinois (Fermanian and Michalski 1992), and a system to accelerate responses to water-pollution crises in Czechoslovakia (Vrtacnic et al. 1992).

A few of these applications are up and running in the South. A system in use in the Dominican Republic for improving land use has drawn attention to some incongruities between the geographic boundaries of responsibilities for extension services and the agroecological characteristics unique to each region (Mendez Emilien and Grabski 1992). A system is being applied in Indonesia that helps new migrants from densely populated Java adjust to more acidic soil conditions, which require unique soil-management techniques (Yost et al. 1992). In Tigre Province of northern Ethiopia, a system helps diagnose the five most common diseases in the area (Porenta et al. 1992).

(Virtually all my ideas on technology blending were conceived and nurtured in close collaboration with A.S. Bhalla; thus, I regard this material as a joint product. However, we may very well differ on details, nuances, and emphases.)

# Technology-related experiences: the informal sector, MSEs, and NGOs

## The informal sector

Maldonado and Sethuraman (1992) have produced the best collection of studies on technological capabilities in the informal sector of developing countries. The informal sector has long been recognized as a useful vehicle for recycling materials and equipment and conserving capital in a number of ways (adapting existing equipment, constructing equipment and tools, and operating from a residence or in the open). The most important finding, however (one surprising to many, including me), is that microenterprises occasionally exhibit innovative behaviour, despite being beset with a legion of difficulties. Thus, the challenge of rendering the sector more technologically dynamic is one of improving on existing and latent creative abilities.

Technological capacity-building is evident in capital accumulation by informal enterprises in India (Sethuraman 1992) and Ecuador (Farrell 1992) and by investment in human capital in Dhaka, Bangladesh (Khundeker 1992). Some innovations involve designing new products, improving product quality, self-constructing hand-operated equipment or tools, adapting equipment, and undertaking repairs and maintenance. In many cases, firms gradually upgrade their equipment as their personnel's learning proceeds. For example, Ecuadorian metalworking enterprises specializing in grillwork for residences would start with a welding set, grinding machine, compressor, hand drill, pincers, saw, and sometimes a forge bellows. The next rung on the technological ladder might be the acquisition of sheet-metal shapers and sheet-metal cutters and, by a few, equipment to impart rope-like twists to iron used for grills. A higher level is attained when an enterprise produces components for light vehicles or uses stand-mounted drills and autogenous welding sets. Eventually, when an enterprise acquires its own lathes, it has reached the top technological echelon for this type of producer.

The imagination of the owner spawns many innovations, but innovations may also emanate from friends, neighbours, and equipment suppliers, as well as the owner's observation of formal or informal production. Innovations seem to occur more frequently with subcontracting arrangements, although these arrangements are rare. Education helps, but training and years of experience are more robust indicators of the incidence of innovation.

Not all informal-sector enterprises are innovative, but the supply of entrepreneurial ideas does not appear to constitute a bottleneck, or to put it another way, a great many latent ideas for change languish just below the surface. Small-scale enterprises sometimes fail to initiate changes because of financial constraints. Many entrepreneurs initiated innovations but had to abandon them when funds became scarce. Many entrepreneurs claim that they have not tried some of their ideas because of limited space or materials or some other problem.

Two telling findings demand some attention. The first is that contact with government agencies gives rise to very few ideas for technological change. The second is that only a small fraction of MSEs in the informal sector graduate to tax-paying, registered firms in the main-stream of the economy.

One of the most imposing barriers to continued innovation and expansion is limited space for production. If you think that 228 m², the area of most shops in Bangalore (Sethuraman 1992), is small, con-sider the 91 m² of those found in Bangkok (Amin 1992) and reserve sympathy for the 15 m² shops sometimes found in Peru (Chaves 1992). A definite dilemma is that most informal enterprises thrive when prox-imity to customers maximizes contact and interaction, saves time, and reduces transportation costs, but for most informal enterprises, space is at a premium.

Shortage of credit is an important obstacle, but sometimes shortage of material inputs looms even larger. A serious encumbrance emanates from the political arena. At best, officialdom is likely to ignore the welfare of the informal sector; at worst, it may actively and purposefully throw up roadblocks and harass informal-sector entrepre-neurs. Much of this obstruction to informal-sector activities is initiated by formal-sector entrepreneurs, who are understandably miffed about competition from nonregistered firms that pay no taxes.

## Micro- and small-scale enterprises

Many MSEs are in the informal sector, so there is considerable overlap. This is illustrated by data provided by Villarán de la Puente (1989): only about 20% of small-scale producers (those with 5–19 workers) in the Peruvian metal–mechanical sector are in the formal sector; 2 970 microenterprises (those with 1–4 workers) are in the formal sector; and about 10 000 more are in the informal sector. No universally accepted criterion exists for measuring the size of enterprises. Any one of capital investment, net worth, sales, energy use, etc., could serve as a criterion, but the most common variable used is the number of employees. If we accept the number of employees as the criterion, there is still a prob-lem, as no one agrees on the numbers for micro-, small-, medium-, and large-scale enterprises. However we define the cutoff points, we can be confident that MSEs are extremely important in providing jobs in devel-oping countries. Empirical studies of rural Africa, for example, indicate that MSEs account for 20–45% of full-time employment and 30–50% of household income (Liedholm et al. 1994). Furthermore, sound evidence indicates that the smaller enterprises can be a dynamic factor in employment creation. In empirical studies of Botswana, Kenya, Malawi, Swaziland, and Zimbabwe during 1980–90, the smaller enterprises pro-vided jobs for about 2.3 million of the 4.9 million increase in the labour force. It is often argued that smaller firms use raw materials and capital more efficiently and that the remuneration to labour is closer to its actual opportunity cost. Smaller firms provide opportunities for accumulating experience in management, marketing, and the financial aspects of operating a business.

Hyman (1989) described some of the recent research on MSEs: stages I and II of the Program for Investment in the Small Capital Enterprise Sector; the Growth and Equity through Micro-Enterprise Investment and Institutions; the Michigan State University studies; the Rural Small Industrial Enterprises; the Asian Development Bank studies; and some others. Much has been learned about the operation and financing of the smaller enterprises, but in the next two subsections I will focus on facets that appear especially relevant.

## Graduation rates

Beyond a threshold of about 10 workers, it appears that managerial complexities, technological deficiencies, and the need to find additional workers from outside the family constitute a barrier to enlarging the firm's operations. During the 1980s, in the five African countries mentioned above, less than 1% of the smaller firms graduated to the stage of having more than 10 employees (Mead 1994). This is a very serious matter because the currently expanding firms make a significant contribution to the increase in employment. No doubt, there are more reasons why smaller firms drop out without graduating, but reducing the obstacles could pay big dividends.

## Technology: the bright side

The technological picture is undoubtedly bleak in regions that host poor populations, but many examples can be given to show that progress is not impossible. When Herbert-Copley (1992) reviewed IDRC's programs in Africa, he found considerable differences in productivity, sometimes within the same industry and same country, which indicates that some enterprises are doing some things well.

I have mentioned some successful appropriate technologies, technology blends, and technological upgrading in the informal sector. I can also point to many other technical-learning experiences involving MSEs in the South, such as hydroponic cultivation of seedlings in Zimbabwe (Tiffin and Osotimehin 1992), cloning of tea in Malawi (James et al. 1988; Mytelka 1990), rice milling in Bangladesh (Mytelka 1990), manufacture of Hotchkiss™ and other wheelchairs in Colombia (de Wilde et al. 1991), production of treadle pumps and ceramic-lined stoves in Senegal (ATI 1994), production of Mark II™ pumps in India (Fricke 1984), and commercial small-scale *tambak* (brackish ponds) farming for large prawns and milkfish in Indonesia (de Wilde et al. 1991).

In a study of small-scale enterprises in Sierra Leone, covering 1975–80, 48% of the entrepreneurs surveyed had introduced some form of technical change (Chuta and Liedholm 1985). Villarán de la Puente (1989) uncovered innovations in MSEs in the metal–mechanical industry in Peru. Langdon (1984) found technical learning among firms in his study of textile and wood production in Kenya. SMEs have been involved in innovations in the agricultural equipment and food industries (Cortes et al. 1987). Electric Arc Limited evolved from a financially troubled firm to one that was extremely successful, through the deliberate accumulation of technological mastery — a small enterprise in a small country (Jamaica) that forged ahead during terrible economic times (Girvan and Marcelle 1991). Ebunso Nigerian Limited has been able to provide local designs for processing plants using local raw materials (Chuckwjekwu 1991).

Only 2 of 15 field-tested innovations in agricultural equipment identified in Nigeria made it to commercialization (Tiffin and Osotimehin 1988), but the number was not zero. Mishra (1994, p. 216) was justified in labeling it a "dismal picture indeed" when he found that 55 of 78 farm-machinery producers in Uttar Pradesh had failed to introduce changes in their designs, but the point I would like to make is that some did — the survey was not completely devoid of innovating firms. Innovations happen in poor regions. The trick will be to discover ways to make them less exceptional and idiosyncratic and, in our more optimistic moments, to hope that innovations in poor regions can eventually become infectious.

## Nongovernmental organizations

NGOs have become something like the darlings of many interested in or actually engaged in fostering socioeconomic development in the South. It is frequently remarked that it is desirable to forge better links and establish more effective cooperation between governmental entities and NGOs; it is also the recommendation of official aid agencies that NGOs have a greater part in project implementation in areas traditionally the province of government agencies. The United Nations Development Programme (UNDP) estimated that the world has 50 000 NGOs (UNDP 1993), but we have no accurate count, and the count could be even higher. NGOs come in a rich assortment of species. Some NGOs rely on government funding, whereas others are supported by private sources. Some are "base" NGOs, or NGOs with local origins and agenda, whereas others are "intermediate" NGOs, or NGOs that provide resources and technical assistance to base organizations. Some are structured around a membership, whereas others have professional staffs and target groups without considering a roster of members. Some

NGOs are from the North but are active in the South, whereas others are Third World NGOs. NGOs range from very large organizations, like Amnesty International and the Earth Council, to cell-like local base organizations. NGOs are prominent in the empowerment and advocacy arenas — UNDP (1993, p. 98) asserted that "advocacy is clearly the NGOs' greatest strength" — but many NGOs attempt to upgrade technology to benefit lower income groups. Our attention will be on these latter activities, although gains in the advocacy and empowerment arenas, such as fewer violations of human rights or greater security of land ownership, can have positive influences on innovative behaviour and the willingness to take risks.

NGOs have been operating in developing countries for some time. What accounts for their recent popularity and their move closer to centre stage? Carroll (1992) provided some answers. In an unusual convergence of admiration, the conservative factions seem to approve of NGOs because of their potential for reducing the role of the state and making life more tolerable during structural adjustment, and the more liberal factions are attracted by the grass-roots, people-oriented participatory activities often claimed to be the hallmark of NGOs. Intermediate NGOs can reduce transaction costs in dealing with base organizations and are especially effective in accumulating expertise at the regional level. This means that compared with governmental organizations, NGOs have both greater flexibility and less top-down determination of the ways development undertakings will be formulated and implemented. Furthermore, some believe that the intimate feel of NGOs for local needs and conditions, coupled with local participation, makes them more effective in mobilizing local resources to complement outside support.

NGOs and their operating environment, including donor agencies, operate in a framework circumscribed by several trade-offs or tensions. However, these and other policy issues connected with NGOs will be discussed in the closing section.

### The Mexican model

Mexico has a program well under way that pulls together some of the threads in this discussion (Aspe 1993). In 1987, Mexico's national industrial development bank, Nacional Financiera (NAFINSA), allocated 94% of its credit to large parastatal agencies and a scant 6% to SMEs. In 1991, the proportions were exactly reversed. NAFINSA is now set up to work with small firms without access to the commercial banking system.

The first tier is aimed at microenterprises (those with four or fewer employees and annual sales no greater than $100 000), most of which are in the informal sector. NAFINSA provides credit to locally established NGOs (sometimes with the state government as an intermediary), who monitor the credit provided by NAFINSA and pro-vide the required training, financed by private-sector contributions. The credit, which is limited to $10 000, is not subsidized and has a 3-year limit. Technical assistance is provided by the staff of the NGOs or through the cooperation of universities whose students have an obliga-tion to provide community service.

When microenterprises go beyond the stipulated employee or annual sales limit, they have graduated to the next tier for small enter-prises (5–14 employees and sales between $100 000 and $250 000). Commercial banks and other financial institutions allocate credit, now at a $250 000 maximum, according to a point system for evaluating the credit rating of small enterprises and then discount these loans with NAFINSA. The borrowing entrepreneur is issued a plastic identification card, and on presentation of the card, the entrepreneur receives the amount requested within 24 h, which saves time previously spent in lengthy and complicated negotations. Once these firms grow beyond the stipulated limits, they graduate once more and are ready for ordi-nary commercial loans. However, the Government of Mexico also encourages entrepreneurial associations to guarantee loans; this can reduce the cost of loans from commercial banks or of those available directly from NAFINSA through special trust funds.

It is too early to evaluate the Mexican scheme, but it deserves scrutiny as it unfolds. In 1989, 40 firms a day received credit, a num-ber that grew to 250 by the end of 1991. During that time, 74 000 firms received credit. Repayment rates are running close to 100%. The suc-cess of the scheme will depend not only on repayment rates but also on the incidence of graduation, the degree of technological capacity accumulated, and the impact on Mexico's competitive capacities. Clearly, Mexico has seriously studied the Italian economy, in which firms with fewer than 15 employees export $30 billion annually and account for almost half of the industrial output of the fifth largest West-ern industrial economy.

# Now what? A selected portfolio of issues and suggested actions

## Technological pragmatism

The term *humane technology* is merely catchy shorthand for applying technology to humane ends. Properly used, the ventilated, improved pit latrine is a humane technology, but without a fly screen it becomes a health threat. Asbestos–cement roofing sheets keep the rain out of dwellings in many parts of the Third World, but they are a health hazard if those doing the cutting and drilling neglect to dampen the sheets and wear a face mask (Dudley 1993). Furthermore, technology can be humane by degrees. Wood-burning stoves cause death from smoke inhalation, but if no reasonable substitutes can be found for heating and cooking, an improved, efficient stove is more humane than an inefficient, unimproved one.

By looking at appropriate technology and technology blending, I have been arguing that a multilayered technology approach, or technological pluralism, is a wise course of action. What this really means is technological pragmatism, which is perhaps a better way of addressing the problem. Technological pragmatism looks for the best technical means for satisfying basic needs while recognizing the harsh realities of resource availability. We need to avoid being caught up in the fervour of an appropriate-technology movement, a technology-blending movement, or an emerging-technology movement. Very sophisticated techniques were used to develop ORS, and sophisticated computer techniques were used to perfect windmills for developing countries, to determine the right porosity for small dams in India, and to design a more environmentally friendly kiln for small-scale brick makers in Juárez, Mexico. Whether these are examples of appropriate technology, technology blending, or emerging technology is far less important than the fact that they work. For that matter, conventional technologies, such as the old tried and true biotechnology techniques, still have much to offer in basic-needs satisfaction.

The practical and helpful technologies are in constant flux and must be continually monitored. For example, research on photovoltaic power is continuing, especially on new methods for direct casting of silicon and thin films (Caldwell 1994). Investigations are also under way to improve oral rehydration therapy by experimenting with amino acids and the addition of powdered food to slow diarrhea and better protect cells in the intestine (Hirschhorn and Greenough 1991).

### Appropriate technology

Advocates of appropriate technology have come a long way toward technological pragmatism. The movement phase appears largely to have faded, and many appropriate-technology units, like the Intermediate Technology Development Group and the Volunteer in Technical Assistance program, will recommend emerging technology if it makes more sense in a particular context. Moreover, the misplaced preoccupation with things has, as a result of more than two decades of learning from experience, given way to a realization that coming up with a novel gadget is analogous to an ante in a poker game — you have to do it, but what happens after that is what is important. Commercialization as a mode of dissemination is far more prevalent than in the past. In short, much of what needs to be done involves building on progress that has already been achieved. However, I will touch on two more issues.

Undoubtedly, a better job could be done, but in general, the world is doing fairly well at coming up with alternative technologies. The problem is that although the world as a whole is performing reasonably well, low-income countries and areas are definitely not. Low-income areas desperately need to accumulate internal technological capacity to meaningfully complement technology acquired externally. Because of the tacit and cumulative nature of technology, technological capacity-building is the only hope for sustainable progress in very low income regions.

The second issue concerns the international community, which can encourage countries to examine macro policies systematically to remedy those that discriminate against smaller firms in particular and labour-intensive techniques in general. Haggblade et al. (1990) gave an extremely useful inventory of macro policies: trade policies (import restrictions, foreign-exchange controls, etc.), monetary policies (interest rates, banking regulations, etc.), fiscal policies (tax structure, provision of infrastructure, etc.), labour policies (minimum-wage laws, legislation governing working conditions, etc.), pricing policies (price controls on consumer goods or inputs, etc.), and direct regulatory controls (monopoly privileges, zoning, etc.). Country studies along this line might look at some possible changes and their overall impact on innovative behaviour and technological capacity-building, including those in the smaller enterprises.

**Technology blending**

Not until very recently have deliberate experiments in technology blending been initiated. We simply do not know whether beneficial technology blends are rare and idiosyncratic or whether robust technological trajectories are possible. We know still less about whether blending can favourably affect the very poorest populations (the projects initiated by Swaminathan, discussed earlier, are the most promising).

This being the case, we obviously need to initiate more blending experiments and from day one (if not in the preplanning stage) to begin gathering information on socioeconomic and technical variables. Providing a greater awareness of technology blending could be helpful. Review the literature on the application of artificial intelligence in developing countries, and you will find no discussion of technology blending, thus foreclosing any cross-fertilization. Review the experience of World Bank financial assistance for computer technology in Africa, and you will find little or no evidence of blending used as an alternative to straightforward insertion (Gahan 1992; Moussa and Schware 1992).

## Reaching the lowest strata

In general, basic-needs efforts do not effectively reach the poorest of the poor. UNDP (1993) estimated that NGO interventions probably miss the poorest 5–10%. Carroll (1992, p. 67), after examining the highest rated intermediate NGOs from a sample of 30 operating in Latin America, concluded that they "have relatively few direct beneficiaries among the poorest rural households." This means that, like it or not, basic-needs efforts have a salvaging dimension, and this is not confined to sporadic famine and refugee movements but is endemic and long term. It also means that we cannot become excessively doctrinaire about pure market forces. Seldom will people in the lower category of the poor qualify for even a microloan, and when one is struggling to keep body and soul together, it is unrealistic to suppose she or he will come up with an innovative idea and have the energy to pursue it. Some subsidization from somewhere is inevitable. (Incidentally, contrary to widespread belief, Pakistan's Grameen Bank does not recover costs on loans to microenterprises [see Wahid 1994].) The international community could serve as a catalyst for encouraging the exploration of financing mechanisms, delivery agencies, and implementation strategies for the poorest of the poor to advance their condition. In addition, it would be useful to know whether successful programs for the people in the upper category of the poor have or could have a beneficial impact on those in the lower category of the poor. Perhaps the trickle-down effect is more robust when the economic distance between up and down is minimal.

## Nongovernmental organizations

NGOs have to do a number of balancing acts, not the least of which is between the time horizons dictated by the sources of their funding and the time required to introduce and nurture technical changes. Technical learning involves tacitness and is cumulative, each of which implies that ample time is needed to establish a needs-based technical change; to generate participative community support; to identify regional cultural, social, and geographic distinctions that might affect the adoption of technology; to smooth out linkages with the relevant state agencies; and to go through a phase of trial and error and experimentation with technical changes. Intermediate NGOs are under too much pressure to produce quick results. Too much emphasis is on producing how-to manuals as a gauge of progress. Short financing cycles force NGOs to spend inordinate amounts of time preparing proposals and lobbying for funding.

Both donors and NGOs need patience and perseverance. For example, at first, Sri Lanka had terrible problems replicating electronic-load-controlled mini-hydroelectric projects (Smillie 1991). Seeing it through was time consuming and expensive, even though this technology is often mentioned as a showcase example of technology blending. China's program for improved cookstoves also took years of experimentation and learning from mistakes.

An additional trade-off concerns the optimal size of NGOs. Up to a point, scaling-up can reduce transaction costs and get an organization beyond a critical minimum size needed to be effective. However, realizing economies of scale and scope through increased size may threaten the flexibility, alacrity of decision-making, and intimate contact needed to foster community participation. Yet, from a political-economy standpoint, it is difficult, if not impossible, for a small NGO to affect the centre of gravity of regional or national policy. Several strategies are available, including the cloning of promising NGOs; spin-offs, whereby autonomous NGOs are created from others to take on new tasks; and clusters of specialized NGOs. Regional or national NGO associations and fora can help give NGOs, collectively, a more audible voice in policy formulation, with an eye to servicing basic needs.

Frequently, serious tensions emerge between NGOs and state agencies. As Smillie (1991, p. 62) stated,

> despite the obvious advantages and potential of NGOs, many governments remain openly hostile to them — at both political and technical levels. They focus exclusively on the weaknesses and behave as though they are directly or indirectly threatened by NGO growth and achievement, sometimes treating NGO activities as attempts to subvert government policies or as an unwelcome involvement in politics.

The international community might consider fora for donors and NGOs to discuss a reasonable time horizon for showing results and fora to explore mechanisms for easing these tensions between state agencies and NGOs. People interested specifically in technology for basic needs could use conferences and networking to encourage NGOs without a technology orientation to add technical-learning programs to their repertoire.

## The informal sector

Apart from Maldonado and Sethuraman's (1992) collection of case studies, only a few ad hoc investigations take a serious look at innovations in the informal sector. Additional systematic research is needed, especially in sectors outside the metal–engineering occupations about which our knowledge is virtually nil. Also, the development community needs to keep a close eye on projects such as the International Labour Office project funded by the Swiss Technical Co-operation Fund and UNDP in Rwanda, Mali, and Togo (Maldonado 1989). In Rwanda, the focus is on training and gaining access to capital inputs through collective savings and loans. Incomes of participants have gone up significantly. In Mali and Togo, emphasis is on forming organizations better equipped to negotiate with administrative agencies and on setting up workshops for hiring out equipment, using catalogues and technical information, obtaining raw materials, and designing prototypes for small machines and tools. More experiments along these lines are warranted.

In the matter of political economy, avenues need to be found for decreasing the hostility with which officialdom views the informal sector. Kenya, a country that reputedly takes a friendly attitude (Hyman 1989), and Mexico (Aspe 1993), with its national incubator program to facilitate a two-tier graduation of MSEs, are two countries from which lessons may be learned.

## Innovation systems, vested interests, and institutional change

To inaugurate sustainable, endogenous technological progress for reducing basic-needs deficits will take nothing short of a transformation of some elements and the creation of other elements throughout the entire innovation systems of low-income nations or regions. I earlier argued about the dangers of any specific level of technology being associated with a movement, but here I assert that the drive to improve the condition of the planet's very poor populations will require a movement, with all of the commitment, tenacity, fervour, and emotional energy that movements imply. An overhaul of innovation systems that to a great extent eliminates large-scale industrial projects and slavish reliance on imported technology and technicians will be opposed by very powerful and well-entrenched vested interests. Foreign interests, domestic capitalists, the managerial and technical staffs of parastatals, work-force elites in unionized occupations, and established rural interests can be expected to exert pressure to preserve the status quo.

If reform entails the elevation of the director of S&T to true ministerial level, with the recognition of the head of state, if a program is installed to train local talent to carry out feasibility studies, if very small or ineffective RDIs are curtailed or merged, if appropriate technology entails product variations that compete with standard imports, if rules of the game favouring large-scale, mass production are dissolved, and so on, then it would take little effort to identify the opposition to an overhaul of the innovation system in low-income nations or regions. The opposition to change will be strengthened if people in low-income segments of society see novel alterations in the scheme of things as a zero-sum game, as if saying "if they gain, then ipso facto we lose."

Once again, we in the basic-needs movement — and I include myself in that camp — find ourselves in the arena of political economy. To prevail over a number of vested interests and conservative elements (including the poor themselves) fearful of change in the nature, direction, and pace of technological progress, we must seek political allies sympathetic to our cause. Today there is a confluence of synergistic and supportive interests that has been unmatched in recent times. Improving women's quality of life in the South is one. The deepening concern for environmental conditions is another. Support for smaller enterprises is in vogue with established and leading development institutions, as are faith in and reliance on NGOs as a medium for delivering and nurturing technology-laden projects. All of these supportive interests are, to a great extent, compatible with the objectives of technology for basic needs.

In closing, I suggest that although the task is challenging, even daunting, nothing short of a long-term program for fostering local technological capacity-building in low-income countries or regions can lead to sustained progress in goals espoused by those of us devoted to the cause of satisfying basic needs. We need all the complementary help that we can muster.

Chapter 6[1]

# Sustainable Human Development in a Fractured Global Order

*Francisco R. Sagasti*

A new and, as yet, fluid world order is in the making as we approach the 21st century. The multiplicity of changes and trends observable at present indicates that an accelerated, segmented, and uneven process of globalization is under way. The worldwide expansion of production and services, the diminishing importance of national frontiers, and the intensive exchange of information and knowledge coexist with the concentration of "global" activities in certain countries, regions, cities, and even neighborhoods and with the marginalization of many local production and service activities and the people engaged in them.

As we make the transition to the 21st century, we are witnessing the emergence of a fractured global order, an order that is global but not integrated, an order that puts most of the world's people in contact with one another but simultaneously maintains deep fissures between diverse groups of countries and between diverse peoples within countries, an order that segregates a large portion of the world's population and prevents it from sharing the benefits of scientific advances and technological progress. A brief review of the main changes taking place in the mid-1990s will help explain the extent and depth of the fractures in this emerging global order, the complexity of

[1]This chapter builds on work carried out by the author with the support of the Carnegie Corporation of New York.

the challenge of sustainable human development in the transition to a new century, and the role that science and technology (S&T) can play in meeting this challenge.

## Politics and security

The end of the Cold War undermined the ideological, military, and political foundations of the international order that prevailed during the last half century. The world is in transition to a postbipolar political order, the nature of which is still being defined but will require a profound reexamination of the ways we provide local, national, regional, and international security as preconditions for development (Stremlau 1989; McNamara 1992; UNDP 1994). Some of the elements of this new order are the virtual elimination of the threat of an all-out nuclear war, an increase in the number and intensity of regional conflicts, the likelihood of a more cooperative approach to conflict resolution among key political and economic players, and a greater role for international institutions in fostering and maintaining international security.

The effects of these elements may be very wide ranging. The demise of East–West rivalry has complex implications for national security and governance in developing countries. Conflict and insurgency based on Cold War ideology, once generously financed by the superpowers, have all but vanished, along with the possibility of playing one camp against the other. Soviet and American disengagement, however, could encourage other countries and regional powers to build and exercise military power with the enthusiastic support of arms merchants.

Ethnic and religious tensions within countries have aggravated these trends because the factions can attract support from neighbouring states. New regional conflicts over natural resources, such as water, oil, and tropical forests, and over environmental spillovers could also aggravate them. Such tensions and conflicts may be kept in check through the concerted actions of the major military powers, regional and international organizations, or both. However, so far, despite diminished rivalry among the global superpowers, there is no evidence of a decline in regional disputes or in organized violence by ethnic groups, religious fundamentalists, secessionist movements, terrorists, or drug traffickers.

At the same time, states are becoming less important as political units, that is, less able to control whatever economic, social, environmental, or technological events occur in the world. The preeminence and sovereignty of states are being eroded in many aspects

of foreign and economic policy, as highlighted by the renewed importance of the United Nations in conflict prevention and resolution, the
proliferation of regional trade and economic agreements, the growing
economic power of international corporations, and the conditions
established by international financial institutions for access to
resources under their control. The movement toward supranational
action is likely to proceed by fits and starts, with temporary reversals
and renewed bouts of nationalism, but will probably gain momentum
as the world moves into the new century.

Political pluralism, popular participation, and democratic
movements are becoming a fact of life everywhere. It is now almost
unthinkable to accept any government's imposition of a repressive
regime on its citizens, at least not without outrage, loud protest, and
international sanctions. By the mid-1990s, Eastern European countries
had their first open elections in half a century; almost all the countries
of Latin America had democratic regimes; a military coup failed in Russia; the central Asian states of the former Soviet Union were struggling
to become modern nations; more pressure was being applied for political liberalization all over Asia, including China; white rule disappeared
in South Africa; and attempts were made to abolish one-party rule in
many African countries. However, the civil wars in the former
Yugoslavia and Somalia and the self-inflicted coups of elected leaders
in countries as diverse as Russia and Peru have shown that advances
toward democracy, respect for human rights, and peaceful coexistence
are by no means guaranteed (Dahl 1989; Diamond and Plattner 1993;
Revel 1993).

The new international political context radically alters the balance in favour of democratic forms of governance (Slater and Bennis
1990). Without East–West conflict as a justification, it has become much
more difficult for Western industrialized countries to accept friendly
authoritarian regimes in the developing world. After the collapse of
one-party rule and the spread of democratic practices, Eastern European countries and the former Soviet Union are in no mood to support
authoritarian regimes in developing countries, even if they could afford
to do this.

## Governance

In parallel with these changes in the political and security arenas, governance issues became important in developed and developing countries for a variety of reasons, such as the erosion of the power of nation
states, the spread of democratic practices, and the threats posed by
internal disruptions, such as terrorism, drug trafficking, corruption,

and crime. The salience of governance issues has also been reinforced by advances in telecommunications, mass media, and information processing. These advances were instrumental in hastening the demise of communism in Eastern Europe and the former Soviet Union, are changing the nature and functioning of democracies, and are creating a more open and transparent setting for politics in developing countries (Rosell 1993).

In the industrialized nations, a variety of political events have led to what is perceived as a widespread crisis of governance. Corruption and scandals have undermined people's confidence in the political system in Japan, Italy, France, Spain, and Germany. Right-wing, xenophobic political groups have emerged in Germany and France. A constitutional crisis and its conflicts have surfaced in Canada as well as Japan. Citizens have expressed their dissatisfaction with the functioning of political systems, as is evident from the setbacks experienced by traditional and ruling political parties in the United States and several countries of Europe. The prolonged economic decline of the United Kingdom, Australia, Canada, Spain, Sweden, and other countries led to disillusionment with the political establishment. The spread of organized crime, drug trafficking, and terrorism throughout Europe, North America, Japan, the former Soviet Union, and Eastern Europe has generated a new sense of insecurity and instability that is breaking the social compact between the state and civil society and between governments and the people (Michel et al. 1975).

Governance problems have intensified in developing countries because of the sharp contrast between the growth in social demands and the capacity of the institutional frameworks — of the state, private sector, and civil society — to satisfy them. Governance issues have also been made more prominent by the need to marshall political support for economic reforms, by the precariousness of new democracies, and by the need to have legitimate and effective mechanisms for citizen participation and political intermediation.

The emergence of governance as a critical development issue coincided with attempts to redefine the roles of the public and private sectors, markets, and state intervention in fostering economic growth and social justice. Government failures in economic-policy management, production, and the provision of services, along with a renewed confidence in the positive role that market forces can play, prompted the international development community to pay greater attention to the ways in which state institutions exercise power and authority to pursue development objectives.

Governance and good government have also emerged as an area of concern for international development organizations. Throughout most of the period after World War II, development assistance focused primarily on investment in infrastructure, agriculture, industry, and the social sectors. However, by the early 1980s it had become clear that many of the projects supported with external technical and financial resources failed to yield the expected rates of return. One reason for this was that investments were made in highly distorted policy environments, which prevented the benefits from materializing. By the end of the 1980s, most developing countries had accepted the need for policy reforms and sought a better balance between market forces and state intervention. These developments underscored the importance of government's capacity to formulate and manage policy reforms and the ability of the private sector to assess the impact of the policy environment on enterprise performance (World Bank 1992a; Tomassini 1993). Policy reforms had important social consequences, many of which were not anticipated in the early 1980s. The interventions needed to ameliorate the impact of macroeconomic stabilization, trade liberalization, deregulation, and privatization were lacking, so social conditions worsened in many developing countries, prompting a renewed concern with the political sustainability of economic reforms.

## International economy

Major transformations are taking place in the patterns of world economic interdependence, including the rapid growth and globalization of financial markets, fundamental changes in trade patterns, and deepening inequalities between developed and developing countries. The effects of these changes on practically all aspects of the international economy may be much more wide ranging in the 1990s than at any other time in the last four decades. Growing interdependence and globalization, primarily a consequence of advances in communications and information technologies (ITs), have created an international economic environment that transmits disturbances, magnifies disruptions, and creates uncertainty. This is exacerbated by the absence of effective international rules and institutions to regulate financial and trade flows and by uncoordinated economic policies among the world's leading economies (Solomon 1990, 1991).

International financial markets now constitute a tight web of transactions involving global securities trading, arbitrage in multiple markets and currencies, portfolio investments through a bewildering array of international funds, and massive transborder capital movements (witness the recent debate over ways to regulate the international market for financial derivatives). Financial transactions have acquired a life of their own and are becoming detached from the production and distribution of goods and services (Drucker 1986; Fardoust and Dareshawar 1990). The globalization of financial markets has taken the form of an explosive growth of transactions among the financial centres of a few cities (New York, London, Tokyo, Frankfurt, Paris, Chicago, Zurich, and Hong Kong) located primarily in the industrialized countries. Although the recent growth of the emerging capital markets of Asia and Latin America is beginning to register in international financial transactions (primarily because of the high profits they yield to speculative investors), these markets are a long way from challenging or even joining the established centres of global finance.

Changes have also occurred in the direction and content of international trade, as exemplified by the emergence of the North Pacific as the world's largest trading area; the movement toward worldwide trade liberation, as exemplified by the General Agreement on Tariffs and Trade and the creation of the World Trade Organization; the rise of regional trading blocks, such as the European Union and that of the North American Free Trade Agreement; and the shift in the content of international trade away from primary commodities (exported primarily by developing countries) and toward high-technology services and products (exported by industrialized nations). New commercial linkages among transnational corporations have now emerged in the areas of manufacturing, finance, trade, and services. These linkages are characterized by complex and continuously shifting cooperative and competitive arrangements. Strategic alliances among corporations in precompetitive research and development (R&D), coupled with fierce competition in final-product markets, are a prime example of these new trends. A significant shift is occurring in the organization of production and service activities in the globalized segments of the world economy: the economic unit is no longer the enterprise (either local, international, or transnational) but a specific network created for a particular purpose at a particular time, which operates largely independently of the enterprises that established it. (I am grateful to M. Castells for insights into the new forms of industrial organization emerging in the globalized economy.)

The pace of the globalization of the economy is now set by a core of strategic economic activities operating in real time and simultaneously throughout the globe in capital markets, business services, travel and tourism, technology, and a few production lines, such as automobiles, computers, and electronic goods. At the same time, many people in both developing and industrialized nations are being marginalized and run the risk of becoming irrelevant to the functioning of an increasingly globalized economy in which, for the first time in history, the rich do not need the poor.

# Social conditions

There have been dramatic improvements in life expectancy and standards of living in many parts of the world in the last several decades. For example, the average per capita consumption has increased by 70% in real terms; average life expectancy has increased from 51 years to 63 years; and primary-school enrollment has reached 89%. Despite these changes, there are still enormous and persistent economic differences between regions and countries, particularly between the industrialized and the developing countries.

According to the World Bank (1994b), in 1992 the average per capita gross national product for the 43 low-income economies was $390, but the average for the 23 high-income economies was $22 160, about 57 times higher. The total population of the low-income countries was approximately 3.2 billion, nearly four times as high as the 828 million in the member countries of the Organization for Economic Co-operation and Development, although both groups of countries cover roughly the same area. The absolute number of poor people in the world has continued to increase, and disparities between the rich and the poor have widened even more. In the 1980s, the rate of improvement in economic and social indicators began to slow down (World Bank 1993a). Among developing countries, a few outstanding successes, notably in Southeast Asia, coexist with many stagnant or even regressing situations, particularly in sub-Saharan Africa but also in Asia, Latin America, and the Middle East.

Between 1960 and 1991 the share of world income for the richest 20% of the global population rose from 70% to nearly 85%, whereas the share of the poorest 20% declined from 2.3% to 1.4%. In 1991, the ratio of the income share of the richest 20% to that of the poorest 20% was about 61 : 1 (UNDP 1994). The fracture between poverty and affluence has proven to be one of the most enduring and alarming features of the emerging global order.

The explosive growth in social demands in the developing regions, triggered largely by population increases in the last 30 years, and the significant slowdown in population growth in the industrialized nations have led to a highly skewed worldwide distribution of social needs and capacities to satisfy them. The dynamics of population growth strongly affect the demand for food, education, employment, housing, and other social benefits. Demands for food and nutrition have multiplied many times over, particularly in the poorest countries. Although world aggregate food production is sufficient to provide each and every human being with adequate nourishment, this is thwarted by existing political, social, and institutional arrangements at both the national and international levels. As a result, more than 800 million people in the world go to bed hungry every night. Armed conflicts, droughts, and natural disasters have conspired to make access to food even more difficult in many developing countries.

Demands for basic health care and elementary education have expanded at a rapid pace in the last four decades, and developing countries have tried to improve their provision of these services. Nevertheless, disparities between developed and developing countries are huge: for example, there is one doctor for every 400 people in the industrialized countries; one doctor for every 7 000 people in the developing countries; but one doctor for every 36 000 people in sub-Saharan Africa.

Unemployment has emerged as perhaps the most troublesome and persistent problem in developing countries. The modern sectors of these countries' economies cannot absorb new entrants to the labour force, and this has led to a variety of informal arrangements for workers. Developing countries face the difficult challenge of raising the productivity of labour to improve standards of living and competitiveness while absorbing the growing number of entrants to the labour force.

The rate of population growth in industrialized countries is expected to drop from an average of 0.5% per year in the 1980s to an average of only 0.3% per year in the 1990s. This implies a rapid increase in the number of elderly people (particularly in Japan, France, and Germany, where people aged 65 or more will constitute one fifth of the population by 2020), a significant increase in the ratio of dependents (children and old people) to workers, and a further shift in the balance of world population. Aging in industrialized nations will have a major impact on the demand for social services, as well as important consequences for the patterns of consumption, employment, and savings. Because investments in scientific research and technological innovation are highly concentrated in industrialized countries, the population trends of these countries have important consequences for the direction of technical progress, which is likely to move further in the direction of labour-saving innovations.

In developing countries, rapid population growth is expected to continue through the 1990s, although at a moderately slower pace, dropping from an average rate of 2.0% per year in the 1980s to 1.8% per year during the 1990s. As a consequence, youth will remain by far the largest segment of the population in most of these countries, whose economies must expand at rates significantly above those of population growth to satisfy the growing demand for work (Fardoust and Dareshawar 1990).

Population imbalances could pose the problem of uncontrolled mass migration from developing countries to industrialized countries, threatening social cohesion and international solidarity. In some Western European countries, a backlash against foreigners is already occurring, although the feared massive inflows of workers from the East has as yet failed to materialize. In Asia, migration pressures are likely to build up as a result of the growing demographic imbalance between Japan and the poorer, overpopulated countries of the region. Despite the increased participation of women in the labour market, the Japanese will experience a decline in the labour force after 2000, and labour shortages will be compounded by moves to reduce the number of working hours (OECD 1991). In the next decade, the role of human capital and technological capabilities will become even more important as a major determinant of long-term growth in the developing countries. The level and quality of investments in human resources will have to increase significantly in the 1990s to deal with the rapid rise in the number of young people and to enable the developing countries' labour forces to use new technologies that increase productivity.

A prominent and disturbing feature of the global situation is the large disparity between men and women as measured by social and economic indicators. Despite two decades of efforts devoted to women in development, women and children remain the poorest of the poor, and the gender gap in development is widening. In industrialized countries, sexual discrimination appears in employment and wages: women often have one-third fewer employment opportunities and earn about half as much as men. In developing countries, the greatest disparities, outside the job market, are in health care and nutritional support. Women make up two thirds of the world's illiterate population, and the 1989 *World Survey on the Role of Women* stated that women do 66% of the world's work, own 10% of the land, and have only 1% of the world's income (see United Nations 1993; Gender Working Group–UNCSTD 1995; UNDP 1994). This is another fracture in the global order that demands urgent attention.

## Environmental sustainability

In the last two decades, environmental concerns have risen to the top of the international public-policy agenda. We are now more aware of the limits that the regenerative capacity of natural ecosystems imposes on human activities, of the dangers of uncontrolled exploitation of natural resources (fisheries, forests, land, and rivers), and of the overload of the Earth's capacity to absorb waste (air and water pollution, acid rain, and toxic and nuclear wastes). The 1980s and early 1990s witnessed the emergence of truly global environmental problems, such as global warming and the depletion of the ozone layer, which underscored the danger that ecological instabilities could cause irreversible environmental damage.

The problems of environmental sustainability and resource use are closely related to population growth and poverty in the developing countries and to the often wasteful consumption habits of rich nations. Major changes in lifestyle will be essential for both groups of countries in the transition to the 21st century. According to the World Bank (1992b, pp. 2–3),

> the most immediate environmental problems facing developing countries — unsafe water, inadequate sanitation, soil depletion, indoor smoke from cooking fires, and outdoor smoke from coal burning — are different from and more immediately life-threatening than those associated with the affluence of rich countries, such as carbon dioxide emissions, depletion of stratospheric ozone, photochemical smog, acid rain and hazardous wastes.

The Earth Summit in Rio de Janeiro endorsed Agenda 21, a wide-ranging world program of action to promote sustainable development, but the negotiations exposed the divergence of perspectives between industrialized and developing nations on appropriate approaches (UNCED 1992; Carrol-Foster 1993a,b). Questions about lifestyles, national sovereignty, barriers to trade, financial assistance, and access to less-polluting technologies are now at the centre of the debate about sustainable development.

Because of the greater awareness of environmental problems, international governance issues have also acquired greater importance. Proposals have been tabled to redefine national security in environmental terms, and moves to strengthen international institutions have led to the creation of the Commission on Sustainable Development at the United Nations. According to Mathews (1989),

> Global developments now suggest the need for another ... broadening definition of national security to include resource, environmental and demographic issues .... Environmental strains that transcend national boundaries are already beginning to break down the sacred boundaries of national sovereignty ... forcing governments to grapple in international forums with issues that were contentious enough in the domestic arena.

See also Myers (1989), Harris (1991), CDCGC (1992), French (1992), Gardner (1992), and Kimball (1992).

A further consequence of the greater importance of environmental concerns is that access to development assistance in the 1990s will be increasingly linked to environmental objectives. Another result is that some industrialized countries, notably Japan and Germany, are positioning themselves to compete in one of the most dynamic markets of the future: environmentally sound technologies. The ability to deliver green technologies could soon become a source of competitive advantage in the global search for new markets (Heaton et al. 1992; Rath and Copley 1993; Heaton et al. 1994).

## Cultural factors

Three powerful cultural forces are shaping the international scene in the transition to the 21st century: first, the growing importance of religious values and the rise of fundamentalism as a driving force behind economic and political actions in many parts of the world; second, the tensions between the drive to cultural homogenization, brought about by the pervasive influence of mass media, and the desire to preserve cultural identity; and, third, the emergence of spiritual and ethical issues at the forefront of debate about inter- and intragenerational equity, particularly in the areas of human rights, the environment, income distribution, and poverty reduction. The rising importance of cultural factors was recently underscored by Huntington (1993), who argued that conflicts between civilizations will replace other forms of conflict in the transition to the 21st century, and also by Ajami et al. (1993), who strongly criticized Huntington's views.

The revival of religious and spiritual concerns has been a characteristic of the last two decades, which have witnessed a renaissance of Islamic values in northern Africa, the Middle East, and central Asia, a revival of the Orthodox Church in eastern Europe and the former Soviet Union, the spread of evangelical churches in Latin America and other developing regions, a surge of popularity of the Roman Catholic pope, the growing influence of Christian fundamentalism in American political life, and a renewed interest in mysticism and Oriental religions, often associated with New Age movements. This points to the fact that the spiritual dimensions of human development have been neglected since World War II because of the overriding concern with improving material well-being and standards of living. For a review of religious movements in contemporary society, see Beckford (1986).

Globalization and the pervasive influence of the mass media as a result of advances in communications during the last two decades allow us to see two contradictory cultural forces at play: the drive toward the standardization of aspirations and cultural values; and the desire to reassert individuality and preserve cultural identity. These forces create cultural tensions and emotional stress, particularly in developing countries, where the images of affluence brought by television programs from industrialized nations contrast sharply with the harsh reality of mass poverty and depict worlds of plenty that are simply unattainable for the vast majority of the population.

Moral and ethical questions, once the province of academics and religious activists, are finding their way into public debates on the right of future generations to sustainable development and on a variety of other issues, such as racism, abortion, corruption, crime, and drug trafficking. The extent to which moral and spiritual issues are moving to centre stage in international politics was underscored by Brzezninski (1993):

> The West should understand that a billion Muslims will not be impressed by a West that is perceived as preaching to them the values of consumerism, the merits of amorality, and the blessings of atheism. To many Muslims, the West (and especially America's) message is repulsive .... The American society cannot be the model for the world — both morally and as a matter of practical economics — if a pre-dominantly cornucopian ethic defines its essence, while a sizable but impoverished minority is simultaneously excluded from meaningful social participation .... The global crisis of the spirit has to be overcome if humanity is to assert command over its destiny.

A renewed concern with human rights throughout the world has led to a debate about the principle of nonintervention in the internal affairs of states in which governments do not respect basic human rights (ODC 1992; Bloomfield 1993). Finally, in contrast to the trend that prevailed during the 1980s, equity is finding its way onto the political agendas of many industrialized and developing countries. At the same time, moral and ethical aspects of economic behaviour have begun to receive greater attention. For a thoughtful and well-argued report on the relations between global trends and religious and spiritual concerns, see Barney (1993).

## Humanity in transition

The fractured global order is emerging amidst a fundamental reappraisal of the human condition. New findings, discoveries, and speculations are challenging centuries-old ideas about human nature and the place of humanity in the order of things, as well as prevailing conceptions of human potential (Bezanson and Sagasti, unpublished).[2] These

---

[2] Bezanson, K.; Sagasti, F. The elusive search: development and progress in the transition to a new century. Unpublished manuscript.

new findings suggest that humanity is in the midst of a bewildering and paradoxical transition to something that cannot as yet be clearly visualized; some intellectuals have referred to this as the post-modern condition (Lyotard 1984).

For example, people are increasingly aware of the close relationship between the activities of human beings and the physical and biological world and accept the fact that we can no longer act with impunity or blindly trust the regenerative capacities of ecosystems. This implies a radical shift from the ideas prevailing in the 18th and 19th centuries and much of the 20th century, when human beings were thought to be lords and masters of creation with the right to do to the planet as they saw fit. Human beings are now considered stewards of a precious heritage that must be passed on to future generations.

Advances in IT are creating a new level of reality — virtual reality, or cyberspace — that lies between the tangible and real world, which has always been with humanity, and the world of abstract concepts, which was discovered by the Greeks about 2500 years ago with the invention of theory. Communication technologies are also generating new modes of human interaction and, in the process, altering the meaning of experience, privacy, selfhood, cultural identity, and governance. The explosive growth of the Internet provides the most startling example of these new developments (Benedikt 1991; Batty and Barr 1994).

In addition, humanity is becoming aware of its newfound capacity for consciously altering the direction of human evolution, along with the possibility of overcoming the limitations of an individual's biological and genetic hardware (Orlich and Erlich 1989). Although it may be possible to manage our biological evolution, we still need to develop the ethical and moral foundations for a conception of the governance of evolution. Such a conception is needed to meet humanity's newly acquired responsibility for its biological, as well as its cultural, future (Anderson 1987; Jonas 1990).

Advances in expert systems, artificial intelligence, and robotics are also forcing us to reconsider the attributes once believed unique to human beings. As we become more aware of the impacts of artifacts and machines on living systems, the idea of a co-evolution of humanity, nature, and machines is beginning to emerge. The concepts of processes such as natural selection, once thought to apply only in the realm of living organisms, are now also applied to computer programs and technological systems (Mazlish 1993).

Finally, speculations about the origins and the ultimate destiny of the universe and new discoveries about the origin of life and human beings are putting the Earth and humanity in a cosmic context whose history spans billions of years. Against this backdrop, the ephemeral character of the few thousands of years of human civilization contrasts sharply with the human capacity to transcend its limitations and comprehend the vastness of the world humanity inhabits.

## Knowledge in the emerging fractured global order

Scientific advances and technological innovations are at the root of the complex processes of transformation that have led to the emerging fractured global order. Changes in the political, economic, social, environmental, and cultural fields have also stimulated and supported the growth of S&T and have shaped its evolution.

Since World War II the products of scientific research and technological innovation have become more and more deeply enmeshed in all aspects of human activity, and there have been profound modifications in the way knowledge is generated and used. A problem — which could also be seen as an opportunity — is that too little of the great power of modern S&T has been directed at development. The attempted mobilization of scientists in developed countries to deal with problems found mainly in developing countries has not been very successful, and the S&T capabilities of developing countries are far too limited to deal adequately with the enormous problems of development in the fractured global order.

Only about 4% of the world expenditure on R&D and about 14% of the world's supply of scientists and engineers are in developing countries, where more than 80% of the world's people live (CCSTG 1992; UNESCO 1993; Annerstedt 1994). Discrepancies like these, which have persisted for a long time, are a distinguishing feature of the emerging fractured global order. The role that knowledge now plays in the process of development is so critical that *development* could be redefined in terms of the capacity to generate, acquire, disseminate, and use knowledge, both modern and traditional. The presence or absence of this capacity marks a crucial division between the developed and developing nations and between regions of the world where people have the potential to decide and act autonomously and those where people are unable to realize their potential (Sagasti 1990a, b).

Two aspects of S&T merit particular attention during the transition to the 21st century: the changes in the way scientists are conducting research; and the increasingly systemic character of technological innovation (Salomon et al. 1994).

# Scientific research

In the five decades since World War II, knowledge has grown at an astonishing pace: the stock of knowledge doubled during the first half of the 20th century, and now it doubles every 4 or 5 years (Linowes 1990). The growth of scientific research, supported by advances in information and computer sciences, has primarily been responsible for this explosion of knowledge. An increased cross-fertilization has taken place between scientific research, technological innovation, and the commercial exploitation of research results.

The multiple and complex interactions between research, innovation, and commercialization have shown the inadequacy of the linear model of progress in S&T, in which scientific findings lead directly to new technologies to be incorporated in goods and services. It is now clear that the accumulation of technological innovations provides a base of observations for science to delve into; technological progress plays an important role in defining the agenda for scientific research; high-tech industries are continually identifying new problems to be addressed by science; and techniques of observation, testing, measurement, and instrumentation are major determinants of scientific progress. All of this has dramatically reduced the time between scientific discovery and commercial exploitation (Rosemberg 1982; Mowery and Rosemberg 1989).

The institutional settings for basic research, for applied research, and for the development of new products and processes are changing, particularly as a result of shifts in the sources of funding and a more prominent role for the private sector. Links between universities and industries are being strengthened; industrial research and technological alliances have become imperative in certain fields; and venture-capital firms and some specialized government agencies are playing a greater role in funding the commercialization of new technology. These changes have been made largely in response to major increases in the cost of basic and applied research, increases that have also led to greater concentration in fields in which large facilities are needed and getting results may take a long time.

Certain fields of research, such as chemical synthesis, have become increasingly dependent on advanced and expensive instruments that combine advances in electronics, optics, analytical techniques, and data processing (NAS 1982). The high cost of advanced instruments and financial constraints have been creating difficulties for university laboratories in industrialized nations and have effectively put many fields of research out of the reach of the vast majority of scientific institutions in developing countries. However, there is still ample scope for developing countries to become actively involved in many aspects of scientific research, even in areas that seem to be closed to them (Salam 1991).

The accelerated pace of scientific progress requires a continuous effort to keep up with current advances, as the stock of knowledge and the capabilities acquired through training and research become obsolete rather quickly. This has important implications for human-resources development and for training researchers in advanced scientific fields, particularly in the developing countries, where high-level professionals are in short supply.

The closer links between scientific capabilities, developments in technology, and economic growth, as well as the increasing costs of scientific research, the accelerating obsolescence of research capabilities, the emergence of new transdisciplinary fields, and the growing complexity of the institutional setting for research, all make it more difficult for most developing countries to push quickly toward the frontiers of knowledge and take advantage of advances in S&T. At the same time, the slowdown in the rates of economic growth, severe resource constraints, and growing social demands undermine any long-term efforts to build S&T capabilities in developing countries.

## Technological innovation

The innovation process, particularly in science-intensive industries, has become more complex: it is more expensive; it requires more sophisticated management techniques; it has intensified international collaboration and competition; and it has expanded the government's role in the support of innovation. These changes are closely associated with the emergence of a new technoeconomic paradigm that makes microelectronics (primarily the microprocessor) rather than energy (mainly oil) the key factor in the organization of production and service activities. (The key factor in production is an input or set of inputs that has a clearly perceived and rapidly falling relative cost, an apparently almost unlimited availability over long periods, and a clear potential for use or incorporation in a great variety of products and processes [Freeman and Perez 1988; Perez 1989].)

The innovation process is systemic in at least two ways: the technical advances required for any one innovation complement each other, and a large network of institutions and support services is needed for innovation to take place. New technologies are more combinative than old technologies, which means that individual advances in IT, automation, new materials, chemical synthesis, and biotechnology require complementary inputs from other technologies. This has become clearly noticeable in automation, which fuses microelectronics, computers, telecommunications, optoelectronics, and artificial intelligence into an integrated technology system closely associated with the new technoeconomic paradigm (Kaplinsky 1984).

The technological convergence implied by the systemic character of innovation demands that firms quickly develop expertise in a broader array of technologies and scientific disciplines. This is evident in the food-processing and pharmaceutical industries, which have had to develop competence in biotechnology, molecular biology, and advanced electronic instrumentation (Mowery and Rosemberg 1989). The increasingly systemic character of innovation is also reflected in the increasing number of players needed to bring major innovations to the market. In addition to the firms directly involved, this process may require subcontractors; suppliers of inputs and equipment; laboratories and other organizations that provide technological services; management consultants; educational and research institutions; marketing research units; distributors and trading companies; financial institutions and venture-capital firms; and government agencies and departments.

The costs of incorporating research results into goods and services and of bringing new products to the market have been steadily increasing in the past few decades. The higher costs of innovation and the greater risks faced by firms in a more competitive environment have in effect increased barriers to many fields of industry (Ernst and O'Connor 1989). Paradoxically, the increased competition has generated a host of cooperative arrangements between industrial firms, primarily in precompetitive research and marketing, giving rise to new specific-enterprise networks in which the interests of a number of enterprises converge at a specific time for a specific purpose. However, only firms with substantial financial or technological assets (including small firms focusing on specific technological niches) can be expected to become players in the complex competition–collaboration game of international technological alliances.

New technologies make it cost effective for industries to produce more diverse products and to accelerate innovation by adopting shorter product cycles. Flexible automation is lowering the minimum efficient plant size in several industries. Advances in communications and IT permit a just-in-time approach to production management, reducing inventory costs but requiring close interactions with suppliers and markets. Low labour costs are no longer the dominant criterion in locating production sites, and corporations are finding it increasingly difficult to establish production facilities far from their markets, suppliers, and R&D centres.

The systemic character of innovation and the changes brought about by the new technoeconomic paradigm have led to greater emphasis on management skills and capabilities. To realize the full potential of new technologies, it has become necessary to introduce innovations in organization and management, a task for which advances in IT have provided the tools (Hoffman 1989; Hanna 1991). In addition, innovation requires the support of a well-developed infrastructure, including a good network of roads, transportation facilities, telecommunication and data-transmission networks, a reliable supply of electricity, waste-disposal facilities, and clean water supplies. Advanced repair and maintenance services may be needed for a variety of laboratory and industrial equipment. Some of the infrastructure requirements are well beyond the capabilities of most developing countries.

These changes in the innovation process have mixed effects on the prospects for developing countries. On the one hand, advanced-technology components may be incorporated into traditional and conventional technologies in developing countries. This is known as technology blending, which can lead to more appropriate and productive technologies (Bhalla and James 1988; Bhalla 1993). On the other hand, the comparative advantage of these countries is shifting away from low labour costs and natural resources, forcing a major adaptation in industrialization and development strategies.

# S&T for sustainable human development in the fractured global order

## Two civilizations with a multiplicity of fractures

The fractures that characterize the emerging global order overlap partially and often shift direction, sometimes reinforcing each other and at other times working at cross purposes. The overall picture is of a multiplicity of paradoxical and contradictory processes creating enormous turbulence and uncertainty and giving rise to an extremely wide range of possibilities.

One salient feature of the contemporary scene, however, provides a clear point of reference for all the changes occurring in the fractured global order. The enormous impact that advances in S&T have on all aspects of human life, including our very conception of humanity, makes it abundantly clear that the world is witnessing the rise of the "knowledge society" (Drucker 1993). Among the bewildering multiplicity of fractures that are evident in the emerging global order, the knowledge fracture — the great divide between those who have and those who do not have the capacity to aquire and use knowledge —

could rapidly become an abyss. It may now be appropriate to speak of the emergence of "two civilizations" (Sagasti 1980).

The first of these two civilizations is characterized by the growth of science; by the rapid evolution of technologies; by the incorporation of these technologies into industry and society; and by the emergence of new ways to work and live, deeply influenced by the worldview of modern S&T. The second is characterized by an inability to generate scientific knowledge on a large scale; by passive acceptance of the scientific results generated by the first civilization; by a technological base with a substantive component of traditional technologies and a veneer of imported ones; by a production system whose modern segment depends on the expansion of production in Western industrialized nations and the absorption of imported technology and whose traditional segment depends on an often stagnant technological system; and by a coexistence of disjointed and even contradictory cultural forms.

These two civilizations interact strongly, although the interaction is one-sided. The second civilization is dependent on and deeply affected by the first but lacks the capacity to influence it to a matching degree. The first civilization, found in the developed or highly industrialized countries such as the United States, Japan, and the countries of Europe, has an endogenous S&T base, in which science, technology, and production interact strongly. The second civilization has an exogenous S&T base, in which science, technology, and production remain separate (Sagasti 1979, 1988). This holds true for the vast majority of developing countries, even though, during the last three decades, a handful have begun to reduce their distance from the nations of the first civilization and to develop an endogenous S&T base.

Modern S&T has always been ambiguous, but in the culture in which it developed from the 17th to the 19th centuries its promises were never really treated as threats to the survival of humanity. However, S&T does not always bring about improvements. Despite what was promised by the rationalism of the Enlightenment and, even more, by the positivism of the 19th century, S&T progress does not necessarily coincide with social or moral progress. The complex and rapidly shifting context of the emerging fractured global order is making this point in a painfully obvious way.

The nations of the second civilization face difficult choices about the importance of tradition, with its hierarchies, codes, and rites, and that of rationality — the hallmark of modern science — with its capacity to create order and disorder, to transform, and to destroy. From one perspective, scientific and technical thinking, taken to extremes, threatens to reduce human beings to purely instrumental rationality. From another perspective, attacks on rationality leveled by particular faiths or traditions threaten to retard or prevent progress and lead to stagnation. The nations of the second civilization, with their legitimate diversity of cultures, perspectives, and viewpoints, face the challenge of harmoniously integrating the pursuit of modern S&T and its material intellectual manifestations with the social and cultural heritage that provides these nations with a sense of identity.

## Beyond the two civilizations: toward sustainable human development

The most important challenges humanity faces in the transition to the 21st century are, first, to prevent the multiplicity of fractures of the emerging global order from creating self-contained, partially isolated pockets of mutually distrustful peoples, ignorant and suspicious of each other's viewpoints, aspirations, potentials, and capabilities; and, second, to prevent these fractures from creating inward-looking groups of people relating only through tenuous links forged by mass media or economic transactions or interacting in ways fraught with conflicts, threatening human and environmental security. To meet these challenges will imply a commitment to building bridges across the multiple fractures of the emerging global order, to give all human beings as individuals and as groups the opportunity to realize their full potential. The knowledge fracture must be prevented from creating a world with two distinct civilizations, and there must be a determination to embrace and put into practice a new conception of sustainable human development.

Sustainable human development could provide all individuals, both now and in the future, with equal opportunities to expand their capabilities to the fullest possible extent and to put those capabilities to the best use in political, economic, social, environmental, and cultural fields. Development patterns that perpetuate today's inequities and deepen the fractures of the emerging global order, particularly the knowledge fracture, are neither sustainable nor worth sustaining. The essence of sustainable human development is that all human beings of both present and future generations should have equal access to development opportunities (Dahrendorf 1983; Sen 1984, 1992; UNDP 1994). Moreover, sustainable human development must have replicable and desirable models of material production and consumption that guarantee that future generations will have opportunities similar to the ones enjoyed by previous generations. Because the accumulation of human capital can replace some forms of exhaustible resources, human development should be seen as a major contribution to sustainability. As J.S. Speth (1994), the administrator of the United Nations Development

Programme, stated in a speech to the Executive Board of the United Nations Secretariat,

> *Sustainable human development should join sustainable development and human development every day, in practice, on the ground, around the world. It is development that does not merely generate growth, but distributes its benefits equitably; it regenerates the environment rather than destroying it; it empowers people rather than marginalizing them; it enlarges their choices and opportunities and provides for peoples' participation in decisions affecting their lives. Sustainable human development is development pro-poor, pro-nature, pro-jobs, and pro-women. It stresses growth with employment, growth with environment, growth with empowerment, growth with equity.*

Sustainable human development is not just for the developing countries. Its lessons are lessons for the industrialized nations as well. It is a new paradigm, or a new synthesis of development needs. Moreover, along with this new concept of development it is necessary to evolve new approaches to development cooperation (CCSTG 1992; IDRC 1992b).

However, it is important to emphasize that sustainable human development cannot take place without interaction between cultural heritage and instrumental rationality, even though the two may not be entirely reconciled in all places and at all times. S&T can contribute a great deal to sustainable human development, but S&T does not offer a ready-made solution to the problem of values raised by the clash between tradition and modernity. Therefore, from the perspective of S&T the quest for sustainable human development has to be considered an uncertain one, in which the seekers rely heavily on the knowledge and innovations produced by modern S&T (Salomon 1994; Salomon et al. 1994).

## Knowledge for sustainable human development

In the transition to the 21st century, S&T will continue to be essential for achieving sustainable human development. We must be aware of the problems, threats, and limitations of the instrumental rationality that is characteristic of modern S&T, but through the creation and use of knowledge it is possible for scientific research and technological innovation to expand the range of goods and services available, lead to improvements in productivity, help build educational systems that open up new opportunities for human betterment, and provide the technical options and means for achieving the sustainable use of the

Earth's resources. In short, S&T provides the means for bridging the multiple fractures in the emerging global order.

Moreover, without an appropriate level of S&T capability, no country can make the major decisions that affect its policies and strategies for achieving sustainable human development; absorb, adapt, or improve on imported technology; expect to develop its production potential, even when it has competitive advantages; or be able to follow international advances, particularly those with potential impact on the country's strategies to achieve sustainable human development.

It is clear that developing countries at different levels of socioeconomic development, with different social and economic objectives and varying degrees of S&T capability, have to mobilize S&T for development in different ways. Policies, strategies, and priorities for action will differ according to the specific conditions prevailing in particular developing countries and the options those countries can identify or construct for themselves.

In the transition to the 21st century, however, the mobilization of S&T for sustainable human development is likely to take place in the context of severe resource constraints, which will tend to reinforce the multiple fractures in the new order. This context will test the political will of the leaders of developing countries to embark on the uncertain and long-term enterprise of building S&T capabilities, particularly when these countries are facing a multiplicity of urgent short-term needs. Many successful examples in fields such as health and agriculture suggest that much more could be profitably invested in the development of S&T capabilities.

In the last analysis, without S&T there can be no belief in and commitment to the future and no means of dealing with the multiple fractures in the emerging global order. Future generations in developing countries must rely on their access to accumulated S&T knowledge to understand and interact with the environment, not only to satisfy their most basic needs and establish their position in an increasingly interdependent world, but also to realize their potential contribution to sustainable human development and to reaffirm their sense of identity.

## Gender and environmental sustainability

The report of the Gender Working Group–UNCSTD (1995) starts with the explicit recognition that development is gender specific and that S&T for development must systematically and purposefully recognize this if it is to respond to the concerns, needs, and interests of both women and men appropriately and equitably. As a tool to serve society, S&T has a specific and far-reaching potential but cannot be assumed or expected to have a homogeneous impact on society. Which part of society benefits from this tool depends to some degree on whose needs and whose interests are being addressed. Because the roles, responsibilities, needs, and interests of men and women are often different, the tools to address one set of needs and interests often neglect or even harm the other competing sets of needs and interests.

Whether the impact of S&T on women or men is negative or positive, development initiatives in S&T should, from the outset, consider the needs and interests of people in a gender-desegregated manner. Only through a gender-specific approach, with a clear understanding of whose needs and whose interests are being served in each instance, can resources and research be equitably directed to serve all of society. Moreover, the fact that development is gender specific makes it difficult to assess the real role and potential of women in development and the ways S&T can advance their particular interests and respond to their specific needs.

The report of the Gender Working Group–UNCSTD (1995) also focused on the gender-specific impact of technical change and on the gender-specific distribution of science education and scientific careers and made recommendations that are valid for both developed and developing countries.

## Integrated approaches to land management

The United Nations Commission on Science and Technology for Development's panel on S&T for integrated land management (ILM) focused on one of the most important issues in environmental sustainability. The essential role of land and water resources in supporting all current and future human activities makes the management of these resources one of the primary tools in sustainable human development. The methodology known as ILM offers a single framework and provides an overall perspective from which to approach a multiplicity of problems in the sustainable use of land and water resources.

Because land has multiple functions in society, diverse social, economic, and environmental considerations influence current and future land uses. Systematically examining the potential uses of land makes it possible to improve social and economic development while protecting and enhancing the environment. In this context, ILM is an essential tool for achieving sustainable human development. Moreover, poor land management has negative consequences, such as degradation of the land, waste of resources, and even international conflict. A fundamental goal of ILM is to use S&T to prevent the degradation of the land's ability to support human activities, particularly the production of food.

Modern S&T can play an important role in ILM:

▼ ITs for monitoring and diagnosing land use;

▼ Evaluation technologies for interpreting and identifying options for land use;

▼ Application technologies for using the land for specific purposes; and

▼ Support technologies for providing the infrastructure that allows the efficient and sustainable use of land.

However, one limitation is that the various technologies that can contribute to ILM are unavailable in the developing countries, where they are most needed.

The panel on S&T for ILM identified five objectives in the effective implementation of ILM to achieve sustainable human development:

▼ To improve the availability of information on technologies for ILM;

▼ To improve developing countries' ability to educate professionals and technical staff;

▼ To increase public involvement in land-use and development issues;

▼ To increase developing countries' capabilities in problem evaluation and goal prioritization; and

▼ To target research to critical-applications technology.

# Chapter 7

# Science for Sustainable Human Development, Technologies for Vital Rights

*Oscar Serrate*

This is not an essay about technical instruments for poverty reduction or about scientific formulas for development. Does it present hardware or software mechanisms that can be used to feed, provide health care for, or teach people? Not really. Is it about the physical elements required to satisfy the basic needs of the Third World? No. This is an essay about people and the kinds of relationships that human beings forge with their neighbours and their environment to feed themselves, to live, and to learn. With this perspective, I have analyzed the issue of the means available to the poorest of human beings and required by them to build a healthy life in harmony with their fellows and with nature. By focusing on the problem this way, I have tried to avoid the trap of instrumentalism.

Means are important, and they are even more important for those who lack them because they then become vital. However, to understand how people can have the means they require, or which means they should have, we must first ask ourselves why people lack the means they need. That is a multidimensional problem, involving both the actors and the system. Accordingly, this paper starts with a humanistic perspective on the contemporary world, analyzes the historical connections between technology and primary needs and between science and the human condition, and refers to some of the development theories and practices of recent decades.

The present analysis shows the transformations in production systems that have taken place lately and the processes that have been experienced — advances in liberty, delays in justice — and connects these transformations and processes in the technological and scientific context. Reality is not so pleasant after a couple of centuries of modernity. This is particularly obvious in the poor areas. The myths that promised salvation are disappearing, but new paradigms are emerging at different latitudes. For instance, the focus on sustainable human development is giving fresh life to anthropocentrism in a context of systemic, universal integration, and that means restating the question about people's rights to education, health, and food.

The globalized and divided world is compelling countries to accept the need for a dual strategy to deal with the dual challenges of modern competitiveness and extreme poverty. Technologies to meet these challenges may not come in the form of new recipes but in the form of knowledge in action as a way to open avenues to participation. Hence, new possibilities for change are emerging that may not be very evident today but are certainly in a formative phase.

# The international context

## Globalization

As the world draws closer to the third millennium, the development prospects that heralded the 20th century are increasingly fading away. The gleams of hope that lit up the beginnings of industrialization are threatened by the new doubts and fears emerging in a daunting and contradictory world that has gone from the steam-engine to the computer and from class struggle to globalization in less than 100 years.

The engine of this process is unquestionably the growth of science and technology (S&T), or the development of productive forces, that has been steadily breaking new ground, at first year by year, then day by day, then hour by hour, and nowadays in nanoseconds. Humanity has accumulated an unprecedented store of knowledge and production, but huge problems of human livelihood have been left unresolved, which at first affected thousands, then millions, and today billions of people.

The integrating power of electronics, the growing strength of an increasingly service-oriented economy, and the astonishing diversification of worldwide markets are remarkable signs of a modernity that many are calling into question. We seem to be hearing the echoes of the crumbling of an old model even as, we hope, new ways of thinking are emerging. These new ways of thinking are still unknown, still unclear, but humanity, in its continuous quest, has always founds ways to build and to rebuild.

Many currents of contemporary thought share a common view of the transition that is taking place at a global level. Postmodernism, hypermodernism, or however this time of constant change ultimately comes to be known, does not yet have clear features. What is clear is that the changes are not yet finished and that they are not going to stop, because history is, after all, not going to end. Science, which wrought this present technological civilization, is now faced with the challenge of either a rebirth or a fading of its power to transform.

Science and Technology for Development, the name given to this commission by the United Nations, clearly expresses a desire for reform and a confidence in human endeavour and in the positivist contribution of knowledge to the happiness of world's inhabitants. However, famine and poverty are showing us that we have not yet managed to connect thoroughly with the amazing experience and value of human life or with all the wise teachings of nature. Amid the rubble left by the wayside as progress has forged ahead, we see glaring instances of hunger and poverty going unheeded and new kinds of conflict to be faced.

Worldwide, globalization seems, as yet, to be only skin deep. It answers fundamental questions in the universe of production with unquestionable effectiveness. However, the basic questions concerning the inner life of the human person and of individual and collective welfare around the Earth still do not fit into the rational logic of modern knowledge. This disparity has been characterized as a growing estrangement between science and culture, but in fact this disparity is a separation of human beings from themselves, leading people to turn for safety to the traditional beliefs of their own group. Thus, a paradoxical dual trend is emerging: globalism–tribalism.

This new clash is potentially even more stark than the one in the industrial era between employers and workers, who in their own way, shared the common aim of becoming the vanguard of progress. The struggle that pits culture against culture leaves no room for mediation. When the globalists look down, sometimes with an almost racist scorn, on individualists, the latter start to develop feelings of hatred toward the globalists whom the individualists perceive as destroying their people, their environment, and their habitat in the name of technologies or total success. Thus, on one side is utilitarianism; on the other, a focus on the particular. The one side, with a majority in the North and a minority in the South, is creating its technical and economic circles; the other side, with a majority in the South and a minority in the North, is entrenching itself behind defensive walls of cultural identities.

This gap also appears between economy and culture. As production started to shift from an emphasis on material goods, characteristic of the industrial era, to an emphasis on the new symbolic goods, characteristic of the information age, some people boarded the spaceship of change, like alert pilots, looking to market opportunities. Others came on as passengers and customers. But many were simply left behind or rejected as excess baggage. Still, modern production has increased the technical potential of human beings, thus also increasing the level of their needs and demands. It now remains to be seen whether the pressure of largely unsolved problems and the increasing entropy are leading us to chaos or to a higher standard of life on Earth.

## Dualization

One of the cycles that is coming to a close with this century is related to the permanent quest for greater productivity, particularly through techniques of scientific management. These techniques were basically aimed at improving mass production when the vast majority of industrial labour activities were mechanical and manual. As the century draws to a close, labour no longer accounts for a substantial share of the production process. The most important asset contributed by productive technologies is no longer physical: it is symbolic, and it is beginning to be called knowledge.

Windmills, waterwheels, and the stirrups that allowed knights to ride and control horses were the technological symbols of the feudal period of kings, gentry, knights, and crafts people. Just as the steam-engine marked the beginning of the end for the crafts people of that period, technology seems to be marking the twilight of the age of manual labour. Producers who have not adapted themselves to modern methods are being driven out of product markets, and traditional workers are also being driven out of the labour market. At the beginning of the century, the major concern was the exploitation of humans by machines or by other humans; today, on the threshold of the 21st century, the main problem for many is the lack of exploitation.

The comparative advantage of cheap labour is losing significance. Many underdeveloped workers, who have low purchasing power and limited access to educational and health-care systems, are becoming less and less necessary, although they were once useful to the system. It is becoming more and more difficult to justify new investments in infrastructure or in basic needs, because the productive integration required by the labour–management partners is no longer an absolute condition. Certain centres of excellence are becoming concentrated in technological islands, establishing contacts with their counterparts at other latitudes via satellite. As if in a return to feudalism, insuperable electronic walls are going up around the "gentry" of information and finance, and some of these people are beginning to raise the drawbridge to keep out the commoners.

Technology is advancing so quickly that many countries have already given up trying to catch up. For every step these countries' professionals took, the creative avant-garde took at least two or three more, widening their lead over local producers, inefficient researchers, career professionals, or national scientists and gaining an even greater lead over players who were no longer in the running at all — people who no longer counted, people without money, nonpeople, the marginalized.

The boom in communications has also produced an increase in expectations and therefore in demands and unmet needs. Requirements for education and housing are increased by burgeoning populations, by migrations of people who have aspirations but who do not necessarily constitute markets, and by people who do not always have purchasing power and who have very little hope of one day becoming part of the middle class. Many of these people have become so weakened that they have even lost the capacity to take action on their own initiative; they are undefined, sometimes immobilized, and often anonymous or outside the law. These shadows of a two-track economy become increasingly evident as one moves from the world economy's centre of gravity out to its periphery.

This trend toward marginalization is also encouraging ethnicity, the tendency to turn inward. The Third World, which after all implies nonalignment and the hope of discovering a future, has to one degree or another spread all around the globe. It now hovers around the outskirts of the universe of productive technology and mass consumption. The Third World is resigned to lurking in the shadows in frustration. In fact, some people are beginning to point to the emergence of a "Fourth World" in quantitative and qualitative terms.

The economic interdependence of the powerful and the powerless, the haves and the have-nots, is breaking down. Those connected to the world market can keep going, raise their standard of living, educate their children, and enjoy their holidays, even if their community is not producing properly, is not producing at all, or is not consuming. Through mutual disregard, the gulf between fellow citizens grows wider.

The reduction of transport and communication costs will probably also increase demand for experts and reduce demand for unskilled labour, further eroding the incomes of unskilled workers. Both trends will complicate efforts to implement or improve social services or public health services. To this must be added the further costs of measures to prevent or combat crime, which usually get higher priority than health issues.

Nowadays, according to the United Nations Development Programme (UNDP), one fifth of the world's population is suffering from famine; one fourth does not even have drinkable water; and one third is living in extreme poverty, under conditions remote from any reasonable concept of human existence. This is not the promised land of S&T.

## S&T and human needs

The modern era was inaugurated in the 18th century, when the instruments and technologies of crafts people began to be described, analyzed, and disseminated by processes of learning and teaching aimed at generalizing and improving their application. The study (*logos*) of the abilities and inventiveness (*techne*) of producers gave us technology, that is to say, the systematic development of knowledge applied to the concrete goal of manipulating or transforming some aspect of the mineral, vegetable, or animal world for the benefit of human beings.

In that way, the operation and control of instruments and means that could be useful for the activity and life of human beings became part of science. Previously, sciences were supposed to respond to spiritual or universal concerns, far from the realm of manual activity, which was scorned and compartmentalized. Knowledge started to follow two different paths: that of pure science and that of applied science. Pure science enjoyed the glory, but it is now in disfavour because it is thought to be too unreal and speculative. Applied science, which was once considered only a concern of vocations and crafts, is now touted as the road to development or salvation.

Later on, technology, which had been the study of techniques, became identified with the instrument itself: the new machines that replaced older ones were called new technologies. Technology came to be considered the bridge between humanity and nature.

Utilitarianism was primarily addressed to the improvement of conditions for both the individual and the community; it was concerned with day-to-day problems of physical existence, such as water, food, housing, roads, and even war. But a moment in history came when production also became a concern for philosophers or psychologists, among others: progress and inner life came into conflict, and progress emerged victorious. That was when science gave up its leading role to technology, and technology, in turn, became emblematic of social organization.

History then began to be told in reference to the means of operation peculiar to each period: the paleotechnical era, the era of the railroad, the industrial era, the electronic age, the era of data processing, and similar labels. These labels are indicative of the common understanding that the highest form of knowledge, inner or external — in a word, science — has come to be viewed in terms of its principal heir, operational technology. In this way, a connection was established between science and the improvement of the human condition through technology, which was supposed to be directed to the greatest good. This image oriented the sciences toward new inventions promoting wealth and well-being, which in turn became the core values of culture and became synonymous with society's striving to better the human condition.

In this historical process, several cleavages emerged. People became separated from their instruments, and these instruments generated rules and methods for social development, rather than vice versa. Technology became an art and departed from the science that gave birth to it, sometimes defying the premises that presided at its creation. Science focused on mechanics, and humanity was almost forgotten as the centre and subject of every action. People became alienated from themselves and from each other and raised up the idols of the material world to replace ethical and moral values that they regarded as outmoded.

A striking cleavage that became evident was the separation between man as "reason" and woman as "sentiment." Man was predestined to make the best use of the tools of modernity, and woman was supposed to take care of tradition and family life. Man, well equipped with muscles, could move heavier machines, and therefore it was normal for him to assume command of instrumental life and business, whereas woman was oriented to the domain of soul or nature.

Another salient division emerged between human activity and nature, with nature relegated to the role of an inexhaustible supplier of raw materials and used as a mechanism for dominance or a weapon of destruction.

It is also true that during this long evolution of modernity, many human needs were satisfied in many places, but the instruments for doing this broke down when efforts to use them lacked a comprehensive vision, sectoral specialization overwhelmed context, social action took second place to the technical, and the trend toward one-dimensionalism came to reduce development to merely a matter of production. Technology, which was originally devised precisely to increase humanity's options, became in many cases one more obstacle to this and one more factor working toward humanity's isolation and marginalization. This will continue as long as the gaps widen between the how and the why, science and technology, nature and society, man and woman, development and the human being, and object and subject.

## S&T: for development?

### The myths that failed

Many lessons have been learned in recent decades about development and in particular the technological aspects of basic needs. Today, without ideological prejudice, it is possible to analyze the mechanisms and the myths that failed. We must understand them explicitly if we are to abandon practices that do not work and clear the ground for alternatives that look to the future.

The main myth that is winding down at the end of this century is that development will come from society. The French Revolution liquidated the myth of the divine origin of salvation on Earth. After it, humanity, in search of its fate, contractually assigned to an abstract mediator — society — the care of people's material welfare. The problem was that the mediating entity took on a life of its own, developed its own rules, and finally imposed itself on the subject that had created it. Society acquired different forms in the 20th century — socialism, fascism, nazism, liberalism, technocratism, and other variations on the same theme: a metaphysical dynamic with strength superior to our own would bring us happiness and prosperity.

According to some, an invisible hand would distribute the dividends of production throughout the market. Others claimed that the state would provide these dividends to each according to need. The satisfaction of needs became associated with a higher authority. Something would come down from above, but each of us was fated to wait our turn to receive. One side said that the results of entrepreneurial activity were soon going to work their way down (trickle down); others regretted the absence of complete proletarian power to control the party that was supposed to control the state. Consequently, in many places, the "creative destruction" of innovation remained just "destructive destruction." In other places, people waited for the seeds of self-destruction to undo a mode of production that they viewed as doomed to failure. Nowadays, we have come to understand that development is not something one receives but something one does.

Part of the reason for the failure of the basic-needs strategies is the vertical conception of the top-down approach, which is a paternalistic way of facing the problem. Another part of the reason is the fact that the basic-needs strategies were generally global strategies devised in laboratories and presented as if they were the only solution. However, experience has taught us that social situations are so complex that no single answer is appropriate for all circumstances. It is not enough to remove the obstacles to profit or to exclusively develop appropriate technologies, without considering all the dimensions. We are not traveling a road already laid out; we are building our own road to the future, along all fronts. This was the scientific methodology adopted by medical and health specialists when they discarded the generalized diagnoses and panaceas and started to seek specific remedies for specific illnesses. However, for decades planners had been evoking the image of a goal, the image of a utopia that was unattainable and therefore paralyzing, and the image of utopias that tended to divide human thinking into different schools of thought and therefore failed to achieve their goals. Also, some complex mathematical models tended to oversimplify reality, seldom helping to redirect meaningful resources to the poor. In most cases, bureaucratic planning and technocratic methodologies hitched many countries to the last cars of the development train. Today we know that we need straightforward blueprints that can be accepted and implemented by everyone.

Another utopian impulse that tended to stagnate was the revolution against bonds of dependency. In most societies with violent movements, machinery for repression was generated by both sides, and this rarely led to significant social advances because the priorities were the weapons. In most cases, national security or the will of the people prevailed over the essential pluralism of human beings and the formidable complexity of their environment. Force was used to impose the market or the state with a firm hand, in the name of a fictitious unity conceived as something more important than the people concerned — movements synonymous with the forms of totalitarianism that are happily on their way to extinction nowadays, with the exception of some recent demonstrations of xenophobia. Many times, people justified their hatred technically or scientifically or by reference to laws of nature and ended by creating communities of people subjected to the power of the society they had originally created to serve them.

The take-off approach to development or to stages of development did not work either, nor did the nostalgic form of populism that takes shelter in itself against changes in the world. Those who naively called for a return to humanity's roots, some of them still using terrorist weapons to assail the system, also failed. Neither the aggregate sum of individual projects not the proliferation of foreign investments has been able to fill the gaps opened by the engines of so-called development. It is not difficult today to discern the hollow shafts of mines that have been exhausted and the misery of people who were once the wealth of humanity. Exploitation broke camp and moved its operations elsewhere as soon as natural and human resources were depleted, leaving behind holes in the earth and in the lungs.

A growing dualization has today become so widespread a phenomenon that not even the most partial of observers can underestimate it. The differences now revolve around a debate that is itself becoming anachronistic: should meeting basic needs be left to the market or to the state? Neither approach can be said, in empirical terms, to have worked, because each is the reflection of a threadbare approach: salvation by forces beyond ourselves.

## The market

Today, it is very easy to see why a pure and simple market approach will not automatically lead us to the solution of the basic-needs problems of populations with scarce resources. The statistical proofs of this are so abundant that it is unnecessary to insist on the widening abysmal differences in standards of living or the long-term tendency to their worsening, demonstrated by the empirical results of growth without employment. According to the trickle-down theory, jobs are the essential means to meeting human requirements, but investment is no longer necessarily correlated with employment. When the member countries of the Organisation for Economic Co-operation and Development double their gross domestic product, the corresponding growth in employment is less than one fourth; in the rest of the world, it may be only about one half. That is because production is growing, but it is growing by virtue of increases in productivity resulting from advances in technology.

Most of the technologies in developed countries must be seen in a context of relative demographic stagnation. They are labour-saving technologies that, in their design, reflect the international distribution of income: the fifth of the world that earns 80% of the world's income has four times the purchasing power of the poorest 80%; therefore, it is evident that technology will be guided toward the preferences of the richest members of international society. Moreover, these disparities are increasing: the countries in the North have 9 times more scientists and technologists than those in the South, 18 times more telephone connections, 20 times more computers, and 24 times more investment in technological research.

## The state

The state has experienced many failures, even though, in some cases, it did manage to make some contribution to efforts at modernization. Although the individual entrepreneur played a decisive role in certain cases of industrialization, one cannot deny that the national conscience promoted by the state also played its part, with remarkable results in Germany, Japan, and Brazil, as well as many other countries in the East, the West, the North, and the South. In many cases, the state contributed to the growth of a significant middle class, which is still seeking its identity. The problem, however, is not the success or failure of avenues to certain forms of industrialization, which are now being closed off; the question is how to reform a state that has become bureaucratic, client centred, authoritarian, unwieldy, static, and lacking in flexibility and initiative.

In many paternalistic states, the governments sought their justification in helping the poor. This century was ushered in by many public-works projects for water supply, schools, and hospitals, as well as by social-security campaigns, some of which were proclaimed by socialism and others of which were designed to prevent it. By the 1950s, from England to the colonies, everyone was redesigning the state in terms of social priorities. Similarly, some countries of the Third World supported a strong state to redistribute income and take action in the social arena in response to industrial and technological development and to mediate between capital and labour.

Before long, the state became a jack of all trades, expected to plan, organize, direct, execute, and coordinate. In some developing countries, even ice-cream production and hotel management became synonymous with state action. Much of this was supposed to have been done for the benefit of the poor, and taxes began to be justified by reference to a hypothetical redistribution. In many fields, even international cooperation contributed to justifying bureaucracy, charged against basic needs that did not always turn out to be the basic needs of the intended beneficiaries. Now, at the end of this century, we are realizing that not even 13% of national budgets is oriented to basic needs and that not even 10% of international assistance is geared to that purpose. That is not the kind of state to which citizens can continue to entrust the satisfaction of basic needs. So useless did the state become that it began to engender an extreme backlash, which is equally dangerous: leaving everything to the private sector or to market forces, which is tantamount to the state's abdicating a primary duty that had been assigned to it by the other parties to the social contract.

**International negotiations**

The international arena in earlier decades had the Cold War, which created major distortions in many states that entered the arms race to a greater or lesser extent and began to assign higher priority to military activities than to social requirements. The world environment also directed technology to national security, which implied capital-intensive instruments that gradually spread into other productive areas. Sovereignty and the great nation-state became the rationale for research, for protection, and, in some cases, even for confrontation.

At the beginning of this century, the state began to levy duties as a kind of national bulwark. This became a bone of contention between the ardent defenders of nationalism and the liberals. The defenders of nationalism saw themselves as foes of oppression, and the liberals saw themselves as friends of trade. Mass production began to drive a search for new markets in as yet unindustrialized regions, and nations began to compete among themselves, each proclaiming loyalty to its patriotic symbols and to the goods produced at home. The expansion of markets brought the issue of imperialism to the foreground, and powerful states began to contend for spheres of influence.

On all sides, the order of the day was to train more scientists and engineers so that the state could compete on more favourable terms with other countries, and the state then found itself foursquare in the race to support technology. Large companies were zealous custodians of their know-how and proudly flew the flag of their country. In some cases, companies even financed invasions in defence of their interests or encouraged armed conflicts to secure control of resources for production.

Negotiations for transfer of technology were launched in this framework of nation-state tensions. Several attempts were made to find a middle ground to ease the looming polarization. The aim was to gain control of the natural resources or raw materials, the technology needed to process them, and the markets in which to sell the products. However, within three or four decades, the stakes had changed, the rules of game had changed, and the negotiations shifted to another playing field. Resource–technology–market became an almost indivisible triad, and the most important thing was no longer the control of one of these three points but the power to connect all three and put forward global solutions.

This strategic shift began when, at the global-market level, production started to move from the high-volume economy to the high-value economy (Reich 1993). Within two or three decades, there emerged competitive companies that had the comparative advantage of cheap labour and could also sell their products in distant markets because of improvements in transportation. Protectionism became ineffectual because the margins it provided were not wide enough. Wage reductions, which had their limits, and financial tactics could not fulfill the expectations of large companies. Both production and technology began to be oriented to the needs of certain consumers, those who desired sophisticated goods. From special steels to computer software, from magnetic-resonance imaging to the entertainment industry, the markets that today promise large earnings are those for goods with a high technological value. All the staple items that can be standardized can now be manufactured or copied in many places around the globe. Staple items are no longer the main problem, at least as far as transfer of technology is concerned. The main field for the technological contest is no longer in markets, where competition is about volume and price, but in the search for connectivity between specialized technologies and selective consumers.

Many things are changing with this new shift. The nationalities of global companies are no longer so important. The activities of global companies have been decentralized. The geographical provenance of products is no longer clear. Products cannot be clearly distinguished from services. Even financial sources are not easy to distinguish, and the owners of technologies are not the same as before.

The sovereignty traditionally associated with territory is now beginning to be redefined because borders no longer enclose or protect either markets or patents. Nobody now speaks of nationalization to take over assets whose real location in time and space is nebulous. Furthermore, the owners of capital or the owners of the means of production have become a mix of shareholders, investors, managers, pension funds, employees, and even unions.

The national bourgeoisie is also becoming ill defined, and many negotiations among nation-states have lost significance. Some of the rigid structures of nation-states have become barriers to the spread of techniques and mechanisms. Further, many governmental organizations designed to accomplish technological tasks are losing motivation, and several universities in developing countries are no longer playing the leading role they had always assumed in changing their communities. It is not surprising, therefore, that international negotiations for technology transfers should so often fail, perhaps because they are not really connected with the real world. The movement of diskettes, funds, and professionals is outpacing any official agreement, and the movement is not normally in the direction where 80% of humanity is located. Maybe both sides of the table are debating obsolescent issues or perhaps the people seated around the bargaining table are not the ones involved directly in technological issues. For example, more than three quarters of the value of microelectronic products accrues to technical services, designs, and patents. The owner of the asset is no longer the factory owner or the employer, much less the government: the valuable employees count very much. In some cases the company holds the patents, but innovation moves so quickly that the capacity to create more and more new things is much more important than the installed capacity by itself. This considerably enhances the value of the specialist, so much so that now it is no longer a question of acquiring the racquet or of transferring the tennis-playing skill; rather, the tennis player can be the principal bearer of added value in a technological transaction.

However, the most sought-after specialists are no longer the pure experts in the traditional sense. In symbolic production, the most valued people are those who know how to connect their expertise with the concrete desires of the consumer and how to articulate sources of inputs, production, and distribution points. Precisely when the auditors of the world are commemorating the 500th anniversary of the work of Pacioli, who devised the accounting methodology for evaluating the flows of money and goods, that method is beginning to be questioned because now many assets are not physical. The intangible assets of advanced companies may represent three or four times their book value, and intellectual-property assets are no longer structural: they are basically human. Although the accounting problems of corporations are becoming complex, the idea of evaluating a country merely in terms of its national accounts is becoming meaningless.

The main powers in the world compete or agree with each other, depending on their concrete interests, and make the principal decisions about the global market. The Group of Seven has much more bargaining power than the almost 200 developing nations. Some progress has been achieved in common directions because knowledge allows nations to move closer and have more and more frequent interaction. However, the concrete results still leave much to be desired, and the great majority of technological transactions are still taking place between countries in the developed regions. The 20% of the world's population with the lowest incomes transacts less than 1% of the world's trade.

## Democratization

After considering the dramatic panorama of events, the conceptual obstacles, the unfortunate experiences in the field of development, the shortcomings in markets, the unwieldy states, the excluding international environment, now what? Despite all this, one must give credit to modernity for the most important of its victories: democracy. With all its blemishes, with all the unresolved problems, and with the burden and the as yet unpaid price of the world's divisions, no one today denies that the greatest progress that humanity has made in its quest for development has been in the realm of political freedom. If development means happiness and opening up more and more options in life, it can be confidently asserted that before the end of the second millennium, the world has opened the doors to a sphere of collective action never before attained. It is not easy to glimpse the future; however, one can clearly discern that the solutions to come will need to build on the foundations of that challenging participatory approach.

Technology has played a role in both development and underdevelopment, as well as in the development of underdevelopment, but one must also recognize the essential role of technology in the process that led the world toward the democratic revolution. Decentralization, transparency, flexibility, and accountability of rulers were unthinkable without the advanced communications available today. Economies of scale, for example, were in themselves conducive to authoritarian methods or even to dictatorial hierarchies, but now, in these times of innovation, those structures too have become anachronistic.

Given the failure of justice to keep pace with liberty, the use of S&T for development raises the following question: Development of what and for whom? The strategies for satisfying basic needs were born out of an important attempt to respond to human problems that not only persist but have grown vastly larger and more complex. However, the progress achieved in recent decades in reducing infant mortality and increasing life expectancy indicates that some success in narrowing vital gaps is possible.

Approaches that reinforce the Cinderella complex are not going to work any more: they merely encourage people to wait for a Prince Charming, who never arrives. Although the market is a necessary condition for modernization, there is more to it than that. Even to take part in a market economy, contemporary elites need to have some kind of a state, just as they cannot do without the rest of the citizenry. How can we ensure that both the state and the market are guided by those they affect, that is, by the citizenry, and that human beings become active agents, both in their own eyes and vis-à-vis society?

Ample demonstration has been given of the loss of wholeness between science and culture and between science and technology, of the gaps between possibilities and needs and between production and consumption, of the break between the global and the particular and between nations and regions, of the separation between human beings and between man and woman, of the withdrawal of the specialists from contact with people, and of the large barriers between life aspirations and public obligations. Many believe that technology itself has much to do with this and that the technological defeats suffered by entire continents can also be chalked up on the debit side of the experts' ledgers. That is sometimes the case. We do have an outstanding debt to ourselves and to our people.

Men and women of science cannot remain indifferent to the major contradiction between liberty and justice that has emerged at the millennium's end. Scientists cannot exclude themselves from, or be excluded by, the world. They cannot become prisoners of their books or isolated in an elite, leaving the whole range of human understanding to the mercies of popularization. Scientists should not wholly reject utilitarianism, nor should they become completely wedded to it. Scientists cannot indulge a certain type of consumption pattern if elsewhere many people are unable to consume even a life-sustaining minimum. Similarly, to apply knowledge in carrying out an analysis and arriving at a diagnosis is not enough: the scientists must then propose solutions. Nor should scientists assume the role of prophets or saviours. Above all, this is no time for scientists to exclude themselves.

# Toward sustainable human development

## A new paradigm

Physicists have managed to reconcile the atom and the expanding universe; biologists have integrated human beings with nature; sociologists consider both the actor and the system; and many branches of research are gradually becoming anthropocentric. So, too, we must strive for a meeting between the part and the whole, a meeting between the individual and his or her complex surrounding and his or her life, a meeting with one's self, one's neighbours, one's community, one's environment, and (why not also include) one's instruments of production and creative transformation. The inspiration for this renewal could be found again in the sciences that are part of Science with a capital S, not only instrumental or utilitarian science. What is needed is Science that puts humanity at the centre of the universe and closely links humanity to its cosmic dimension, which goes beyond the merely material.

It is not a question of simplifying but of recognizing complexity. It is not a question of extrapolating from one specific source of knowledge but of drawing sustenance from each source of knowledge and opening up the possibilities for doing so. The Gaya hypothesis, for instance, expresses the concept that we belong to a larger whole, to an ecosystem, and that our planet is a common house (*eko*) that we must make sustainable. Gaya was a Greek goddess, perhaps the equivalent of the *Pacha Mama* of the Incas or the Earth Mother of many religions. For many cultures, the whole of life is interrelated, and what directly affects one person actually indirectly affects everyone else. That is why the human being and the universe are joined through two basic principles: the anthropocentric principle and the ecosystemic principle. Human endeavour can be guided by two complementary orientations: the human and the sustainable components. In this approach, human life is judged not just by what individuals can produce but also by its own qualities. Accordingly, vital rights are given their legitimacy, which is the first step to making vital rights universal.

The concept of development in this vision has much to do with the etymology of *development*, or the Spanish *des-arrollo*, or the Portuguese *des-envolvimento*, that is, "de-envelopment." De-envelopment in many languages means to untie something that is tied, enveloped, closed, or locked, that is to say, to remove all the obstacles that block life or any individual or collective action. This concept of development implies eliminating hindrances to the creative energy of persons and nations, the only types of being that can determine their own fate. This kind of development would not waste time programing paralyzing objectives or designing unattainable utopias. This idea of development implies trust in human strength and people's ability to know what they need and how to obtain it, people who demand nothing more than a fair chance to work out their own solutions.

To accomplish these ends, a radical change in the style of development is needed. Paternalism failed as an approach to development because it neglected the work of those who really know the needs and failed to mobilize the most important asset: the people. When there are no set formulas for success, the only way to act is through unity and consensus. The unity of the people can be catalyzed, allowing them to conduct their own programs and actions. The biggest investment must be in peoples' self-esteem. Communities should not be called on for support; rather, they should be supported and inspired, insofar as this is possible, with the confidence to frame their own changes.

If this is an option, and if this is the right choice, then technologies will have to be made easy and methods will have to be simple. Technologies must be easy to transfer, learn, and teach. However, making it all easy may be the most difficult task, given a past that is weighed down by complex techniques that brought more problems than solutions. Virtually all the explicit policies of the present era are based on vital rights: education, health, and food. This is not a question of importing or creating something new; rather, it is bringing back a vision as old as humanity, as deeply rooted as civilization, and giving people the opportunity to re-create the ethical option of sharing the potential of the present with those who are to come.

The first principle of the Rio Declaration, universally approved in 1992, states that the human being is at the centre of sustainable development, with all the implications that flow from this. This new paradigm of sustainable human development is the most important conceptual contribution to vital rights made by the United Nations in this century. The Secretary-General has referred to this paradigm as the salient epistemological breakthrough of our times.

Agenda 21 is an extraordinary program of action, and with 40 chapters and more than 100 programs, is the most exhaustive framework to date for making decisions and for taking action at the national and international levels. It would have been impossible to adopt by consensus such an instrument in a world divided by hot or cold wars. Agenda 21 addresses the main issues of development and environment, trade and investment, poverty and pollution, health and technology, and education and population, as well as many other topics.

Never before has the world adopted a program so comprehensive and backed by so wide a consensus. Agenda 21 also covers the questions of capacity-building and the need for the participation of young people, women, indigenous peoples, entrepreneurs, peasants, and workers. This program calls for a global partnership for sustainable development, in which all peoples and nations undertake new social, economic, and political commitments. This spirit of Rio has been called an eco-revolution, heralding a change in world perceptions and attitudes.

This monumental piece of work and the consensus it represents open up new possibilities for dealing with the issue of basic needs in the realm of ideas. Although the objective conditions for satisfying material basic needs have grown worse, the subjective conditions are improving, at least in some respects. As Kuhn would say, a new paradigm is being born. A new movement is being prepared, perhaps along the lines anticipated by Dilmus James in Chapter 5. This time, let us not make the mistake of making Agenda 21 a new bible and seeing sustainable human development as the new saviour, confusing ideas with realities. As in love and war, the crux of the art is in doing: the most important thing is not to interpret the world but to change it. For that, a program helps, but the changes are made by the actors of social movements.

## Basic social needs or vital human rights?

Experts can help by refining Agenda 21 and implementing many of its proposals. Scientists must continue to explore the human and universal dimensions, the axiomatic accuracy, and the categorization of the new encounter with wholeness. We should reclassify the so-called basic social needs as vital rights. *Social needs* still has a connotation of passivity, of dependence on a metaphysical entity called society for the satisfaction of social needs.

The imposed provision of goods and services diminishes the personal satisfaction in satisfying a basic need. In a human environment, technologies must be accessible so that individuals can use them to increase their own creative potential and personal development. We should therefore try to cultivate a holistic knowledge that goes beyond instrumental acquisition, a holistic knowledge in which all would agree on an ethic in which human development is linked directly to the sustainability of the environment and in which the needs of the planet become human needs and human rights become universal rights.

Replacing *needs* with *rights* is a small but very meaningful change. The terms are considerably different, so the practical consequences of making this change could be capital. The modern world measures the value of everything by its practical effects, forgetting, sometimes, that nothing is more practical than a good theory. With the change from *needs* to *rights*, technologies would have to provide equal opportunity and equal access. Technologies for sustainable human development, technologies for vital human rights, or simply vital technologies must meet this equal-access requirement. Furthermore, such technologies must be user friendly. Additional research and, in certain cases, up-to-date techniques may be needed.

The main guarantee of the sustainability of human development is the scope of the vital rights, which guarantee the continuity of life in its broadest sense. The issue of the right to development and its links with human rights and technologies have been a major concern of the United Nations for many years. Some progress has been made in interrelating the three concepts of development, technology, and human rights. Life, education, health, and nutrition have been identified as the most essential of human rights. The studies, breakthroughs, agreements, and conventions of recent decades could be the diplomatic basis needed for a change and for implementing a fresh strategy for ensuring these vital rights become universal.

The Universal Declaration of Human Rights (1948) stated that each individual is entitled to a healthy standard of life, including nutrition, clothing, shelter, and all the appropriate social services (Art. 25). The right to education was also expressly provided for (Art. 26), as well as special care for mothers and children (Art. 25). Progress since then has been made step by step, as shown in the following UN documents:

1. In 1966 the international covenants on Economic, Social, and Cultural Rights and on Civil and Political Rights reiterated these vital concerns.

2. In 1968 the International Conference on Human Rights adopted the Teheran Declaration to mark the 20th anniversary of the Universal Declaration of Human Rights. The Teheran Declaration dealt with issues pertaining to developing countries.

3. In 1974 the World Conference on Nutrition supported the right to food as a human right.

4. In 1978 the Alma-Ata Declaration recommended that primary health care be considered a basic human right.

5. A decade later, the Declaration of the Right to Development stated that development is an inalienable human right and that every human being deserves to share in, contribute to, and benefit from economic, social, cultural, and political development. This is the basis for all human rights and political freedoms.

6. In 1990 the UN Declaration on Education for All recalled that education is a fundamental right and that learning is a basic need. Similarly, health is a right, food is a right, agriculture is a basic need.

All these vital rights, rights of subsistence, should be made universal, and ensuring them should be made workable.

7. In 1991 the Rights of the Child were enhanced.

8. In 1992 the Rio Declaration introduced recognition of the right of every human being to have a healthy life in harmony with nature.

9. In 1992 the World Conference on Nutrition and the Declaration of Barcelona underscored the right to food as a human right.

10. In 1993 the World Conference on Human Rights drew attention to economic, social, and cultural rights.

11. In 1994 the Cairo meeting on population and in 1995 the Fourth World Conference on Women drew attention to gender discrimination in ensuring rights that are ostensibly universal.

12. In 1995 the Social Summit also focused on human rights in the struggle against poverty.

Thus, a closer link between development and human rights has been steadily developing. At the operational level, the United Nations Committee on Development Planning has linked poverty reduction to sustainable development and has given priority to the human right to a fair share of national welfare, education, health, and employment.

In parallel, since the Teheran Declaration in 1968, another universal concern began to appear, through the specific resolution on human rights and the S&T progress. That process reached a benchmark in 1975, when the General Assembly decided to promote the use of S&T not only for peace and security but also for social and economic development, with a view to the protection of human rights. The aim was to strengthen national capacities to hasten the realization of the social and economic rights of peoples.

In 1986, on the basis of the Vienna Program of Action for Science and Technology for Development, the Commission on Human Rights invited the United Nations University to study the interactivity of development, S&T, and human rights. The conclusions of this project, which attracted contributions by experts and specialists the world over, showed the close links among these three concepts and concluded that it was urgent to orient S&T to the improvement of human rights, particularly in developing countries. The project coordinator, who is now a judge of the International Court of Justice, recommended (Weeramantry 1993, p. 10) that the focus of this effort be on

> *health, education, and environment as the best entry points,*
> *representing the rights broadly accepted by the international*
> *community. Advances in science and technology enable*

*education to spread through the dissemination of informa-*
*tion and promote universal health care and provision of*
*clean water and air.*

These steps taken by the United Nations provide a solid basis for transforming basic social needs into vital human rights and giving weight, legitimacy, and universality to these critical rights of poor people around the world.

## Global cleavage, dual strategy

The global cleavage, now clearly perceived and thoroughly documented, has reached such proportions that it has become inconceivable that a single strategy would adequately meet the demands of modernization and resolve the plight of the extremely poor. These two goals are in a sense antagonistic, but they need to be pursued lest entire peoples are driven over the brink into nonviable situations. In some regions, it is no longer possible to think in terms of half measures: modernization is necessary if one is trying to survive in more and more competitive markets. For people living in extreme poverty, the only choice is survival. In the first case, the challenge is to grow; in the second case, the challenge is to keep up hope. In the first case, one has to find contracts; in the second case, one has to find food. In the first case, one has to promote the commercial life of a product; in the second case, one has to keep the children alive.

There is no other choice: a dual reality needs a dual strategy. Action is needed in two directions, at two different speeds, with different executing machinery, different rules, different actors, different processes, and different goals. Global cleavage has become so wide that the two strategies must each be allowed to follow its own ways and its own rules while trying not to ignore the other. One strategy is for poor people, their sustainable livelihood, and their vital rights. The other strategy is for modernization and is going to be determined by the markets; to guarantee its success, it cannot be burdened by internal restrictions. Integrating with the world economy is no longer a matter of choice; one simply has to achieve it, and for all countries, the sooner the better. However, the richest 20% of a population will never benefit from their success while they remain surrounded by the 20% on the other end of the social scale, or more accurately, off the end of the scale. Furthermore, competition is now a systemic problem, and every product bears the stamp of the physical or human unsustainability of its place of origin.

The governments of the future will be judged on, first, the help they give their economic actors to enter and compete in the global market, and second, the opportunities they open up for the survival of people excluded from the economic system without closing off opportunities for future generations. If this sounds like a problem in linear programing, let us make no mistake — the world is not linear, and no mathematical model can optimize these inequalities. The solutions, if any, are in the political realm, which is technical but primarily social and basically human, with all the complexity that that implies. When the issue of power is being discussed, scientists usually absent themselves. Sometimes, though, the discussion is said to be about art, not science, precisely to exclude the scientists. However, with the present state of the art in development, one cannot fail to factor S&T into the equation.

The aim of modernization is to become as modern as possible, to find out and master the best techniques, and to establish a systematic unity of management, production, and marketing. This unity should not be static; it should be dynamic, changing. This is a concern not only of governments but also of the private sector. The Manichean view of the state as good and private industry as bad, or vice versa, is a thing of the past. Negotiations in the fields of management, production, and marketing take place among investors. The state may be of some help, but ultimately the decisions are made by people who buy and people who sell. These negotiations are a matter of management policy and microeconomics. In these, a traditional industrial policy is almost impossible.

The question I am addressing is what kind of S&T is needed for the poor and especially for a special category of the poor, those of the Fourth World. The Fourth World no longer embraces nation-states or even entire geographical regions; rather, it embraces geographically scattered human beings who are being denied the right to life in material and nonmaterial terms. This change in the geography of poverty is not due to a lack of modernization; indeed, it may sometimes be due to the fact that modernization has undermined traditional strategies for survival. This poverty is not only ethically intolerable but politically dangerous, economically unsustainable, and environmentally corrosive. This poverty can be seen in La Paz or New York, in Paris or Lagos. The strategy of using technology to protect vital rights has to be directed to supporting these human beings. The instruments are of two complementary types: the global technologies, which can have an indirect influence on poor people, and the vital technologies, which are directly linked to survival and can open up opportunities for the poor to work for themselves.

The word *knowledge* carries the connotation that it must be transmitted via the computer, which is not always true. Vital technologies are not necessarily electronic, even though some use electronic tools. The vital technologies may be developed with contributions from lawyers, sociologists, economists, biologists, politicians, nutritionists, psychologists, and many other specialists who also are, or should be, considered as being in the applied sciences.

Because the sciences are split into various specialties or subspecialties, a closer focus in one area sometimes leads to the loss of a holistic vision of the world. Technologies for human beings have to be T-shaped: in-depth in one specialty but horizontal to communicate with the others. Most vital techologies have to have an interdisciplinary character, serving both human beings and nature, which is, in the end, the *raison d'être* of science. If hardware goes with software, they should both go hand in hand with "human-ware" so that we could say these are human technologies, or humane technologies, or better still, sustainable human technologies.

Following these guidelines, I have selected 10 types of global technologies that are indirectly pertinent to vital rights and 10 types of vital technologies, which I will discuss in greater detail. This is not an exhaustive list; these are technologies in a broad sense, based on the etymology of *technology*. They should not be confused with the human-centred technologies, which are user-friendly machines and programs, but these 20 types of technologies also exemplify that valuable idea. They are more than physical instruments: they are knowledge in action.

## Global technologies

### Modernization technology: competitiveness
Modernization technology is the main element in an outward-oriented strategy for development. To different degrees in different countries, an outward-oriented strategy aims to establish a country's international position and build as many bridges for doing this as possible, as soon as possible. This objective cannot wait for bureaucratic decisions to be put into action. Competition requires pursuing technologies on a day-to-day basis, one after another, company by company. With the present state of the art in technology, no industrial, agricultural, or service policies can be generalized. What we know indicates only that countries have to engage in the interplay of the markets, trying to make them as fair as possible, which is not always the case. The best comparative advantage that developing countries still have is their own market; although they cannot protect it, they can at least try to serve it better. In addition, some bilateral conventions and multilateral agreements

are showing positive results in many regions of the world: the tailoring of these internal and regional opportunities will continue to be one of the most appropriate techniques for development, although most high-volume products no longer hide any technological secrets.

### Production technology: growth

For developing countries especially, growth is not only a right but an obligation. Increasing the gross national product will continue to be a technique of economic policy or political economy that affects the life of a nation's citizens. Growth is an imperative and requires a national consensus on, and collective awareness of, the need for it. Many countries have not yet learned that lesson. Forming a national consensus is an advanced technology, and its implementation is a skill successful countries mastered some time ago.

### Investment technology: privatization

The public sector is most unlikely to be the major agent of investment for development in years to come. The trend observable in most countries is to reduce public-sector investment. Moreover, the megaprojects that led many Third World countries into debt are no longer so common, which is as it should be. Additionally, it is more and more difficult to clearly differentiate national and foreign investments; in other words, the geographical origin of capital is no longer as clear. Capital is now financial, technological, and as we have seen, human. As growth is an imperative, present and future investments in technology will mostly be guided by trade agreements and the market. Many productive units have been privatized in the developing countries, with all the advantages and disadvantages privatization implies. The integration of global resources in vulnerable economies will undoubtedly become one of the many arts of local technologists. Research and the exchange of experience will be of cardinal importance.

### Economic technology: the balance

Another inescapable aspect of today's economic environment is structural adjustment and the balancing of national accounts. Anti-inflation measures are very well known and have been applied with varying success around the world. Undoubtedly, a very close relationship exists between macroeconomic variables and technological policy; where vital rights are concerned, budgets and redistribution are the main issues. The transfer of funds to vital areas will have to take into account a country's complete financial position. Moreover, it is essential to exchange experiences from the renegotiation of foreign debt, a process that has permitted the release of some funds for human development.

The art will be in striking a balance that respects vital rights and does no further injury to the weak.

### Articulation technology: integration

A dual strategy for development is needed to address the dual reality in developing countries, not because a dual strategy is desirable but because this is the reality. However, there is nothing sustainable about supporting countries with areas or concentrations of profit that become physically, economically, and socially divorced from broad sectors of the population. In other words, a necessary corollary of a dual strategy is a conscious collective process of national integration that can be shared by the whole community via infrastructure (such as roads, telecommunications, and power generation), cultural integration, and the mutual enrichment of the various sectors of each country.

### Institutional technology: capacity development

Another technological course of action is to strengthen institutions for sustainable human development. This opens up major prospects for the future, from the bottom up and from the top down, in both the public and the private sectors. The obsolescent edifice of technology in most countries needs to be redesigned to function in the dual strategy. Some institutions will have a global function, some a vital function, and others a mixed function. Universities, for example, should have both global and vital functions: some university–enterprise organizations or foundations have been successful and decisive in the global dimension. On the other hand, as Fernández mentioned (in Chapter 3), nothing prevents university students and young professionals from taking part in internal plans for horizontal technical assistance, mobilizing the knowledge and national experience applicable to disadvantaged areas.

In technological terms, capacity has to be a dynamic and holistic concept, involving the possible innovation, adoption, and adaptation of tools. At the same time, capacity has to be the measure of appropriate use of funds for vital rights, for the development of human energy and local techniques, and for the construction of grass-roots organizations and their participation in the development process. In other words, capacity development has to be understood as the technology that empowers human beings and their organizations to resolve their own problems.

### Research technology: blending

Research in developing countries has to be determined by the needs of the global market and the vital sector to give local experts who have this sense of dual commitment the strongest possible motivation. This means continuing to explore, in a pragmatic spirit, appropriate technology and the blending of technologies, with the intention of applying these innovations on one side or the other of the dual strategy. The global market requires speed and flexibility, and certain local products can reach the global market if they are backed up by research on the management–production–marketing triad. On the other hand, the vital sector calls for research on the whole range of tools needed in all the economic, social, political, and technical dimensions of the struggle against extreme poverty. It is also becoming very important to know, and perhaps to systematize, the methods and the processes used in many of the activities in the so-called informal economy, which has often generated more alternatives for survival than the formal economy.

The system of innovations has to develop according to the dual strategy at every level, from consultancy firms to parents' associations. Job growth, which responds mostly to the capacities and interests of the private sector, will need support, particularly in the case of small businesses and productive activities in agriculture. Again, the predominance of the tertiary sector will orient more and more activities toward services, and because most services are vital services, these will continue to be partly public concerns.

**Power technology: feminization**
Social structures that still exclude half the population from decision-making and action are clearly no longer sustainable. The legal, administrative, cultural, and economic obstacles that limit the participation of women are ethically unacceptable, as well as being one of the most serious constraints on the prospects for sustainable human development. Moreover, women are the most staunch supporters of a new encounter with nature, against the exclusivity and the dehumanizing effects of technologies, from many of which women have been barred. Equal opportunity for the sexes could also serve as a benchmark for the growth of options for poor people. What is more, the majority of the poor are children, and the majority of children are poor. Both women and young people are especially concerned with changing this.

**Financial technology: the 20 : 20 covenant**
The *Human Development Report, 1994* (UNDP 1994) presented a feasible alternative for reaching objective targets for ensuring the vital rights of humanity. The proposal is to promote an agreement between governments and the international community for each to earmark 20% of its budget for human basic needs. This document sets forth the following goals as attainable within the next 10 years, to be agreed on by governments:

▼ Universal access to basic schooling;

- ▼ Immunization for all children;

- ▼ 50% reduction in maternal mortality;

- ▼ General access to family planning services;

- ▼ 50% reduction in the adult illiteracy rate;

- ▼ Eradication of severe malnutrition;

- ▼ Movement toward population stabilization; and

- ▼ Establishment of credit systems for the poor.

**Mobilization technology: Agenda 21**
Development always proceeds on the basis of human labour and nature, that is, the mineral, animal, and vegetable kingdoms. The dual challenge for countries today is sustainable livelihood and productive transformation with sustainability. One has to invest in environmentally sound technologies, which is a major argument for the paradigm of sustainable human development.

Agenda 21 is the most complete agreement for a program of action that has ever been reached. Beyond being technically motivating, Agenda 21 can generate domestic currents conducive to human objectives and collective sustainability. Agenda 21 covers the broad range of topics necessary for a program of action to build a sustainable covenant, one that, in the developing countries especially, must include a way of combating poverty. Agenda 21 is viewed as the best existing pragmatic instrument for the common cause of vital rights, thanks to its comprehensive content and the legitimacy of its underlying consensus.

## Vital technologies

Vital technologies have a much closer bearing than other technologies on the problems of the poorest of the poor. In that sense, vital technologies can be regarded as those technologies specifically designed to address the vital rights that are most neglected. Like the other 10 technologies discussed above, these 10 technologies are only some of the possibilities a country could adopt for the principal target groups of the dual strategy.

**Political technology: governance**
The political system is seriously affected by dualization, and this is further aggravated by a lack of adequate democratic mechanisms for reconciling two apparently antithetical objectives: participation and governability. Marginality, which is the way extreme poverty finds

political expression, threatens the political life of nations with regional, sectoral, and cultural fragmentation. The intermediary role played by parties is complicated by corruption, subservience to constituencies, and other dubious aspects of politics, which can attain violent proportions. Some critical technological elements, such as electoral mechanisms and the media, are not immune to this. Also part of the picture are the forms of management, adoption, and enforcement of laws, as well as specifically juridical techniques.

It is unrealistic to try to use S&T to strike a balance between liberty and justice if one excuses the political institutions from giving due attention to basic needs. Those needs require a suitable system of governance, one that is flexible and modern and includes machinery for the defence of people and their elementary rights. Some may say that this is beyond the realm of electronics, which of course it is. However, adequate governance and the protection of vital rights cannot be secured without technological components, which can be understood as instruments of applied political science in the service of the citizenry. Various examples can be given: the instruments used to conduct parliamentary debate, to document persons, to simplify bureaucratic procedures, to organize security forces, and to detect crime and drugs. We need to look at the broad sphere of work pursued in different countries if we are to rediscover what Ventura and Henry (in Chapter 4) have called the forgotten strategy.

### Administrative technology: decentralization

Decentralization is the predominant trend in modern administration. Decentralization is occurring in corporations, governments, religious and academic institutions, sports, culture, the military, and so on. As hierarchical structures change into networks and people learn increasingly more about the logic of decision-making, an irresistible wave of transfers or delegations of power has emerged, in both functional and geographic terms, because the end-users of public or private functions are trying to gain more direct control over the power and circumvent cumbersome intermediaries.

Where the state is concerned, the link in the chain that is closest to the citizen is the local community, which should gradually gain more powers. The provinces and districts will become points of articulation for economic or political programs.

Administrative science has undergone major changes in recent decades. There has been a shift from the classical approach to the systems approach, with its action-oriented and other variants, which has led to more efficient results. Accountability, clarity of responsibilities, methods of executing and monitoring projects, and many other areas related to vital rights are being decentralized, with the result that many different kinds of units are being integrated into collective action. The techniques and instruments for redistributing functions vertically and horizontally will become routine parts of the dual strategy.

## Planning technology: participation

We must try to achieve as much bottom-up planning as possible and as little top-down planning as necessary. Many mistakes in traditional planning have led to its methods being discredited, either because of overzealous actions of the state or because of results that have not been in keeping with intentions. Almost always, what was missing was the necessary dovetailing of planning and reality, and this has been due to the methods not having been developed on the ground. A systematic approach, integrating a bottom-up perspective, would contribute most to the coherence of development plans. This means trusting in the strengths of the people and in their wisdom to know what they need and how to achieve it, and it means giving people a fair chance to work out their own solutions.

People's energies need to be catalyzed so they can take charge of their own programs. Such actions dispel complexes, diminish paternalism, and build people's self-esteem. If obstacles are removed, the creative energies of people and communities will be released, enabling them to take the initiative. People are the best productive force, the one that makes the best use of human, natural, physical, and financial potentials, as well as institutional and cultural heritage. It is the people who will best ensure their vital human rights without endangering those of future generations.

Top-down mechanisms need not be abandoned, but they must be supportive and function with minimal intervention. The support they give must be focused. Bridges to supply technical assistance are important, primarily in reconciling conflicting demands. When fair and transparent rules are set out, communities have shown the wisdom in setting priorities for the use of available resources.

## Action technology: sustainability

The concept of sustainable livelihood was enshrined in Agenda 21 in the context of an antipoverty program. The bases for technological action derived from that approach deserve special attention because the goal of such action is to provide everyone with an opportunity for survival by attacking the causes of poverty, hunger, inequity, and meagre human development. This means protecting natural resources.

Any policy for protecting natural resources should take into account the people who depend on those resources for their livelihood, or the policy may negatively affect the struggle against poverty, which in the long term will also affect resource conservation. Similarly, any attempt to increase the production of goods should take into account the sustainability of the resources used in making those goods; otherwise, productivity is bound to fall sooner or later, and this in turn can lead to increased poverty. A basic requirement of sustainable development is a concrete strategy to combat poverty.

A strategy to combat poverty must aim to create the best possible conditions for a sustainable development that eliminates poverty and reduces inequality among population groups. Action must focus especially on women, children, and young people, as well as on small-scale property owners, herders, crafts people, associations of producers, grass-roots organizations, neighbourhood councils, landless families, indigenous communities, migrants, and those in the informal sector of the urban economy. The year 1996, which is the Year for the Eradication of Poverty, should provide a fitting context for thinking globally, but the action needed is local because the cause of self-sustainability will be won or lost locally.

## Credit technology: popularization

Credit and financial facilities are needed for the marginal sector, as well as improved access to land and resources. Experience shows that credit can be extended to the poor because the poor are responsible borrowers and do not need subsidized interest rates. Well-known proven management methods are being used by bankers and borrowers in Bangladesh, Bolivia, Costa Rica, India, Indonesia, Mexico, the Philippines, and many other countries, with surprisingly positive results. Credit operations for small businesses have not only contributed to job creation but also brought about innovations in the delivery of certain services. Credit for small businesses is an encouraging avenue of action for vital rights, which can result in the beneficiaries' satisfying their basic needs.

## Organizational technology: citizenship

Communities and all other expressions of civil society have begun to reject the passive citizenship role they played in the past. The involvement of communities, neighbourhoods, and town councils in conducting their affairs is an observable trend. Some of these groups are even suggesting new organizational subdivisions for provinces or districts. With the creativity typical of human beings, diverse organizations are springing up in all countries; some of these organizations are going so far as to take control of community projects and services for water supply, education, health, land management, roads, and technology. This trend implies the growth of a third sector, which can be seen as one answer to problems of the Fourth World. The vacuum left by the state and by failed political structures is in many cases providing room for changes in social relations to resolve civil-rights issues. The vacuum is being filled by development associations, civic committees, cooperatives, foundations, and many other forms of organization striving to overcome poverty, promote rights, and protect women, children, and the environment.

This third sector is also known as the nonprofit sector or the nongovernmental sector. The organizations in this sector are called "human change institutions" and address very specific tasks. They represent a shift to the paradigm of "social ecology" in postcapitalist society. Some of these entities are small, whereas others have major vertical or horizontal links. Some, like the Campaign Against Hunger in Brazil, arouse mass enthusiasm, whereas others capture and channel financial resources and exchange experiences and techniques. These entities express civil society in its multiple forms and varied origins, interests, and goals. The best name for an entity of this type seems to be "organization of civil society" (OCS), as this characterizes it by saying what it is rather than what it is not, as with *nonprofit* or *nongovernmental*. The OCSs open up a vast area of action for solving many technical problems. If the OCSs join with other actors and involve the excluded, who are not organized, they can achieve the goal of every organization, which is to transform knowledge into reality.

Both the centrifugal forces changing the features of nations and the lack of centripetal forces that has brought about crisis for some states may compel people to look for a sense of belonging to a civil society near them. The discussion of basic needs seemed so far removed, so lofty, that those concerned have decided to take the matter in hand and assume responsibility for satisfying basic needs. Assuming responsibility means feeling that one is a citizen in the sense in which the Greeks and Romans understood it: feeling that one is part of a civil society, with civil rights and the right to participate in and to own what society builds.

This community-based approach to satisfying basic needs does not mean forgetting about the privileged sector of society, which owes a social debt to its fellow citizens, nor does taking this approach mean absolving the state of its social obligations. The community-based approach means creating for both privileged society and the state a way of taking action for the sake of rights. However, in a world gradually becoming dominated by the first and second sectors, it also appears to be the only choice. This is, indeed, a change in the dimensions of our problem. We can no longer speak of basic needs without taking into account the citizen, meaning a human being in action, with a definite purpose, surrounded by those who are geographically or culturally his or her fellows. This could be described as an advanced technology that is turning passive subjects into active subjects: the technology of citizen-making.

## Coordination technology: communication

The goals of sustainable human development imply establishing bonds of mutual cooperation and solidarity. Interdependence is becoming increasingly prevalent, making the exchange of information about S&T advances and other knowledge and experience imperative. Information is a right, and the need for communication can be satisfied by modern means that afford ever more powerful instruments at ever lower costs.

Information for basic education, preventive medicine, agricultural or climatic problems, and so many other purposes can be transmitted and received by radio, television, or computer. The contribution of information to international development can be extremely positive, provided that in transmitting or receiving this information we have a real respect for each others' cultures. The information highway should be used to supplement other forms of communication between people and between communities.

Communication is the best way of refining human knowledge, but in times of change, the most important thing is creativity, the ability to create new things on an ongoing basis, the capacity to do better tomorrow what was being done yesterday. A piece of information that was obtained today can be of use if it has been improved on, elaborated on, and supplemented. Communication is useful if it inspires innovation, does not make recipients passive or simply induce them to copy, stimulates recipients to learn how to learn and how to renew themselves every day, and induces recipients to transmit the information to others, to teach others. Under those conditions, two-way communication networks between countries and regions can have a major impact on international cooperation to combat extreme poverty.

## War technology: against famine

Hunger is the most severe manifestation of extreme poverty. Where hunger has been successfully attacked, this attack has usually been called a campaign or war against hunger. Humanity has had the technology to deal with acute crises, such as famine, since the time of Sun-Tzu, who referred to war as an art (see 1994 translation). The war against hunger is an art because survival is a necessary but not a sufficient condition for financial activity or activity aimed at creating an economic environment for combating hunger.

The managerial machinery used in dealing with war can also be applied as instruments of peace and justice, because emergencies cannot be remedied merely by exercises in mitigation. The techniques of war can be used to combat insensitivity, slowness, and other limitations, which implies that the combatants against hunger need to agree on the target groups. Today, we no longer have any doubt that the weaker social sectors are those with above-average infant mortality and below-average literacy rates, nutrition, basic sanitation, and access to productive infrastructure.

The battlefronts are where we find those vulnerable groups, because it is there, with the full participation of those groups, that concrete action can be framed and tangible results can be sought. That is also the logic that should govern efforts to ensure food security, which can be measured by the qualitative and quantitative access to nutrition needed for the healthy reproduction of the human organism. Chronic malnutrition afflicts 800 million people, more than one third of the people who live south of the Sahara and one fifth, on average, of the people in developing countries. According to the Food and Agriculture Organization of the United Nations (FAO 1993), the people in more than 60 countries have no prospect of satisfying their nutritional requirements, even by 2000. Optimistically, by 2010, we could expect to have "no more" than 650 million people affected. These figures are enough to justify a systematic effort on all fronts and at local, national, and international levels.

Agriculture is crucial to the dual strategy because agricultural technology comprises productive technologies, indispensable technologies, and survival technologies that are vital. The territorial, social, and functional blendings will depend greatly on whether participatory efforts are made and whether OCSs can tip the balance against poverty. Everyone would benefit if markets stopped raising barriers against agricultural products from developing countries.

**Life technology: health**

Life is foremost among human rights, and technology has already accomplished a great deal to protect this right, although even more remains to be done. Health is directly correlated with economic, social, and spiritual development because health is determined by people's surroundings while contributing to their development. This, too, implies a holistic vision of the operational aspects of development. Functionally, some health measures will be preventive, whereas others will be corrective and therapeutic. The vital thing for the poor, especially in rural and suburban areas, is to satisfy their needs for primary care, which includes the issues of basic infrastructure and monitoring mechanisms. The problem is in implementing systems of primary health care that are practical, scientific, socially acceptable, based in the community, and adequate for people's requirements.

As part of the dual strategy, health measures should include traditional knowledge compatible with health and foster research aimed at including appropriate technologies in the health infrastructure. To include appropriate technologies is to adapt technologies to local needs and provide for local maintenance of these technologies. For transmitted diseases, I must draw attention to advances in vaccination and chemical treatment. However, virtually all countries find it difficult to provide medical and related services, such as water supply, as a result of a lack of materials, personnel, or organization. Accordingly, some of the challenges in health are to establish the machinery to coordinate efforts in the health and related sectors, obtain financial and administrative solutions, educate for health, promote rural extension services, foster nutritional and environmental hygiene, offer family-planning services, provide health care for girls, adapt techniques and procedures, train people, and start maternal and public information programs. In general, health requires technologies of knowledge in action. In this field, it is especially clear that the important thing is not the hardware.

The field of health is a very clear point of departure for a new systemic approach to using S&T for development. In most cases the knowledge is available, the products exist, the many dimensions of the problems are known, yet the problems persist. Everyone knows that one person's health problem is everyone's health problem. This is an area in which the interrelationship of people's lives is clearly evident because health for one is health for all. Improvements in general health have perceptible and quantifiable results, and the benefits are clear, especially for children, women, and other vulnerable groups.

**Technological technology: education**

The human being is more important than any technology. Technology counts by virtue of the ways it expands or narrows life and its potential. Technology counts by virtue of the changes it helps to bring about in both the creators and the users of technology. However, all technologies are replaceable, whereas life and the miracle of transmissible memory are irreplaceable.

It was not the steam-engine that ushered in the industrial era, and it was not the computer that ended it. Behind the steam-engine and the computer were human beings with creativity and admirable intentions, who charted a course that others followed. The challenge in using technology for development is not technology itself, but the use we make of it. Instruments have become ever faster and programs ever more complete, but human knowledge is ever more important. Technology has strikingly enhanced the value of the human person, and with information having become decentralized, it has opened up unimagined horizons.

Postman's (1993) "technopoly" is still the prevalent ideology in many places, and the vaccination against this, the key to a universe of possibilities, is education. Education is the most basic of rights and the most technical of technologies: that of learning, of learning to learn, and of learning to teach. This is the technology that creates options and satisfies the most basic of basic needs, the need to feel equal to others, and this is the technology that builds, separates, or unites cultural centres and makes us into actors in our own story.

In practical terms, the Framework for Action to Satisfy Basic Needs for Learning and the UN Declaration on Education for All, of Jomtien, Thailand, in 1990, cannot be improved on. Here are the guidelines and tools, the broad vision, and the themes of means, conditions, curricula, programs, mobilization, and solidarity. This is the line to be followed. It only remains to add that education is a continuing endeavour, now more than ever, and that having chosen to work on the topic of technology for poverty, we are bound to follow education as one of the fronts in the dual strategy. However, a human being is not a duality but a unified whole, and human beings are not split by the fissures in the world that is home to us all.

# Conclusions and recommendations

Tools acquire validity only after they have been tested by the people who are going to use them. In the following sections, I present some recommendations for discussion, debate, and analysis.

## Science for sustainable human development

We must strive for the lost wholeness of science so that we can assemble the parts within the whole, which means a new encounter between humans, their complex environment, and life. This new encounter can only be found in a science that places the human being at the centre of the universe, using two basic principles, anthropocentrism and the ecosystem, as the two perspectives for promoting sustainable human development. The development of this new science must take place in the laboratory of life, relying on forms of communication other than the traditional reports and scientific papers. Simplicity may help us reach mass audiences; however, we want to avoid both oversimplified popularization of science and the isolation of science from ordinary people.

## A global technological facility

Technologies are made to serve human beings, so the more complex a technology is, the lower the level of satisfaction will be. To provide universal access to techniques essential for life, a set of rules should be established to ensure that products like vaccines can be incorporated into a "Technical Heritage of Mankind," subject to adequate compensation as defined by an appropriate authority to protect intellectual property rights. This may require the creation of a Global Technological Facility to address vital human claims without discouraging research.

## Maximum support, minimum intervention

The poor should take charge of their own options. The role of the external agent should only be to support and possibly to help channel some of their initiatives. A creative capacity would be promoted by letting the poor know about some of the available technologies, by providing financial options and access to new materials, and by helping target groups to form contacts with other communities or persons affected by similar problems. Technological options should be assumed by local men and women, and support from outside must be in the form of informing, rather than doing.

## The right to information

The most operational of basic needs at present is the right to information. If people have the right to profit from S&T developments, then people must also have the right to adequate and simple access to information, at least in the case of the vital or essential technologies. The establishment of easy to handle networks for personal and technical exchange of information at a very low cost would be of great service.

## Capacity development

Capacity depends on people and their organizations having sufficient awareness of their problems to choose the right options. Thus, although support should be from the top down, from the international to the local level, learning and teaching should be done with a bottom-up approach, enhancing the understanding of the methods people use and the ways people organize locally. Technology can be negotiated but should not be used paternalistically. Technology should bring people together, rather than separating them; respect traditions but avoid paralyzing nostalgia; minimize petty self-interest and build broad options; and be based on an effort of human solidarity to seek a sustainable course.

## Major groups

There is a virtually worldwide consensus about the roles of women, youth, and indigenous and local communities in directing sustainable human development. The high-priority endeavours and the main strategies for ensuring vital rights to education, health, and food should be determined by these main actors.

## The social responsibility of experts

At the present stage of global development and underdevelopment, scientists and technologists can no longer ignore the evidence that the effects of technology can be negative. Scientists are sometimes the victims and sometimes indirectly the authors of these negative effects. By isolating ourselves in the sciences and focusing more on the big bang than on population explosions, by delving into human psychology while disregarding humanity's natural environment, by probing the atomic nucleus but ignoring the social universe, scientists make it seem that science is too important to be left up to scientists. This is unacceptable. An important step would be to promote a new, universal code of professional conduct, including a global commitment to putting scientific knowledge at the service of human beings and their vital rights.

## A joint meeting on S&T and human rights

A proposal could be made to the Economic and Social Council that it agree to meet with the Commission on Science and Technology for Development and the Commission on Human Rights to discuss common issues, in particular those related to the building of a framework for sustainable human development. The tenor of such a meeting might be constructive, rather than normative or defensive.

## A new agenda for development

The strength of the paradigm of sustainable human development is in the direction it may give to an action plan for universalizing vital rights. If the potential created by new technologies is placed at the service of all men and women and this vector is added to the powerful synergy created by the idea of vital human rights, which could be the most influential idea of the century, then a new theory could emerge and new practices could be generated and these could contribute to the United Nations' new agenda for development.

## The universal recognition of vital rights

The spectre that haunts the modern world from the South to the North is dualization. Those who can and those who cannot must work together to build bridges between those who have and those who have not. The main step at the global level, in the domain of seminal ideas, is promoting the subjective awareness required for action. We need unity and consensus, that is to say, common objectives and methods. A new collective ethic may create a keener awareness that freedom demands justice, and that awareness could be based on the universal recognition of vital human rights as a necessary condition for change.

## A world social charter

Resources and agreements are both necessary conditions for ensuring vital human rights. The World Social Charter, suggested by UNDP, is part of a global strategy to create an environment favourable to change in the conditions of the poor. However, change has to originate at the local level in the organizations closest to the people, where the sense of citizenship is being rebuilt. If a new strategy for basic needs is to be successful, the most important technological change we can seek is a means of promoting participation in the strategy's implementation.

## Permanent education

Education should be at the centre of concern in developing technology for the future. Education should be a permanent activity, linked with knowledge in action. Continuing education will always be needed for professionals with human sensitivity.

The main challenge for the dual strategy will be to secure its acceptance. A human being is not a duality but is unique, and the gaps dividing people can, I hope, be closed by knowledge, because now the planet has become everybody's home.

# Technology and Basic Needs in Ethiopia

*Getaneh Yiemene*

The population of Ethiopia is an estimated 55.1 million, and the annual growth rate is estimated at around 3.2%. The overwhelming majority of the population (about 47 million, or 85.3%) live in the rural areas. With an estimated gross national product (GNP) of $120 per capita, the number of people believed to be living below the absolute poverty line is estimated at 28 million, or 50.8% of the population.

The main characteristic of the Ethiopian population is its youthfulness. People below the age of 15 account for 49.1% of the total population; those between 15 and 59 years old account for 46.1%; and those 60 years or older account for 4.8%. The dependency ratio is as high as 124%, which implies that every 100 persons of working age have to support themselves and another 124 dependents. The sectoral distribution of the labour force reflects the agrarian nature of the economy: agriculture and allied activities engage about 88.6% of the labour force; manufacturing, 1.6%; construction, 0.3%; wholesale, retail trade, and catering, 3.8%; transport, 0.4%; and public administration and social, cultural, recreational, personal, and household services, 5.3%.

In rural areas, 96.3% of the labour force are "own-account" workers and unpaid family workers. In urban areas, the self-employed constitute a significant share of the labour force (40.8%), and the public- and private-sector employees account for 32.8 and 18.6%, respectively.

---

[1] The statistics presented in this chapter have been extracted from documents of the Government of Ethiopia, many of which are unpublished.

The health status of the Ethiopian people is extremely low. Life expectancy at birth is only 53.8 years. Health coverage is less than 46%. Statistical reports from different health institutions reveal that communicable diseases and malnutrition account for the highest proportions of morbidity and mortality. Communicable diseases now constitute 60–80% of all diseases in the country. The majority of the Ethiopian population have no access to modern health services and depend on traditional remedies and medical practices.

In the past two decades, Ethiopia has experienced serious economic difficulties. As a consequence, human deprivation and poverty are widespread. More than 50% of the population, as already remarked, live below the poverty line. Available data on health and nutrition show that only 46% of the population have access to health facilities; only 21%, to safe drinking water and proper sanitation facilities. Daily caloric intake is only 67% of requirements, compared with 90% for the rest of Africa and 132% for the industrialized world.

At present, the educational infrastructure is far from desirable. Because of its limitations and uneven regional distribution, the overall levels of participation are about 15% for pre-primary education, 22% for primary education, and 20% for secondary education. The overall level of participation in primary education (22%) is one of the lowest in Africa, and it has fallen sharply in recent years as a result of crisis, civil war, and rapid population growth.

The pace of social and economic development in Ethiopia has been slow because of severe structural weakness, poor economic performance, and inappropriate policies. In the field of science and technology (S&T), scientists, engineers, technicians, and skilled workers are in short supply.

To discuss technology to address basic needs is to discuss national development. Ethiopia has very limited resources at her disposal to allocate to the building up of a national S&T capability, although extensive and sustained development of S&T capability is required to bring about massive social and technical changes, to rapidly achieve increases in agricultural and industrial productivity, to rationally conserve and use natural resources to provide for basic human necessities (for example, food, clothing, shelter, education, and energy), to modernize communication networks — in general, to improve the standard of living of the people. Such long-term undertakings, with limited resources, can only succeed if guided by a coherent S&T policy.

In the past, in the absence of an S&T policy and a strategy document for S&T development, S&T activities were undertaken without any systematic planning at the national or sectoral level. Hence, the country has not built the research capacity to solve the fundamental development problems. In view of this, the Transitional Government of Ethiopia issued an S&T policy in December 1993 to address the basic needs of low-income people in Ethiopia. The S&T policy was based on the *Charter and New Economic Policy of the Transitional Government of Ethiopia.*

The aim of this paper is to broadly assess the S&T situation in the high-priority sectors. The paper identifies major obstacles to building S&T capabilities. The priority sectors and programs are also indicated. These priority programs have far-reaching implications for the satisfaction of the basic needs of the low-income people and for the long-term development of the country.

## Assessment of the current S&T situation

In this section, some aspects of the S&T situation are assessed under specific sectoral headings, and the major problems are identified to provide a clear definition for programs of action in high-priority areas.

### Agriculture

The area of Ethiopia is $122 \times 10^6$ ha, of which an estimated $82 \times 10^6$ ha is potentially arable. Various sources indicate that of the total area, about $18.5 \times 10^6$ ha is under annual or perennial crops.

In general, the productivity of land, labour, crops, and livestock is very low, even by the standards of many developing countries. For example, the major crops, maize and wheat, yield an average of 1.8 and 1.2 t/ha, respectively, whereas the world average yields for maize and wheat are more than 5 and 2.5 t/ha. Some research results indicate that crop and livestock yields can be increased through improved materials and better management practices. If the country is to attain self-sufficiency in agricultural production, it has to improve its agricultural practices and provide farmers with incentives to use their existing resources to the fullest extent for maximum production. This is where greater S&T capability would play a decisive role in the growth and development of the agricultural sector.

Agricultural research is a recent phenomenon in Ethiopia. The principal agricultural research institution, the Institute of Agricultural Research, conducts and coordinates agricultural research activities at the national level. It also conducts research programs, in 12 research areas, through its 22 centres in different agroecological zones of the country. The other bodies involved in agricultural research and development (R&D) are the Alemaya University of Agriculture and three colleges (Ambo, Jimma, Awasa), whose primary function is training professionals and technical and field assistants. These institutions conduct research on livestock, poultry, crop production and protection, and soil science and socioeconomics, although their research results have not had any consistently significant impact.

Other major R&D institutes (RDIs) include the National Veterinary Research Institute; the Rural Technology Centre, under the Ministry of Agriculture; and the various organs of the Ministry of State Farms, Coffee and Tea Development. Although the R&D infrastructure appears solid and research efforts are being made in many spheres, agricultural production is still faced with many problems. In particular, although the peasant is the main contributor to agricultural production, the socioeconomic and technological setup has not been transformed. The peasants and their production systems have not been studied well enough to identify the real bottlenecks and determine possible solutions for improvement.

## Environmental protection and rehabilitation

Human activities are changing the environment of Ethiopia in many ways, too often to its detriment and the detriment of the people. The country is also experiencing recurrent droughts. The cause of the devastating famine and drought is the deterioration of the environment that has resulted from massive ecological disruption and the unabated growth of the population. The accelerated population growth and its uneven distribution in the country have placed considerable pressure on natural resources, such as the soil, water, plants, animals, grasslands, and forests.

Soil productivity can be lowered by a number of factors, such as salinization, alkalinization, soil erosion, and chemical degradation. The area of salt-affected soils in Ethiopia is estimated at $11 \times 10^6$ ha, of which $10.3 \times 10^6$ ha is in the saline phase and 425 000 ha is in the alkaline phase. At present, it is estimated that more than 82% of the country is affected by soil erosion to varying degrees, which causes a loss of about 200 t of top soil/km$^2$, or $1.5 \times 10^9$ m$^3$, from the whole country every year. According to the Ethiopian Highlands Reclamation Study, 50% of the highlands ($27 \times 10^6$ ha) is seriously eroded and more than $2 \times 10^6$ ha of farm land has reached a stage of irreversible destruction, unable to sustain cropping in the future.

Lack of efficient sewage-disposal and sewage-treatment systems in areas of concentrated settlement has resulted in the deterioration of environmental quality. An environmental impact assessment, to study the ecological relationships among agriculture (irrigation), urbanization, human settlement, industrialization, modern technology, and mining, should be undertaken before any development programs are launched. Human resources and appropriate S&T services are not well enough developed in Ethiopia to meet the requirements for environmental protection and development.

## Water

The limited available data indicate that Ethiopia possesses rich water resources, with an estimated annual surface runoff of $104 \times 10^9$ $m^3$ in 10 of its 14 major catchment areas. But Ethiopia has not made much use of its water potential. Adequate clean water is available to only 19% of the population. The potentially irrigable area in the country is estimated at $3 \times 10^6$ ha. Of this potential, 150 000 ha, or only 5%, has been put to use. It is clear that more irrigation is essential to Ethiopia's agricultural development. Hydropower exploitation stands at less than 2% of its potential. Conservative estimates place the potential sustainable yield of inland fish resources at 30 000 t/year. However, the contribution of fisheries to national income and food supply is a negligible fraction of this potential.

The involvement of S&T in the development, conservation, and management of water resources is a recent phenomenon in Ethiopia and is at a low level. Some R&D activities have been initiated to control salinity in irrigated lands; to classify the climate; to determine rainfall variability; and to develop appropriate technologies for defluoridation and desalination. Adaptive research on the effective use of subsurface dams is also in progress. Other R&D activities include work on low-cost water-lifting devices and shallow- and deep-well hand pumps. There is also a wind-power project for borehole pumping and low-lift irrigation.

The impact of these R&D activities is far from significant. However, the recently established Arba Minch Water Technology Institute is expected to supply intermediate- and high-level training in water technology and strengthen and promote R&D activities in the field.

## Energy

Ethiopia's energy resources are said to be plentiful, but the level of exploitation is very low. Of the total nonmuscular energy used in the household and in production and services, 94.1% is drawn from traditional biomass fuels, such as firewood, charcoal, crop residues, and cow dung. Of this nonmuscular energy, 93% is used in the household, mainly for food preparation, and only 7% is used in modern transportation, industry, agriculture, and services. However, the use of fuel in the household, in most parts of Ethiopia, continues to be extremely wasteful. The nation's traditional biomass resources are quickly depleting. The country once had up to 16% forest coverage, but now this is estimated to be only 2.7%.

Of the nontraditional energy resources, petroleum products account for 85% of consumption, and hydroelectricity represents only 15%. Imported oil accounts for 5.3% of the total energy supply, whereas hydroelectricity accounts for only 0.6%. The gross hydroelectricity potential of Ethiopia is estimated at 650 TW·h/year, of which 70–120 TW·h is economically exploitable. The current rate of generation of hydroelectricity is only 1.28 TW·h/year, which is less than 0.2% of the potential rate. Recent explorations indicate that Ethiopia is endowed with considerable geothermal energy, with about 700 MW in the lake district, Afar region, and Danakil Depression. But the present level of exploitation is nil.

Another source of energy, which is gaining importance in the world, is the sun. Ethiopia is well endowed with solar energy. Recent attempts to estimate this energy resource indicate that for Ethiopia as a whole the average daily radiation reaching the ground is about 5.2 kW·h/m², or $6.34 \times 10^6$ kW·h/day, the equivalent of $193 \times 10^9$ t of oil/day. In addition, total wind energy is estimated at an equivalent of $474 \times 10^6$ t of oil/day. Neither of these energy resources is presently being tapped for use.

Coal resources appear to be quite widespread in Ethiopia. However, the coal is low-quality lignite that occurs in thin layers under fairly deep overburden, which discourages large-scale mining and local development. The potential coal energy identified so far is estimated at 304 TJ ($72.6 \times 10^{12}$ cal). Other potential energy resources include $20 \times 10^6$ t of oil shale and traces of radioactive minerals, but no attempt has been made to exploit these.

Although the importance of developing energy resources is recognized, the critical shortage of energy and the low level of exploitation in an environment of abundance are a contradiction. The use of S&T is a top priority in the exploitation of available energy resources, reduction of energy waste, and substitution of nontraditional energy resources for traditional energy resources, whose excess use is resulting in catastrophic environmental damage.

Organizations engaged in energy R&D include the Ethiopian Energy Authority, the Ethiopian Electric Light and Power Authority, Addis Ababa University, the Ministry of Education, a number of nongovernmental organizations, and the Ethiopian Geothermal Survey. The absence of clear policy and strategy, a weak institutional capacity, and a lack of coordinated effort in the application of S&T are manifest in the energy sector.

## Industry

Ethiopia's industrial sector is backward in its sectoral structure, employment, and technological content. The current contribution of the sector to the GNP is about 12%, about one third of which comes from handicrafts and small-scale industries. Although it is hard to obtain reliable statistical information, some estimates indicate that the sector as a whole employs no more than 3% of the total labour force, and nearly half of this is in handicrafts and small-scale industries.

A survey of 112 manufacturing enterprises in 1987 revealed that 78% of these enterprises had been in operation for 19–74 years and were obsolete. The magnitude of dependence on imported machinery and spare parts is high in the metal and chemical industries, exceeding, according to some estimates, 95%. By the same token, the imported industrial inputs for the metal and chemical industries are about 95 and 80%, respectively.

Basic industries, such as design, fabrication, and metallurgy, which are crucial for the development of the industrial sector, are hardly existent. For example, the value of metallic products and electrical manufacturing is about 5% of that of total industrial output. The metal and engineering firms, such as the Akaki Spare Parts and Hand Tools Factory, Truck and Bus Assembly, Kotebe Hand Tools Factory, Kaliti Steel Works, and Ethiopian Iron and Steel Industries, are important institutions but have low capacities for adapting, developing, and producing the technologies required by the economy. There are some industrial activities in the areas of sugar, textiles, leather, and flour and oil mills, but when you consider the country's potential, it seems that the agro-industry is still in its infancy.

Organized research within the industry system is just being considered. There have been initiatives to establish and develop a food-technology research centre, a chemical R&D centre, and textile and sugar research institutes. However, there is a lack of relevant human and material resources, effective management, clear purpose and direction, and an integrated S&T system at the sectoral level. This situation is due to the absence of an S&T policy and strategic master plan and effective coordinating and promoting mechanisms.

## Construction

Construction is second to agriculture in generating employment in Ethiopia. Capacities in construction, as well as in manufacturing of construction materials, are in a better setting than in other sectors. This is because fairly reasonable institutional and infrastructural bases exist for design and construction in both the public and private sectors. The sector can also be said to have better developed skilled labour.

At present, R&D in the construction sector is conducted mainly in the production of wall and roofing materials. R&D on domestic raw materials to reduce the sector's dependence on imported materials is far from what it should be. R&D has been conducted by various institutions, departments, and units in a scattered and uncoordinated manner. Little progress has been made in generating efficient and effective indigenous technologies to fit the available material and human resources, especially in low-cost housing construction. The sector has no centrally organized institution to support and carry out R&D.

## Transport and communication

The transport and communication sector in Ethiopia embraces four subsectors: inland transport, which includes road and rail transport; marine transport; air transport; and communication, which consists of telephone, telegram, and postal services. In the subsectors the leading role in Ethiopia is played by road transport, which accounts for 93% of freight and passenger transport. Road transport is widely used but is possible in only a limited portion of the country. Currently, every 1 000 km² of land area has about 12.3 km of roads.

All the machinery and equipment and almost all the spare parts used in this sector are imported. There are few local industries and workshops engaged in bus and truck assembly, sheet-metal body work, parts rectification, or general maintenance.

The promotion of R&D, design, and technology-acquisition capabilities is virtually nonexistent, in institutional form or otherwise, although these are needed to solve the technological problems of the sector. Only the Ethiopian Air Lines and Ethiopian Telecommunication Authority have clearly set criteria for acquiring new equipment and developing human resources to operate and maintain new technologies. The sector's problems that could be solved by indigenous R&D will continue unless RDIs are set up and people are trained.

## Mineral resources

The mineral wealth of Ethiopia has not been extensively assessed. Most of the technologies used in the mining sector for mineral exploration and development are imported. This has led to the accumulation of a variety of technologies that cannot be effectively used because of a lack of spare parts and maintenance capability.

Although some encouraging steps have been taken to identify the mineral resources, gather data, and train human resources, the achievements are far from adequate. Little work has been done to make economic use of Ethiopia's easily traceable and accessible mineral wealth. It needs a well-conceived policy and strategy to guide the use of modern S&T in the economic exploitation, beneficiation, and use of mineral resources.

The Ethiopian Mineral Resources Development Corporation (EMRDC) was established in 1982 to develop the country's commercially important precious and industrial minerals. EMRDC has changed the trend in Ethiopia of producing only gold and platinum. Now some steps have been taken to commercially exploit tantalum, soda ash, ceramic clays, and other industrial minerals. Some R&D is taking place in one of EMRDC's enterprises. Although these efforts are in the right direction, they require proper institutional arrangements and a legal framework with adequate resource allocations.

## Health

The major health problems in Ethiopia are communicable diseases and disorders arising from nutritional deficiency. The prevalence of intestinal parasites and infections reflects poor sanitary facilities and a lack of education.

For a while, health services in Ethiopia were focused on three major urban areas. Lately, as a result of a deliberate policy to give priority to rural health, the focus has been on the prevention and control of mortality and morbidity, and the government has promoted primary health care. Despite the priority given to rural health services and primary health care, the distribution of modern health services remains extremely sparse and still favours the urban areas.

The sparse coverage of health services can be illustrated by the population–bed ratio, which stands at about 4 300 : 1, and by the population–doctor ratio, which stands at about 31 000 : 1. These are among the worst ratios in the world. Institutions that undertake health research include the Ethiopian Nutrition Institute (ENI), the Institute of Pathobiology, the National Research Institute of Health, the Armans Hausen Research Institute, the Ethio-Swedish Pediatric Clinic, the Gondar Faculty of Medicine, the Coordinating Office for Traditional Medicine, and the Jimma Health Sciences Institute. Judging from published works, one has to conclude that the bulk of health research has come out of ENI, the Ethio-Swedish Pediatric Clinic, and the Gondar Faculty of Medicine. Research has concentrated on nutritional disorders, communicable diseases, and maternal and child-care health issues. Most of the studies have been carried out in two hospitals, rather than in the community, and deal mostly with biomedical research, rather than public-health research.

S&T is especially important in the development of health services. The world is fast advancing in the use of S&T for both the diagnosis and the treatment of health problems. Disease prevalence is not universal but depends very much on socioeconomic and ecological variations, so research is needed on treating area-specific diseases. As well, adapted technologies in the field of microelectronics, microbiology, and radiology are essential for an effective health service. Local capability in both the investigation and the treatment of disease are vital to overall social development. Little research has been done on using modern S&T to improve and develop traditional medicine. Ethiopia is known for its fauna and flora, which are the basic inputs to traditional or modern medicine. Ethiopia has made no use of this wealth.

As a result of a lack of conscious effort to make use of S&T in health services, even the few R&D activities undertaken are uncoordinated. No coordination exists among the institutions that do health research, which leads to duplication of effort. The R&D capacities of the health-services sector are weak and need to be expanded and strengthened to promote sustained health services and to keep up with emerging technologies. To accomplish these objectives, the sector requires a clearly defined policy and strategy and needs to strengthen its policy-formulation and planning capacities.

## Education

A sound education for creative S&T is a foundation that has to be laid early. At the early stages, education to cultivate an interest in the study of nature or experimental work is of paramount importance. Furthermore, educational infrastructure is the basic springboard for S&T activities in general and R&D in particular.

The educational infrastructure in Ethiopia is far from desirable. Its limitations and uneven regional distribution result in low levels of absorption of school-age children into the educational system. The quality of primary and secondary education has been unsatisfactory, as a result of several factors, among which are ineffectual teachers and unfavourable student–teacher ratios.

The same is true of technical and vocational education and training. The country has more than 18 technical and vocational schools and institutes. Fourteen of these are administered by the Ministry of Education and provide broad training in agriculture, construction, home economics, commerce, and industrial technology. The other four schools are under the control of missionaries and provide training with curricula similar to those administered by the Ministry of Education. There are some specialized institutions, controlled by agencies. Also offered are on-the-job training, apprenticeships, and short-term in-house and external training by the many public and private production and service enterprises. However, this training is dispersed and uncoordinated and emphasizes the short-term requirements of their respective enterprises, rather than the overall systematic building of technological capability.

The universities suffer heavily from inadequately equipped and furnished laboratories and a lack of workshop equipment and teaching materials. A conducive environment for learning and effective R&D hardly exists. About 14 specialized research institutes, inside or outside the higher education system, undertake R&D. Like the higher education system itself, these research institutes lack adequately trained staff and research materials. It has been established that within these 14 institutes, only 6% of the staff have doctorates.

The educational system neither lays the required foundation nor provides the right type of trained personnel for R&D. Because R&D is not coordinated with production and development programs, little use is made of R&D results. To date, with only a few exceptions, research results end up merely as reports or as published articles in periodicals and journals. Because of the lack of research coordination and the absence of a clearing mechanism for research activities, duplication of research is common.

## Assessments of problems and needs

The major problems in S&T development in Ethiopia are the following:

▼ Absence of well-elaborated and detailed S&T policies and strategies, at national and sectoral levels, to build national S&T capability;

▼ Lack of a well-defined plan based on identified priorities and integrated with the national economic planning process;

▼ Little consideration given to S&T activities to promote, develop, use, and conserve natural resources rationally and effectively for sustainable development;

▼ Undue reliance on foreign sources of technology, instead of conscious use and promotion of indigenous technology;

▼ Low priority given to R&D activities and absence or underdevelopment of S&T terms and concepts in different languages;

▼ Low productivity of traditional technologies and inadequate attention given to their improvement and development;

▼ Nonexistence of a strategy to build managerial and administrative capability in S&T;

▼ Absence of conscious effort to increase the participation of women in S&T activities;

▼ Low priority given to S&T activities to address women's needs;

▼ Poor-quality S&T education at the primary, secondary, and tertiary levels and inadequate availability of vocational training institutes in various technical fields (in general, the educational system fails to inculcate curiosity about research and a sense of the priority of inquiry);

▼ Inadequate university programs and facilities for postgraduate research;

▼ Absence of conditions conducive to technological culture in society and absence of rewards or an effective incentive system to enhance S&T activities;

▼ Insufficient S&T human resources at all levels of activity and underuse of the existing S&T human resources;

▼ Lack of strong professional associations, along with limited financial resources from nongovernmental scientific societies and learned bodies, resulting in an inability to create science awareness in the nation or involve the people in the development of technology;

▼ Lack of effective S&T institutions at the grass-roots level (for example, field experimental stations and production and service centres) for creating site-specific technologies;

▼ Inadequate research facilities for undertaking S&T activities in the critical new and emerging technologies;

▼ Inadequate support services for R&D or for development, dissemination, acquisition, or application of technologies (ESTC 1993);

▼ Lack of capability in identifying, transferring, and adapting technologies appropriate to the country's needs;

▼ Weak engineering and consultancy capabilities;

▼ Lack of a well-coordinated and strong S&T information system;

▼ Lack of effective S&T popularization programs, resulting in inadequate promotion of S&T in the society;

▼ Lack of appreciation in various production and service sectors of the importance of building S&T capabilities; and

▼ Lack of effective coordination among scientific establishments, leading to the fragmentation of national research efforts.

The degree of deficiency in S&T capability varies from one sector to another and may vary among subsectors. Where serious inadequacy or complete lack of capability can be perceived, it is imperative to formulate strategies, measures, and programs to build and bring specific elements of S&T capability to the required levels rapidly and then harness these elements for sustainable development.

# Priority sectors and programs

Although the Ethiopian government wants to promote balanced and integrated development, the S&T capability necessary in all sectors is difficult to develop because of the limited financial resources. Hence, because of the country's need to alleviate the basic and urgent problems of the people, the national S&T policy identifies programs to be undertaken in priority sectors: agriculture and fishing; natural resources and environmental protection; water resources; energy; industry; construction; transport and communication; mineral resources; health and population planning; education; and new and emerging technologies. To encourage and promote S&T activities in the priority sectors, the transitional Government of Ethiopia is committed to allocating up to 1.5% of the gross domestic product annually to meet the following objectives:

## Agriculture and fishing

1. Support activities that lead to food self-sufficiency:

▼ Support and encourage research to raise the productivity of food crops and animal resources and improve the means of production in kind, quantity, and quality by making it compatible with environmental protection and with the culture and traditions of Ethiopian society.

▼ Encourage the use of irrigation schemes of different scales and forms to secure reliable production.

▼ Encourage and support research on methods using appropriate technologies to reduce pre- and postharvest loss during agricultural production.

▼ Support and encourage techniques for developing appropriate and productive fish species in rivers, lakes, and ponds and promote fish in the diet in Ethiopia.

▼ Diffuse large-scale storage and preservation technology for food products in every locality.

2. Promote and support S&T activities to help produce agricultural products in adequate quantity and desired quality for use in the industrial sector.

3. Develop and support S&T techniques for raising the quantity, quality, and diversity of agricultural products for export.

4. Study and upgrade traditional technologies and methods handed down for centuries and support and strengthen strategies for disseminating appropriate technologies for integrated rural development.

## Natural resources and environmental protection

1. Encourage studies and research to map out proper land use. Survey the country's ecological systems, identify the biological resources, and create a system to collect, register, store, apply, and preserve plant and animal genetic resources.

2. Support research on appropriate land-use and soil-conservation techniques.

3. Encourage the use of mechanisms to control deforestation and other ecological imbalances, to protect the forests.

4. Establish R&D programs to discover, develop, and popularize species of fast-growing, drought-resistant, multipurpose trees to rehabilitate degraded environments.

5. Conduct research on controlling atmospheric, soil, and water pollution caused by chemicals used in agriculture and industry.

6. Set up educational methods and programs in the communal way of life to increase people's awareness and knowledge of and participation in environmental protection and rehabilitation.

7. Strengthen techniques for tracking changes in the environment and for predicting, averting, and minimizing natural disasters.

## Water resources

1. Support research to improve the quantity, quality, and conservation of groundwater and surface water.

2. Develop a system to integrate the use and reuse of water for agriculture, energy, transportation, and private consumption.

3. Encourage the discovery of ways of supplying urban and rural people with reliable, potable water.

4. Raise public awareness of sedimentation control, watershed management, and rain-water use.

## Energy

1. Promote the use of diverse and integrated energy resources to attain a sustainable and reliable energy supply:

   ▼ Support research to discover, develop, and popularize fast-growing tree species and strengthen the development of biomass energy.

   ▼ Lay the groundwork for the application and expansion of water resources as a source of energy.

   ▼ Encourage research that will increase the exploitation and use of fuel oil, natural gas, coal, and geothermal energy.

   ▼ Support techniques for finding and exploiting alternative and renewable energy sources.

2. Support and encourage efficient and economic use of energy in all sectors.

3. Support R&D on devices for energy generation and use.

4. Encourage the development, popularization, and dissemination of appropriate energy technologies in the rural population.

## Industry

1. Encourage efforts to build and strengthen the capacity for producing essential inputs for the agricultural sector.

2. Support measures and activities that help with the production of basic consumer goods, implements, and equipment.

3. Encourage R&D on the manufacture of production equipment to help expand small-scale and rural industries.

4. Encourage the use of methods to enable the local production of industrial raw materials and other inputs.

5. Support research to modernize traditional and handicraft technologies and make them more productive.

6. Foster the use of technology to help prevent environmental pollution caused by industrial activities and by-products. Promote the use of recycled by-products.

7. Encourage and facilitate capacity-building in basic design and manufacturing, project engineering, and technology transfer.

## Construction

1. Create enabling conditions to support the production and use of appropriate construction materials and equipment. Popularize appropriate construction technologies that do not aggravate deforestation.

2. Develop the necessary construction, design, management, implementation, and follow-up capacity in priority economic sectors, particularly in the development of waterworks (dams and irrigation systems), transport and communication (roads, ports, airports, etc.), and industry.

3. Support research on technologies that speed up overall construction and development and widely employ human labour.

4. Support efforts to improve and disseminate traditional construction technologies.

## Transport and communication

1. Support capacity-building in the selection, application, and repair of modern and alternative transportation.

2. Encourage research to produce appropriate technology for public and freight transport and establish capacity-building programs for repair and maintenance in the rural areas.

3. Encourage and support research on simple telecommunications instruments that can be produced and used to expand, develop, and disseminate modern communication services in various parts of the country.

## Mineral resources

1. Assist in expanding appropriate techniques and modern technologies to help identify the mineral resources of the country.

2. Support the development and dissemination of simple techniques to promote strategies for mineral exploration, study, and application, particularly methods that ensure the participation of people in rural society.

3. Support the building of the capacity to study, explore, and develop crude oil, natural gas, coal, iron, and industrial minerals.

4. Strengthen S&T in hydrology and seismology.

## Health and population planning

1. Support R&D on methods to prevent and control communicable and parasitic diseases.

2. Promote maternal and child health care, youth-improvement programs, and family-planning programs.

3. Support and encourage studies and research on the causes of, and solutions to, health problems in both rural and urban populations.

4. Strengthen and promote methods for ensuring adequate food supply and better nutrition systems.

5. Support and encourage research on sanitation, traditional medicines and methods in health care, and beliefs and attitudes about health.

6. Support studies and research on environmental pollution and health problems arising from activities in industry, agriculture, transport, and other sectors.

7. Strengthen research on potable-water supply and environmental sanitation.

8. Assist in studies and research on the prevention of new disease outbreaks.

9. Support and encourage research on health-services systems.

10. Support research on population planning.

## Education

1. Identify ways to strengthen S&T education at all levels.

2. Support the domestic production and maintenance of instruments and materials for S&T education.

3. Encourage the application of the available research results from Ethiopian universities and colleges.

4. Encourage basic research and support the development of professional human resources for basic research.

5. Explore ways of making education relevant and complementary to people's daily activities.

## New and emerging technologies

1. Assist in strengthening the use of biotechnology in agriculture, health care, and industry.

2. Organize and support the development of centres, facilities, human resources, journals, and workshops that promote, coordinate, and strengthen the application of biotechnology.

3. Support institution building and training to strengthen and enrich knowledge and develop the application of microelectronics, especially computers.

4. Assist in increasing the awareness, knowledge, and application of new and emerging technologies in the transport and communication sector, especially telecommunications devices and new materials.

# Part III

# UN Contributions

Chapter 9[1]

# United Nations System and Selected Organizations: Activities Involving Technologies for Basic Needs

*United Nations Conference on Trade and Development*

The Commission on Science and Technology for Development (CSTD), at its first session, held in New York in 1993, chose the "use of technology for small-scale economic activities to address the basic needs of low-income populations" as a theme for its intersessional work. In accordance with Economic and Social Council (ECOSOC) decision 1993/320, CSTD established the Panel on Technology for Basic Needs (PTBN) to conduct an in-depth study of this theme and to prepare a report on it for consideration at CSTD's second session, in 1995. ECOSOC resolution 1993/74 indicated that the work of PTBN should build on relevant studies from inside and outside the United Nations system, including the regional commissions, the United Nations Conference on Trade and Development (UNCTAD), the United Nations Industrial Development Organization (UNIDO), the International Labour Organization (ILO), the Food and Agriculture Organization of the United Nations (FAO), the World Bank, and the regional development banks. Additionally, at its first meeting in June 1994, PTBN asked the UNCTAD Secretariat to review the work of the United Nations system and selected organizations dealing with technologies for basic needs.

---

[1] This chapter represents an edited version of document UNCTAD/DST/Misc. 14, entitled "Review of the Work of the United Nations System Selected Organizations Dealing with Technologies for Basic Needs." Chapters 10–13 represent edited versions of substantive papers submitted to the Panel on Small-scale Economic Activities to Address the Basic Needs of Low-income Populations.

In response to that request, the UNCTAD Secretariat undertook the present review. A sample of 68 organizations, including organizations within the United Nations system, intergovernmental and non-governmental organizations (NGOs), and national organizations in developed countries providing development assistance, were invited by UNCTAD to provide information on their activities in connection with technology for basic needs. In recognition of the fact that basic needs is a dynamic concept, the analysis of which calls for an interdisciplinary, integrated approach, the organizations were asked to give special attention to the three issues with which PTBN is particularly concerned: food production and processing, education — especially technical and vocational training — and health care.

## Overview

This section presents an overview of the respondents' activities addressing the three main issues of particular concern to PTBN. The sample of responses received from 36 organizations indicates that a considerable amount of work is being carried out on the issue of basic needs, but these inputs often provide an obscure picture of the role played by technology for basic-needs satisfaction in these organizations' endeavours. In general, the information on basic-needs-related programs is extensive, and the activities take a variety of forms, including small-scale activities. The role of technology, its application and diffusion, and policy-related aspects of technology in the satisfaction of basic needs are less evident in some of the material. Technology does not always emerge as a dynamic factor, one that is fundamental in the provision of goods and services, is essential for upgrading production systems and processes, and embodies a developmental dimension.

### Food production and processing

Work in food production and processing appears to be led by organizations such as FAO, the Consultative Group on International Agricultural Research (CGIAR), and the International Fund for Agricultural Development (IFAD). An important role is also played by UNIDO and the regional commissions, such as the Economic and Social Commission for Asia and the Pacific (ESCAP). Food production and processing are a priority in the work of most of the responding organizations. Technology is an essential factor in food production and processing and is certainly critical for meeting the basic needs of low-income populations in developing countries.

Activities in food production and processing cover the major elements, such as procurement of raw materials, major technical improvements of production and processing, and distribution- and trade-related aspects, although the latter appear to receive less emphasis. All these major elements would allow one to develop an integrated approach to food production and processing, with alternatives for diverse stages of technological development and for specific basic needs, including consumer-oriented priorities.

The information provided by the organizations has a broad scope and is not limited to the traditional emphases on, for example, developing hybrid crop varieties or efficient and appropriate machinery. This broad scope is seen in FAO work in research and technology development, which aims to increase and intensify food production, improve consumption and nutrition, add to the market value of agricultural produce, improve income-earning capacity, and create opportunities for employment in the production, processing, and marketing of agricultural goods. The organizations emphasize postharvest technologies in developing countries, using loss assessment as a tool in the rural handling and storage of farm inputs and outputs. IFAD noted that technologies to increase production and productivity have little success in the absence of proper postharvest and processing technologies near the farm. However, all organizations stressed the importance of the development of skills to accomplish diverse tasks in food production and processing. The human-resource development programs vary extensively, and FAO stressed the need to carry out systematic and continued training in techniques, as well as technological upgrading.

Many organizations give priority to work in biotechnology, which is seen as having great potential for improving productivity in food production. Various activities occur in this domain. Apart from the development of improved crop varieties undertaken by CGIAR, FAO, and IFAD, other examples of biotechnology are the use of integrated pest-management systems to reduce dependence on chemical pesticides in crop farming and the use of deoxyribonucleic acid (DNA) fingerprinting techniques to control livestock diseases.

The overall strategy of the main organizations dealing with food- and agriculture-related issues is to focus on the sustainable management of natural resources. CGIAR noted that increased demands on the resource base mean that future increases in agricultural production and rural livelihood will require a multifaceted approach to natural-resource management and a policy environment designed to maximize the benefits of new technologies. IFAD's programs, therefore, incorporate socioeconomic elements to facilitate the dissemination of technologies and enhance their impact on smallholder farming systems.

## Education (especially technical and vocational training)

The United Nations Educational, Scientific and Cultural Organization (UNESCO) plays a prominent role in education. The World Conference on Education for All, organized by UNESCO in 1991, launched the process of reviewing the concept of basic learning needs so that it would include the promotion of literacy, numeracy, and life skills, with particular attention on the basic skills related to health, family welfare, civic responsibilities, and vocational training. Project 2000+, undertaken by UNESCO in cooperation with the United Nations Children's Fund (UNICEF), the United Nations Development Programme (UNDP), the World Bank, the International Council for Scientific Unions (ICSU), and a number of other organizations, endeavours to establish appropriate structures and activities in all countries to ensure scientific and technological literacy for all by 2001. UNESCO also aims to adapt university engineering education to industrial needs, enhance the role of technical and vocational education, and strengthen relevant facilities. In these endeavours, UNESCO promotes cooperation, mainly through the International Project on Technical and Vocational Education (UNEVOC), which was launched in 1992. An international network of educational institutions is being established within the framework of UNEVOC, which has three programs: international exchange of experience and promotion of studies on policy issues; system development in technical and vocational education and strengthening of national research and development (R&D) capacities (that is, the development of infrastructures); and access to databases and documentation in its broadest sense (that is, information and communication).

ILO deals with issues of employment and vocational training as they affect technology and basic needs and has also done pioneering conceptual work in this domain. Its international training centre in Turin is committed to the principle that the most efficient form of technical cooperation and the best investment for sustainable advancement lie in human-resource development. Technology-related activities to promote education are carried out by the Committee on Science and Technology in Developing Countries (COSTED), which has been involved in the development of computer software for science education. The Third World Academy of Sciences (TWAS) operates a fund for spare parts for laboratory equipment, thus assisting many laboratories in developing countries, where experiments are often interrupted for long periods because of equipment failure or lack of spare parts. From the material reviewed, though, it appears that technology for the promotion of education is not, in itself, a priority concern. However, education to promote technology is very much a priority in the work of, for example, Project 2000+, a joint endeavour of major intergovernmental organizations, agencies, and bodies. Their aim is to establish appropriate structures and activities in all countries to ensure scientific and technological literacy for all.

The World Bank is keenly aware of the importance of science and technology (S&T) for development and has significantly increased its loans to the S&T sector in recent years. Both the private and public sectors benefit from World Bank loans: loans are made to institutions of higher education, mainly universities, as well as to polytechnics and other more specialized post-secondary professional training institutions. The World Bank has expanded its portfolio of loans to support public and private research institutes to help industry develop products for local consumption. The World Bank's recent activities include a focus on interactive technologies in higher education programs and the use of these technologies in both on- and off-campus learning. Examples are computer-mediated instructional technologies and technologies based on telecommunications networks. Recent publications have identified a number of potential obstacles to the implementation of these technologies, including constraints stemming from inadequate technical, educational, economic, administrative, and cultural environments.

## Health care

Health-care technology has been at the centre of World Health Organization (WHO) activities. The major emphasis is on support for countries' health-care policy analysis and development. WHO has developed a training program for health-care equipment management, and this is being implemented in all WHO regions. WHO provides continuous support for the development of national technical expertise and the promotion of awareness and information exchange. Of particular importance to basic needs are WHO's efforts to provide guidance on equipment essential for health facilities, particularly at primary and district levels. WHO is assuming a leadership role in strengthening national capacities for efficient, safe, and cost-effective use of health technology as an integrated component of the development of overall health systems.

About 1 billion people live without adequate water and sanitation, and this is the cause of many of the most prevalent diseases in developing countries. The United Nations Centre for Human Settlements (Habitat) has promoted appropriate technologies, affordable to low-income communities, in the field of sanitation and waste management. UNIDO has promoted technology development in vaccines and diagnostics, and the Commonwealth Secretariat has promoted a project on ethnobotany, which focuses on the use of plants for medicinal use.

Despite the apparent lack of a clear technology focus in this sector, health is a priority in the work of numerous organizations. Project 2000+ gives special attention to education in basic skills related to health. UNESCO's activities in education, health, and nutrition provide direction for small-scale economic initiatives that respond to basic needs.

Although renewable energy is not PTBN's particular concern, it is important to many organizations, especially those working in rural areas where traditional sources of energy, for example, firewood, are becoming scarce. Activity in renewable energy is concentrated mostly on solar energy and biogas. The World Solar Summit Programme is a major initiative to develop and disseminate technologies and make the widespread use of renewable energies possible. Many organizations, such as FAO, UNESCO, UNIDO, the regional commissions, Habitat, and the Asian and Pacific Centre for Transfer of Technology (APCTT), are trying to popularize the use of renewable energy in rural areas — small quantities of electricity can help meet essential health needs, can improve the quality of life, and can provide small-scale industries with the means to generate income. Nevertheless, extensive application of well-proven, mature, renewable-energy technologies has yet to occur, and much of the work is still in an experimental phase.

The material submitted by different organizations varied in scope and detail but pointed to the importance the international community attaches to the development of technology for meeting basic needs. The technological solution to meeting basic needs may vary from country to country or from community to community and can be found both through a more efficient use of improved traditional technologies and through the application of the most recent technological advances. The experience of the organizations, guided by a clear understanding of the role of technology and its translation into specific priorities and projects, demonstrates that the systematic application and dissemination of technologies contribute significantly to a change in the lives of low-income people, as well as helping them meet their basic needs. This experience also indicates that the dissemination and use of technologies for basic needs may succeed with a coherent S&T policy framework that covers macro- and micro-level aspects and takes into account more than S&T solutions. Relevant social, cultural, environmental, and gender-related elements and the interplay among major economic sectors — agriculture, industry, natural resources, education, and health — have been highlighted. An integrated policy framework includes the careful setting of priorities; the interaction and participation with and among diverse economic and social actors; specifically targeted technology generation and R&D efforts; the availability of sufficient financial resources; and a new emphasis on the application of R&D and the dissemination of technologies. For this purpose, we need renewed international efforts and programs of an interdisciplinary nature, with emphasis on human-resource development.

# Activities of selected organizations dealing with technologies for basic needs

## United Nations organizations and related specialized agencies

### Department for Policy Coordination and Sustainable Development

Within the Commission on Sustainable Development (CSD), the Department for Policy Coordination and Sustainable Development (DPCSD) has addressed the issue of technologies for basic needs in the context of the transfer of environmentally sound technologies, cooperation, and capacity-building. At its second session, CSD stressed the importance of involving small and medium-sized enterprises (SMEs) in technology transfer because SMEs are the backbone of business and industry in most developing countries. CSD therefore invited UNCTAD, UNDP, UNIDO, United Nations Environment Programme, and appropriate organizations of the United Nations system, among others, to assist countries in applying new modalities for the involvement of SMEs in long-term international technology partnerships, including assistance in the preparation, execution, and postservicing of sustainable-development projects at the local level and to report to CSD at its third session.

One of the sectoral issues considered by CSD in 1994 was that of human settlements, an essential area in meeting basic needs. CSD underlined the role of the private sector in the development and dissemination of cost-effective and sustainable building materials, increased energy and materials efficiency, and sustainable waste management. CSD highlighted the need to encourage local micro- and small-scale enterprises (MSEs) and then called on governments to strengthen the networks of SMEs in rural regions to provide attractive settlement opportunities and ease the migratory pressure on large metropolitan areas. CSD recommended that governments implement programs of rural development: expanding employment opportunities, providing educational and health facilities, strengthening technical infrastructure, encouraging rural enterprises, and fostering sustainable agriculture. CSD also called on the international community to support such rural development programs.

Another aspect of DPCSD's work is monitoring the follow-up to the Global Conference on the Sustainable Development of Small-Island

Developing States. The program of action resulting from that conference stresses the need to improve access to environmentally sound
technologies for economic activities in small-island developing states.
The program of action also recommends that measures be taken at the
national level to enhance the indigenous capacity to manage, assess,
acquire, disseminate, and develop technologies. At the regional level,
the cooperative development and sharing of appropriate technology
through the regional organizations' centres and networks are encouraged. At the international level, the program of action recommends the
following:

▼ Disseminate information on available technology.

▼ Provide education and training to improve the endogenous
capacity of small-island developing states to absorb, manage, and use environmentally sound technologies.

▼ Promote, facilitate, and finance access to and the transfer of
such technologies and corresponding know-how.

▼ Ensure the adequate and effective protection of the technology, knowledge, and customary and traditional practices
of local and indigenous people.

### Economic Commission for Africa

The activities of the Economic Commission for Africa (ECA) in the area
of S&T have focused on technologies to solve the problems faced by the
majority of the continent's people. ECA advocated this focus in the
regional strategies for S&T, for example, in the Lagos Plan of Action for
the Economic Development of Africa. One of the immediate follow-ups
was a collaborative project with the government of India to transfer
appropriate rural technologies from India to Africa. The project set up
a demonstration centre to demonstrate the technologies and provide
training in their operation, maintenance, and replication. The project
focused on three main fields of postharvest technologies: food processing (millet milling) and preservation and the conversion of agricultural
waste into materials for making paper; energy technologies and biogas
generation, including the use of power in small grain-grinding
machines; and technologies for women, the manufacture of leaf cups
and plates, and water purification. An earlier phase of this project supported long-term demonstration of rural technologies in various fields,
including the use of solar energy for cooking, pumping water, and operating domestic utilities, such as television and lighting.

The ECA Secretariat has also focused on technology in rural
development, which invariably touches on such basic needs as food,
shelter, and energy. The Secretariat has sponsored a number of activities,
including expert consultations on technology and rural development; on

culture, gender, and S&T in Africa (with a strong bias on the acquisition and application of technologies in African communities); and on technology policy and planning in the informal sector, with special reference to food, agriculture, and energy.

The African Regional Centre for Technology (ARCT), sponsored by ECA and located in Dakar, Senegal, has an important mandate to promote the development and diffusion of practicable local technologies. Some areas of focus are food production — including processing and preservation — and energy, particularly renewable energy, with emphasis on biogas digesters and the use of renewable energy for food production. ARCT has had successes in these areas by establishing production and demonstration units in various parts of the region. In 1985, ECA, in cooperation with ARCT and the German Foundation for International Development, held a workshop, Technology Policy and Planning in the Informal Sector: The Case of Food, Agriculture and Energy in the Eastern African Subregion. The workshop emphasized the importance of training informal-sector entrepreneurs and engineers; strengthening R&D on renewable energy; and establishing R&D priorities, including the informal sector's designs and prototypes for production of improved equipment.

In 1986, ECA held the Regional Expert Consultation on the Impact of Technology on Rural Development in Africa. The consultation concerned S&T and self-sufficiency in the provision of food in Africa, and ECA concluded that S&T alone would be insufficient to boost agricultural production and that S&T should be adapted to local conditions. This would have to take into account the special structure of the given society or community. Accordingly, ECA concluded that socioeconomic research needs to accompany agricultural research.

**Economic and Social Commission for Asia and the Pacific**
Technology is a crucial and strategic variable for socioeconomic development. The activities of the ESCAP Secretariat in the area of technology for development, including basic-needs strategies, emphasize institutional reform and the strengthening of the infrastructure for technological development, including human resources, to meet the changing needs of the developing countries of the region. The ESCAP Secretariat has organized various training courses, seminars, and technical advisory services and has provided relevant information.

A seminar with forum was convened by ESCAP at Vanuatu in 1990 in connection with a project to develop and popularize appropriate industrial technology for food storage and processing. The following issues were discussed: food supply and distribution; currently available food technologies and government policies and programs for their development and popularization; and market-related aspects of processed food products. The participants at the Vanuatu seminar also developed guidelines for strategies to develop and popularize appropriate technologies for food storage and processing, with emphasis on their diffusion and on the promotion of technical cooperation among developing countries.

In the area of R&D, training programs on solar photovoltaic technology were organized for the member developing countries, including in rural areas, to promote better understanding of the economic feasibility and the technical requirements. The programs included activities undertaken in cooperation with the Pacific Energy Development Programme to develop national training courses and prepare training materials. ESCAP organized an expert group meeting in Bangkok to discuss the technological upgrading of agro-based industries and the development and popularization of appropriate industrial technology for food processing in least-developed and land-locked developing countries. The group recommended strategic guidelines for developing, upgrading, and popularizing food-processing technologies. ESCAP, FAO, and UNIDO have been jointly sponsoring the Fertilizer Advisory, Development and Information Network for Asia and the Pacific. The network is designed to assist in solving problems in the supply, marketing, distribution, and use of fertilizers. Improved plant nutrition raises agricultural productivity, especially that of small-scale farmers who produce food, and prevents or reduces land degradation. Activities for human-resource development have also been carried out.

Proposals for possible implementation in 1994/95 included sustainable development and the enhanced participation of women in the development and commercialization of environmental biotechnology; poverty alleviation through the technological development of rural areas; and the promotion of the participation of low-income women in household-based manufacturing and processing. A regional workshop and study tour will be organized in India, at the community level, to promote low-cost, high-quality assistive devices for people with disabilities. The project is expected to promote access to and adaptation of technology and South–South transfer of technology.

A workshop and study tour was organized in Beijing, China, in 1994, to examine R&D, the use of technologies to regulate plant growth, and types of technical cooperation among developing countries. In connection with the "Developing Building Component Industries Through the Application of Updated Modular Coordination Rules" project, an international training course on applicable construction technology and materials was organized in China in 1994. The course had the objective of having students learn from research and application experiences.

To alleviate poverty through market-generated rural employment, national and regional training courses were organized in 1994/95 for nine developing countries to assist the rural poor in obtaining non-farm or off-farm income.

The Regional Network for Agricultural Machinery project has the objective of increasing agricultural output and labour productivity through mechanization and, ultimately, improving the working conditions and incomes of farmers. The project is designed to promote technical cooperation among developing countries through the exchange of information on selection, design and development, adaptation, and popularization of agricultural machinery. Recent activities have included study tours and an agricultural machinery exhibition. UNIDO has developed a special project for the promotion and development of agro-related metalworking industries in least-developed countries.

ESCAP has established the Regional Co-ordination Centre for Research and Development of Coarse Grains, Pulses, Roots and Tuber Crops in the Humid Tropics of Asia and the Pacific. One of its objectives is to solve technical problems related to crop production of smallholder farmers, particularly in remote areas, thereby increasing employment opportunities and achieving better income distribution and a balanced diet. Another objective is to forge closer linkages between the livestock sector and related industries. The centre has several ongoing projects: assessing the role of women in upland farming development; measuring the effects of the generation of rural employment; establishing a database on crops; and training researchers and policymakers.

**Asian and Pacific Centre for Transfer of Technology** — APCTT operates as a regional institution under ESCAP. APCTT's objective is to help the member and associate member countries of ESCAP strengthen their capacity to develop, adapt, and apply technology, with the main focus on SMEs. APCTT's core activities pertain to technology information and exchange. APCTT also executes projects funded by bilateral and multilateral donors. Of particular relevance to technology for basic needs are the Transfer of Small-scale Productive Technologies and Encouragement of Entrepreneurship Among Rural Women project and the Make Your Own Solar Cooker project. Most of these activities have no special focus on a particular industrial sector, such as food production and processing or health care, but are cross-sectoral.

UNDP financially supported APCTT's technology-information activities in 1991 and 1992 through the Mechanism for Exchange of Technology Information (METI) project. One thing the METI project is doing is creating a database on technology offers, requests, institutions, and consultants. The project has established a network of focal points in 11 Asian countries for the exchange of information on technologies and has trained 300 technology information officers as part of its efforts to stimulate regional cooperation on technology transfer.

APCTT has promoted technologies through technology missions, expositions, techmarts, and catalogue exhibitions, resulting in the publication of several technology handbooks aimed at facilitating the access to information on technologies and thus promoting South–South transfer of technology. APCTT publishes a bi-monthly journal, the *Asia–Pacific Tech Monitor*. The January–February 1994 issue focused on food processing and highlighted a number of selected technology offers especially relevant to small-scale industries. In addition, APCTT publishes bi-monthly updates in five different areas under the title, "Value Added Technology Information Service." One of the areas covered is food processing.

**Economic Commission for Latin America and the Caribbean**
In connection with technology and basic needs, the Economic Commission for Latin America and the Caribbean (ECLAC) has been involved in activities to boost the region's productivity to achieve international competitiveness and contribute to greater social equity. Attaining that objective has required the development of technological and physical infrastructure, organizational capacity, and human resources. In the framework of this systematic approach, the social sectors — in particular, the health sector — have an important role to play in maintaining and enhancing human resources.

The proposal "Health and Changing Production Patterns with Social Equity" (1994) aims to achieve greater equity in relation to health risks and access to health services, which in turn requires greater efficiency in resource allocation and more effective health interventions. The proposal suggests several components for an action plan:

▼ Mobilize intersectoral and multisectoral action for health.

▼ Implement a basic basket of health services.

▼ Target specific groups for health programs and interventions.

▼ Reform the health sector. This would include institutional change at the cultural level, decentralization, community participation in health promotion, and a recognition of the growing diversity of agents and their roles in the financing, regulation, management, and delivery of health services.

▼ Develop the capacity to monitor the profiles of priority health problems in different social sectors and the impact of interventions on the inequalities in health.

▼ Invest in the recovery and expansion of the productive capacity of both the health system and the basic health infrastructure.

Another priority area of activity for ECLAC is education and training. Despite enormous progress, the average length of schooling in the region is still too low, as are attendance rates and quality of education. Generally, the educational systems have expanded at the expense of quality, and many countries have significantly low educational levels, incapable of meeting the needs of development. The low quality of primary education is reflected in high rates of late entry, repetition of courses, temporary dropouts, and premature final abandonment of the system. Efforts to universalize the system have been accompanied by a failure to pay attention to both quality and equity. The majority of the population has access only to low-quality education. The reform strategy suggested by ECLAC focuses on integrating education into changing production patterns. The main guidelines of this strategy are as follows:

▼ Ensure universal access to modern education by expanding preschool attendance, extending the coverage of basic education, lengthening the school day, and encouraging attendance.

▼ Establish an educational system that is open to the needs of society by creating autonomous educational units, mechanisms for public regulation, and arrangements for coordination.

▼ Professionalize the role of educators and improve their profile through recruitment and training, remuneration, and incentives.

The main objective in the overall area of training is to improve the general level of education for the present and future labour force. The main targets include the labour employed in SMEs, labour in the urban and rural informal sectors, the unemployed, and unskilled recent entrants into the labour market. ECLAC suggests that training be included as an explicit component of an integrated assistance package for SMEs; that training assistance for the informal sector and microenterprises be more general in scope, be promoted by the public sector, and provide the opportunity for participants to earn money during training; and that training of unemployed workers be specific and aimed at enabling these workers to rapidly rejoin the active workforce. Training should allow first-time entrants into the labour market to bridge the gap between formal education and the working world and provide contacts and opportunities for finding jobs. ECLAC has pre-pared special financially self-sustaining training modules for such pur-poses, adapted to each country's conditions.

### United Nations Centre for Human Settlements

Habitat has been engaged for more than a decade in promoting and facilitating the transfer of technologies to developing countries and assisting in domestic capacity-building to meet the basic needs of pop-ulations, through international cooperation. Habitat's activities cover R&D, technical cooperation, information dissemination, and training.

In the energy sector, Habitat's activities for the 1992/93 work program focused on conserving energy in human settlements and using renewable, low-polluting energy sources in the development, provision, and operation of low-cost infrastructure. The emphasis of Habitat's current work is on promoting biomass-energy technologies to meet the needs of both the urban and the rural poor. Habitat's strategy is to identify appropriate biomass-energy technologies; have an expert group meeting to analyze the current constraints on their wide-scale use; and suggest effective promotional measures, such as technical publications, films, slides, and graphics, for the commercialization of these technologies. Habitat also assisted in the preparatory process for the United Nations Conference on Environment and Development by preparing a report on energy-related issues, which provided a basis for action for the international community. Habitat has also been looking at other renewable sources of energy, such as solar energy, wind energy, and small-scale hydropower, mainly in terms of the availabil-ity, adaptability, costs, and development of the technology required.

In the field of environmentally sound infrastructure, Habitat has published several technical manuals on appropriate technologies for low-cost water and sanitation that are affordable to low-income communities. Some of these manuals are on shallow sewer systems, water-conserving technologies, and low-cost water-supply systems. In the area of waste management, Habitat's efforts have focused on pro-moting capacities in developing countries for environmentally sound solid-waste management. Habitat recently carried out a research pro-ject on the promotion of small-scale waste-recycling technologies. The project covered five countries in Asia and reviewed environmentally sound and economically efficient waste-recycling practices. Habitat's activities in this field are widening to cover Africa and Latin America. Habitat has also developed computer software to assist developing countries in selecting appropriate technologies for waste collection. A special program has been launched for planning, management, and mitigation in disaster-prone areas. The program uses emerging technologies with a high potential for appropriate transfer to assist in the assessment of vulnerability and hazards.

In the construction sector, Habitat has promoted appropriate technologies for the production and use of locally produced building materials. Initiatives include training programs, technical publications, technical assistance in the transfer of technologies, and improvements in the efficiency of production processes, especially energy efficiency through renewable sources of energy, including agricultural and industrial wastes. To address environmental and health concerns, Habitat conducted baseline studies in the construction sector in all three developing regions, with the objective of documenting trends in the consumption of resources, especially nonrenewable resources, and the levels of environmental pollution caused by on-site and off-site activities. Habitat produced a technical publication on the development of national technological capacities for environmentally sound construction and jointly organized with UNIDO the first global consultation on the construction industry, in Tunis in 1993. This consultation focused on the management of nonrenewable resources, the control of physical disruption, and the minimization of air pollution from construction-related activities and emphasized the importance of incorporating principles of sustainability in national development planning and S&T policies. Information networks can help disseminate information on the environmental and health aspects of building materials in developing countries, at little cost to recipients. The organization of staff exchange and joint research programs among building research institutions of industrialized and developing countries accelerates the information-sharing process. In carrying out these activities, Habitat collaborates with ECA, UNIDO, UNDP, and international NGOs such as the Intermediate Technology Development Group (ITDG) and the German Appropriate Technology Exchange (GATE).

### United Nations Conference on Trade and Development

UNCTAD undertakes its activities most closely related to the issues of technology for basic needs in the framework of its mandates on the transfer and development of technology. At the intergovernmental level, this work has followed the recommendations of the Ad Hoc Working Group on the Interrelationship Between Investment and Technology Transfer, established in 1992, after an UNCTAD-VIII decision. UNCTAD's work principally aims to assist developing countries in formulating and implementing technological policies, with a view to strengthening their capacities to adapt, master, and develop technologies, including those at the level of SMEs. A number of the UNCTAD Secretariat's research projects and technical-cooperation activities have focused on technologies to meet the basic needs of low-income populations in developing countries. Particular mention should be made of research in the areas of food processing, energy, pharmaceuticals, and capital-goods construction services. Recently, technical-cooperation projects aimed at technological capacity-building have been initiated in selected least-developed countries of Asia and Africa. At the intergovernmental expert level, aspects of technology policy specifically related to some of these sectors were highlighted at meetings, resulting in concrete recommendations (UNCTAD 1982a, b, c, 1986).

The Ad Hoc Working Group paid particular attention to the problem of technological capacity-building in developing countries, especially least-developed countries. The group concluded that technology is vital for achieving economic development and sustaining competitiveness. However, technological capability cannot be an instantaneous, cost-free, or automatic achievement, even if the technology is well diffused elsewhere. Apart from physical inputs, technological capacity-building calls for various new interactions among firms, equipment suppliers, and standards' bodies, for example. Setting up this dense network of cooperation requires the development of special skills and favourable economic, institutional, and legal environments.

The Ad Hoc Working Group recommended, *inter alia*, that UNCTAD, in coordination with other appropriate international organizations,

▼ Undertake a project specifically designed to foster technological capacity-building in the least-developed countries;

▼ Assist developing countries, especially least-developed countries, in fostering entrepreneurship through the transfer of technology and managerial skills and developing the framework and mechanisms for technology partnerships between enterprises, with special attention to SMEs and their representative organizations; and

▼ Examine measures, especially in training and education, that would more fully engage the creative potential of SMEs to generate and disseminate environmentally sound technologies through networks and other channels of information.

After the restructuring of the economic and social sectors of the United Nations in 1993, UNCTAD became responsible for servicing CSTD, through which the work of PTBN is taking place.

Issues related to meeting the basic needs of the poor are also considered in UNCTAD's activities in least-developed, land-locked, and small-island developing countries and in poverty alleviation. Within the framework of the Program of Action for the Least Developed

Countries for the 1990s, UNCTAD seeks to overcome the structural bottlenecks and extreme economic difficulties experienced in those countries and thus to support the modernization of their economic base, including rural development. Of special relevance are the activities to help develop MSEs, including those in the informal sector, along with women's involvement in the production process and the improvement of education and health in least-developed countries. UNCTAD's Standing Committee on Poverty Alleviation, established following UNCTAD-VIII, has among its program priorities the facilitation of developing countries' access to productive and labour-intensive employment opportunities, productive assets, technology, and technical training.

## United Nations Development Programme

After the recent restructuring process, UNDP's main divisions whose work is related to technologies for basic needs are the Social Development and Poverty Elimination Division (SDPED) and the Science, Technology and Private Sector Division (STPSD).

SDPED supports UNDP's efforts to promote development, giving priority to the needs of the poor and to the advancement of women and other disadvantaged groups. SDPED will seek to infuse all of UNDP's work with a concern for equity, empowerment, and broad participation of civil society in development initiatives. SDPED is to assume a lead role in supporting the agreements of the International Conference on Population and Development (held in Cairo in 1994), the World Summit for Social Development (held in Copenhagen in 1995), and the Fourth World Conference on Women (held in Beijing in 1995). More specifically, SDPED will have responsibility for the following areas:

▼ Poverty elimination through food security, sustainable livelihoods, and job opportunities for the poor, including efforts to strengthen the informal sector, microenterprises, and microcredit arrangements;

▼ Advancement of women in development, along with the empowerment of disadvantaged groups;

▼ Strengthening of civil society, including efforts to foster grass-roots participation and involve NGOs and community-based organizations;

▼ HIV–AIDS and development programs;

▼ Human-resource development, including strategies for the education, health, and other social sectors; and

▼ Culture and development.

STPSD supports UNDP's efforts to put science, effective technologies, and the private sector at the service of sustainable human development in program countries. STPSD will bring together much of the science-based work of the former Division for Global and Interregional Programmes, the UNDP's initiatives to support private-sector development, and other efforts. The staff of the United Nations Fund for Science and Technology will be integrated into STPSD, which will manage the available resources. Specifically, STPSD will have responsibility for the following areas:

▼ Support for the creation of new applied science directly relevant to sustainable human development, including joint efforts with United Nations agencies and other bodies from both the South and the North to coordinate R&D;

▼ Access of program countries to internationally available information on S&T for sustainable human development;

▼ Collaborative research efforts among scientists in developing countries, including collaboration with people with appropriate expertise from the North;

▼ Policy development, international cooperation, and capacity-building for the diffusion, transfer, and adaptation of environmentally superior technologies and other technologies to promote sustainable human development, with public and private NGOs' cooperation;

▼ Development of policy frameworks and private-sector support programs to further entrepreneurship, private-sector initiatives, and mobilization of local investment in program countries, using a sustainable-human-development framework to generate employment and environmentally sound productive activities;

▼ Direct foreign investment for sustainable human development; and

▼ International private-sector support for sustainable human development in program countries.

### United Nations University–Institute for New Technologies

Technology for basic needs is not of direct major concern to the United Nations University–Institute for New Technologies (UNU–INTECH). Current and future research at UNU–INTECH will address the relationship of new technologies to education and training and, to a lesser extent, food and health.

A recent study of technology, trade, and industrialization in selected sub-Saharan African countries indicated that firms that invested in training to adapt workers to the changing requirements of new technologies have been able to maintain their position in export markets. Research on industrialization in Taiwan focuses on the role of various mechanisms and policies for technology transfer in the creation and diffusion of technological capabilities, particularly among SMEs, and analyzes the impact on firms of the transfer of knowledge from citizens who had studied or worked abroad. Two studies on the effect of microelectronics and automation technologies on women's employment in developing countries analyzed the changing job-skill and training requirements for women and identified new occupational and entrepreneurial opportunities for women. A research project is being considered to explore the process of building capabilities in microelectronics-based technologies in selected developing countries. Meetings are also being planned to address the question of whether Latin American and Caribbean universities and technical training institutes are supplying the scientists, engineers, managers, technicians, and skilled workers in the number, type, and quality required for the new technologies and the increasing international competition.

UNU–INTECH published an interpretive survey on biotechnology that highlighted developed and developing countries' agricultural and food-processing innovations, such as bovine hormones and corn-based fructose sweeteners, as well as medical innovations, such as diagnostic kits, proteins, and vaccines.

**Food and Agriculture Organization of the United Nations**
FAO assists developing countries in the generation and transfer of science-based technologies to support small-scale farmers and rural communities. The focus of assistance is on the men and women who produce most of the food in developing countries. FAO's work in research and technology development has a wide range of objectives: to increase and intensify food production; to improve consumption and nutrition; to raise the value added of agricultural produce; to improve income-earning capacity; and to create opportunities for employment in the production, processing, and marketing of agricultural goods. FAO also promotes new and renewable sources of energy to meet the requirements of rural populations in developing countries. See Chapter 10 for descriptions of FAO's activities in these fields.

Technical and economic cooperation among developing countries and South–South transfer of technology are high priorities in FAO, cutting across the whole spectrum of activities funded from the Regular Programme, as well as extrabudgetary activities. FAO fosters inter-country training, exchange of expertise, technology transfer, and networking in the fields of agriculture, fisheries, forestry, nutrition, and rural development. FAO supports about 100 networks in the four developing regions. The 23 operational networks supported by the FAO Regional Office for Latin America and the Caribbean offer a good example of such activities.

In FAO's view, education, especially technical and vocational training, will have to be improved if the basic needs of rural people are to be met. A major factor contributing to the migration of massive numbers of rural people to urban areas is the lack of equitable education opportunities in rural areas. Furthermore, FAO has found a need for the retrieval of indigenous knowledge about the technology of traditional production, collection, storage, and processing of food and for the development and dissemination of appropriate technology. This would contribute to household food security and provide adequate nutrition for people in marginalized rural households, as well as poor consumers. FAO has produced technical documentation on nutrition and has undertaken the training of field staff from different sectors (agriculture, community development, health, education, and adult education). FAO is also preparing a set of booklets for use with a program of food-based interventions to prevent micronutritient deficiencies.

In FAO's opinion, the development of new technology should be supplemented and complemented by innovative educational and self-help approaches geared to various interests and literacy levels. The promotion of people's participation and the recognition of the different roles played by men, women, and youth in rural development deserve close attention. Comprehensive rural development programs could benefit from interdisciplinary approaches, which bring the combined strengths of different United Nations agencies to bear on a number of key issues. FAO recommends that CSTD examine both the new technologies and the methods that lead to their successful adaptation and adoption.

### International Fund for Agricultural Development

IFAD is a multilateral financial institution with the specific mandate to reorient technological systems to address the issues of smallholder farmers and, in general, the rural poor. The focus is on the development of sustainable farming systems in rainfed and marginal environments. IFAD places special emphasis on the development of frontier technology for achieving maximum impact and the adaptation of technology to fit particular farming systems, which requires close relations with the ultimate beneficiaries.

The IFAD grant program for practical research has focused on food crops and livestock that the rural poor of developing countries have traditionally produced and consumed. For example, IFAD has been involved in research projects on rice in Bangladesh, Indonesia, the Philippines, Sri Lanka, and Thailand. The objectives are to increase cropping intensity and productivity, to solve problems related to cultivation techniques and pest control, and to increase the stress resistance of high-yielding varieties. IFAD has been conducting tests on special sorghum and maize varieties under diverse ecological conditions in Africa and has set up research projects on wheat and barley in North Africa. The active involvement of IFAD in faba (broad beans) projects in Egypt and Sudan has contributed to increased productivity. In Latin America, IFAD's activities have focused mainly on increasing the yield and pest and disease resistance of field beans under smallholder production systems. Similar research projects on roots and tubers have been undertaken in Ghana, Malawi, Nigeria, Sierra Leone, and Zaire.

IFAD's livestock research is mainly focused on small ruminants, which are very important in the traditional farming systems of the rural poor. The research has been largely concentrated in West Africa because conditions there have led to serious shortcomings in the livestock-linked elements of smallholder farms. Recent experiences show that sustainability of small farming systems in areas with marginal land for crop production, too dense a population, or uncertain weather conditions depends on the availability of technology for efficiently integrating livestock with other farming activities. Projects related to nutrition and the reproduction of small ruminants have been concentrated mainly in sub-Saharan Africa, and projects related to the biological control of insect pests have been strengthened successfully in southern Africa.

IFAD first evaluates the requirements for, and the sustainability of, technology for the agroecology and farming systems of areas in developing countries and then begins the arduous process of transferring techniques for better production. Transferred technology is generally not self-implemental. This is especially true of innovative technologies, particularly in least-developed countries, where information exchange among smallholder farmers is deficient or absent.

Production technology represents only one of the essential components of a strategy for poverty alleviation in the rural areas. IFAD's experience shows that technology to increase production and productivity has little success without available postharvest and processing technologies for handling, storing, preserving, and adding market value to products at or near the farm. By incorporating socioeconomic elements in its programs, IFAD hopes to facilitate the adaptation and adoption of useful technologies and ensure or enhance their positive impact on smallholder farming systems. Socioeconomic elements include human nutrition, women's labour, relevant policies, and information exchange in IFAD's target population, which is usually site specific. In IFAD's view, a complete package of various elements for action is the key to poverty alleviation.

## International Labour Organization

Technology — the skills, knowledge, and procedures for providing useful goods and services — has been a principal underlying theme of ILO's thinking and activities since the organization was established in 1969. The World Employment Conference in 1976 and its discussions on technologies for productive development gave a new impetus to the organization's work on technologies for basic needs, particularly in the context of the program of action adopted at that conference (ILO 1976, 1977). The core of the related ILO work, especially its Technology Programme, has had a clear antipoverty thrust and has concentrated on the complex relationships among technological choice, employment, and basic needs, as well as on research and technical-cooperation projects to assist in the implementation of appropriate technology for basic needs. ILO has made a substantial effort to disseminate information on appropriate technology for rural development, small-scale and agrobased industries, and construction. ILO has developed guidelines to help managers and management trainers make technological choices that take into account the potential to generate employment. ILO's activities have been guided by the perception that technology is the servant of social and economic objectives and not the master and that S&T efforts should be directed toward the welfare of the villager, the peasant, and the worker in small-scale industry, as well as the modern-sector managers and employees (see Chapter 11).

## United Nations Educational, Scientific and Cultural Organization

The World Conference on Education for All, organized by UNESCO in Thailand in 1990, provided a major opportunity for the United Nations system to integrate strategies to meet basic learning needs into an overall basic-needs approach. In many developing countries, the concept of basic learning needs has since been reviewed and broadened to include the promotion of literacy, numeracy, and life skills appropriate to the cultural and socioeconomic setting of each country. This process has also focused attention on basic skills related to health, family welfare, civic responsibilities, and vocational training. Many countries have instituted measures to monitor the extent to which their populations have acquired these basic skills. UNESCO has, in this endeavour, closely cooperated with other United Nations bodies and organizations, notably UNICEF, UNDP, the World Bank, the United Nations Population Fund, and the World Food Programme.

Project 2000 + (involving UNESCO, UNICEF, UNDP, the World Bank, ICSU, and the International Council of Associations for Science Education) aims to prepare educational programs, provide guidelines for the continuous development of S&T educators and leaders, support the development of projects enhancing cooperation in S&T education, and support the establishment of national task forces to initiate programs for greater S&T literacy.

Another priority for UNESCO is the Programme on University–Science–Industry, which aims to adapt university engineering education to industrial needs, retrain practicing engineers, establish UNESCO chairs sponsored by industry, and develop the UNESCO Series of Learning Materials in Engineering Sciences. Furthermore, the newly created International Fund for the Technological Development of Africa has received UNESCO's contribution of $1 million. The fund aims to strengthen R&D activities that would contribute to the development of small-scale industry in Africa. In 1980, UNESCO established the African Network of Scientific and Technological Institutions (ANSTI) with funding from UNDP and the Federal Republic of Germany. ANSTI aims to bring about close and active cooperation among the high-level S&T training and research institutions in the UNESCO Africa region.

UNESCO's activities in education, health, and nutrition are intended to provide direction for small-scale economic initiatives that would respond to basic needs in poverty situations. More particularly, UNESCO is focusing on health, nutrition, and other poverty-related problems of school-age children in the least-developed countries. UNESCO has long been involved in the development of intermediate and appropriate technologies for rural development. In 1980, UNESCO, in cooperation with the Belgian government, held an expert meeting in Brussels to discuss new ways of promoting technologies for rural development. The report of the meeting contains a number of ideas discussed at the meeting (UNESCO 1981).

UNESCO has been very active in the field of technical and vocational education since the early 1960s. In 1991, UNESCO decided to launch the first phase (1992–95) of its UNEVOC project. See the discussion of the UNEVOC project in Chapter 12.

At its regional offices, UNESCO has been actively involved in matters related to basic needs. The Nairobi Regional Office, for example, plans to encourage country-wide use of certain appropriate technologies that are as yet used only randomly. The sail-propelled fishing vessels from the East African coast are now being introduced in Lake Victoria. In Uganda, UNESCO is encouraging the country-wide use of animal-propelled technologies, such as carts and ploughs, to boost the economic returns of Ugandan peasants. UNESCO is also promoting small-scale mining and agrogeology, which help bring sustainability to agriculture in developing countries by supplying fertilizers, such as phosphates and nitrates.

The Nairobi Regional Office is also involved in the World Solar Summit Process, which will culminate in 1996 in the World Solar Programme. Some of the aims of the process are to enhance the

understanding of the benefits of renewable energy sources and to foster regional, interregional, and international cooperation in research
and training in renewable energy. As part of this process, UNESCO held
a high-level expert meeting for Africa in Zimbabwe in 1995 to discuss
the benefits of solar energy for rural development and for the development of Africa as a whole. UNESCO aims to popularize the use of solar
energy, especially in rural areas, where the availability of modest quantities of energy could help meet essential health needs and substantially improve the quality of life.

The work of the UNESCO Regional Office for Science and Technology for the Arab States covers education and scientific research but
does not deal directly with technology for basic needs. The same is true
of the Regional Office for Science and Technology for Latin America
and the Caribbean, which, among its main activities for 1992/93,
undertook major programs in science and engineering and the
environment.

### United Nations Industrial Development Organization

The Investment and Technology Promotion Division of UNIDO promotes the transfer of technologies to meet basic needs. The division
also helps developing countries increase their technological capability
to respond more effectively to basic needs, such as food supply, basic
health care, and basic power supply in rural areas.

The Technology Acquisition Subprogramme supports techmarts, which are technology market fora for access to and adaptation
of technology and for North–South and South–South transfer of technology. At a techmart, a technology seeker can directly buy the rights
to manufacture and upgrade existing products and processes from technology suppliers from developed and developing countries. The techmarts have a special emphasis on the needs of SMEs.

Consultative and training workshops, field visits, and pilot
demonstrations enable the Technology Acquisition Subprogramme to
promote and facilitate technology transfer. These technologies include
gari-processing and other cassava-processing technologies in Africa;
food-fermentation technologies to improve the traditional fermented-
food industry (through the Lactic Acid Bacteria Network, LABNET) in
Asia and Africa; bioconversion of agricultural and agro-industrial
wastes (through the Mushroom Biotechnology Network, MUSHNET);
and marine technology, including seaweed-processing technology, in
the Asia–Pacific region. The Technology Acquisition Subprogramme
extends support to the African Agency for Biotechnology and the
Regional Network for Biotechnology in Latin America and also promotes the development and transfer of technology for vaccines and

diagnostics and their application in the treatment of such diseases as hepatitis, malaria, and AIDS.

The Technology Acquisition Subprogramme helps developing countries take advantage of small hydropower and solar-energy applications, especially for target beneficiaries in the rural areas. UNIDO established the Network on Mini-Hydropower Generation in Asia with the aim of supplying electric power to remote and isolated areas not already covered by the national grid. Similarly, UNIDO's Technology Service Programme is active in promoting the commercialization and application of photovoltaic solar energy, especially in the rural areas, where prices for this source of energy are competitive. The photovoltaic technology thus provides an immediate solution to certain basic needs. UNIDO has been promoting commercialization, the improvement of small-scale enterprises, and the development of new small-scale industries, based on local resources, to generate employment and income opportunities for combatting poverty. The delivery of services often favours the employment of women: many of the small-scale enterprises, such as food fermentation and processing, are home based.

UNIDO has established several mechanisms for effective dissemination of information and delivery of services. It has established, strengthened, and promoted many databases and information networks, as well as R&D networks. The Investment and Technology Promotion Division contributes to the Industrial Technology Information Bank and the "Technology Monitor," which provides information on current and advanced technology in biotechnology, biosafety, electronics, materials, and industrial marine sciences. In addition, a number of information networks have been established to support the various technological-cooperation networks, such as LABNET, MUSHNET, and ICGEBNET. More recently, in cooperation with FAO, UNIDO initiated an information network on biotechnology and biodiversity in Asia. The network disseminates information on technologies, expertise, and practices that are appropriate for farming communities to use in support of participatory development and conservation of biodiversity.

Capacity-building is a major objective of the Technology Service Programme. Through interrelationships with other endogenous capacity-building and R&D activities, most of UNIDO's promotional activities have been supported by a parallel program that establishes centres of excellence to train scientists in developing countries and give them access to advanced R&D facilities. These centres include the International Centre for Genetic Engineering and Biotechnology (ICGEB) and the Centre for Application of Solar Energy. ICGEB has a network of more than 20 affiliated centres to carry out collaborative research relevant to local needs. In addition, ICGEB provides advice to countries on policy and program formulation in relevant industry-related areas, such as biotechnology. Expert group meetings and workshops are conducted at national, regional, and international levels to review state-of-the-art developments.

## World Bank

The World Bank's loans to the S&T sector focus on projects for higher education and industry-related applications. Private industry benefits from the World Bank financing: firms can borrow money on subloan terms, through intermediary financial institutions, to develop and produce items for local and international sale. The World Bank also supports major public or parastatal infrastructure and energy projects with specific S&T components. The World Bank has financed project components in three basic categories: infrastructure, training, and management. The infrastructure component refers both to civil works and a wide variety of equipment. Civil works often involve creating facilities, such as laboratories and classrooms and, occasionally, administrative buildings, libraries, and maintenance and repair facilities. Related equipment may include laboratory and other technical equipment, scientific literature, and computers.

Scientific research and training are essential to development, and a recent publication (Boh 1994b) highlighted basic scientific research, applied research, and mechanisms to improve the use of research outputs. This publication also contains a summary of the World Bank's experience and pitfalls in its projects for the support of research in capacity-building.

Another publication of the World Bank (Boh 1994a) examined interactive technologies in higher education programs and their use in both on- and off-campus learning. Two main types of educational technologies were reviewed: computer-mediated instructional technologies, that is, individual, stand-alone units, of which multimedia technology is the fastest growing example; and technologies based on telecommunications networks. The use of these technologies improves the effectiveness of education; increases efficiency through low-cost alternatives to conventional instruction; extends access to geographically, economically, or socially isolated students; and produces graduates with a heightened capacity to adapt to technological change and innovation. Potential obstacles to the application of these technologies include inadequate technical, educational, economic, administrative, and cultural settings.

In the World Bank's experience, projects promoting S&T capacity need to include

▼ Training and research resources to accompany the provision of equipment;

▼ Incentives for researchers to undertake both basic scientific research and studies that directly serve national goals;

▼ Mechanisms to monitor and direct these activities;

▼ Plans for disseminating research results in the form of publications, technologies, or products;

▼ The alignment of loan management and evaluation with requirements for the implementation of technical projects; and

▼ The promotion of a policy environment that is conducive to the development of S&T and takes into account marketplace composition and orientation, distribution of administrative and financial controls between government and institutions, travel and exchange options, and support for an information infrastructure.

## World Health Organization

Technology based on physical and engineering sciences has provided health-care professionals with many devices and techniques for functioning more effectively. For the past two decades, the development and transfer of technology have moved at an unprecedented pace, with thousands of new items available each year. Rapid proliferation of new and existing technologies has far-reaching social, ethnical, legal, and economic consequences for health care, going far beyond the clinical implications. Technologies are frequently identified as major factors in rapidly rising health-care costs, but technology also underpins medical progress. The effective introduction, use, and maintenance of technologies require sophisticated managerial, medical, and engineering talent. Although they hold the promise of great potential health benefits, technologies confront health authorities with a bewildering array of choices when they are trying to evaluate health priorities and allocate scarce resources.

The rapid growth of technology markets has led to a certain degree of misuse in a number of countries. Low-volume, high-cost health technology often absorbs an unduly large proportion of health resources, and, consequently, some high-priority health programs suffer. In many countries, indiscriminate use of high technology means sophisticated medicine for the few and poor-quality or no care at all for the great majority. At present, the efficiency and cost-effectiveness of health care in any country depend largely on wise judgments being made about the value of specific health technologies, their true possibilities, and their limitations. As part of a worldwide concern over quality assurance and cost containment, health-technology options should be assessed and chosen with reference to purpose, quality, and cost.

Many health problems can be prevented, diagnosed, and treated with available, relatively simple, affordable equipment.

All countries need an explicit policy on the management of health-care technology that covers all levels of a national health system, is consistent with the country's needs, and is targeted to the solution of the health problems of the majority of people. Such a policy should cover needs-assessment and planning procedures; selection and procurement strategies; regulations and standards governing quality, safety, and efficiency; the budget and infrastructure for maintenance and repair; human-resources development; information support systems; and many other factors.

Nearly all kinds of health-care technologies are available in the medical marketplace, and developing countries find themselves under pressure to import modern technology. However, the rate of absorption is governed by a country's scientific and professional level, the ability of competent authorities to differentiate between need and demand, the existence of necessary infrastructure for the technologies' use and service, and the ability of a country to pay. In the view of WHO, a pressing problem now in almost every developing country is not merely the substantial amount of health-care technology that is often inappropriate to a country's health priorities but the even greater amount that is appropriate and could contribute to the country's health goals but lies idle because of inappropriate management. In many developing countries, more than 50% is unusable or not used.

The people at WHO have been deeply concerned about the need for expanded international collaboration, information exchange, and strong national capacities to deal with the variety and complexity of problems in the management of health-care technology. A number of WHO programs have dealt with this subject in a variety of activities.

The major emphasis of these programs is on assisting countries in policy analysis and development. WHO developed a health-care equipment-management training program, which is being implemented in all WHO regions. Information support, promotion of awareness, and advocacy are being facilitated by publication and dissemination of selected materials. Important areas for information exchange, sharing of knowledge, and international collaboration have included medical devices, regulatory affairs, and health-care technology-assessment methodologies. WHO has made systematic efforts to provide guidance on essential equipment for health facilities, particularly at the primary and district levels, as well as designing specific equipment for worldwide use. The results of these designs are visible in the Basic Radiological System, cold-chain and sterilization equipment for the Expanded Programme of Immunization, health laboratory equipment, and a number of other specific types of equipment. WHO's technical efforts are also reflected in the clinically efficient use of specific technologies, such as diagnostic imaging, and technologies used in specific areas of medicine, such as cardiovascular diseases, cancer, and diabetes.

WHO is committed to supporting its member states in strengthening national capacities for efficient, safe, and cost-effective use of health technology as an integral component of overall development of health systems. Assuming a leadership role in this area, WHO is making every effort to mobilize human, technical, and financial resources. The WHO Global Action Plan on Management, Maintenance and Repair of Health Care Equipment, started in 1987, and the WHO Programme on Health Technology, started in 1993, have led to considerable progress in strengthening international cooperation, coordinating related activities, and exchanging information. WHO is establishing a worldwide network comprising pertinent United Nations agencies, NGOs, bilateral donors, and many other institutions from both industrialized and developing countries. See Chapter 13 for descriptions of some of WHO's activities.

## World Intellectual Property Organization

Among the responsibilities of the World Intellectual Property Organization (WIPO) is cooperation with developing countries in their development efforts related to intellectual property. WIPO deals with a few areas relevant to technologies for basic needs: access to and adoption of technology; North–South and South–South transfers of technology; and the related dissemination mechanisms.

To these ends, WIPO sponsors workshops and regional seminars on the use of industrial property and on technology transfer in sectors of relevance to developing countries, such as the food-processing industry. Target groups include both the government and private sectors. Although patents usually relate to advanced techniques, rather than to small-scale, traditional food production, many contributions commissioned by WIPO have dealt with basic needs because of the intimate relationship between food and human survival. Thus, reference has been made to the dualistic nature of the food-processing industry in developing countries, with capital-intensive, large-scale plants (usually around urban areas), on the one hand, and widely dispersed small enterprises (usually in the rural areas), on the other. The latter often use age-old techniques, and even small technological improvements could have a significant effect on the income and waste management of these small enterprises and thus on food availability.

In WIPO's view, the future development scenario suggests a transformation from small-scale to large-scale operations. Thus, the issue of patents will become more pertinent to a larger portion of the food-processing sector and other sectors relevant to basic needs in developing countries. The vast majority of patents have their origin in industrialized countries; therefore, a trend such as this will have implications for basic-needs technologies.

## Intergovernmental organizations

### African Development Bank

The African Development Bank (ADB) has undertaken no studies that directly deal with technologies for basic needs. Any actions in education, health, housing, and food are delivered through the projects ADB finances; these actions tend to be project specific. ADB has expressed interest in the work of PTBN in the hope that the panel will provide guidance in ADB's endeavours to reduce poverty in its member countries.

### Association of Southeast Asian Nations

The activities of the Association of Southeast Asian Nations (ASEAN) cover many aspects of the development of S&T expertise and human resources and the transfer of technology. Food S&T has been identified as a priority area for action. The development of therapeutic and biologically important substances from plants and the production and use of cells and enzymes for improved carbohydrate conversion have been important components of ASEAN's work. In the field of marine sciences, ASEAN supports management plans on the use of coastal resources, with a particular focus on commercial fisheries. All of ASEAN's programs involve workshops and training, the exchange of information, the establishment of databases, and the wide dissemination of ASEAN's publications in the region.

### Commonwealth Secretariat

A number of divisions in the Commonwealth Secretariat assist member countries in their efforts to satisfy the basic needs of low-income populations, most notably needs in the areas of food production, rural development, and S&T.

On food production and rural development, the work of the Commonwealth Secretariat's Agricultural Development Unit (recently replacing the Food Production and Rural Development Division) is mainly in the area of small-scale agricultural mechanization, from the manufacture, testing, and commercialization of small agricultural tools to the promotion of agroprocessing. The work of the Commonwealth Secretariat began as far back as 1979, when the first meeting of Appropriate Technology Co-ordinators from East, Central, and southern African Commonwealth countries was held, in Lusaka. The meeting reviewed developments in appropriate technology in those countries and was followed in 1981 and in 1982 by other activities focusing on a set of standard procedures for testing the performance of tractors and ox-drawn machinery, as well as other equipment, such as hand tools and small-scale machinery. Similar activities were undertaken in Pacific-region countries. The Agricultural Development Unit has published directories of firms that manufacture small implements in African and Pacific countries. Following a desk study of the work done by other multilateral and bilateral organizations in agricultural mechanization in the last decade, a regional workshop in Nigeria in August 1990 examined issues related to the development of national strategies. A similar study was undertaken for the Commonwealth countries in the Caribbean. To follow up on the studies, the unit decided to establish two networks, one for southern, Central, and East African Commonwealth countries and another for West African countries. These networks have become operational. The first project undertaken by the networks was the publication of a quarterly newsletter on regional developments. The Commonwealth Secretariat also provided to member governments the technical assistance and training facilities needed for designing prototypes of agricultural equipment suitable for local conditions. These prototypes were tested on farmers' fields and have since been commercialized.

The Industrial Development Department (IDD) helps developing countries develop industries, mainly small- and medium-scale industries in the private sector, focusing on quickly maturing projects and a combination of local and external skills and resources. IDD places particular emphasis on technical assistance to the small-island and least-developed countries. IDD's role in technology is to promote the transfer and adaptation of technology in developing countries by helping to develop and strengthen private-sector business enterprises, which are considered key vehicles for the delivery of technology.

IDD has provided assistance to Commonwealth developing countries across a wide spectrum of technologies. Technical-assistance projects related to small-scale economic activities have focused primarily on basic needs for food, shelter, and clothing. IDD has implemented about 200 technical-assistance projects in the food-processing sector, such as projects concerning dairy products, meat and fish processing, and solar salt production and refining. To address the need for shelter, IDD has assisted in the development of projects throughout the Commonwealth for the extraction and processing of a range of building materials, such as lime–cement mixes, timber, bricks and tiles, stone, and lateritic soils. In the area of low-cost housing, IDD has been promoting prototype house units that halve the cost of conventional building methods and use local materials and unskilled labour. IDD's objective in the clothing industry has been to help upgrade technology to improve the quality and diversity of products. With regard to health care, the Commonwealth's Biological Diversity and Genetic Resources Programme is responsible for a project dealing with ethnobotany, with specific reference to the use of plants for medicinal purposes.

The overall S&T concerns of the Commonwealth Secretariat are to increase the capabilities of Commonwealth countries to apply S&T for their economic, social, and environmental development and to develop human resources and national S&T infrastructures. The Commonwealth Science Council's key aim is to enhance developing countries' ability to generate technology for small-scale economic activities to address the basic needs of low-income populations. Current programs marginally address the problems in food production and processing and health-care services. In the area of food production and processing, the Commonwealth Science Council has initiated a network in the Asia–Pacific region to promote underused fruits by upgrading production through propagation, processing, and marketing. Related to this activity is a project to seek alternatives to the use of maize by promoting cassava, for example.

### Preferential Trade Area for Eastern and Southern African States

The scope of the technological cooperation program in the Preferential Trade Area (PTA) for Eastern and Southern African States derives largely from PTA's wide objective: the economic integration and development of its member states. To pursue this objective, PTA countries undertake to cooperate in industry, for example, to create wealth and employment. PTA's concern with technology, therefore, derives from the pursuit of integrated industrial development. The treaty establishing the Common Market for Eastern and Southern Africa, which was signed in 1993, further strengthens PTA's cooperation program for technological development. The thrust of PTA's activities is largely directed to building capacity and capability because PTA believes that efforts to promote socioeconomic development will be futile without the appropriate levels of endogenous capacity and capability.

In the last 11 years, PTA has developed many technology-related projects, some of which are being implemented and some of which are in the pipeline. The Metallurgical Technology Centre was established in 1990, with the aim of enabling the eastern and southern African regions to acquire the technological capability to develop its metallurgical and related downstream industries. The Leather and Leather Products Institute was set up in Addis Ababa, Ethiopia, to enhance productivity, competitiveness, trade, and cooperation in the leather-industry subsector. Similar project proposals include centres for sugar technology, food technology, and textiles. A technology market forum (techmart) for SMEs in the region was planned for 1995, to be undertaken in collaboration with donor agencies. A project is ongoing to develop prototype mobile seed-dressing applicators suitable for African countries. This project aims to validate the technoeconomic feasibility of seed-dressing technology through research, design, and local fabrication of a prototype seed-dressing applicator specifically designed for the needs of African small-scale rural farmers, with a view to promoting its widespread application in the region.

PTA's member states identified energy self-sufficiency as the key to alleviating social and economic hardships, particularly the hardships of low-income, urban households. Renewable-energy systems were to play a critical role. Assistance was requested from UNIDO to develop energy systems based on locally available resources, such as biomass and solar energy. The region acquired two biomass gasifiers from India and Italy, which were then modified by a Zimbabwean company to suit PTA regional requirements. The technology of biomass gasification is now being transferred to other PTA countries. PTA has also established demonstration units to introduce photovoltaic technology in rural areas beyond the reach of the national electricity grid. The private sector is being encouraged to take the lead in disseminating this technology as widely as possible.

### Consultative Group on International Agricultural Research

The whole range of CGIAR's work embraces the issue of technologies to address basic needs. Consequently, CGIAR possesses a vast amount of information on the subject. The 18 international centres supported by CGIAR are part of a global agricultural research system. CGIAR seeks to function as a guarantor of developing countries, ensuring that international scientific capacity is brought to bear on the problems of the world's disadvantaged peoples. For many years, CGIAR has been working for sustainable development by focusing on programs dealing with sustainable productivity, agricultural policy, capacity-building, integrated pest management, and conservation of genetic resources. More recently, CGIAR has placed special emphasis on integrating Agenda 21, including the World Declaration and Plan of Action for Nutrition adopted at the FAO–WHO International Conference on Nutrition in 1992 in Rome, into programs at CGIAR centres.

Food productivity in developing countries has increased through the combined efforts of CGIAR centres and their associates. The same efforts have brought about a range of other benefits, such as increased farm income, reduced prices for food, better food-distribution systems, better nutrition, more rational policies, and stronger institutions. CGIAR centres play a central role in the alleviation of poverty by developing technologies to help farm families achieve sustainable food increases on both favourable and marginal lands. To more effectively address this challenge in the future, members of CGIAR endorsed a comprehensive set of priorities, arranged by region, activity, production sector, and commodity, to guide the evolution of the system's programs. The purpose of establishing these priorities, recommended by CGIAR's Technical Advisory Committee, is to ensure that the policies and operations of CGIAR systems strengthen the connections between research on productivity and research on natural-resource management. CGIAR's strategy for implementing its priorities will involve both global and ecoregional research. CGIAR's global program will concentrate on strategic research on wheat, rice, maize, sorghum, millet, bean, cassava, potatoes, sweet potatoes, fisheries, and livestock. Ecoregional activities will cover strategic and applied research on natural-resources management, production systems, and location-specific aspects of commodity improvement in regionally defined agroecological zones.

A key research activity is commodity improvement through the application of technologies, such as germplasm enhancement and breeding, in which CGIAR has a well-established comparative advantage. An example is the breeding of varieties of pearl millet in Rajasthan, India, that are tolerant of the severe heat and drought typical of the semiarid tropics. Such research would benefit large numbers of people for whom pearl millet is a staple food in the harsh environments of the semiarid tropics. Banana, plantain, and coconut are other crops for which CGIAR research centres around the world are developing hybrids resistant to common pests and diseases and tolerant of extreme soil and climatic conditions.

The conservation of genetic plant resources is crucial to the survival of agriculture in a changing environment because many plants have already naturally adapted to deficient rainfall, extreme temperatures, and disease. CGIAR centres play a leading role in this conservation by establishing major collections of germplasm of numerous crop species.

Pest-management strategies are a major focus of CGIAR research. Integrated pest-management technologies can help reduce dependence on chemical pesticides. Such strategies include breeding genetic resistance to the world's most widespread rice disease, using DNA fingerprinting; and breeding weevil resistance in beans, using a weevil-resistant wild, primitive bean vine found in Mexico. The resistant beans can help some 300 million people across Africa and Latin America store beans without pesticide protection, thus saving millions of dollars annually. Similar results have been obtained by developing hybrid potato varieties, notably a "hairy" variety that traps and kills pests. CGIAR research centres are also working on the control of diseases that afflict livestock, notably trypanosomiasis, by using tests that detect the DNA of parasites in cattle. Such tests will help us understand the causes and dynamics of various livestock diseases.

A CGIAR research centre is working as an aquaculture research partner in a major United States Agency for International Development (USAID)–Bangladesh agricultural project. Small-scale aquaculture has been adopted by thousands of resource-poor farmers to produce a new purebred strain of tropical fish, with superior growth. In a project undertaken in 1992 in cooperation with the German Agency for Technical Cooperation (GTZ), CGIAR found that the integration of aquaculture and agriculture sustained household incomes and food supplies during a severe drought in Malawi.

In many agroecological systems, the demands on the resource base have reached the point where further increases in agricultural production and improved rural livelihoods will be difficult to achieve without resolving basic issues in the management of natural resources. CGIAR research centres are therefore developing approaches to systematically analyze the technical, institutional, and policy issues that affect natural-resource management by farmers and rural communities and then testing these approaches through a small number of in-depth case studies of important ecosystems. The general focus of CGIAR research centres has been on policies to promote technological change, increase food production, and ensure that the poor benefit from agricultural growth. CGIAR emphasizes that a correct policy environment for equitable agricultural growth is an important complement to the work of CGIAR centres to develop technology.

## National organizations

### German Appropriate Technology Exchange

GATE is part of GTZ, whose main task is the implementation of programs and projects cofunded by the German government in cooperation with partners in developing countries. GATE's scope of activities includes sectoral consultancy and capacity-building in the use of appropriate technologies. In this framework, the German Ministry for Economic Co-operation and Development sponsors a long-term supranational project, the Information and Advisory Service on Appropriate Technology (ISAT). ISAT maintains and disseminates continuously updated appropriate-technology documentation (about 12 000 titles) and publishes a quarterly magazine, books, and information sheets. ISAT also answers inquiries on appropriate technology.

ISAT sponsors about 20 NGOs that work on appropriate technology. This sponsorship includes financial assistance, as well as transfer of know-how through short-term consultancies and capacity-building activities. ISAT has supported the establishment of a network for southern and East Africa (RATIS, Regional Appropriate Technology Information Service) and one for West Africa (SIATA, Service interafricain de technologie appropriée). RATIS and SIATA are based, respectively, in Harare, Zimbabwe, and Ouagadougou, Burkina Faso.

In Germany, ISAT is one of the founding members of Appropriate Technology Forum, a working group. The purpose of this forum is to safeguard appropriate technology in development cooperation, as well as coordinating German support for projects related to appropriate technology. ISAT is a member of various European, mostly sectoral, networks of NGOs that disseminate appropriate technology.

## Swedish Agency for Research Cooperation with Developing Countries

The Swedish Agency for Research Cooperation with Developing Countries (SAREC) has a long history of technological capacity-building and has contributed to the building up and strengthening of S&T capacity in research institutions around the world. To help provide technology to meet the basic needs of low-income populations, SAREC is supporting both academic training and research in, for example, food technology, energy, water conservation, waste recycling, and rural industrialization. SAREC is carrying out a project with a focus on the role of township enterprises in China and is also coordinating a network of African researchers working on energy policy and planning in the field of renewable-energy technologies. Special mention should be made of a number of health- and nutrition-related projects in three Latin American countries and six African countries. In the African countries, SAREC is working on chemical and nutritional aspects of cassava processing, aquaculture, molecular biology of plant resistance, and assessments of national health policy.

## Swedecorp

Swedecorp is an agency created by the Swedish government to promote a favourable business environment and sustainable profitable enterprises in developing countries and Eastern Europe. Swedecorp provides assistance in three main areas: competence development, business development, and risk capital. Swedecorp's mission is mainly to assist SMEs, that is, the formal sector. Swedecorp's activities are not significantly related to basic-need issues and the microbusiness sector.

## Nongovernmental organizations

### African Centre for Technology Studies
The African Centre for Technology Studies (ACTS) was established in 1988 as a nonprofit organization with an international mandate to undertake policy research on S&T for sustainable development in Africa and to identify facilities to implement its findings. With a focus on key issues of contemporary development, ACTS is involved in three main activities: research, capacity-building, and outreach. ACTS carries out research and formulates, directs, and implements programs. Some research projects concentrate on methods of using technology in sustainable-development programs and activities; some focus on sustainable land use; and others focus on identifying policy and practical options for integrating gender awareness into development activities. To build capacity, ACTS provides general training in policy analysis and supervises postgraduate students, from local and foreign universities, who are studying S&T and environment policy. ACTS's Outreach Division issues publications and organizes consultations, conferences, and the Public Policy Outlook Seminars for the discussion and dissemination of research findings.

### Appropriate Technology International
Appropriate Technology International (ATI) is a private, nonprofit development corporation with offices in Africa, Asia, and Latin America. ATI targets assistance to groups of small-scale producers in strategic economic subsectors and works with a wide range of local, national, and international partners to devise and diffuse small-scale solutions worldwide. ATI has special programs to commercialize technologies that low-income entrepreneurs need to forge feasible businesses and sustainable livelihoods. ATI also has initiatives to develop business plans for basic industries and small-scale farmers.

ATI is mainly funded by USAID and assists animal herders, fibre processors, oilseed farmers and entrepreneurs, dairy producers, and tree-crop farmers. ATI provides advice on management and technology, such as irrigation systems, biofertilizers, and biopesticides, as well as advice on adding value to their products and on conserving the environment through alternative processing opportunities.

### Board on Science and Technology for International Development
The Board on Science and Technology for International Development (BOSTID), created in 1969, is an NGO with an annual budget of about

$6 million, much of which comes from USAID. Four major objectives have guided BOSTID's program from its inception:

▼ To help developing countries strengthen their own capabilities to deal with development-related problems and move toward greater S&T self-reliance;

▼ To effectively use S&T and engineering in solving problems of high priority for economic development and human welfare;

▼ To increase the access of developing countries to the S&T and engineering resources and expertise in the United States and other industrial countries; and

▼ To interest the US S&T and engineering community in assistance to developing countries and encourage greater interaction with colleagues in the Third World and to advise US and international development agencies on policy for S&T and engineering.

BOSTID uses a wide variety of mechanisms — workshops and advisory visits to developing countries, study reports and computer-linked conferences, research grants, and short-term courses — to carry out its comprehensive program. BOSTID's investigations of innovative uses of technologies, plants, and animals include biotechnological aspects. BOSTID has published a report on ferroconcrete applications in developing countries and has also focused on *Leucaena leucocephala*, a Mexican leguminous tree; the winged bean, a high-protein legume for the humid tropics; microlivestock; fishery technologies; and saline agriculture. BOSTID also provides assistance for sustainable agriculture and natural-resource management in Burkina Faso, El Salvador, Guatemala, and the Philippines. In Indonesia, BOSTID's recent activities include a marine science exchange program and workshops on systems analysis as a tool for examining food systems, rural technology, and food policy.

### Latin American Association of Development Financing Institutions

The 1994/95 working program of the Latin American Association of Development Financing Institutions (ALIDE) was concerned with finance and the promotion of SMEs. The program focused on the support and promotion of micro-, small-, and medium-scale enterprises (MSMEs) because these can make a significant contribution to economic and social growth. The difficult environment for Latin American domestic economies, resulting from a process of development in the framework of structural adjustment policies, compels these countries and their various economic agents to promote new fields and mechanisms for action to contribute to development. The mechanisms and instruments that development banks can make available to MSMEs play an active role in overcoming the gaps and imperfections in financial markets.

In 1994/95, under the guidance of its Small and Medium-Scale Companies Technical Committee, ALIDE planned technical meetings, training and technical-assistance activities, and studies concerning the financing and promotion of MSMEs. One study, "Development Banking, Social Equity and Environment," aims to use national experience as a background for examining the participation of development-financing institutions in designing and applying new forms of finance. The aim of this endeavour is to improve the productivity and well-being of sectors of the population with the lowest income levels by meeting their training and technical-education demands and housing needs. The study also considers the most suitable forms of finance for ecological and environmental preservation projects. ALIDE is preparing a report on systems for loans to MSEs in Latin America that evaluates the results of seven guarantee funds established in Colombia, Ecuador, El Salvador, Honduras, Mexico, Peru, and Venezuela.

Three regional seminars on promotion and finance for small-scale companies were set up in 1994 for the countries of Central America, the Andean Group, and the Southern Cone. The seminars gave these countries an opportunity to jointly analyze the development of MSMEs in the process of economic globalization, following up on a 1993 international seminar on this subject in Mexico City. Another seminar on business finance and the promotion of MSMEs covered such aspects as the role of development banks in supporting MSMEs, the preparation and evaluation of projects, and the mobilization of financial resources.

**World Assembly of Small and Medium Enterprises**
The World Assembly of Small and Medium Enterprises (WASME) is an NGO devoted to promoting rural SMEs in member countries. WASME carries out substantial work on food-processing technologies and the marketing of processed food and beverages, South–South and South–North cooperation, and human-resource development, with special attention to rural and small-scale industries.

WASME recently organized two national symposia on food-processing technologies and international marketing of food products and beverages, focusing on entrepreneurship and food-processing machinery. WASME has conducted seminars to promote South–South technology transfer, upgrading of locally available technologies, and trade among member countries. In an effort to promote economic cooperation between specific countries, WASME has carried out extensive studies with specialists from these countries. In the field of human-resource development, WASME has organized several international seminars in member countries. Recently, WASME was approached by the Government of India to share responsibility for providing the skills training people needed to start micro- and small-scale rural industries.

## World Association of Industrial and Technological Research Organizations

The World Association of Industrial and Technological Research Organizations (WAITRO) works on technological capacity-building, especially in developing countries; technological service in the SME sector; and North–South linkages. WAITRO brings together industrial and technological research institutions from developed and developing countries. Its 1993/94 work program emphasized capacity-building and institutional restructuring, especially for developing countries and countries in transition to market economies.

Among WAITRO's activities, one project centres on building capacity for research in traditional fermented-food processing. Another project, begun in September 1994, aims to establish a network of African institutions involved in the study of fermentation of traditional foods. This project helps these institutions develop modern techniques for food analysis, experiment in the development and use of starter cultures, and introduce quality-assurance systems. Six African institutions, in Burkina Faso, Ghana, Kenya, Nigeria, Tanzania, and Zimbabwe, as well as two European institutes, in Denmark and Germany, are involved in this project. WAITRO has a training course in laboratory and field techniques for the optimization of biogas production. An integrated pest-management project uses biological control to combat major pests in staple-food crops in West Africa.

## African Biosciences Network

The African Biosciences Network (ABN) was established in 1981 by UNESCO and ICSU to encourage and provide support for bioscience research and training. ABN's mandate is to provide the African region with competent skills in basic and applied biology to tackle the critical problems of hunger, disease, and poverty. UNDP provides support to ABN.

In 1989, ABN organized, in Yamoussoukro, Côte d'Ivoire, the International Symposium on the Role of Biology in the Solution of the Food Crisis in Africa. Following the recommendations of the symposium, the Yamoussoukro Programme was established. This program adopts an intensive approach to the appropriate use of biotechnologies to tackle the problems of hunger, disease, and poverty. ABN also promotes research in a wide variety of fields, such as sustainable land use, disease control, and health care.

## Development Alternatives, Inc.

Development Alternatives, Inc. (DAI) is a group established to promote and develop appropriate technologies for meeting basic needs and generating income. For the last 10 years, DAI has focused on appropriate shelter technologies, improved weaving technologies, upgraded silk-reeling devices, and handmade-recycled-paper technology. Appropriate technologies must be equitable, environmentally sound, and affordable and have the ultimate aim of generating sustainable livelihoods for marginalized and socially disadvantaged groups by improving the productivity and economic feasibility of enterprises.

Appropriate technologies promoted by DAI include Technology and Action for Rural Advancement (TARA) handmade-recycled-paper technology, which uses recycled cotton rags, waste paper, and agricultural residues. The TARA Handmade Recycled Paper Unit, on the outskirts of Delhi, demonstrates that this can be a profitable enterprise. The favoured options for dissemination of this technology are wholly owned units, franchised units, and joint ventures with buy-back arrangements. The TARA Balram is a machine for making compressed-earth blocks. This technology combines centuries of experience and the replicability of modern science. The TARA Balram is manually operated and can be used anywhere by either men or women. DAI's Technology Systems Branch runs training programs to familiarize masons and builders with appropriate building techniques in earth construction. The TARA microconcrete roofing (MCR) system was developed by adapting fibre concrete-roofing technology to Indian conditions. The system allows the creation of MCR tiles that are affordable to people who currently make do with thatch and tin sheets. The TARA vibrator, which is used for making these tiles, was indigenized so that all materials and spares are easily available in rural areas. The tile-making mixture, too, was developed to suit local conditions. The system comes with detailed manuals for operation, quality control, machine maintenance, and roof installation and is accompanied by a quality-control kit. Training is also provided. The MCR technology has resulted in some very successful enterprises.

## Intermediate Technology Development Group

ITDG is an NGO for promoting the use of intermediate technology. Much of ITDG's work follows a participatory approach to technological development, which combines the indigenous knowledge of local producers with the exogenous knowledge of the wider world. Recently, ITDG has made efforts to consolidate this approach under the concept of participatory technological development and to incorporate this approach in working practices. To accomplish this, ITDG has been collaborating with various European agencies to prepare a report to clarify the issues raised by this approach and to identify the gaps in current understanding.

ITDG's strategy for food production concentrates on the choice of technology for achieving food security and influencing decisions in favour of farmers, herders, and fishers. This strategy combats the increasing loss of entitlements among vulnerable groups of food producers caused by national and supranational policy changes, local pressures on resources, and adverse production conditions. ITDG disseminates ideas on low-input, sustainable agriculture and biodiversity. ITDG has further developed practices and processes for improving food security through cereals production and for dealing with pests, such as those affecting sorghum, through experimentation with local plants with the potential to kill pests.

ITDG's work in Kenya and Peru illustrates its concern with technology for basic needs. ITDG works in regions of Kenya with marginal farmers and pastoralists and does joint work with government services to develop strategies and train staff to help farm communities treat simple diseases. In Peru, ITDG has initiated an integrated rural concentration on livestock. Also, ITDG has developed an institution in Peru to focus on irrigation technology for peasant farmers.

ITDG has also taken a leading role in activities of the NGO Aquaculture Forum, in Bangladesh, which is concerned with poverty alleviation. Following a major workshop in October 1992, ITDG published and distributed a report, addressed to policymakers and practitioners alike, in the wider South Asian region. In addition, ITDG advises NGOs in Bangladesh on poverty-focused, fish-culture projects.

**International Council of Scientific Unions' Committee on Science and Technology for Development**
The main objective of COSTED is to stimulate selected S&T activities in developing countries and to direct these activities toward capacity-building and national development. The International Biosciences Network (IBN) was merged with COSTED in 1994. The registered COSTED–IBN is cosponsored by UNESCO. COSTED–IBN is involved in various activities, such as education, training, and publishing, and also organizes scientific meetings. Many of these have specific technology aspects related to basic needs, such as the meetings entitled The Role of Science and Technology Education in Capacity-Building in Developing Countries; The Role of Science in Food Production in Africa; and Basic and Applied Science Education in Developing Countries; and the workshops entitled Applications of Remote Sensing for Developing Countries; and Application of Satellite Remote Sensing for Identifying and Forecasting Potential Fishing Zones in Developing Countries. Concerning technology for education, COSTED–IBN has been involved in

the Development of Computer Software for Science Education project in India and computer courses catering to the needs of local students and researchers. COSTED–IBN has also organized university training programs for Asian and African scientists on such subjects as biotechnology and remote sensing.

COSTED–IBN believes that recent global trends in S&T and development and the increasing role of new and high technologies in the 21st century will force developing countries to consolidate and nurture a sound and self-reliant capacity in science if they are to participate effectively in the global march of development and provide the essential needs of their peoples.

## Third World Academy of Sciences

TWAS, a nonpolitical, nonprofit NGO established in 1983 to provide an international forum for distinguished scientists from the South, promotes scientific capacity and excellence for sustainable development. The current activities of TWAS can be grouped under five program headings: awards and prizes, capacity-building for research, fellowships and associateships, meetings and lectures, and publications. In addition to these programs, the TWAS Secretariat is responsible for the affairs of the Third World Network of Scientific Organizations (TWNSO) and is cosponsoring all of TWNSO's activities.

In the area of capacity-building for research, TWAS collaborates with the International Centre for Theoretical Physics to provide books and journals to a number of libraries in developing countries facing severe shortages in foreign currency. TWAS also provides funds to cover the cost of small-item spare parts that cannot be obtained or manufactured locally. TWAS is collaborating with TWNSO, UNIDO, ICSU, and UNESCO in an ambitious project to upgrade a number of competent scientific institutions in the South to international centres of excellence. As centres of excellence, they will provide the South with advanced training and research opportunities in S&T and environment, areas that are critical to sustainable development.

## International Federation of Consulting Engineers

The International Federation of Consulting Engineers (FIDIC) represents the interests of independent consulting engineers worldwide. FIDIC believes that the work of the engineering profession is critical to the achievement of the sustainable development of both society and the environment. FIDIC prepares proposals for training, technology transfer, mentorship, and other assistance programs for developing countries on a volunteer basis. However, FIDIC carries out no work directly on technologies for small-scale activities.

# Technology for Small-scale Economic Activities to Address the Basic Needs of Low-income Populations

*Food and Agriculture Organization*

The Food and Agriculture Organization of the United Nations (FAO) assists developing countries in the generation and transfer of science-based technologies, with the aim of supporting small-scale farmers and entrepreneurs in rural communities. The focus of assistance is on the men and women who produce most of the food in developing countries. FAO's work in research and technology development has a wide range of objectives: to increase and intensify food production; to improve consumption and nutrition; to raise the value added of agricultural produce; to improve income-earning capacity; and to create opportunities for employment in the production, processing, and marketing of agricultural goods. A large part of FAO's work in research and technology development is conducted in close cooperation with researchers and research institutions in developing and developed countries.

The application of science and technology to the improvement of living standards in developing countries has been a primary goal of FAO's activities since its foundation. To pursue this goal, the functional focus has traditionally been on activities that address the most basic needs of people and would, in addition, have a positive economic effect. Small-scale economic activities are a major source of rural and coastal livelihoods in developing countries. Much of this employment and income may be of a semisubsistence nature and poorly remunerative, but some enterprises are profitable and, occasionally, grow to a significant size. Even the semisubsistence enterprises are important because they reduce open unemployment and are accessible to the disadvantaged segments of society, such as women and the landless. Although the basic focus on the poor in developing countries has remained the same over the years, general approaches to assisting the poor have been modified to take advantage of experiences gained and to accommodate changes in the recipient environment.

The focus of technical assistance may have to be reconsidered because of the general move toward private-sector development. In the past, research and development (R&D) capacity has been geared toward helping national institutions, which, in turn, were to transfer R&D capability to local people. This approach has achieved very limited success on the ground. In future, it may be more worthwhile to concentrate less on research capacity per se and focus more on mechanisms to transfer this capacity to the sectors that can turn it into practical economy-building activities.

FAO operates with a very wide range of technology-transfer activities to address the basic needs of low-income populations, even if we consider only FAO's activities in food production and processing. The range of commodity coverage spans virtually all the known edible animal, aquatic, and plant products. The scope of technical activities employed to assist in the execution of small-scale economic activities is equally vast and includes basic production and all postharvest activities, including storage, transformation, and analytical technologies. In some cases, these technologies are used to stabilize perishable goods so that they may be marketed over an extended period, but in other cases, technologies are used to transform basic commodities into more marketable forms. The technologies used in this process may include traditional and modern technologies to reduce natural toxicity and specific antinutritional factors in certain foods.

It is beyond the scope of this paper to describe in detail the wide range of small-scale, technology-based economic activities covered by FAO. For example, the unit of FAO dealing with the processing of plant products covers close to 100 different commodities, which are convertible to items in more than 30 product groups (for example, juices, flours, baked or fermented products, and infant foods). More than 50 types of technology (for example, milling, extraction, extrusion, and dehydration), from rudimentary-cottage scale to small-industrial scale, are used. When additional sectors, such as meat, fish and other aquatic resources, and nonwood forest resources, are considered, the range of technologies employed is enormous. The following is a brief account of the work of FAO in developing research and technology for small-scale economic activities to address basic needs, with special emphasis on food production and processing.

# Basic production

## Crops

FAO promotes technologies for the sustainable production of cereals and food legumes, roots, tubers, vegetables, and fruits, which constitute staple-food crops for the majority of people in developing countries. In recent years, FAO has elaborated an integrated plant-nutrition system and an integrated pest-management approach that are environmentally sound and socially and economically feasible. The focus of attention is the cropping system, rather than an individual crop.

FAO conducts field trials with farmers to demonstrate options for improved production. Among the improvements introduced by FAO are increased access to marginal growing areas for different crops, appropriate agronomic practices, and identification and field introduction of improved varieties. Special emphasis is given to testing locally available and low-cost inputs, tailoring input applications to specific localities, and training national research and extension staff.

For some perishable crops, such as roots and tubers, or protein and oil crops, such as tropical soybeans, increased production should be linked to increased capacity for postharvest processing and handling at the village level. Therefore, FAO promotes technologies to generate more value added in the processing of such crops and is also developing projects to integrate processing with improved production techniques.

FAO also promotes home gardening and fruit-tree development, linked with nutrition education, and has prepared technical material for specific country conditions and national languages, as well as generic technical documentation for use in a wide range of countries.

## Livestock

Ruminant livestock is the most important animal resource in many developing countries and for the smallholders who are FAO's assistance priority. FAO gives some attention to camelids and small-animal production. FAO concentrates its R&D on large and small ruminants in the developing regions of Asia, Africa, and Latin America.

FAO conducts training, demonstration, and research in a regional cooperative network related to sheep and goats. FAO has made a computerized global inventory of activities related to small ruminants and has set up networking and training activities covering pigs and poultry. FAO has established a network on draft-animal power in Africa that provides information on the design of tools and harnesses for the better use of the animals.

FAO has taken the lead in coordinating international efforts in prevention, diagnosis, control, and eradication of livestock diseases. The FAO reference laboratories and FAO–WHO collaborating centres dealing with diagnosis constitute a global network of 20 units (9 of these are in developing countries), covering 29 diseases. These centres assist with diagnosis of diseases, preparation and distribution of diagnostic reagents, and training of specialists in laboratory diagnostic procedures.

Large populations of cattle and buffalo in the developing world are still at risk from rinderpest. FAO established two veterinary vaccine centres in East and West Africa to test rinderpest vaccine for the Pan African Rinderpest Campaign, and these centres have also held subregional seminars on vaccine quality control.

A regional project has been promoting the use of trypanosome-tolerant livestock, such as the n'dama cattle of West Africa, for rural development in areas infested by the tsetse fly. This project is making progress in n'dama-genome mapping. A program for the control of ticks and tick-prone diseases in East and Central Africa is in its second phase. In cooperation with the International Atomic Energy Agency, several governments, and donors, FAO was instrumental in quickly eradicating the screwworm fly from North Africa.

## Fisheries

FAO work in fisheries focuses on conservation and rational use of fisheries resources; development of small-scale fisheries and aquaculture; and improved fish use and marketing, with emphasis on the reduction of waste and postharvest losses. Research on better fishing technologies promoted by FAO has led to the introduction of appropriate new types of vessels, fishing gear, and energy-efficient water transport.

A project to develop small-scale fisheries in the Bay of Bengal was implemented by FAO more than a decade ago. The project has introduced technical advances to increase production, such as beach landing craft and improved fishing gear, supporting their use with social improvements, such as credit schemes (particularly for women) and nonformal education and training.

About 35 African countries participate in an FAO program for applied research on fish use, mainly at artisanal levels. FAO has done work on locally constructed smoking ovens that are more fuel efficient and on insulated storage containers that retard the melting of ice.

# Rural industry

## Farming systems

One of the keys to sustainable development in resource-poor areas is better management of farm production systems to minimize risks and enable the farm household to withstand shocks and stress. For small farms, FAO places special emphasis on efficient, sustainable operation that uses available material and labour resources, raises farm output, and increases farm and farm-family income.

FAO has supported studies on integrated crop and livestock farming systems in circumstances of pastoralism, shifting cultivation, and plantation cropping. The objective of such studies is intensified livestock production, coupled (when nomadic pastoralists are being settled) with increased fodder and crop production. The provision of animal feed is also promoted, for example, through a research network on the use of crop residues and agro-industrial products in West Africa.

Through the introduction and support of a wide range of engineering technologies, FAO seeks to improve production, reduce the risk of failure, and alleviate drudgery for farm families, especially for women in developing countries. National agricultural research institutions, extension agencies, and end-users are encouraged to select technologies appropriate to the relevant farming systems.

## Rural energy

Agriculture is an important user of energy in rural areas. Fuelwood accounts for about 60% of the energy consumed in Africa. About 30 developing countries depend on it for more than two thirds of their energy. However, the energy inputs required by rural populations is still in deficit in most developing countries. Heating, electricity, or mechanical power is needed for cooking food, transportation, and other local services. More energy is needed, but in many cases, per capita energy consumption has declined with population growth, as a result of shortage of fuelwood supplies, transportation problems, and high costs. FAO promotes new and renewable sources of energy to meet the requirements of rural populations in developing countries.

FAO's largest program on renewable sources of energy concentrates on solving the problems of fuelwood-deficit areas. Modern technologies are available to generate energy in various forms, but these technologies need to be adapted to local needs and possibilities. Biogas production, based on anaerobic digestion of organic wastes and residues, is expanding in many developing countries. FAO supports the greater diffusion of technologies through national projects for both small- and large-scale systems. Solar- or wind-energy sources are used for cooking, heating and pumping water, heating greenhouses, and refrigeration. However, the efficiency and reliability of solar- and wind-energy systems need to be improved and their costs reduced for these sources to be used widely.

## Food handling and processing

Too much of the world's food harvest is lost to spoilage and infestations on its journey to the consumer. Losses occur in all operations, from harvesting through to handling, storage, processing, and marketing. Proper evaluation of postharvest technologies should consider the entire postharvest chain, using loss assessment as a tool for understanding when, where, and why losses occur. Such an evaluation should include technical, economic, and social components and involve beneficiary participation throughout. Small-scale agro-industries are the major pipeline of food, fibre, and agriculturally based industrial commodities to the population. The small-scale agro-industry sector ensures that any comparative agricultural advantage that a country may have is sustained through the preservation and shelf-life extension of these materials in the most convenient and usable form. Thus, meeting the basic needs for food, clothing, and construction materials depends on a country's agro-industrial base.

The technical-assistance community is clearly giving more attention to small-scale food and agricultural enterprises. This is understandable because the agro-industries sector contributes significantly to the economies of developing countries. Agro-industries, regardless of scale, are generally defined as those industries engaged in a full range of economic activities involving raw materials derived from natural resources. Because the economies of most developing countries are agriculturally based, agro-industries generally contribute more than 50% of the overall manufacturing sector's added value. Agro-industries also have an extraordinary ability to generate employment opportunities. In many developing countries, small-scale agro-industry is often the largest employer in the manufacturing sector.

## Handling and storage of products

For rural handling and storage of farm inputs and outputs, FAO seeks to develop and make available farm- and village-level technologies that use locally available construction materials and building designs that reflect social and cultural traditions. The individual farmers make the decisions to adopt new or improved technologies. Application of simple techniques for harvesting, postharvest treatment, grading, sorting, and presentation of many fruits and vegetables, at village and community levels, has proven profitable for small-scale growers in numerous countries. The introduction of controlled-atmosphere techniques (where feasible) has provided access to more local and export markets.

## Agro-industries

The role of agro-industries in economic development is often underestimated. These industries aim to improve the quality and increase the value of primary agricultural products. Appropriate technologies are particularly needed for processing food in rural areas of developing countries. Traditional technologies can sometimes be upgraded to enhance the shelf life and consumer acceptance of indigenous foods, as well as developing value added for products with export potential.

FAO has issued a compendium of traditional food-processing technologies in Africa and supports research for, and establishment of, small- and medium-scale food-processing industries. The emphasis has been on food preservation in rural and semiurban areas, on small-scale, labour-intensive industries with low-cost available materials, and on import substitution.

FAO has promoted research on the processing of cereals, legumes, roots, and tubers into flours for indigenous convenience foods. In Africa, FAO has helped women's groups improve the handling, storage, and processing of cassava, maize, and other staples, contributing to food security at the village level. In other regions, rice milling has been made more efficient through the rehabilitation of existing mills and the establishment of new processing units. Rice parboiling has been introduced as a means of extending the yield and improving the nutritional value of rice.

New or modified technologies for slaughtering and meat handling and processing have been introduced in areas with an undeveloped infrastructure. Among these technologies are small-scale abattoirs for hygienic slaughtering in the absence of electricity and an adequate water supply, as well as mobile slaughter facilities. Because refrigeration is rarely available in the rural areas of developing countries, FAO focuses on traditional and modern, low-cost meat-preservation methods, such as meat-drying and other technologies yielding low- or intermediate-moisture products.

As a result of population growth and increased per capita incomes, demand for milk and dairy products exceeds supply in most developing countries. This is felt most acutely in urban areas, where people often resort to costly imported milk powder to meet requirements. The resulting increase in consumer demand provides an opportunity for year-round employment in smallholder dairy operations, thus making use of family and local labour resources. Establishing a functional link between small-scale milk producers and the growing markets requires the transfer of appropriate technologies for collection, processing, and distribution, and this is an area where FAO is very active. In addition, the conversion of milk to various dairy products, such as cheese and yoghurt, results in expanded markets for products with a longer shelf life. FAO is developing a low-cost, village-level processing model and is studying village-level use of microbial starters and possible rennet substitutes for cheese making.

Special efforts have been made to promote apiculture through improvements in beekeeping technologies, hives, equipment, and management methods. Enhanced control of processing has increased the yield and improved the quality of honey and beeswax. FAO has given special support to sericulture development through training in technology for the production and processing of natural silk. FAO has promoted improvements in mulberry-tree cultivation and harvesting, silkworm breeding, cocoon production and disease control, silkworm-egg production, and silk reeling. Such technology can bring high returns for small-scale farmers, including women.

Agricultural products other than food should also be processed to increase value, secure markets, and raise returns for the primary producers. FAO has assisted in the development of processing techniques for natural fibres at the farm and village levels. These techniques include the scouring, grading, testing, and processing of wool, mohair, alpaca, cashmere, cotton, and jute. Labour-intensive small-scale or cottage industries, such as spinning, dyeing, and weaving, require relatively low capital investment and have benefited rural women in particular.

The use of animals for other than meat commodities is another basis for small-scale industry. Improved techniques are now available for flaying, curing, and preserving hides and skins and for using blood, bones, horns, hooves, and intestines to produce marketable commodities, such as glue, sausage casings, animal feed, and fertilizer. FAO has also facilitated the introduction of the wet-salting technique for curing hides and skins from goats and cattle, which in many instances increases their value by as much as 150 and 200%, respectively.

Small-scale agro-industries provide for basic food, shelter, and energy needs and are centrally involved in health through medicinal plants. Until 150 years ago, crude plants were central to all medicine, and herbs are humankind's most ancient therapeutic aid. Their central role in medicine throughout the ages eventually led to these plants becoming part of a folkloric tradition. Because developing countries, particularly those in tropical or semitropical regions, have a comparative advantage in the production of medicinal plants, a number of FAO technical units are providing assistance to this sector.

## Nonwood forest products

More than a decade ago, FAO launched the Forestry for Local Community Development program to help forestry play a more effective role in rural development. The program continues but is now called Forests, Trees and People. In this program, FAO has targeted for study small-scale, forest-based enterprises for the creation of off-farm employment and income opportunities in rural areas.

Small-scale, forest-based enterprises generally have 1.8–3.8 workers, including the owner. More than 60% of these enterprises are one-person operations, that is, the owner is also the only worker. In many countries, enterprises based on nonwood forest products, such as grasses, leaves, cane, and bamboo, are smaller but far more numerous than enterprises based on wood. If enterprises involving fruit, honey, mushrooms, and wildlife meat are added, the dominance of nonwood forest industries in the category of small-scale enterprises becomes even more marked. In promoting the development of nonwood forest products, FAO does not look at the product or commodity in isolation but at a wide range of factors that could help people exploit and manage these resources for sustainability and market the final products for profit.

# Information and technology transfer

FAO most often disseminates technology for small-scale economic activities through its technical bulletins and newsletters. The bulletins contain complete factual information on a wide range of small-scale technologies, along with associated economic, management, and marketing information where appropriate. The newsletters keep extension agencies and individuals informed about technological innovations and provide additional information on where to get more data.

In certain cases, when warranted, FAO has established networks to disseminate technologies for the small-scale food industry in Latin America and Asia. These networks work fairly well if only a few government agencies are involved but have definite limitations in reaching a wide client base of entrepreneurs. Cooperative research programs are a cost-effective way of dealing with technological issues: professional resources can be consulted close to where the issues arise. Expert technical consultations are also used to focus on specific technical interventions. When low-orbit satellite communications technology is more firmly established, it may be possible to use cellular transmission technology to reach a much wider client base directly. This would greatly enhance the extension infrastructures in most developing countries.

To achieve a higher rate of adoption of recommended technologies and to spread the know-how, FAO has been promoting the development and use of agricultural extension systems, agricultural schools, and farmers' organizations. In 1990, FAO's Global Consultation on Agricultural Extension reported that the world had about 600 000 trained extension workers, who could be used to spread available technologies for small-scale farming.

## Future issues

The political mood in the developing world has changed dramatically in the last decade. An almost universal shift has taken place away from centrally planned economies and toward market-driven economies. As a result, technical assistance to the developing world has to shift away from government and toward the private entrepreneur. A radical rethinking of the entire technical-assistance process will be required if we are to effectively contribute to private-enterprise development. Future initiatives will have to be directed to fostering new alliances to effectively meet these challenges. We must be innovative enough to serve private entrepreneurs with programs that support economic development and provide the information, expertise, and contacts that result in profitable and sustainable enterprises.

Despite major efforts to maintain in developing countries an up-to-date awareness of the potential benefits of modern, small-scale technologies, certain trends in the dissemination, ownership, and distribution of technical knowledge may negatively affect developing countries. Our knowledge base in the sciences has traditionally been anchored in research at public universities. However, a large and growing part of university research is funded by private interests that exert a certain degree of control over the dissemination and use of this information. This has resulted in the private sequestering of an inordinate level of scientific information, excluding it from science's global intellectual base. The developing countries are most severely affected by this trend because they are entirely dependent on the public information base for their scientific knowledge.

# Chapter 11

# Technology-related Work for Basic Needs of Low-income Populations

*International Labour Organization*

## Why a basic-needs framework?

Most poor people, including the very poorest, live in rural areas. Even with an antipoverty slant in development programs, Third World countries have yet to make any significant dent in poverty. It is not surprising, therefore, to observe that the level and growth of incomes are not correlated with basic-needs' achievements in Africa.

Paucity of jobs, limited purchasing power, and socioeconomic inequalities contribute to the inability of poor countries, poor families, and poor individuals to fulfill their basic needs. For these reasons, the Technology Programme of the International Labour Organization (ILO) has had a clear antipoverty thrust that relies on employment generation as a major instrument for improving the poor's access, particularly in rural areas, to basic goods and services.

259

# Conventional technologies

The following are highlights of our proposal for a new international mechanism to promote sound national technological capability in generating indigenous technologies best suited to the particular conditions of developing countries and disadvantaged groups:

▼ The mechanism should be a flexible entity, not dominated by donors from the developed countries or from the developing countries, but with greater participation of the developing countries.

▼ The mechanism should be formally outside the United Nations system but closely associated with the United Nations organizations currently engaged in technology-related work for basic needs.

▼ The mechanism should not be responsible for coordinating United Nations activities in the field of technology for basic needs that should be undertaken by appropriate bodies in the United Nations system.

A critical review of the contribution of the ILO Technology Programme to income generation and employment creation for target groups in different sectors of developing countries resulted in the following conclusions:

▼ Intermediate technologies available in agriculture, forestry, and women's processing activities in rural areas can be labour saving. In general, intermediate technologies lead to greater productivity than traditional techniques and to less labour displacement than the more capital-intensive technologies.

▼ Intermediate technologies can be disseminated directly to the target groups by working through their participatory organizations at the grass-roots level.

Evidence collected by the ILO from its work in East and South Africa clearly suggests that expanded use and local manufacture of simple, innovative but well-adapted farm equipment can make a significant contribution to farm productivity and income and to the growth of rural-based manufacturing and the expansion of nonfarm output and employment. The experience derived from an ILO forestry-technology project in the Philippines reveals that intermediate or improved labour-intensive technologies are feasible and commercially attractive.

Intermediate technologies generate productive employment and offer, in varying degrees, the advantages of improved working conditions, decreased risk of injury, and greater protection of the environment.

## Gender aspects of conventional technologies

In the mid-1980s, several studies looked for areas where improved technology could both reduce the workload of and generate income for rural women in South Asia. These studies found that production linkages may or may not always be beneficial for women. Some examples are the following:

▼ The mechanization of the fishing industry in Kerala, India, has resulted in a large increase in the volume of the fish catch and increased women's employment in net making, coir and prawn processing, marketing, and trade.

▼ An alternative technology for milk preservation introduced in the Punjab, Pakistan, has strengthened the backward production linkage with villages near a sterilization plant, but the tendency in the rural family has been for men to pocket the earnings generated by women's additional work.

Field-based ILO technical-cooperation projects for women from three developing subregions (South Asia and West and South Africa) indicate that it is feasible to widen and diversify women's income-earning opportunities by introducing improved technologies. Applying improved technologies could generate women's employment in nontraditional areas, and upgrading the technologies in women's traditional occupations could simultaneously raise their productivity and reduce the drudgery of their work. Channeling improved technologies through rural women's participatory organizations contributes significantly to women's empowerment. Fostering of linkages with commercial suppliers of technology, training institutes, and marketing channels has been a key element in the strategy for women's empowerment.

The emerging experience of developing countries suggests that the kinds of jobs women will be able to get will continue to be associated with women's comparative advantage, that is, with gender traits that are not recognized, or paid for, as professional skills. When industries adopt improved technologies, the women are relegated to the industrial periphery, stressing, therefore, the core–periphery segmentation of the labour force. In traditional industries, such as textiles, footwear, and rattan furniture, the technological improvement of the production process seems to exacerbate the existing gender division of labour, where the better paid jobs with higher skills content are undertaken by men and the lower paid jobs with lower skills content are undertaken by women.

In the metal industry in Indonesia, the introduction of electrical power for the operation of casts has led to work fragmentation, and more tasks have been undertaken by women. Men are concentrated in the finishing process and in the maintenance section. In this case, too, the differential between men's and women's wages illustrates the trend toward the relegation of women to the industrial periphery.

Technical and professional education for women has become a necessary, if not sufficient, condition for changing the gender-based labour-market segmentation of skills and salaries.

# New technologies

Some new technologies for meeting the basic needs of low-income groups are microelectronics, remote sensing, and biotechnology. Microelectronics and remote sensing are applied more to planning, management, control, and data collection and processing than to direct production processes. Microelectronics technology can advance rural nonfarm development and industrialization if it is not too costly but is easy to maintain and repair and requires simple skills and little additional infrastructure. Remote-sensing satellites can provide improved information on natural resources and contribute to increased agricultural production, further facilitating rural development.

Biotechnology can help small-scale producers in developing countries by providing enhanced production methods and environmentally safer inputs that increase farm productivity and, therefore, increase income and employment opportunities for rural producers and wage workers. Some evidence suggests that biotechnology can help reduce seasonality in agricultural employment and enhance aggregate rural employment through strengthened intersectoral linkages, additional use of land, enhanced cropping intensity, and increased demand for hired labour. Hunger in Third World countries could be reduced by using more productive microbial strains to upgrade traditional fermentation processes. Biotechnology offers, therefore, good potential for meeting the basic needs of low-income groups. Through the application of these technologies in agriculture, the following advantages can be achieved:

> ▼ Farmers' production costs can be reduced by eliminating their dependence on agrochemical inputs.

▼ Agricultural productivity can be raised, helping to reduce food prices and offering significant benefits to the landless workers and the urban poor.

▼ The availability of food and the nutritional value of staple crops can be increased, thus reducing the malnutrition so widely prevalent in many developing countries.

## Gender aspects of new technologies

### Microelectronics

The introduction of microelectronics tends to displace jobs with a high information content, and these jobs are invariably occupied by a disproportionately high number of women — office and clerical workers, bank tellers, and telephone and computer operators. Women whose jobs are threatened by microelectronics applications need to be included in an aggressive retraining program to upgrade and diversify their skills if the newly emerging jobs and occupations are not to be cornered by the men.

### Biotechnology: pros and cons

Modern agricultural biotechnologies have the potential to create jobs and incomes for the poorest people by extending cultivation to remote areas. These technologies could also make a dent in seasonal underemployment by allowing multiple cropping. Peasant households, though, would have to rely largely on the pool of unpaid female family members to take care of the extra work generated. Thus, even greater use of unpaid female labour would be required.

The commercialization and worldwide distribution of genetically engineered plant varieties will lead to a substitution of chemical herbicides for manual weeding, largely performed by female wage labour on whose earnings the poorest households depend for their survival. At the same time, the new varieties will introduce a new fixed cost for farmers by compelling them to purchase the herbicide tied to the seed, both supplied by the same multinational enterprise.

# Technologies for sustainable livelihoods

An ILO survey of rural Kenya revealed that socioeconomic sustainability and environmental sustainability are not only interrelated but also mutually supportive. The attributes of socioeconomic sustainability include land rights, equitable farm ownership distribution, stability of incomes and employment, and satisfaction of basic needs (access to water, sanitation, and housing). Other factors that have contributed to sustainable livelihoods are the application of productivity-enhancing agricultural and soil-conservation technologies, awareness of water-treatment and improved sanitation technologies, and use of waste-management techniques.

Chapter 12

# Activities in Technical and Vocational Education

*United Nations Educational, Scientific and Cultural Organization*

The United Nations Educational, Scientific and Cultural Organization (UNESCO) has been very active in the field of technical and vocational education since the early 1960s. UNESCO has organized conferences, seminars, and workshops, undertaken studies, and disseminated publications and information. The aim of these endeavours was to contribute to the development and improvement of technical and vocational education in UNESCO's member states.

The idea of a comprehensive project in technical and vocational education dates back to 1987, when UNESCO held its first International Congress for the Development and Improvement of Technical and Vocational Education, in Berlin, Germany. Member states strongly supported the suggestion that mechanisms be established for the international exchange of information on technical and vocational education. It was proposed that UNESCO support the establishment of an international centre for research and development (R&D) in technical and vocational education.

In 1989, the General Conference (the main decision-making body of UNESCO) made two important decisions related to technical and vocational education: it adopted the Convention on Technical and Vocational Education and it invited UNESCO's director-general to carry out a feasibility study on the establishment of an international centre for technical and vocational education. Based on that feasibility study, which was completed early in 1991, the General Conference decided to launch the first phase of the UNESCO International Project on Technical and Vocational Education (UNEVOC) during 1992–95.

# The UNEVOC project

## Financing

UNEVOC is financed through UNESCO's regular budget, together with a grant from the Government of the Federal Republic of Germany. Germany also provided premises in Berlin for the project Implementation Unit. Several other member states have also made contributions to UNEVOC. For instance, the Government of the Republic of Korea sent an expert to work for UNEVOC and funded a fellowship program to train technical and vocational educators from developing nations. The Government of Japan has also decided to provide an expert to the project. Currently, we are making great efforts to allocate more financial resources from UNESCO's member states, other organizations, and the private sector.

## The program

### Program area A: system development
The basic concept behind program area A is to enhance the role and status of technical and vocational education in national education systems. UNESCO held a consultation in 1993, with experts from different regions of the world, to identify some of the factors determining the role and status of technical and vocational education. Currently, a series of case studies is being prepared on the relevance of these factors in given national education systems.

To promote cooperation between educational authorities and the world of work in technical and vocational education, UNEVOC will study existing policies and legislation that enhance such cooperation in selected countries.

As soon as these case studies are completed, the information gathered will be made available to all interested countries and presented to policymakers through regional symposia.

A gender-related survey on the relevance of vocational information and guidance to access to technical and vocational education was carried out as a contribution to the Fourth World Conference on Women, held in Beijing in September 1995.

**Program area B: infrastructures**

Program area B is devoted to strengthening national R&D capabilities through the development of infrastructures. In 1993, UNESCO held a workshop that convened experts from all the regions of the world. Participants compared different methods for developing vocational curricula. UNESCO has initiated certain follow-up activities. UNESCO places special emphasis on the international transfer and adaptation of existing curricula. Differences in applied technologies, norms, legislation, teacher training, and so on have to be taken into account when curricula are to be adapted to a new environment. UNESCO will document the methods applied and experience gathered in the course of such curriculum adaption.

Cooperation between educational institutions and enterprises is needed not only at the system level but also at the training level. The workplace provides a valuable environment for systematic vocational learning. But how can this potential be exploited for the improvement of training? UNESCO is studying mechanisms for cooperation between educational institutions and enterprises and will make the results available to the member states.

With the support of a partner institution in an industrialized country, a seminar for key personnel was scheduled for 1995 to address the modalities of cooperation between educational institutions and enterprises.

UNESCO will also take steps to define its future role in the promotion of nonformal technical and vocational education. A survey will be prepared on the activities of various agencies of the United Nations system specializing in this field. That survey will be used as a basis for consultation with these agencies.

**Program area C: information and communication**

Program area C deals with access to databases and documentation in its broadest sense. This concept includes the development of information and communication structures among specialized institutions. The program is devoted to enriching the flow of information between specialized institutions in the member states and aims to increase the transparency of information and enhance the access to databases and documentation. UNEVOC will not compete with specialized documentation centres but will assist member states in efficiently using existing data and documentation.

*UNEVOC Info*, which is published quarterly in English and French, is one of the activities under program area C. Some technical documents dealing with specific topics in technical and vocational education are being prepared and will be disseminated.

## UNEVOC centres

As an important component of the UNEVOC project, efforts are being made to establish a worldwide network of technical and vocational institutions. At the beginning stage, each member state has been invited, through its National Commission for UNESCO, to nominate a leading technical and vocational institution in the country as the national focal point of the network. These institutions will be called UNEVOC centres. There is a possibility that more than one UNEVOC associate centre might be established in each country. To date, more than 70 member states have nominated about 100 institutions to be involved in the UNEVOC network. Once the key institutions are identified, a directory of UNEVOC institutions will be available.

To promote the network, UNESCO organized regional UNEVOC networking workshops in Australia (for the Asia–Pacific region), Kenya (for the African region), Uruguay (for Latin America and the Caribbean), and Bahrain (for Arab States) in late 1993 and early 1994. More than 50 member states participated at these meetings, where interlinkage among UNEVOC centres was discussed and joint activities to meet the regional needs were initiated.

# Chapter 13

# Technology for Health, Particularly for Low-income Populations

*World Health Organization*

*Technology* has been defined by Kenneth Galbraith as the "application of scientific and (or) organized knowledge to practical tasks." Because of the amazing advances in biomedical knowledge, we are now faced with a large discrepancy between the capability to diagnose and the capability to treat.

The term *equipment-embodied technology*, introduced by the Committee on Medical Technology and Health of the National Research Council (NRC 1979), refers, in part, to equipment, procedures, services, or systems that depend primarily on capital equipment. Health-care technology can also be classified according to the function it performs. Clinical technology is used in the provision of direct patient care. Ancillary technology is used directly to support clinical services, such as anaesthesiology, diagnostic radiology, radiation therapy, clinical laboratories, and respiratory therapy. This technology represents more than half of the medical electronics market. Coordinative, educational, and research technologies are used to facilitate, support, improve, and evaluate health-care services but are not directly associated with patient care. Management technologies at all levels represent probably one of the most critical issues for the performance of any modern health-care system.

The role of indirect technologies in the elimination of a large class of diseases through improvements in nutrition, sanitation, education, housing, and hygiene is evident. For most of the Third World countries, the use of these technologies is still a prerequisite for basic health improvements. In fact, these technologies are becoming even more important throughout the world as we try to deal success-fully with the health consequences of pollution and various forms of environmental destruction.

Health technologies, from the point of view of destination, may be categorized as preventive, diagnostic, therapeutic, and enabling technologies, derived mainly from advances in the biological and phys-ical sciences.

## Preventive technologies

Preventive technologies are used for screening and early detection of diseases, such as cancer. Advances in molecular genetics are progres-sively confirming the association between gene defects and specific cancers, as is the case for breast and lung cancers. With the rapid unravelling of the human genome, knowledge about genetic determi-nants of disease will grow exponentially, and with that knowledge, pos-sibilities for early intervention will develop, leading to primary and secondary prevention.

Early detection is also feasible with physical techniques, such as endoscopy and imaging. Reconstruction methods using advanced hardware and software have already revolutionized radiological and ultrasonographic imaging. With faster machines, higher levels of inte-gration, and the ubiquitous use of artificial intelligence, more sophisti-cated algorithms will permit the dynamic investigation of vital organs, like the brain, heart, and liver.

Other well-established preventive technologies are used for vaccinology, nutrition, and environmental engineering. New vaccines will be developed to allow single-dose, multiantigen immunization for children under 1 year old. The constraints imposed by the cold chain in developing countries could lead to the production of lyophilized products. New knowledge about the relationship between nutrition and several noncommunicable diseases is rapidly accumulating, and new food-processing and food-conservation techniques facilitate distribu-tion and diet optimization. Advances in civil and mechanical engineer-ing, materials science, surface technology, and related disciplines will help improve the cost-effectiveness of delivering water and sanitation services. With the rapidly accelerating pace of urbanization in the Third World, faster and less expensive methods of installing infrastruc-ture will be developed.

# Diagnostic technologies

One of the most important developments in diagnostic technologies is the use of the hybridoma technique for producing monoclinal antibodies. The development of the biotechnology industry has been a major result of, and influence on, many such advances. Recombinant DNA techniques are available for prenatal screening and, where necessary, for postnatal examination for inborn errors of metabolism. A variety of other new diagnostic aids are being introduced. Particular types of tumour, for example, generate specific proteins; some may provide opportunities for developing specific assay techniques for early detection of some tumours. The general conclusion from this successful experience must be that deeper knowledge about the biochemistry of normal and pathological conditions will lead to the development of detectable and measurable disease-specific elements and thus to improved diagnostic procedures.

In the realm of physical science and technology (S&T), three major kinds of development have dominated the advance of diagnostic procedures: first, simple, commercially produced, disposable kits that allow diagnostic testing of body fluids to be carried out in the field; second, electronic diagnostic equipment with microchip technology and, in some cases, biosensors; and third, imaging and visualization technology.

Disposable self-test kits for estimation of blood glucose level, for pregnancy testing, and for urine testing are now familiar items. Many more such analytical probes are likely to be made available. However, when a precise indication of the concentration of the material being assayed is needed, biosensor technology will become important. Biosensors represent the result of combining two technologies: microelectronics and biological recognition based on enzymes acting as biochemical catalysts. Earlier detection techniques depended on antibody binding reactions, rather than enzyme catalysis. The new techniques offer the possibility of assaying an increasing range of drugs and hormones. Current and future biosensor technology will be used for monitoring water or air pollution, for monitoring bioprocessing in the food industry, for evaluating the quality of food products kept in storage, and for veterinary purposes. Applications in primary health care would also be self-evident because such devices, interfacing biological materials with electronic circuits, are inexpensive and easy to use.

Electronic diagnostic equipment is developing rapidly because microchip technology has made it possible for a microcomputer to be included in the individual instrument or attached to it as a personal computer. Advances in diagnostic procedures, such as electro- and magnetocardiography, electro- and magnetoencephalography, fetal monitoring, vestibular testing, audiometry, ambulatory monitoring, ophthalmography, and the Doppler investigation of regional blood flow depend on quite sophisticated processing that is transparent to the user. Consequently, it will be increasingly feasible to perform dynamic measurements in spatiotemporal terms, that is, displaying surface maps of the physiological variable as a series of snapshots in real time, at a hundred times per second or more.

Imaging technologies, such as ultrasonography, computer-aided tomography, magnetic-resonance imaging, and positron-emission tomography, have grown out of basic research in physics, mathematics, and electrical engineering. Improvements are expected in speed and resolution (for example, 1 000× in the still experimental ion computer tomography), and efforts are being made to extract information about function, as well as state, to allow better evaluation of planned treatments. Of particular interest is ultrasonic imaging, achieved by echo reflection and the Doppler effect, which allows conventional visualization and measurement of flow and tissue movement. Special techniques, such as colour display of flow mapping (which helps visual interpretation) and pulsed Doppler (which measures both range and velocity, thus allowing velocity profiles to be examined), are adding complexity to investigations but are also likely to expand their range.

## Therapeutic technologies

The combined use of advances in biotechnology and advances in chemistry is promising to streamline and enhance drug development, leading to new treatments for Alzheimer's disease, heart disease, cancer, AIDS, rheumatoid arthritis, and multiple sclerosis.

Monoclinal antibodies will be improved by the adjunction of small synthetic molecules that mimic the targeting portion of the antibody, thus facilitating drug delivery. Carbohydrate research will also play an important role because new investigations point to the possibility of interfering with the binding of carbohydrate ligand to certain cell receptors, which would be useful for treating inflammatory processes, such as rheumatoid arthritis. Other research, of a speculative nature, is exploring the potential of antisense technology: short strands of DNA-like chemicals would be engineered to short-circuit harmful genetic messages. Furthermore, the exploitation of computer technology in drug design is opening up new possibilities: 3-D visualization of molecules, such as the enzyme R Nase H, which the AIDS virus needs to replicate, helps in locating the active site of the enzyme, hence facilitating the development of drugs most likely to disable it. Similar strategies apply to the fight against cancer.

In surgical treatment, various technologies and developments from physical science, such as lasers, are becoming important. Ophthalmologists were the first to adopt lasers for surgery, using them to seal blood vessels and repair or prevent retinal detachment. Laser technology may have potential in photodynamic therapy of cancer, especially in conjunction with photosensitizing agents for treating localized malignancy. Neurosurgery and otolaryngological surgery for the removal of tumours have already produced favourable results and appear to have an excellent future. Another area with interesting possibilities is cardiac surgery, where a fibre-optic laser probe might be used to clear an occluded coronary blood vessel.

Microsurgery is becoming much more subtle and sophisticated, partly with the aid of lasers but also with microscopy and other technological innovations. Another development that has been gaining momentum is the use of robotically controlled devices in surgery of the brain or other organs for which precise positioning is vital.

Surgery is often guided by detailed clinical measurement, and especially where the cardiovascular system is involved, flow measurements are needed, which explains the importance of Doppler techniques. Ultrasonic procedures also have therapeutic applications, such as breaking up kidney stones. Pre- and postsurgical control of the patient, using feedback techniques based on modern control theory, is well developed. Automatic control of blood pressure and other physiological parameters is now routine following open heart surgery. Automated anesthesia is also being extensively studied.

Significant advances are occurring in substitution and repair, transplants of various kinds, prostheses and orthoses, and implanted devices to deal with the problem of disablement. Joint replacement depends on the availability of strong, light, biologically inert materials that can be designed to fine tolerances. New materials are contributing to the broad applicability of such procedures.

Organ transplants have undoubtedly a major future. However, it must be noted that organs for transplant (especially kidneys) are seriously lacking at the moment. This problem needs urgent attention at political, planning, and ethical levels. Artificial devices, though relevant, do not seem likely to provide a permanent solution.

## Enabling technologies

Enabling technologies make an indirect but significant contribution to solving various health-sector problems. In biomedical science, for example, the new discipline of protein engineering uses some of the latest developments in computer technology and computer graphics to design drugs that require a shape complementary to that of a specific macromolecular structure. This illustrates the importance of enabling technologies: technologies that directly or indirectly make substantial advances possible in biomedical science, medical practice, and health technology.

New materials continually offer new opportunities for less costly, better, and more novel biomedical devices, equipment, and facilities; products for the disabled; and economical maintenance of a country's physical infrastructure. Advances in waste-water disposal and environmental control are bound to make important contributions to public-health engineering. Developments in management science and decision-support technology will have a major impact on the rationalization of manufacturing and on the generation of new technologies. In addition, advances in decision-support technology are bound to improve planning in the health sector.

Health technologies range from sophisticated and expensive ones, destined to expand the potential of medicine and health, to simpler and inexpensive ones, destined to treat the large groups of vulnerable and underprivileged people in low-income countries. Examples of definite technology, such as immunization and chemotherapy, illustrate that when effective technologies for prevention, control, and cure of disease are developed, they are relatively inexpensive and simple.

## Technology in support of health at the World Health Organization

All health interventions carried out by the World Health Organization (WHO) use appropriate technology. The selection of technologies for specific health interventions is based on the concept of appropriate technology for health endorsed at the 1978 World Health Conference on Primary Health Care. Technology is appropriate if it is not only scientifically sound but also acceptable to those who apply it and to those for whom it is used. Technology is an association of methods, techniques, and equipment that, together with the people using it, can contribute significantly to solving a health problem.

Each WHO technical program has its own strategy for the assessment, transfer, and application of health technologies. Programs with large technology components emphasize affordable and absorbable health technologies with scientifically proven effectiveness in both large- and small-scale operations. Some specific examples are given below.

## Oral rehydration

Oral rehydration salts (ORS) are a key element in the strategy for reducing deaths from diarrhea among young children. A primary concern of the Division of Diarrhoeal and Acute Respiratory Disease Control has been to ensure sufficient supplies of ORS to meet the need of each country. Although the United Nations Children's Fund (UNICEF) and other donors continue to be important sources of ORS, especially for African countries, the production of ORS by the developing countries has increased steadily. This has come about in large part through efforts of WHO and UNICEF to help countries establish and expand local capacity for ORS production.

Annual global production of ORS continues to increase and now includes about 400 million packets produced in 60 countries; about two thirds of all production is now in the developing countries. The annual contribution of UNICEF remains relatively constant at about 80 million packets.

In developing countries, the Programme for the Control of Diarrhoeal Diseases (CDD) has encouraged local production of ORS in both the private and the public sectors. In discussions with ORS manufacturers, it became clear that the fact that the CDD program had approved only one ORS formula was discouraging manufacturers from developing the product for sale in the private sector. The CDD program agreed, therefore, to define an acceptable range of formulas so that companies could develop distinctive products that would, nonetheless, be safe and effective. The resulting guidelines have assisted companies in product development and have also allowed official drug regulators to confirm whether the compositions of different oral rehydration products were within acceptable limits.

In recent years, the CDD program has supported many research projects to determine whether changes in the formula for ORS could improve its efficacy, that is, reduce stool losses, the duration of diarrhea, or the requirement for intravenous therapy. Although most of the experimental formulas have not been more effective, two are promising. A rice-based ORS has been shown to substantially reduce stool losses in patients with cholera. Perhaps more important, a formula with reduced salt and glucose contents significantly reduces stool losses and the need for intravenous therapy in children with all types of acute diarrhea. It is likely that these findings will lead to the introduction and general use of an improved ORS formula in the near future.

## Action Programme on Essential Drugs

Governments recognize health care as a basic right of their people. Although drugs alone are insufficient to ensure adequate health care, they do play an important role in protecting, maintaining, and restoring health. Providing health services with regular supplies of essential drugs, that is, drugs that meet the health-care needs of the majority of the population, is crucial to making primary health care work and to fulfilling one of the basic needs of low-income populations.

The Action Programme on Essential Drugs (DAP) was established in 1981 to provide operational support to countries in the development of national drug policies based on essential drugs and to work for the rational use of drugs. DAP seeks to ensure that all people, wherever they may be, are able to obtain the drugs they need, at a price that they and their country can afford; that these drugs are safe, effective, and of good quality; and that they are prescribed and used rationally. DAP cooperates with member states and international, bilateral, and nongovernmental organizations (NGOs) in implementing all the elements of essential drug programs or national drug policies.

To strengthen its country-support work, DAP conducts operational research on national and global constraints to pharmaceutical supply and use. DAP also develops tools to facilitate the work of national programs, such as improved methodologies to estimate drug needs or a guide to good drug prescribing.

Today, the essential-drugs concept is widely accepted as being in the interests of public health. More than 120 countries have adapted the WHO Model List of Essential Drugs (WHO 1995) to match their own patterns of disease and financial resources. Governments are developing mechanisms to improve the availability of drugs. People are more aware of the problems linked with the irrational prescription and use of drugs. However, although the procurement and distribution of drugs have improved in many countries, progress has been challenged by the economic crisis and structural adjustment process, and access to essential drugs still remains limited and inequitable in many parts of the world. DAP will continue to support countries in identifying and implementing innovative strategies to improve drug availability and use.

## Food safety

### Guidelines for can manufacturers and food canners

In 1986, WHO and the Food and Agriculture Organization of the United Nations (FAO) jointly issued guidelines for minimizing and preventing lead contamination of canned food. By following this advice, even small-scale can manufacturers and food canners can produce products that comply with the safety standard for lead.

### Hazard Analysis Critical Control Point evaluation system

The Hazard Analysis Critical Control Point (HACCP) evaluation system is a relatively new approach to the prevention and control of foodborne diseases. The system is used to identify the hazards associated with various stages of food production and preparation, assess the related risks, and determine the operations where control procedures will be effective. To help people apply HACCP in homes, food-service establishments, cottage industries, or street markets, WHO published a guide (Bryan 1992) identifying hazards and addressing risks associated with food preparation and storage.

### Essential food-safety criteria for street vendors

Street vending of food is a rapidly growing industry, providing job opportunities and economic gain to virtually tens of millions of people, particularly women, all over the world. However, several high-risk foods may serve as a vehicle for the transmission of infectious diseases, such as cholera, salmonellosis, hepatitis A, and poliomyelitis. In 1992, to address this problem and to provide advice to food-control authorities and street vendors, the Food Safety Unit (FOS) issued the HACCP guide (Bryan 1992) in the form of a provisional edition (WHO/HPP/FOS 92.3). An annual edition, field tested and thoroughly revised, was expected to be available in early 1995.

### Mass catering

Mass catering is an economic activity of restaurants and canteens, among others. The risk of spreading foodborne diseases is particularly high in mass-catering establishments, where people eat from the same food source. Because large outbreaks of foodborne disease have been traced back to mass catering, WHO published *Mass Catering* (WHO 1983), *Safe Food Handling: A Training Guide for Managers of Food Service Establishments* (WHO 1989b), and a leaflet, "Hygiene in Mass Catering — Important Rules" (WHO and the German Federal Health Office 1994).

### Food-handling personnel

Food handlers, by failing to observe basic rules of hygiene or basic rules for hygienic food preparation, may be a source of food contamination. To address this concern, FOS convened a consultation in 1988, the report of which was published the next year (WHO 1989a).

### Golden Rules for Hygienic Food Preparation

First issued in 1988, the "Golden Rules for Hygienic Food Preparation" (10 basic rules) provides guidance for preventing most foodborne diseases. These rules are applicable at the domestic level and also at the street-vending and cottage-industry levels. The rules have been adapted for the prevention of foodborne cholera (WHO 1993).

# Clinical technology

## Treatment procedures and related equipment

Delivery of basic emergency treatment at the first (district) level is an essential element of "Health for All." Unfortunately, because of limited resources and access to specialist services, such care is often unavailable to those who need it, especially in rural areas in developing countries. Whether a patient has trauma, obstructed labour, or acute appendicitis, lives are too often lost when emergencies arise.

To address this problem, WHO took a pragmatic approach, concentrating on training general-duty doctors in small hospitals in poor, rural areas to perform essential operations. Initially, WHO collaborated with several specialist societies (that is, NGOs) to identify common emergencies and then select and develop a repertoire of standard surgical and anesthetic techniques simple enough to be mastered by doctors during a short period of supervised training. Procedures were selected for inclusion on the basis of their capacity to save lives, alleviate pain, prevent the development of serious complications, or stabilize the condition of a patient pending referral. The procedures also define the safest line of action to take in small hospitals.

These basic standard techniques have been described in a series of handbooks (Dobson 1988; Cook et al. 1988, 1991; Krol 1993). Lists of essential surgical instruments, equipment, and materials for providing this form of care at such facilities appear as annexes. WHO expects that this basic repertoire will provide a foundation for adding other procedures specific to locally important diseases and emergencies.

## Oxygen concentrator

To improve the availability of oxygen in remote rural health facilities, WHO collaborated with a professional NGO to draw up specifications for an oxygen concentrator suitable for use under adverse conditions. Representatives of industry (that is, manufacturers of oxygen machines for domiciliary therapy) took up the specifications, and three manufacturers have modified their machines to provide models that meet WHO specifications for use in operating rooms or for therapy of children.

## Health Laboratory Technology and Blood Safety

Health Laboratory Technology and Blood Safety (LBS) is part of the Programme on Health Care Technology. The objective of LBS is to promote the establishment and extension of health laboratory and blood-transfusion services (BTSs) in WHO member countries and improve the quality of these services, particularly at the peripheral and intermediate levels. The strategies used for achieving this objective are multifaceted, including

- ▼ Support for national program development;

- ▼ Development and promotion of appropriate technology for laboratories and BTSs;

- ▼ Standardization of, and quality assurance in, laboratory technology and BTSs;

- ▼ Promotion of reagent production; and

- ▼ Education and training.

WHO has provided support to countries through visits by consultants, temporary advisers, and professional staff of the unit for the assessment of national laboratory services and BTSs, in close collaboration with the regional offices (for example, those in Egypt, Ethiopia, India, Jordan, Malawi, Morocco, Nigeria, Syria, Thailand, and Tunisia). Financial support for the development of national laboratory networks was also arranged, from extrabudgetary sources (for example, Nepal).

WHO has promoted internal quality control, workshops, and conferences through intercountry and regional training courses on reagent preparation, maintenance of laboratory equipment, and quality assurance in hematology, microbiology, and clinical chemistry. Specialized training has been provided through fellowship grants. A number of documents for education and training of laboratory professionals, particularly laboratory technicians, were published in several languages. These documents provided detailed information on technical aspects of good laboratory practice and the management of BTSs, including blood-donor recruitment and retention, the appropriate use of blood and blood products, and virus inactivation in blood products. The activities were complemented by the establishment of international external quality-assessment schemes (EQASs) in seven areas of laboratory medicine (clinical chemistry, hematology, blood coagulation, microbiology, parasitology, immunology, and blood-group serology). The schemes provide guidance for establishing national EQASs. The concept has been accepted worldwide: today, national EQASs are implemented in most countries and at least for one laboratory discipline.

The development of appropriate equipment for laboratories in developing countries has focused on portable laboratory instruments with independent power supply and on techniques requiring minimal instrumentation for measurement. Their performance has been tested in Iran, Kenya, Senegal, Sri Lanka, and Uganda. The search for low-cost, simple laboratory methods has focused on tests for early diagnosis of communicable and noncommunicable diseases and blood-group serology.

WHO initiated the development of a cold chain for storage and transport of blood and plasma. Feasibility studies have been carried out in El Salvador, Indonesia, Malaysia, Namibia, Tunisia, and Vietnam, and one field evaluation is going ahead in Zimbabwe. A blood-safety unit has been created to identify areas of need and to monitor progress in all aspects of BTSs throughout the world.

### Radiation Medicine Programme

In current medical practice in both developing and industrialized countries, diagnostic imaging techniques, primarily diagnostic radiology and ultrasound, are indispensable for correctly diagnosing and monitoring traumas, many infectious and noncommunicable diseases, and various pathological conditions in obstetrics. In fact, hardly a hospital of any size is built without basic diagnostic imaging (X-ray and ultrasound). However, it is estimated that about two thirds of the world's population, most living in rural areas and in impoverished districts in big cities in developing countries, have no access to the most basic diagnostic services.

Because of this serious situation, WHO concentrated on developing the Basic Radiological System (WHO–BRS) during 1975–85. WHO–BRS supports primary health care and front-line hospitals in developing countries and consists of a deceptively simple, low-maintenance X-ray unit that is rugged and incorporates designed-in features for the production of low-dosage, high-quality radiographs. Three training manuals are an integral part of the system: *Manual of Darkroom Technique* (Palmer 1985), *Manual of Radiographic Interpretation for General Practitioners* (Palmer et al. 1985), and *Manual of Radiographic Technique* (Holm et al. 1986).

An evaluation of WHO–BRS in eight African countries (Benin, Cameroon, Lesotho, Tanzania, Uganda, Zaire, Zambia, and Zimbabwe) was conducted in 1990–91 by WHO, the manufacturer, and the Simavi Foundation (the Netherlands), which had purchased the units. The system performed very well in the environment for which it was intended.

In 1993, WHO developed the concept of the WHO Imaging System, which includes basic radiographic and general-purpose ultrasound units, and updated the technical specifications for its radiographic unit. This is expected to enlarge the capability of WHO–BRS and improve the quality of diagnostic imaging services in national health-care systems. Currently, the WHO-specified radiographic unit is produced by four leading manufacturers in the industrialized countries, and approximately 1 000 units are installed in about 60 countries. The strategy for further dissemination of this technology includes collaboration with the United Nations Industrial Development

Organization (UNIDO) to promote the manufacture of the WHO-specified X-ray machine in developing countries.

Ultrasound and computer-assisted tomography were the subjects of a WHO report, entitled "Future Use of New Imaging Technologies in Developing Countries" (WHO 1985). This report discusses each technique, outlines the main clinical indications for their use, and specifies the particular areas where the most benefit can be obtained. For the benefit of those considering the acquisition of these technologies, the report also contains detailed technical specifications for ultrasound and computer-assisted tomography scanners suitable for use in developing countries. At least four types of general-purpose ultrasound scanners that meet WHO's specifications are now commercially available. Recognizing the imperative need for proper training, a WHO group of experts prepared, in collaboration with the World Federation for Ultrasound in Medicine and Biology, a basic manual of diagnostic ultrasound (Palmer 1995).

An estimated 9 million new cancer cases are reported in the world each year. There are expected to be about 15 million new cases annually by 2015, with about two thirds of these in developing countries. Radiotherapy is required by more than 50% of all cancer patients, both for cure and for palliation. Radiation therapy in developing countries is often performed with cobalt-60 units, the radioactive sources of which are long decayed; thus, this treatment is inefficient. Additionally, significant expenses are involved in the disposal and replacement of radioactive sources. To improve coverage of radiotherapy services among disadvantaged groups of the population in least-developed countries, a simple and inexpensive megavoltage X-ray teletherapy machine was designed by WHO Headquarters, the WHO Regional Office for the Americas, the International Atomic Energy Agency (IAEA), and UNIDO.

With the aim of improving radiation-protection services in Third World countries, WHO is collaborating with IAEA to provide personnel-monitoring services to many institutions in developing and least-developed countries, such as Afghanistan, Bangladesh, Djibouti, and Yemen.

At present, one of the primary objectives of six collaborating international organizations — FAO, IAEA, the International Labour Organization, the Nuclear Energy Agency (Organisation for Economic Cooperation and Development), the Pan American Health Organization, and WHO — is to revise the Basic Safety Standards for Radiation Protection in light of the *1990 Recommendations of the International Commission on Radiological Protection* (ICRP 1991). The new edition is expected to have a much enhanced coverage of medical exposure, which is the principal source of exposure to radiation in developing countries.

Staff training is vital to improving radiological services in least-developed countries. Since 1985 the WHO Collaborating Centre for the Regional Training of Radiological Personnel at Kenyatta National Hospital, Nairobi, has been collaborating with individual countries to train radiologists from English-speaking African countries (for example, Lesotho, Tanzania, and Uganda). Similar activities are being carried out by the Regional Training Centre in Radiology in Abidjan for training radiologists from French-speaking African countries.

In addition, in response to specific requests, a network of 24 collaborating centres and consultants provides advice to developing countries on the evaluation, planning, and organization of services, training, and technology acquisition.

**Healthy Cities Programme**

Healthy Cities is essentially a facilitating program aimed at health promotion and institutional development at both the municipal and the grass-roots levels. Experience with this project in a number of cities, particularly Accra, Chittagong, Ibadan, Lahore, Rio de Janeiro, and Teheran, has shown that the city health plan, or municipal health plan, is an important tool for addressing basic health needs. Useful documents describing the city health plans produced by the Chittagong Healthy City Project and the Ibadan Healthy City Project, as well as evaluations of various Healthy City activities in Accra and Chittagong, are available.

The Healthy Cities Programme aims to improve environmental and health conditions by raising awareness and mobilizing community participation in partnerships with local (municipal) agencies and institutions, thereby improving the capacity of these agencies and institutions to deliver effective environmental and health services. A priority objective of the program is to develop the role of local governments in public health and to encourage local governments to implement a Health for All policy at the municipal level.

A principle being adopted in the United Nations and elsewhere is that urban-development activities of many kinds (for example, housing, industry, and infrastructure) present not only hazards to health (if health and environment impacts are not considered), but, more important, health opportunities. These may include opportunities to introduce worker training, safe practices, and pollution control in industrial developments; primary health care and health education associated with house-upgrading programs; and water and sanitation improvements. Healthy Cities may be a stand-alone project in a given city, or it may be a health component of a larger urban-development effort that includes urban infrastructure, land management, municipal finance, and industrial development, with the city health plan being an integral part of the wider development plan for the city.

In addressing urban problems, such as water, sanitation, sewage, solid-waste management, and pollution, the Healthy Cities Programme does not seek to take over the management of these functions from competent authorities and agencies. Rather, Healthy Cities merely aims to add the health dimension by measuring the health burden of these problems (for example, death and disability) and pointing out the health opportunities presented by improved practices, greater health awareness, and the partnership approach in the work of authorities and agencies.

Urban-development activities, such as housing and industrial development, have the potential to enhance the health status of the population if health promotion and protection measures such as the following are undertaken in implementing development:

▼ In industrial development, occupational safety considerations and pollution control should be integral.

▼ In housing development, basic environmental services and primary health-care measures should be implemented with community participation.

The municipal health plan is an ongoing process that requires the implementers to

▼ Identify and review all the available studies and reports describing and quantifying the social, economic, and environmental health problems and environmental conditions in the city;

▼ Attempt to rank the contribution that various social, economic, and environmental problems make to the burden of ill health;

▼ Identify the existing municipal agencies and the medical, social, scientific, educational, and technical organizations, including the United Nations, bilateral agencies, and NGOs, that contribute (or can potentially contribute) to solutions to health problems and describe their work;

▼ Identify potential mechanisms that allow municipal agencies and the above organizations and institutions to work together in a coordinated manner to address problems (this involves an understanding of how political and management decisions are undertaken in the city); and

▼ Identify and rank the priority of feasible actions and programs to improve health conditions in the city.

A municipal health plan may include programs or projects for specific settings, such as schools, workplaces, and the marketplace, and health services.

**Schools** — Schools in the city may participate in a Healthy Schools project that includes the following elements:

- ▼ Environment and health education, with grade-appropriate curricula;

- ▼ Parental, teacher, and child participation in relevant school management and decision-making and in projects to improve the school environment, water facilities, toilets, school playgrounds, and classrooms; and

- ▼ A school medical service that emphasizes prevention.

**Workplaces** — A Healthy and Safe Workplace program would necessarily operate at two levels: the traditional occupational health service, which emphasizes factory-level work by health inspectors; and a non-traditional occupational health service for small-scale and cottage industries, which demands a community-based, participatory approach. Important issues that such a program should address will vary from city to city but may include the following:

- ▼ Education of workers (for example, risk-assessment methodology in plain language; safe procedures for various occupational settings);

- ▼ Support and training of NGOs that can undertake worker education in small-scale and cottage industries;

- ▼ Worker participation and representation in industry management and industry or trade associations;

- ▼ Mass media's role in education;

- ▼ Health services for workers;

- ▼ The needs of female workers and support from women's associations;

- ▼ Channels of communication among industry decision-makers, workers, and authorities responsible for environmental protection;

- ▼ Proper management of solid and liquid wastes; and

- ▼ Urban planning for siting of industries, with a view to reducing pollution and environmental damage.

**Marketplaces** — A Healthy Marketplaces program would establish partnerships among all stakeholders and involve people who can address such issues as

- ▼ The health conditions of stall holders and food handlers (water, toilets, and availability of health services);
- ▼ Practices for storing and handling foodstuffs;
- ▼ Ways to minimize any adverse impacts of markets on surrounding residential areas;
- ▼ Solid-waste management for the market area;
- ▼ Methods of government inspectors, such as food inspectors, and the ways they can play an educational rather than punitive role; and
- ▼ The role of the marketplace in health education.

**Health services** — An Upgrading the Health Services program would consider

- ▼ The development of user-community input to the decision-making processes and management of health services;
- ▼ The development and promotion of preventive services alongside curative services; and
- ▼ Equity in provision of health services.

A partnership could be struck among women's organizations, health-oriented NGOs, the national ministry of health, and municipal health agencies responsible for providing health services, running health centres, and managing hospitals. Such a partnership would address local priorities, such as improved accessibility of maternal–child health services in underserved areas; improved family planning; improved health education; and better, more appropriate, readily available drug therapies for common diseases. The participation of community groups in such activities may be formalized in community contracts with the municipality, whereby the municipality gives support and assistance to community groups in recognition of their work in improving local environments and health conditions.

## Nutrition

> *Hunger and malnutrition are unacceptable in a world that has both the knowledge and the resources to end this human catastrophe. We recognize that access to nutritionally adequate and safe food is a right of each individual.*

The countries participating in the International Conference on Nutrition in Rome in December 1992 endorsed the above statement in *World*

286 ▼ AN ASSAULT ON POVERTY

*Declaration and Plan of Action for Nutrition.* Among the major policy guidelines for developing strategies and actions, people's participation was considered a key issue:

> *Local community involvement, including that of families and households, is a prerequisite for improving food production and sustaining access to food and for instituting adequate nutrition improvement programmes and projects. The importance of the informal sector in the processing and distribution of food should be recognized.*

A recommendation was also made to develop and disseminate technologies to respond to women's needs and ease their workload. With regard to household food security, a more precise recommendation was adopted: "improve rural food technologies; increase marketing facilities at the village, cottage and idustrial levels to smooth the food supply flow throughout the year."

The WHO Food and Nutrition Programme has a long-standing interest in the promotion of locally prepared weaning foods in various regions of the world, particularly in Africa and Southeast Asia. The weaning period is a crucial one because, when the baby is moving from its mother's breast to the family pot, the baby is at risk of receiving insufficient energy (calories) and essential nutrients. Complementary feeding, in addition to breast feeding, which should be maintained for the first two years, has received special attention in the last three decades, and various programs for weaning-food production have been implemented, with varying success.

One may consider small units for weaning-food production a good example of preventive technologies. Various such units have been launched, and the standard pattern has been for these to evolve from a semipilot, small-scale unit to one at an industrial stage. At that stage, the sustainability of the unit is highly dependent on its commercial strategies. Some of the best examples are the Incaparina weaning flours in Guatemala; Superamine, in Algeria; Vitafort, in the Congo; and Actamine, in Morocco. These weaning flours were initially produced on an industrial basis to offer local populations a more adapted and less expensive product than imported flours. Some of these local flours still need production development, distribution, and good promotion through clear and adapted educational messages.

Tentative efforts have been made to set up small semiartisanal units, at community or village levels, where groups of women are given resources, equipment, and raw materials for production of weaning foods from home or village gardens. Many units of this kind were developed in Burkina Faso.

WHO reviewed complementary feeding practices and the use of weaning foods in Africa for a workshop in Alexandria at the end of November 1994. One of the expected outcomes of the workshop was the development of guidelines for the quality of weaning foods. Other topics were technology transfer for households and communities; industrial and artisanal production; and social communication strategies for good complementary feeding practices.

Small-scale plants for salt iodization have been developed for prevention and control of major micronutrient deficiencies. These plants should be considered preventive and therapeutic technologies in countries where iodine-deficiency disorders (goitre) are a threat to public health. Although the technologies are a little more sophisticated, communities can be involved in their implementation.

## Health Learning Materials Programme

Poor communication between institutions in the developing world is an important barrier to progress. The telephone is unreliable, and in addition to being expensive, it cannot be used for transfer of the large quantity of data often required by scientific investigators. The Health Learning Materials (HLM) Programme, sponsored by WHO and the United Nations Development Programme, equipped all national HLM projects, as a first step, with fax machines. Although the telephone services are unreliable, fax transmission can be repeatedly attempted until a line is available. However, the phone charges are relatively expensive. The HLM Programme decided, therefore, to experiment with the use of electronic mail. This computer-to-computer transmission, through a local node, is much faster and less expensive than fax and can be used for accessing major databases, as well as for sharing materials with other developing-country institutions.

An African NGO, the African Regional Computer Centre (ARCC) in Nairobi, has established a network of experts in electronic communication in the majority of countries in Africa. WHO contracted with the director of ARCC for the linkup of a number of national HLM projects in 10 countries. This involved the purchase and installation of modems, provision of software, training of local staff, registration with PTT, cost of a year's traffic, and troubleshooting during the initial phase of e-mail use. The system was fully operational by the end of 1994 in Benin, Ethiopia, Ghana, Guinea-Bissau, Kenya, Namibia, Tanzania, Uganda, Zambia, and Zimbabwe. The offices of the WHO representatives in some of these countries have also been connected to this e-mail system.

The aim of this project is to share the e-mail services with other ministry departments and WHO-sponsored projects. It will then be a cost-effective initiative.

# Technology transfer

The experience in developed countries indicates that the transformation in health that took place between the 18th and 20th centuries was essentially due to a decline in infectious diseases, brought about mainly by better nutrition, provision of clean food and water, and improvements in hygiene (WHO 1986). In the 20th century, infectious diseases were further reduced by immunization and therapy. Because of deficiencies and hazards, though, many of these diseases — the diseases of poverty — are still prevalent in developing countries, but they can be dealt with effectively by the determined use of well-established technologies. The developing countries have also begun to experience a rising incidence of the so-called diseases of affluence that are prevalent in the developed countries. These diseases, too, require intervention involving transfer of technology, but this should not be done at the expense of programs for the basic problems of deficiencies and hazards.

The introduction of new technology, particularly high technology, can have major cost and human-resource implications, even in developed countries, resulting in resources being diverted from other areas. This becomes an issue of critical importance in developing countries, which have severely limited resources for large, unresolved problems. Although technology transfer is of great value in bringing about technological growth and development in developing countries, we must avoid uncritical acceptance and indiscriminate acquisition of technologies without properly considering the suitability, disability, and cost effectiveness of these technologies. The choice of technologies and their proper use will depend on the health priorities and health programs of a country.

A great variety of factors might affect the success of technology transfer, including the following:

▼ The priority given by the recipient nation to improved health care;

▼ The awareness the recipient nation has of the need for, and possible benefits of, a new technology;

▼ The economic evaluation of cost and investment in new technology vis-à-vis the benefits; and

▼ The recipient nation's belief in its own ability to success-fully use a transferred technology.

To enhance the technology-transfer process, WHO chose some institutions in the developing world that have experience in design and fabrication of medical equipment and instruments to be WHO collaborating centres. These centres are generally entrusted with the following tasks:

▼ Problem-oriented research and advice on the development and evaluation of equipment and equipment design for specific tasks, with consideration of several special factors, such as operation by personnel with limited skills, different environmental conditions of operation, and limited maintenance facilities; and

▼ Production at a low volume for equipment evaluation.

The ability of developing countries to obtain and absorb technology successfully varies considerably, but many have developed effective mechanisms for achieving it. In some countries, technology transfer could be facilitated by a research and development (R&D) unit of trained resource personnel. Such a unit would evaluate the technology to be transferred in relation to the needs of the country. The R&D unit would give advice on possible equipment, emphasizing such factors as design simplicity, reliability, availability of spare parts, and ease of maintenance. The R&D unit could interact with the suppliers of technology at different levels, such as equipment designers, engineers, and those with an awareness of servicing requirements. Staff of the unit might, when necessary, carry out limited studies to, for example, test equipment for reliability. Additional functions of the unit might be to engage in maintenance services for health-oriented equipment, possibly as part of a national equipment-maintenance network; to provide training, such as the training of future teachers; and to give feedback to the suppliers to help with further improvement. The R&D unit would be based in the user country, not the provider country; consequently, the developing country would visibly and actually have the responsibility for the choice and use of the transferred technology.

# The Panel on Technology for Small-scale Economic Activities to Address the Basic Needs of Low-income Populations

Oscar Serrate
Chair
UN Commission on Science and
  Technology for Development
Bolivia

Niels E. Busch
Carl Bro Energy and Supply Ltd
Denmark

Mussie Delelegn
First Secretary
Permanent Mission of Ethiopia
Switzerland

Fauzi El Mugassabi
Counsellor
Permanent Mission of the
  Libyan Arab Jamahiriya
Switzerland

Messanvi Gbeassor
Doyen
Faculté des sciences
Université du Bénin
Togo

S.P. Kagoda
Director of Industry and Technology
Ministry of Trade and Industry
Uganda

George M. Mhango
University of Malawi
Malawi

Geoffrey Oldham
Science and Technology Adviser
  to the President
International Development Research Centre
Canada

Mikoto Usui
Faculty of Policy Management
Keio University (SFC)
Japan

Arnoldo Ventura
Special Adviser to the Prime Minister
  on Science and Technology
Office of the Prime Minister
Jamaica

J. George Waardenburg
Chief Scientist
Ministry of Foreign Affairs
Netherlands

Serguei Yampolsky
Head
Department of International Cooperation
State Committee on Science and
  Technologies
Ukraine

Getaneh Yiemene
Head
Science and Technology Policy and
  Planning Department
Ethiopian Science and Technology
  Commission
Ethiopia

## Consultants

Gustavo Fernández
Bolivia

Dilmus James
Department of Economics and Finance
University of Texas at El Paso
United States

## International organizations

I. Ahmed
Employment Strategies and
  Policies Branch
Employment Department
International Labour Office
Switzerland

A. Akpa
Liaison Officer
UNIDO Liaison Office in Geneva
Switzerland

Ajit Bhalla
Chief
Employment Strategies and
  Policies Branch
Employment Department
International Labour Office
Switzerland

Lowell Flanders
Chief
Division for Sustainable Development
UN Department of Policy Coordination
  and Sustainable Development
United States

P. Malhotra
Officer-in-Charge
UNESCO Liaison Office in Geneva
Switzerland

B. Mansourian
Director
Office of Research Policy and
  Strategy Coordination
World Health Organization
Switzerland

Y. Maruyama
Scientist
Office of Research Policy and
  Strategy Coordination
World Health Organization
Switzerland

Norton Satin
Chief
Food and Agricultural Industries Service
Agricultural Services Division
Food and Agriculture Organization
  of the UN
Italy

Souren Seraydarian
Director
UNIDO Liaison Office in Geneva
Switzerland

J. Szczerban
Scientific Adviser
Office of Research Policy and
  Strategy Coordination
World Health Organization
Switzerland

Mihael Zinovieff
Deputy Head
Geneva Office
UN Department for Development
  Support and Management Services
Switzerland

## UNCTAD Secretariat

Maurizio Dal Ferro
Economic Affairs Officer
Division for Science and Technology

Gloria-Veronica Koch
Chief
Capacity Building Section
Division for Science and Technology

Dieter Koenig
Scientific Affairs Officer
Division for Science and Technology

Vladimir Pankov
Economic Affairs Officer
Division for Science and Technology

Pedro Roffe
Officer-in-Charge
Division for Science and Technology

Taffere Tesfachew
Economic Affairs Officer
Division for Science and Technology

# Experts Contributing, as "Friends of the Chair," to the Work of the Panel

Fernando Antezana
Assistant Director General
World Health Organization
Switzerland

M.R. Bhagavaan
Natural Sciences, Technology and
  Industrialization
Swedish Agency for Research
  Cooperation with Developing
  Countries
Sweden

Ajit Bhalla
Chief
Employment Strategies and Policies
  Branch
Employment Department
International Labour Office
Switzerland

Claes Brundenius
Research Policy Institute
University of Lund
Sweden

Dilmus James
Department of Economics and Finance
University of Texas at El Paso
United States

Teresa Salazar de Buckle
Austria

M.S. Swaminathan
M.S. Swaminathan Research Foundation
India

Mohamed S. Zehni
Director
Research and Technology Development
  Division
Food and Agriculture Organization
  of the UN
Rome

# The Commission on Science and Technology for Development

**I. What is the Commission on Science and Technology for Development? When did it hold its first session? What is the relationship between this commission and the United Nations Conference on Trade and Development Secretariat?**

The Commission on Science and Technology for Development (CSTD), a subsidiary body of the Economic and Social Council (ECOSOC), meets once every 2 years. CSTD was established in 1992 as a result of the restructuring and revitalization of the United Nations in the economic, social, and related fields. Through this restructuring, the General Assembly of the United Nations abolished the former Intergovernmental Committee on Science and Technology for Development and its subsidiary body, the Advisory Committee on Science and Technology for Development, which had been created at the time of the United Nations Conference on Science and Technology for Development, held in Vienna in 1979, and in their place established CSTD as a new functional commission of ECOSOC.

CSTD met for the first time in April 1993 in New York. It made a number of decisions regarding its future work and established, toward that end, panels of its own members to focus on specific substantive themes that it had identified for the 1993–95 intersessional period.

Since July 1993 the United Nations Conference on Trade and Development (UNCTAD) Secretariat has been responsible for the substantive servicing of CSTD.

## 2. What are the main functions of CSTD?

CSTD was established to provide the General Assembly and ECOSOC with high-quality advice on relevant issues to enable the General Assembly and ECOSOC to guide the future work of the United Nations, develop common policies, and agree on appropriate action. In this context, CSTD acts as a forum for

▼ The examination of science and technology (S&T) questions and their implications for development;

▼ The advancement of understanding on S&T policies, particularly with respect to developing countries; and

▼ The formulation of recommendations and guidelines on S&T matters in the United Nations system.

## 3. What main subjects will be taken up at the second session?

At CSTD's first session, it decided to focus the work of its intersessional period, 1993–95, on the following substantive themes:

▼ Technology for small-scale economic activities to address the basic needs of low-income populations;

▼ The gender implications of S&T; and

▼ The contributions of S&T to an integrated approach to land management.

CSTD also decided that it would continue its examination of the role of research and development institutes (RDIs) in the industrialization process of developing countries. In addition, CSTD decided to consider, in a preliminary fashion, the question of information technologies (ITs) and their role in S&T for the needs of developing countries, with a view to selecting this issue as a substantive theme for the 1995–97 intersessional period.

## 4. What were the main criteria for selecting basic needs, gender, and land management as the main substantive themes for the second session?

CSTD, at its first session, emphasized that an important criterion for choosing the substantive themes was that the themes and the work on them should be timely and directed to meeting the broad interests of the organizations of the United Nations system. Accordingly, the questions of basic needs, gender, and land management were intended as contributions to the processes leading to, respectively, the World Summit for Social Development (Copenhagen), the Fourth World

Conference on Women (Beijing), and the deliberations of the Commission on Sustainable Development at its third session in relation to chapter 10 of Agenda 21.

## 5. What are the other subjects to be discussed at the second session?

The second session of CSTD has a heavy agenda. Besides having to consider the three substantive themes (see question 3 above), CSTD will consider the following:

▼ Coordination of United Nations activities in S&T for development;

▼ The report of the Secretary-General of UNCTAD on the work of the Ad Hoc Working Group on the Interrelationship Between Investment and Technology Transfer;

▼ Financing S&T for development;

▼ A report on progress achieved and problems encountered in the use of S&T in sustainable development;

▼ Conversion of military capacities for civilian use and sustainable development; and

▼ The work plan of CSTD for the 1995–97 intersessional period.

## 6. What are the main findings and conclusions of the work carried out on the main substantive themes under consideration for the 1993–95 intersessional period?

### Basic needs

The fact that today some nations are rapidly entering a global information infrastructure sharply contrasts with the impoverishment of much of the world's population. In 1980/90, the proportion of people living in absolute poverty still ranged from an average of 31% in developing countries to 64% in the least-developed countries. One third of the population in the least-developed countries lacked access to basic sanitation, and roughly half lacked access to health services and safe water. Similarly, education levels remained low in the least-developed countries. By the late 1980s, research and development (R&D) expenditures in all developing countries were only at 3.9% of the world total. CSTD addressed the issues of how S&T and access to technology for a broader part of the world population could contribute to the alleviation of poverty.

The Panel on Technology for Basic Needs (PTBN) discussed how a fresh approach to S&T could ensure that the basic needs of low-income populations are met. Basic needs are defined as those minimal requirements needed for sustaining life for all people. These needs are adequate nutrition, health care, water, and sanitary facilities, as well as access to elementary education and information to enable individuals and communities to participate in productive activities and rationally use available basic goods and services. In the course of its work, PTBN addressed food production and processing, education — especially technical and vocational training — and health care. The fundamental objective of the mobilization of S&T to meet basic needs should be to create conditions to increase the ability of the poor to gain access to, comprehend, and creatively use knowledge and technology to satisfy their basic needs.

In reviewing experience with basic-needs programs, as well as the relevant work on technology and basic needs carried out in the United Nations system, PTBN found that scant attention was given to the role of technology in alleviating poverty. One problem was a failure to replicate successful cases sufficiently or instigate a systematic effort to apply technology to satisfy basic needs. Nevertheless, it was found that those nations that had launched determined and protracted campaigns to satisfy basic needs were, in a number of cases, able to demonstrate progress.

The role of the United Nations in the implementation of the basic-needs objective is crucial. In this connection, it is suggested that the United Nations

▼ Promote and sponsor activities to sensitize the S&T community, policymakers, and decision-makers to the contribution that S&T can make to the satisfaction of basic needs; and

▼ Implement a mechanism for evaluating national S&T policies, with the aim of determining how adequately basic-needs satisfaction is being addressed.

### The gender dimension

The analysis of the gender dimension of S&T for sustainable human development was underpinned by the explicit recognition that development itself is gender specific and that S&T for development must systematically and purposefully recognize this gender-specific nature of development and appropriately and equitably respond to the concerns, needs, and interests of both women and men.

Unfortunately, the effects of S&T on society have not been uniformly beneficial. Even at the close of the 20th century, women in developing countries, especially in the rural areas, are still experiencing serious difficulty in meeting their own basic needs and those of their households. S&T interventions have improved many aspects of women's lives, allowing for important declines in both maternal and infant mortality. However, in the last three decades, women in many developing countries have also become disproportionately worse off than the men in their own communities. This difference between men and women worldwide cannot be understood without explicitly considering the gender-specific nature of development, including S&T contributions to the development process.

The working group on the gender dimension identified many areas in S&T in which the needs and aspirations of women have been relatively neglected, including

- ▼ The decision-making processes in S&T;

- ▼ S&T career prospects;

- ▼ The manner in which statistics are collected;

- ▼ Ethical issues in S&T;

- ▼ Recognition of women's local knowledge systems; and

- ▼ The S&T activities of the United Nations system.

**Land management**

The panel dealing with S&T for integrated land management (ILM) focused on one of the most important issues in environmental sustainability. The essential role of land and water resources in supporting all current and future human activities makes it necessary to consider the management of land resources as one of the primary tools for sustainable human development. The panel agreed that managing land requires a holistic and integrated approach. An integrated approach to land management is not a fixed procedure but a continuous, iterative process of planning, implementation, monitoring, and evaluation. The basic techniques for carrying out each of these steps are already available, but their application in many parts of the world is limited by training, financial, and institutional constraints. Failure to manage land resources in an integrated manner could lead to permanent destruction or degradation of the land's capacity to provide economic and environmental benefits; inefficient use or waste of resources; and cumulative effects that lead to transboundary problems.

The panel report shows that modern S&T plays a most important role in ILM:

- ▼ ITs for monitoring and diagnosing land use;

- ▼ Evaluation technologies for interpreting and identifying options for land use;

- ▼ Application technologies for using the land for specific purposes; and

▼ Support technologies for providing the infrastructure that allows the efficient and sustainable use of land.

However, one of the problems cited by the panel is that the technologies that can contribute to ILM and that have been developed in each of these areas are not available in developing countries, where they are most needed.

### 7. What are the principal results of the work on R&D systems?

CSTD also considered the issue of linkages between national R&D systems and industrial sectors of developing countries and countries in transition. PTBN confirmed the view that the R&D systems in these countries were not up to the task of promoting industrial development. PTBN identified a number of common weaknesses that characterize R&D systems in these countries:

▼ Rates of R&D expenditure are extremely low, compared with those in industrialized countries.

▼ Little or no R&D is undertaken by the enterprise sector, the main agent in the innovation process.

▼ Public-sector R&D is fragmented and insufficiently oriented to the needs of the industrial sector.

▼ The RDIs are not generating a sufficient volume of commercially applicable innovations.

▼ The RDIs emphasize basic research at the expense of applied research.

▼ The scientists at RDIs tend to be more concerned with career prospects than with the needs of industry.

▼ There is a lack of appropriate incentives for undertaking R&D.

While recognizing that the questions of how, when, and whether to intervene in favour of technological capacity-building are contentious, PTBN has singled out three sets of measures needed to strengthen linkages between national R&D systems and productive sectors. First, an environment conducive to R&D and technological innovation should be created. This would involve establishing a stable economy and a competitive market environment. Second, some of the existing public RDIs should be transformed or restructured through increased commercialization and refocusing of activities to make them more responsive to the needs of industry. Third, R&D should be stimulated in the enterprise sector through the use of general measures (for example, tax and credit incentives, levies, subsidies, and duty exemptions) and selective measures (for example, targeting).

## 8. How does the work on information technologies feature in CSTD's agenda?

CSTD, as part of its intersessional work, considered the effect of ITs in the development process. Following decisions made at its first session, the Secretariat has prepared an issues note on the subject for consideration at the second session. This note briefly highlights the magnitude of global and regional IT markets and identifies issues arising from the international diffusion of IT, particularly for developing countries. The IT market in developing countries is relatively small but growing, accounting for about 9% of the global IT market, which was estimated in 1993 at $450 billion. With telecommunications added, the total world market is close to $1 trillion, of which developing countries account for 11%.

The diffusion of IT and telecommunications technology varies widely among developing countries. A few countries have adopted and successfully taken advantage of this technology, but most have not been in a position to do so. The weak telecommunications infrastructure prevailing in many countries, the shortage of foreign exchange and spare parts, and the deficiencies in technical skills are some of the main obstacles preventing the diffusion of IT. It is widely believed that ITs have a generic influence on the development of modern technologies, thereby determining the pace of social and economic progress. However, the effects that ITs have on the development process, especially the technological advancement of developing countries, have not been systematically studied.

Given the ubiquitous nature and increasing importance of IT to trade and development in today's liberalized and deregulated environment, CSTD may wish to consider IT as a subject for its future work.

## 9. The issue of military conversion is also on CSTD's agenda. What is the focus of the Secretariat's work in this area?

CSTD requested that a report on "scientific and technological aspects of the conversion of military capacities for civilian use and sustainable development" be submitted at its second session. The new paradigm of sustainable development has broadened the traditional understanding of security — threats to nations are no longer limited to military aggression. Global environmental change and the destabilizing effects of persistent poverty among large segments of the world population are perceived as equally significant risks. This broadened understanding provides an additional reason for reallocating resources traditionally spent on the military to poverty and the environmental problems. The report by the Secretariat focuses on efforts to redirect parts of a vast S&T reservoir, formerly at the exclusive disposal of the military, to the development of environmentally sound technologies. However, successful conversion schemes require international cooperation. Linking the needs of developing countries with such measures is an important task in the pursuit of sustainable development.

**10. How is the work program of CSTD defined and how often is it reviewed?**

The work program of CSTD is defined at each session for a 2-year period. At its second session, CSTD will determine the priorities and substantive themes to be considered by its members and the substantive support to be provided by the Secretariat during the 1995–97 intersessional period.

**11. Who participates in the preparation of the reports of the main panels established by CSTD? What are the main features of the so-called new working style of CSTD?**

At its first session, CSTD decided to set up ad hoc panels or working groups to broaden the analytical work on the substantive themes chosen for each intersessional period. CSTD further decided to assign responsibility for the intersessional work on each substantive theme to a CSTD member, who would call together a panel of experts, with the help of the Secretariat. Other CSTD members would be invited to join the assigned member in that task. The bureau of the CSTD, with the support of the Secretariat, set up four panels. Through a questionnaire sent to all members who participated in the first session, the bureau invited these members to express their interest in particular areas of work for the intersessional period. On the basis of their replies, the membership of the panels was established. The panels were responsible for the reports to CSTD on technology for small-scale economic activities to address the basic needs of low-income populations, the gender implications of S&T, the contributions of S&T to an integrated approach to land management, and the role of RDIs in the industrialization process.

The new CSTD working style reflects the fact that the panels and working groups bear the responsibility for the reports they submit to CSTD.

## 12. What is the membership of CSTD? How are the members elected, and for how long? Have all the members of CSTD been elected?

CSTD is to have 53 members, elected by ECOSOC for a term of 4 years. Experts nominated by these members' respective governments should possess the necessary qualifications and professional or scientific knowledge. Fifty-one members have already been elected by ECOSOC. Two members, from Europe, remain to be elected.

## 13. What provisions have been made to elect a bureau for the second session of CSTD?

In accordance with previous practice, CSTD, at its first session, elected its bureau for the second session. The bureau has been actively involved in the work of the panels during the 1993–95 intersessional period, as agreed by CSTD at its first session. The bureau is composed of the following:

> Chair:      Oscar Serrate (Bolivia)
> Vice-Chairs:  Vladimir A. Labounov (Belarus)
>              Mohamed M. El Halwagi (Egypt)
>              Jawaharlal Dhar (India)
>              J. George Waardenburg (Netherlands)

At its second session, CSTD will have to elect a new bureau (a chair and four vice-chairs) for its third session. That bureau will also assume responsibilities for the activities of the 1995–97 intersessional period.

# Acronyms and Abbreviations

| | |
|---|---|
| ABN | African Biosciences Network |
| ACTS | African Centre for Technology Studies |
| ADB | African Development Bank |
| AIDS | acquired immune deficiency syndrome |
| ALIDE | Latin American Association of Development Financing Institutions |
| ANSTI | African Network of Scientific and Technological Institutions |
| APCTT | Asian and Pacific Centre for Transfer of Technology |
| ARCC | African Regional Computer Centre |
| ARCT | African Regional Centre for Technology |
| ASEAN | Association of Southeast Asian Nations |
| ATI | Appropriate Technology International |
| | |
| BOSTID | Board on Science and Technology for International Development |
| BRS | Basic Radiological System [WHO] |
| BTS | blood-transfusion service |
| | |
| CAST | College of Arts, Science and Technology [Jamaica] |
| CDD | Programme for the Control of Diarrhoeal Diseases [WHO] |
| CDR | Acute Respiratory Disease Control [WHO] |
| CGIAR | Consultative Group on International Agricultural Research |
| COSTED | Committee on Science and Technology in Developing Countries [ICSU] |
| CSD | Commission on Sustainable Development |
| CSTD | Commission on Science and Technology for Development |

| DAI | Development Alternatives, Inc. |
|---|---|
| DAP | Action Programme on Essential Drugs [WHO] |
| DNA | deoxyribonucleic acid |
| DPCSD | Department for Policy Coordination and Sustainable Development |

| ECA | Economic Commission for Africa |
|---|---|
| ECB | endogenous capacity-building |
| ECLAC | Economic Commission for Latin America and the Caribbean |
| ECOSOC | Economic and Social Council |
| EMRDC | Ethiopian Mineral Resources Development Corporation |
| ENEA | Italian National Commission on Environment, Energy and New Technologies |
| ENI | Ethiopian Nutrition Institute |
| EQAS | external quality-assessment scheme |
| ESCAP | Economic and Social Commission for Asia and the Pacific |

| FAO | Food and Agriculture Organization of the United Nations |
|---|---|
| FIDIC | International Federation of Consulting Engineers |
| FOS | Food Safety Unit [WHO] |

| GATE | Germany Appropriate Technology Exchange |
|---|---|
| GNP | gross national product |
| GTZ | German Agency for Technical Cooperation |

| Habitat | United Nations Centre for Human Settlements |
|---|---|
| HACCP | Hazard Analysis Critical Control Point system [WHO] |
| HIV | human immunodeficiency virus |
| HLM | Health Learning Materials Programme |

| IAEA | International Atomic Energy Agency |
|---|---|
| IBN | International Biosciences Network |
| ICGEB | International Centre for Genetic Engineering and Biotechnology |
| ICGEBNET | International Centre for Genetic Engineering and Biotechnology Network |
| ICSU | International Council for Scientific Unions |
| IDD | International Development Department [Commonwealth Secretariat] |
| IDRC | International Development Research Centre |
| IFAD | International Fund for Agricultural Development |
| ILM | integrated land management |
| ILO | International Labour Organization |
| IMF | International Monetary Fund |
| INTECH | Institute for New Technologies |

| ISAT | Information and Advisory Service on Appropriate Technology |
| IT | information technology |
| ITDG | International Technology Development Group |
| LABNET | Lactic Acid Bacteria Network |
| LBS | Health Laboratory Technology and Blood Safety [WHO] |
| MCR | microconcrete roofing |
| MSE | micro- and small-scale enterprise |
| MSME | micro-, small-, and medium-scale entreprise |
| MUSHNET | Mushroom Biotechnology Network |
| NAFINSA | Nacional Financiera [Mexico's national industrial development bank] |
| NCST | National Commission for Science and Technology [Jamaica] |
| NGO | nongovernmental organization |
| NHT | National Housing Trust [Jamaica] |
| NIEO | new international economic order |
| OCS | organization of civil society |
| ORS | oral rehydration salts |
| PTA | preferential trade area |
| PTBN | Panel on Technology for Basic Needs |
| PTT | post, telephone, and telegraph [the national post and telecommunications service of Switzerland] |
| RADA | Rural Agricultural Development Agency [Jamaica] |
| R&D | research and development |
| RATIS | Regional Appropriate Technology Information Service |
| RDI | research and development institute |
| SAREC | Swedish Agency for Research Cooperation with Developing Countries |
| S&T | science and technology |
| SDPED | Social Development and Poverty Elimination Divison [UNDP] |
| SIATA | Service inter-africain de technologie appropriée |
| SME | small- and medium-scale enterprise |
| SRC | Scientific Research Council [Jamaica] |
| STPSD | Science, Technology and Private Sector Division [UNDP] |
| TARA | Technology and Action for Rural Advancement [India] |
| TWAS | Third World Academy of Sciences |

| TWNSO | Third World Network of Scientific Organizations |
|---|---|
| UNCTAD | United Nations Conference on Trade and Development |
| UNDP | United Nations Development Programme |
| UNESCO | United Nations Educational, Scientific and Cultural Organization |
| UNEVOC | International Project on Technical and Vocational Education |
| UNICEF | United Nations Children's Fund |
| UNIDO | United Nations Industrial Development Organization |
| UNU | United Nations University |
| USAID | United States Agency for International Development |
| WAITRO | World Association of Industrial and Technological Research Organizations |
| WASME | World Assembly of Small and Medium Enterprises |
| WHO | World Health Organization |
| WIPO | World Intellectual Property Organization |

# Bibliography

AAAS (African Academy of Arts and Sciences). 1993. Science in Africa: Women Leading from Strength. A forum organized by the AAAS Sub-Saharan African Program, Washington, DC, USA.

Adriaansen, W.L.M.; Waardenburg, J.G. 1992. A dual world economy: forty years of development experience. Oxford University Press, Oxford, UK.

Ajami, F.; Bartley, R,; Kirkpatric, J. 1993. Foreign Affairs, 1993 (Sep./Oct.), 2–26.

Alvarez, B.; Gomez, H., ed. 1994. Laying the foundation: the institutions of knowledge in developing countries. International Development Research Centre, Ottawa, ON, Canada. 230 pp.

Amin, A.T.M.N. 1992. Bangkok (Thailand). *In* Maldonado, C.; Sethuraman, S.V., ed., Technological capability in the informal sector. World Employment Programme, International Labour Organization, Geneva, Switzerland. pp. 105–129.

Anderson, W.T. 1987. To govern evolution. Harcourt Brace Jovanivich, New York, NY, USA.

Annerstedt, J. 1994. Measuring science, technology and innovation. *In* Salomon, J.-J.; Sagasti, F.; Sachs-Jeantet, C., ed., The uncertain quest: science and technology for development. United Nations University Press, Tokyo, Japan.

Anonymous. 1994. Peru, buen gobierno y desarrollo: hacia una agenda para la gobernabilidad democratica. Foro Nacional/Internacional, Lima, Peru.

Arora, A. 1991. The transfer of technological know-how to developing countries: licensing, tacit knowledge, and the acquisition of technological capacity. Stanford University, Stanford, CA, USA. PhD thesis.

Aspe, P. 1993. Economic transformation the Mexican way. MIT Press, Cambridge, MA, USA.

ATI (Appropriate Technology International). 1994. Talking Points, 1 Jul. 1994.

Barnet, R.J.; Cavanagh, J. 1994. Global dreams: imperial corporations and the new world order. Simon & Schuster, New York, NY, USA.

Barney, G.O. 1993. Global 2000 revisited: what shall we do? Millennium Institute/Public Interest Publications, Arlington, VA, USA.

Batty, M.; Barr, B. 1994. The electronic frontier: exploring and mapping cyberspace. Futures, 26(7), 699–712.

Bebbington, A.; Thiele, G.; Davies, P.; Prager, M.; Riveros, H. 1993. Non-governmental organizations and the state in Latin America. Routledge, London, UK.

Beckford, J.A., ed. 1986. New religious movements and rapid social change. SAGE–UNESCO, London, UK.

Behrman, J.R. 1993. Investing in human resources. In Inter-American Development Bank, ed., Economic and social progress in Latin America. Inter-American Development Bank, Washington, DC, USA. pp. 187–255.

Bell, M. 1984. Learning and the accumulation of industrial capacity in developing countries. In Fransman, M.; King, K., ed., Techno-logical capability in the Third World. St. Martin's Press, New York, NY, USA. pp. 187–209.

——— 1991. Science and technology policy research in the 1990s: key issues for developing countries. Paper presented at the Science Policy Research Unit (University of Sussex) 25th Birthday Con-ference, 3–4 Jul. 1991, Brighton, East Sussex, UK.

Bell, M.; Scott-Kemmis, D. 1985. Technology import policy: have the problems changed? Economic and Political Weekly, 20 (Nov.), 1975–1990.

Benedikt, M., ed. 1991. Cyberspace: the first steps. MIT Press, Cambridge, MA, USA.

Berry, A.; Mendez, M.T.; Tenjo, J. 1994. Growth, macroeconomic stability and employment expansion in Latin America. United Nations Development Programme and International Labour Organiza-tion, Geneva, Switzerland.

Bhagavaan, M.R. 1990. Technology transfer in the Third World: strategies and prospects. Zed Books, London, UK.

Bhagavan, R. 1979. A critique of appropriate technology for under-developed countries. Scandinavian Institute of African Studies, Uppsala, Sweden. 58 pp.

Bhalla, A.S. 1979. Technologies appropriate for a basic needs strategy. In Bhalla, A.S., ed., Towards global action for appropriate technol-ogy. Pergamon Press, New York, NY, USA. pp. 23–61.

——— ed. 1991. Small and medium enterprises: technology policies and options. Greenwood Press, Westport, CT, USA.

———— 1992. Environment, employment and development. International Labour Organization, Geneva, Switzerland.

———— 1993. Technology choice and development. *In* Salomon, J.-J.; Sagasti, F.; Sachs-Jeantet, C., ed., The uncertain quest: science, technology and development. United Nations University Press, Tokyo, Japan.

Bhalla, A.S.; James, D.D. 1986. Technological blending: frontier technology in traditional economic sectors. Journal of Economic Issues, 20(2), 453–462.

———— ed. 1988. New technologies and development: experiences with "technology blending." Lynne Rienner, Boulder, CO, USA.

———— 1991. Integrating new technologies with traditional economic activities in developing countries: an evaluative look at "technology blending." Journal of Developing Areas, 25 (Jul.), 477–496.

Bhalla, A.S.; James, D.D.; Stevens, Y., ed. 1984. Blending of new and traditional technologies: case studies. Tycooly International Publishers, Dublin, Ireland. 305 pp.

Bhalla, A.S.; Reddy, A.K.N., ed. 1994. The technological transformation of rural India. Intermediate Technology Publications, London, UK.

Bloomfield, L.P. 1993. Policing world disorder. World Monitor, Feb. 1993, 34–37.

Boh, B. 1994a. Interactive educational technologies in higher education. World Bank, Washington, DC, USA.

———— 1994b. Scientific information and literature. World Bank, Washington, DC, USA.

Brautigam, D. 1993. South–South technology transfer: the case of China's Kpatawee rice project in Liberia. World Development, 21(12), 1987–2001.

Bryan, F.L. 1992. Hazard Analysis Critical Control Point evaluations: a guide to identifying hazards and risks associated with food preparation and storage. WHO, Geneva, Switzerland. 72 pp.

Brzezninski, Z. 1993. Power and morality. World Monitor, Mar. 1993, 22–28.

Burrows, B.C.; Mayne, A.J.; Newbury, P. 1991. Into the 21st century: a handbook for a sustainable future. Adamant Press, Adamant, VT, USA.

Caldwell, J.H., Jr. 1994. Photovoltaic technology and markets. Contemporary Economic Policy, 12(2), 97–111.

Carroll, T.F. 1992. Intermediary NGOs: the supporting link in grassroots development. Kumarian Press, West Hartford, CT, USA.

Carrol-Foster, T., ed. 1993a. A guide to Agenda 21: issues, debates, and Canadian initiatives. International Development Research Centre, Ottawa, ON, Canada. 124 pp.

———— 1993b. Agenda 21: abstracts, reviews, commentaries. International Development Research Centre, Ottawa, ON, Canada. 322 pp.

Cartwright, A. 1993. World agriculture 1993. Sterling Publishing Group PLC, London, UK.

CCSTG (Carnegie Commission on Science, Technology and Government). 1992. Partnerships for global development: the clearing horizon. Carnegie Corporation, New York, NY, USA.

CDCGC (Commission on Developing Countries and Global Change). 1992. For Earth's sake. International Development Research Centre, Ottawa, ON, Canada. 152 pp.

Chamarik, S.; Goonatilake, S. 1994. Technological independence: the Asian experience. United Nations University Press, Tokyo, Japan.

Chaves, E. 1992. Lima (Peru). In Maldonado, C.; Sethuraman, S.V., ed., Technological capability in the informal sector. World Employment Programme, International Labour Organization, Geneva, Switzerland. pp. 151-173.

Chuckwjekwu, S. 1991. Development of design and manufacturing capabilities in a small Nigerian company. In Bhalla, A.S., ed., Small and medium enterprises: technology policies and options. Greenwood Press, Westport, CT, USA. pp. 175–181.

Chuta, E.; Liedholm, C. 1985. Employment and growth in small-scale industry: empirical evidence and policy assessment from Sierra Leone. Macmillan, London, UK.

CIDEAL (Centro de Comunicación, Investigación y Documentación entre Europa, España y América Latina). 1993. Human development report 1993. United Nations Development Programme, Madrid, Spain.

Cimoli, M.; Dosi, G. 1990. The characteristics of the development process: some introductory notes. In Chatterji, M., ed., Technology transfer in the developing countries. Macmillan, London, UK.

Colombo, U. 1991. The role of technology blending in development. In Swaminathan, M.S., ed., Biotechnology in agriculture: a dialogue. Macmillan, Madras, India.

Colombo, U.; Oshima, K., ed. 1989. Blending technology: an appropriate response to development. Tycooly International Publishers, London, UK.

Congdon, R.J. 1975. Lectures on socially appropriate technology. Enschede, Eindhoven, Netherlands.

Cook, J.; Sankaran, B.; Wasunna, A.E.O., ed. 1988. General surgery at the district hospital. World Health Organization, Geneva, Switzerland. 237 pp.

———— ed. 1991. Surgery at the district hospital: obstetrics, gynaecology, orthopaedics, and traumatology. World Health Organization, Geneva, Switzerland. 207 pp.

Cornia, S.A.; Jolly, R.; Stewart, F. 1991. Adjustment with a human face: protecting the vulnerable and promoting growth. A UNICEF study. Volume I. Clarendon Press, Oxford, UK.

Cortes, M.; Berry, A.; Ishaq, A. 1987. Success in small- and medium-scale enterprises: the evidence from Colombia. Oxford University Press, New York, NY, USA.

Crozier, M.; Friedberg, E. 1977. L'Acteur et le système. Éditions du Seuil, Paris, France.

Dahl, R. 1989. Democracy and its critics. Yale University Press, New Haven, CT, USA.

Dahrendorf, R. 1983. Oportunidades vitales: notas para una teoría social y política. Espasa-Calpe, Madrid, Spain.

Davis, O.; Witter, M. 1986. Food security in the 1980s and beyond. Caribbean Food and Nutrition Institute, Kingston, Jamaica.

de Wilde, T.; Schruers, S.; Richman, A. 1991. Opening the marketplace to small enterprise: where magic ends and development begins. Kumarian Press, West Hartford, CT, USA.

Diamond, L.; Plattner, M.F. 1993. The global resurgence of democracy. Johns Hopkins University Press, Baltimore, MD, USA.

Dobson, M.B. 1988. Anaesthesia at the district hospital. World Health Organization, Geneva, Switzerland. 143 pp.

Drucker, P.F. 1986. The changed world economy. Foreign Affairs, 64(4).

———— 1990. The new realities. Harper & Row, Publishers, New York, NY, USA.

———— 1993. Post-capitalist society. Harper Business, New York, NY, USA.

Dudley, E. 1993. The critical villager, beyond community participation. Routledge, London, UK.

Een, G.; Joste, S. 1988. One hundred innovations for development. Intermediate Technology Publications, London, UK.

———— 1991. More innovations for development. Intermediate Technology Publications, London, UK.

Eide, A.; Eide, W.B.; Goonatilake, S.; Gussow, J. 1984. Food as a human right. United Nations University Press, Tokyo, Japan.

Eisemon, T.O. 1986. Foreign training and foreign assistance for university development in Kenya: too much of a good thing? Journal of Educational Development, 6(1), 1–13.

Eisemon, T.O.; Davis, C.H. 1991. Can the quality of scientific training research in Africa be improved? Minerva, 29, 1–26.

———— 1992. Universities and scientific research capacity. Journal of Asian and African Studies, 27(1/2), 69–94.

Enos, J.L. 1982. The choice of techniques vs. the choice of beneficiary: what the Third World chooses. *In* Stewart, F.; James, J., ed., The economics of new technology in developing countries. Pinter, London, UK. pp. 69–81.

——— 1991. The creation of technological capacity in developing countries. Pinter, London, UK.

Enos, J.L.; Park, W.-H.. 1987. The adaptation and diffusion of imported technology in the case of Korea. Croom Helm, London, UK.

Ernst, D.; O'Connor, D. 1989. Technology and global competition: the challenge for the newly industrialized economies. Organisation for Economic Co-operation and Development, Paris, France.

ESTC (Ethiopian Science and Technology Commission). 1993. National science and technology policy. ESTC, Addis Ababa, Ethiopia.

FAO (Food and Agriculture Organization of the United Nations). 1988. Review and analysis of agrarian reform and rural development. FAO, Rome, Italy.

——— 1993. Agricultura: acia el año 2010. FAO, Rome, Italy.

Fardoust, S.; Dareshawar, A. 1990. Long-term outlook for the world economy: issues and projections for the 1990s. International Economics Department, World Bank, Washington, DC, USA. Working Paper Series, No. 372.

Farrell, G. 1992. Quito (Ecuador). *In* Maldonado, C.; Sethuraman, S.V., ed., Technological capability in the informal sector. World Employment Programme, International Labour Organization, Geneva, Switzerland. pp. 131–150.

Fermanian, T.W.; Michalski, R.S. 1992. AGASSISTANT: a new generation tool for developing agricultural advisory systems. *In* Mann, C.K.; Ruth, S.R., ed., Expert systems in developing countries: practice and promise. Westview, Boulder, CO, USA. pp. 42–69.

Forsyth, D.J.C. 1990. Technology policy for small developing countries. St. Martin's Press, New York, NY, USA.

Fransman, M.; King, K., ed. 1984. Technology capability in the Third World. Macmillan, London, UK.

Freeman, C.; Perez, C. 1988. Structural crisis of adjustment, business cycle and investment behavior. *In* Dosim, G.; et al., ed., Technical change and economic theory. Frances Pinter, London, UK.

French, H.F. 1992. After the Earth Summit: the future of environmental governance. Worldwatch Institute, Washington, DC, USA. Worldwatch Paper No. 107.

Fricke, T. 1984. High impact appropriate technology case studies. Appropriate Technology International, Washington, DC, USA.

Gahan, E. 1992. Computers for industrial management in Africa: an overview of issues. Industry and Development, 31, 1–65.

Gaillard, J. 1991. Scientists in the Third World. University of Kentucky Press, Lexington, KY, USA.

Gaillard, J.; Ouattar, S. 1988. Purchase, use and maintenance of scientific equipment in developing countries. Interciencia, 13(2), 65–70.

Gaillard, J.; Waast, R. 1992. The uphill emergence of scientific communities in Africa. Journal of Asian and African Studies, 27(1/2), 41–51.

Gardner, R.N. 1992. Negotiating survival: four priorities after Rio. New York Council on Foreign Relations Press, New York, NY, USA.

Gbeassor, M. 1994. Experiences in Togo. United Nations Conference on Trade and Development, Geneva, Switzerland. TECH/BASE/10. 6 pp.

Gender Working Group–UNCSTD (United Nations Commission on Science and Technology for Development). 1995. Missing links: gender equity in science and technology for development. International Development Research Centre, Ottawa, ON, Canada. 380 pp.

George, S. 1987. Introduction. *In* Bennett, J.; George, S., ed., The hunger machine. Policy Press, Cambridge, UK. pp. 1–107.

Ghai, D.P.; Khan, A.R.; Lee, E.L.H.; Alfthan, T. 1977. The basic-needs approach to development: some issues regarding concepts and methodology. International Labour Organization, Geneva, Switzerland.

Ghosh, P.K., ed. 1984. Third World development: a basic needs approach. Greenwood Press, Westport, CT, USA.

Girvan, N.P.; Marcelle, G. 1991. Overcoming technological dependence: the case of Electric Arc (Jamaica) Limited, a small firm in a small country. World Development, 18(1), 91–107.

GOJ (Government of Jamaica). 1994. The Throne speech, 1994–1995. Jamaica Information Service, Kingston, Jamaica.

GOJ; GON (Government of Jamaica; Government of the Netherlands). 1993. Out of many one project: evaluation of the GOJ/GON micro enterprise project. Netherlands Economic Institute, Rotterdam, Netherlands. pp. 35–39.

Goodland, R.; Daly, H.E.; El Serafy, S. 1992. Population, technology, and lifestyle: the transition to sustainability. Island Press, Fort Meyers Beach, FL, USA.

Goulet, D. 1976. The uncertain promise: value conflicts in technology transfer. Overseas Development Council, Washington, DC, USA.

Guevara, G.F. 1985. Transfer and adaptation of a technology of milk substitutes production in the Andean Group: a Bolivian case-study. *In* Williams-Silveira, M.P., ed., Research and development: linkages to production in developing countries. United Nations Centre for Science and Technology for Development, Westview Press, Boulder, CO, USA.

Haggblade, S.; Liedholm, C.; Mead, D.C. 1990. The effect of policy and policy reforms on non-agricultural enterprises and employment in developing countries: a review of past experiences. *In* Stewart, F.; Thomas, H.; de Wilde, T., ed., The other policies: the influence of policies on technology choice and small enterprise development. Intermediate Technology Publishers, London, UK. pp. 58–98.

Hanna, N. 1991. Informatics and the developing world. Finance and Development, Dec. 1991.

Harris, J.M. 1991. Global institutions and ecological crisis. World Development, 19(1), 111–122.

Heaton, G.R., Jr; Banks, R.D.; Ditz, D.W. 1994. Missing links: technology and environmental improvement in the industrialized world. World Resources Institute, Washington, DC, USA.

Heaton, G.R., Jr; Repetto, R.; Sobin, R. 1992. Backs to the future: US government policy toward environmentally critical technology. World Resources Institute, Washington, DC, USA.

Heilbroner, R. 1993. 21st century capitalism. W.W. Norton & Co., New York, NY, USA.

Herbert-Copley, B. 1992. Technical change in African industry: reflections on IDRC-supported research. Canadian Journal of Development Studies, 8(2), 231–249.

Herbolzheimer, E.; Ouane, H. 1985. The transfer of technology to developing countries by small and medium-sized enterprises of developed countries. Trade and Development, 6, 131–148.

Hirschhorn, N.; Greenough, W.B., III. 1991. Progress in oral rehydration therapy. Scientific American, 264(5), 50–56.

Hoffman, K. 1989. Technological advance and organizational innovation in the engineering industry: a new perspective on problems and possibilities for the developing countries. Industry and Energy Department, World Bank, Washington, DC, USA. Working Paper Series, No. 4.

Holm, T.; Palmer, P.E.S.; Lehtinen, E. 1986. Manual of radiographic technique: WHO Basic Radiological System. World Health Organization, Geneva, Switzerland. 256 pp.

Hope, K.R. 1983. Basic needs and technology transfer issues in the new international economic order. American Journal of Economics and Sociology, 42, 393–403.

Huntington, S. 1993. The clash of civilizations? Foreign Affairs, Summer 1993, 22–49.

Hyman, E.L. 1989. The role of small- and micro-enterprises in regional development. Project Appraisal, 4(4), 1989.

ICRP (International Commission on Radiological Protection). 1991. 1990 recommendations of the International Commission on Radiological Protection. Pergamon, New York, NY, USA. 215 pp.

IDB; UNDP (Inter-American Development Bank; United Nations Development Programme). 1993. Reforma social y pobreza: hacia una agenda integrada de desarollo. Inter-American Development Bank, Washington, DC, USA.

IDRC (International Development Research Centre). 1992a. 101 technologies from the South for the South. IDRC, Ottawa, ON, Canada. 231 pp.

────── 1992b. Empowerment through knowledge: the strategy of the International Development Research Centre. IDRC, Ottawa, ON, Canada. 32 pp.

────── 1992c. Our common bowl: global food interdependence. IDRC, Ottawa, ON, Canada. 64 pp.

ILO (International Labour Organization). 1976. Employment, growth and basic needs: a one-world problem. ILO, Geneva, Switzerland. 270 pp.

────── 1977. Meeting basic needs: strategies for eradicating mass poverty and unemployment: conclusions of the World Employment Conference 1976. ILO, Geneva, Switzerland. 64 pp.

────── 1992. Strengthening technological capabilities: a challenge for the nineties. ILO, Geneva, Switzerland.

────── 1993. Entrepreneurship and small enterprise development in urban and rural sectors in Africa. ILO, Geneva, Switzerland.

INSTRAW (International Research and Training Institute for the Advancement of Women). 1992. Women, environment and sustainable development. INSTRAW, Santo Domingo, Dominican Republic.

Irle, A. 1989. Education and access to modern knowledge. Daedalus, 118 (Winter).

Jamaican Ministry of Development and Welfare. 1963. The five-year independence plan, 1963 to 1968. Government of Jamaica, Kingston, Jamaica.

────── 1970. The second five-year plan, 1970–1975. Government of Jamaica, Kingston, Jamaica.

James, D.D. 1989. Importation and local generation of technology by the Third World: an institutionalist perspective. In DeGregori, T.R., ed., The development challenge: theory, practice and prospects. Kluwer–Nijhoff, Boston, MA, USA.

James, D.D; Lalkaka, R.; Malik, K. 1988. Cloning of tea in Malawi. In Bhalla, A.S.; James, D.D., ed., New technologies and development: experiences in technology blending. Lynne Rienner, Boulder, CO, USA. pp. 258–268.

Jequier, N.; Blanc, G. 1983. The world of appropriate technology. Organisation for Economic Co-operation and Development, Paris, France.

Jonas, H. 1990. Le Principe responsabilité. Les Éditions du Cerf, Paris, France.

Johnston, A.; Sasson, A. 1986. New technologies and development. United Nations Educational, Scientific and Cultural Organization, Paris, France.

Kagoda, S.P. 1994. Profiles of on-going projects in Uganda which attempt to address the needs of low-income populations. United Nations Conference on Trade and Development, Geneva, Switzerland. TECH/BASE/11. 6 pp.

Kaplinsky, R. 1984. Automation: technology and society. Longman, Harlow, UK.

Keating, M. 1993. Cumbre para la tierra: programa para el cambio. El Centro para Nuestro Futuro Común, Geneva, Switzerland.

Kennedy, P. 1993. Preparing for the twenty-first century. Random House, New York, NY, USA.

Khundeker, N. 1992. Dhaka (Bangladesh). In Maldonado, C.; Sethuraman, S.V., ed., Technological capability in the informal sector. World Employment Programme, International Labour Organization, Geneva, Switzerland. pp. 81–104.

Killick, T.; Bird, G.; Sharpley, J.; Sutton, M. 1986. The IMF and stabilization: developing country experiences. Heinemann Educational Books, London, UK.

Kimball, L.A. 1992. Forging international agreement: strengthening intergovernmental institutions for environment and development. World Resources Institute, Washington, DC, USA.

King, A.; Schneider, B. 1991. The first global revolution: a report by the Council of the Club of Rome. Pantheon Books, New York, NY, USA.

Krol, J. 1993. Rehabilitation surgery for deformities due to poliomyelitis: techniques for the district hospital. World Health Organization, Geneva, Switzerland. 112 pp.

Kurz, R. 1993. O Colapso da modernizacao: da derrocada do socialismo de caserna e crise da economia mundial. Paz e Terra, Brazil.

Lall, S. 1992. Technology capabilities and industrialization. World Development, 20(2), 165–186.

Langdon, S. 1984. Indigenous technological capability in Africa: the case of textiles and wood products in Kenya. In Fransman, M.; King, K., ed., Technology capability in the Third World. Macmillan, London, UK.

Lewin, R. 1994. Complexity: life at the edge of chaos. Macmillan, New York, NY, USA.

Leydesdorff, L.; van den Besselaar, P. 1994. Evolutionary economics and chaos theory. Pinter Publishers, London, UK.

Liedholm, C.; McPherson, M.; Chuta, E. 1994. Small enterprise employment growth in rural Africa. American Journal of Agricultural Economics, 76 (Dec.).

Linowes, D. 1990. Speech to the White House Conference on Libraries and Information Services. Washington, DC, USA.

Logan, B.I. 1987. The reverse transfer of technology from sub-Saharan Africa to the United States. Journal of Modern African Studies, 25(4), 597–612.

Lyotard, F. 1984. The postmodern condition: a report on knowledge. University of Minnesota Press, Minneapolis, MN, USA.

Maldonado, C. 1989. The underdogs of the urban economy join forces: results of an ILO programme in Mali, Rwanda and Togo. International Labour Review, 128, 65–84.

Maldonado, C.; Sethuraman, S.V., ed. 1992. Technological capability in the informal sector. World Employment Programme, International Labour Organization, Geneva, Switzerland. 222 pp.

Marx, K. 1968 [1867]. Capital. Volume I: The process of capitalistic production. International Publishers, New York, NY, USA.

Mathews, J.T. 1989. Redefining security. Foreign Affairs, Spring 1989, 162–177.

Mazlish, B. 1993. The fourth discontinuity: the co-evolution of humans and machines. Yale University Press, New Haven, CT, USA.

McNamara, R. 1992. New thinking for coping with regional conflicts in a post-Cold War world. In Kirdar, U., ed., Change: threat or opportunity, political change. United Nations, New York, NY, USA.

Mead, D.C. 1994. The contribution of small enterprises to employment growth in southern Africa. Growth and Equity through Microenterprise Investment and Institutions (GEMINI), Bethesda, MD. GEMINI Technical Report 72.

Mendez Emilien, D.; Grabski, S.V. 1992. DREAGIS: a knowledge-based agricultural geographic information system for the Dominican Republic. In Mann, C.K.; Ruth, S.R., ed., Expert systems in developing countries: practice and promise. Westview, Boulder, CO. pp. 127–145.

Michel, C.; Huntington, S.P.; Watanuki, J. 1975. The crisis of democracy. New York University Press, New York, NY, USA.

Mishra, S.C. 1994. The small-scale farm machinery industry in Uttar Pradesh. In Bhalla, A.S.; Reddy, A.K.N., ed., The technological transformation of rural India. Intermediate Technology Publications, London, UK. pp. 201–221.

Monkiewicz, J. 1989. International technology flows and the technology gap: CMEA experience in international perspective. Westview, Boulder, CO, USA.

Monkiewicz, J.; Maciejewicz, J. 1986. Technology export from the socialist countries. Westview, Boulder, CO, USA.

Moussa, A.; Schware, R. 1992. Informatics in Africa: lessons from World Bank experience. World Development, 20(12), 1737–1752.

Mowery D.; Rosemberg, N. 1989. Technology and the pursuit of economic growth. Cambridge University Press, London, UK.

M.S. Swaminathan Foundation. 1993. Third annual report, 1992–93. M.S. Swaminathan Foundation, Madras, India.

Myers, N. 1989. Environment and security. Foreign Policy, Spring 1989, 23–41.

Mytelka, L.K. 1990. Transfer and development of technology in the least developed countries: an assessment of major policy issues. United Nations Conference on Science and Technology for Development, Geneva, Switzerland.

Naisbitt, J. 1994. Global paradox: the bigger the world economy, the more powerful its smallest players. William Morrow & Co., New York, NY, USA.

Naisbitt, J.; Aburdene, P. 1990. Megatrends 2000: ten new directions for the 1990's. Avon Books, New York, NY, USA.

NAS (National Academy of Sciences). 1982. Outlook for science and technology: the next five years. W.H. Freeman & Co., San Francisco, CA, USA.

Nelson, R.R. 1990. Acquiring technology. In Soesastoo, H.; Pangestu, M., ed., Technical change in the Asian Pacific economy. Allen & Unwin, Sidney, Australia.

Nelson, R.R.; Winter, S. 1982. An evolutionary theory of economic change. Belknap Press of Harvard University Press, Cambridge, MA, USA.

Noisi, J.; Rivard, J. 1990. Canadian technology transfer to developing countries through small and medium-size enterprises. World Development, 18(11), 1529–1542.

Norman, D.A. 1993a. Things that make us smart: defending human attributes in the age of the machine. Addison-Wesley Publishing Co., Reading, MA, USA.

———— 1993b. Turn signals are the facial expressions of automobiles. Addison-Wesley Publishing Co., Reading, MA, USA.

NRC (National Research Council). 1979. Medical technology and the health care system. National Academy of Sciences–National Research Council, Washington, DC, USA.

ODC (Overseas Development Council). 1992. Humanitarian intervention in a new world order. ODC, Washington DC, USA. Policy Focus Series, No. 1.

OECD (Organisation for Economic Co-operation and Development). 1991. OECD Forum for the Future: Conference on Long-term Prospects for the World Economy, 19–20 Jun. 1991. OECD, Paris, France.

Ogbimi, F.E. 1990. Preparing for commercialization of scientific research results in Nigeria. Science and Public Policy, 17(6), 373–379.

Orlich, R.; Erlich, R. 1989. New world, new mind: moving towards conscious evolution. Doubleday, New York, NY, USA.

Oyeyinka, O.; Adeloye, O. 1988. Technological change and project execution in a developing economy: evolution of Ajaokuta steel plant in Nigeria. International Development Research Centre, Ottawa, ON, Canada. IDRC-MR187e. 80 pp.

Palmer, P.E.S. 1985. Manual of darkroom technique: WHO Basic Radiological System. World Health Organization, Geneva, Switzerland. 25 pp.

——— ed. 1995. Manual of diagnostic ultrasound. World Health Organization, Geneva, Switzerland. 334 pp.

Palmer, P.E.S.; Cockshott, W.P.; Hegedüs, V.; Samuel, E. 1985. Manual of radiographic interpretation for general practitioners: WHO Basic Radiological System. World Health Organization, Geneva, Switzerland. 216 pp.

Pavitt, K. 1987. The objectives of technology policy. Science and Public Policy, 14, 182–188.

Perez, C. 1989. Technical change, competitive restructuring, and institutional reform in developing countries. World Bank, Washington, DC, USA. Strategic Planning and Review Discussion Paper No. 4.

Perrings, C. 1994. World employment programme: sustainable livelihoods and environmentally sound technology. International Labour Organization, Geneva, Switzerland. Working Paper.

Polanyi, M. 1965. The tacit dimension. Routledge and Kegan Paul, London, UK.

Porenta, G.; Pfahringer, B.; Hoberstorfer, M.; Trappl, R. 1992. A decision support system for village health workers in developing countries. In Mann, C.K.; Ruth, S.R., ed., Expert systems in developing countries: practice and promise. Westview, Boulder, CO, USA. pp. 193–207.

Postman, N. 1993. Technopoly: the surrender of culture to technology. Vintage Books, New York, NY, USA.

Ramphal, S.S. 1978. What next? A mandate for developing countries. In Partners in tomorrow: strategies for a new international order. Canadian International Development Agency, Hull, PQ, Canada.

Rath, A.; Copley, B.-H. 1993. Green technologies for development: transfer, trade, and cooperation. International Development Research Centre, Ottawa, ON, Canada. 64 pp.

Redclift, M.; Benton, T. 1994. Social theory and the global environment. Routledge, London, UK.

Reddy, A.K.N. 1979. Some thoughts on traditional technologies. Paper presented at the United Nations University Conference on Sharing of Traditional Technologies with a Human Face, 15–22 Apr. 1979, Yogyarkarta, Indonesia. United Nations University, Tokyo, Japan.

Reich, R.B. 1993. El trabajo de las naciones: hacia el capitalismo del siglo XXIII. Javier Vergara, SRL, Buenos Aires, Argentina.

Revel, J.-F. 1993. Le Regain démocratique. Fayard, Paris, France.

Richards, P.J.; Leonor, M.D. 1982. Target setting for basic needs. International Labour Organization, Geneva, Switzerland.

Rosell, S., ed. 1993. Governing in an information society. Montreal Institute for Research on Public Policy, Montreal, PQ, Canada.

Rosemberg, N. 1982. Inside the black box: technology and economics. Cambridge University Press, London, UK.

———— 1990. Why do companies do basic research with their own money? Research Policy, Winter 1990.

Sagasti, F.R. 1979. Technology, planning and self-reliant development. Praeger Press, New York, NY, USA.

———— 1980. The two civilizations and the process of development. Prospects: Quarterly Review of Education, 10(2).

———— 1988. Reinterpreting the concept of development from a science and technology perspective. *In* Baark, E.; Sveding, U., ed., Man, nature and technology. Macmillan, London, UK.

———— 1990a. Cooperation in a fractured global order. New Scientist, 14 Jul. 1990.

———— 1990b. International cooperation in a fractured global order. Impact of Science on Society, 39(3), 207–211.

Salam, A. 1991. Science, technology and science education in the development of the South. Third World Academy of Sciences, Triest, Italy.

Salomon, J.-J. 1994. Why the quest was uncertain. Lecture given at the United Nations University, 11 Jul. 1994, Tokyo, Japan.

Salomon, J.-J.; Sagasti, F.R.; Sachs-Jeantet, C. 1994. The uncertain quest: science, technology and development. United Nations University Press, Tokyo, Japan.

Sasson, A. 1990. Feeding tomorrow's world. United Nations Educational, Scientific and Cultural Organization, Paris, France.

Saunders, P. 1991. Pakistan: misuse of drugs for childhood illness. Lancet, 338(8764), 438.

Savant, K.P.; Hasenpflug, H. 1977. The new international economic order: confrontation or cooperation between North and South? Westview Press, Boulder, CO, USA.

Schrage, M. 1990. Shared minds: the new technologies of collaboration. Random House, New York, NY, USA.

Schumacher, E.F. 1973. Small is beautiful: economics as if people mattered. Blond and Briggs Ltd, London, UK.

Segal, A.; et al. 1987. Learning-by-doing: science and technology in the developing world. Westview, Boulder, CO, USA.

Sen, A.K. 1984. Resources, values and development. Basil Blackwell, Oxford, UK.

———— 1987. Poverty and famines: an essay on entitlement and deprivation. Clarendon Press, Oxford, UK.

———— 1992. Inequality reexamined. Harvard University Press, Cambridge, MA, USA.

Sercovich, F.C. 1988. Domestic learning, international technology flows and the world market: new perspectives for developing countries. World Employment Programme, International Labour Organization, Geneva, Switzerland. Research Working Paper No. 189.

Sethuraman, S.V. 1992. Bangalore (India). In Maldonado, C.; Sethuraman, S.V., ed., Technological capability in the informal sector. World Employment Programme, International Labour Organization, Geneva, Switzerland. pp. 49–79.

Shahidullah, S.M. 1991. Capacity-building in science and technology in the Third World. Westview, Boulder, CO, USA.

Sheehan, G.; Hopkings, M. 1979. Basic needs performance: an analysis of some international data. International Labour Organization, Geneva, Switzerland.

Singer, H.W. 1972. Technology for basic needs. International Labour Organization, Geneva, Switzerland.

———— 1977. Technologies for basic needs. International Labour Organization, Geneva, Switzerland.

———— 1982. Technology for basic needs. International Labour Organization, Geneva, Switzerland.

Singh, A.; BNDP (Basic Needs and Development Programme). 1983. Industrialization, employment and basic needs in a fast-growing agrarian state: a study of the Indian Punjab. World Employment Programme Research, International Labour Organization, Geneva, Switzerland. Working Paper.

Slater, P.; Bennis, W. 1990. Democracy is inevitable. Harvard Business Review, 1990 (Sept./Oct.), 167–176.

Smillie, I. 1991. Mastering the machine: poverty aid and technology. IT Publications, London, UK.

Smith, K.R.; Shuhua, G.; Kun, H.; Daxiong, Q. 1993. One hundred million improved cook stoves in China: how was it done? World Development, 21(6), 941–961.

Soedjatmoko. 1980. Development and human needs. IFDA Dossier, 1980 (Jan./Feb.), 122–128.

Solomon, R. 1990. A world of uncertainty. International Economic Letter, 10(10).

———— 1991. How the world has changed in ten years. International Economic Letter, 11(1).

Speth, J.S. 1994. Building a new UNDP: agenda for change. Paper presented to the United Nations Development Programme, Executive Board, United Nations Secretariat, United Nations, New York, NY, USA.

SRC (Scientific Research Council). 1990. Science and technology: a national policy. Ministry of Planning and Production, Kingston, Jamaica. 29 pp.

Stewart, F. 1977. Technology and underdevelopment. Macmillan, London, UK.

———— 1985. Basic needs in developing countries. Johns Hopkins University Press, Baltimore, MD, USA.

———— ed. 1987. Macro-policies for appropriate technology in developing countries. Westview, Boulder, CO, USA.

Stewart, F.; James, J., ed. 1982. The economics of new technology in developing countries. Pinter, London, UK.

Stewart, F.; Thomas, H.; de Wilde, T., ed. 1990. The other policies: the influence of politics on technology choice and small enterprise development. Intermediate Technology Publications, London, UK.

Streeten, P.P. 1979. Basic needs: premises and promises. Journal of Policy Modeling, 1, 136–146.

Streeten, P.P.; Burki, S.J. 1978. Basic needs: some issues. World Development, 6, 411–471.

Stremlau, J. 1989. Security for development in a post-bipolar world. World Bank, Washington, DC, USA.

Sun-Tzu. 1994. The art of war [Sawyer, R.D., trans.]. Barnes & Noble Books, New York, NY, USA.

Swaminathan, M.S., ed. 1991. Biotechnology in agriculture: a dialogue. Macmillan, Madras, India.

———— ed. 1993. Information technology: a dialogue. Macmillan, Madras, India.

Szretter, H. 1985. Planning for basic needs in Latin America. Mexico: las necesidades básicas de alimentación. Institute of Social Studies, International Labour Organization, Geneva, Switzerland.

TCMD (Transnational Corporations and Management Division, United Nations). 1992. Small transnationals: no less than larger ones. Transnationals, 4(4), 1, 6.

Teece, D.J. 1977. Technology transfer by multinational firms: the resource cost of transferring technological know-how. Economic Journal, 87 (June), 242–261.

Teekens, R., ed. 1988. Theory and policy design for basic needs planning: a case-study of Ecuador. Avebury Publishing Co. Ltd, Amersham, UK.

Tiffin, S.; Osotimehin, F. 1992. New technologies and enterprise development in Africa. Organisation for Economic Co-operation and Development, Paris, France.

Tiffin, S.; Osotimehin, S.O.A. 1988. Technical entrepreneurship and technological innovation in Nigeria. Journal of Development Planning, 18, 195–220.

Toffler, A.; Toffler, H. 1993. War and anti-war: survival at the dawn of the 21st century. Little, Brown and Co., Boston, MA, USA.

Tolintino, E.E. 1993. Technological innovation and Third World multinationals. Routledge, London, UK.

Tomassini, L. 1993. Estado, Gobernabilidad y Desarrollo. Banco Interamericano de Desarrollo, Washington, DC, USA. Monograph Series, No. 9.

Touraine, A. 1992. Critique de la modernité. Fayard, Paris, France.

——— 1994. Qu'est-ce que la démocratie? Fayard, Paris, France.

Toynbee, A.J. 1934. A study in history. Oxford University Press, London, UK. 12 vols.

UNCED (United Nations Conference on Environment and Development). 1992. Final report of the United Nations Conference on Environment and Development: Agenda 21. United Nations, New York, NY, USA.

UNCSTD; APIC (United Nations Commission on Science and Technology for Development; Association for Promotion of International Cooperation). 1984. Pioneer projects on the integration of emerging and traditional technologies. APIC, Tokyo, Japan.

UNCTAD (United Nations Conference on Trade and Development). 1976. Trade and development issues in the context of a new international economic order. UNCTAD IV, Geneva, Switzerland. Programme Discussion Paper.

——— 1982a. Report of the Meeting of Governmental Experts on the Transfer, Application and Development of Technology in the Capital Goods and Industrial Machinery Sector, 7–16 Jul. 1982, Geneva, Switzerland. United Nations, Geneva, Switzerland. TD/B/C.6/82 and Corr.1 - TD/B/C.6/AC.7/7 and Corr.1.

——— 1982b. Report of the Meeting of Governmental Experts on the Transfer, Application and Development of Technology in the Food Processing Sector, 1–10 Jun. 1982, Geneva, Switzerland. United Nations, Geneva, Switzerland. TD/B/C.6/78–TD/B/C.6/AC.6/7.

——— 1982c. Report of the Meeting of Governmental Experts on the Transfer, Application and Development of Technology in the Energy Sector, 25 Oct.–2 Nov. 1982, Geneva, Switzerland. United Nations, Geneva, Switzerland. TD/B/C.6/AC.6/5.

——— 1986. Report of the Meeting of Intergovernmental Group of Experts on the Transfer, Application and Development of Technology in the Energy Sector, Paying Particular Attention to New and Renewable Sources of Energy, 15–24 Oct. 1986, Geneva, Switzerland. United Nations, Geneva, Switzerland. TD/B/C.6/AC.10/4.

———— 1990. Transfer and development of technology in the least developed countries: an assessment of major policy issues. United Nations, New York, NY, USA. UNCTAD/ITP/TEC/12. 48 pp.

———— 1993. Information technology and international competitiveness: the case of the construction services industry. United Nations, New York, NY, USA.

———— 1994. Least developed countries report, 1993–1994. United Nations, New York, NY, USA. 264 pp.

UNDP (United Nations Development Programme). 1991a. Development without poverty. Regional Project for Overcoming Poverty, United Nations Development Programme. Oxford University Press, New York, NY, USA.

———— 1991b. Human development report, 1991. Oxford University Press, New York, NY, USA.

———— 1992. Human development report, 1992. Oxford University Press, New York, NY, USA.

———— 1993. Human development report, 1993. Oxford University Press, New York, NY, USA.

———— 1994. Human development report, 1994. Oxford University Press, New York, NY, USA.

UNDP; GOJ (United Nations Development Programme; Government of Jamaica). 1992a. Assessment of science and technology in the productive sectors. Strengthening Endogenous Capacity in Science and Technology Project. Trafalgar Advisory and Business Services, Kingston, Jamaica. 27 pp.

———— 1992b. Inter-relationship of the Jamaican S&T system within the UN system with other international agencies and the S&T systems in other states and overseas nationals. Strengthening Endogenous Capacity in Science and Technology Project. Lorraine Blank, Kingston, Jamaica.

———— 1992c. Review/analysis of the S&T system and its interface with government, with special reference to policy, planning and performance. Strengthening Endogenous Capacity in Science and Technology Project. Trevor Hamilton and Associates, Kingston, Jamaica.

UNDP; ILO (United Nations Development Programme; International Labour Organization). 1994. The employment challenge: an agenda for global action. International Labour Organization, Geneva, Switzerland.

UNESCO (United Nations Educational, Scientific and Cultural Organization). 1981. Technologies for rural development. UNESCO, Paris, France.

———— 1992. Science and technology in developing countries: strategies for the 1990's. UNESCO, Paris, France.

———— 1993. World science report, 1993. UNESCO, Paris, France.

UNIDO (United Nations Industrial Development Organization). 1979. Conceptual and policy framework for appropriate industrial technology. UNIDO, Vienna, Austria. Monograph on Appropriate Industrial Technology, No. 1. 144 pp.

United Nations. 1973. Economic Declaration and Action Programme for Economic Cooperation: 4th Conference of Heads of State of Governments of Non-Aligned Countries, Algeria. United Nations, New York, NY, USA. UN Document A19330.

——— 1989. Elements of an international development strategy for the 1990s. United Nations, New York, NY, USA. Committee for Development Planning Report. 11 pp.

——— 1992. ATAS: biotechnology and development expanding the capacity to produce food. Department of Economic and Social Development, United Nations, New York, NY, USA.

——— 1993. Report on the world social situation 1993. Department of Economic and Social Development, United Nations, New York, NY, USA.

——— 1994. Moral implications of a global consensus. Ethics and Agenda 21. United Nations Environment Program, Geneva, Switzerland.

Usui, M. 1994. Newly emerging technologies for blending with traditional technologies. United Nations Conference on Trade and Development, Geneva, Switzerland. TECH/BASE/25. 8 pp.

Vaitsos, C. 1970. Bargaining and the distribution of returns in the purchase of technology by developing countries. Bulletin of the Institute of Development Studies, 3(1), 16–23.

Ventura, A.K. 1992a. Elements of innovation and technological development in Jamaica. Paper commissioned by UNESCO, Paris, France. 69 pp.

——— 1992b. Food and the future. In Proceedings of the 6th Annual National SRC Conference on Science and Technology, 9–12 November 1992, Kingston, Jamaica. Scientific Research Council, Kingston, Jamaica. pp. 75–150.

——— 1992c. The role of innovation and invention in building endogenous technological capacity. United Nations Development Programme, Geneva, Switzerland. 25 pp.

——— 1994. Technology creating competitive advantages in production. In Lewis, P., ed., Jamaica preparing for the twenty-first century. Ian Randle Publishers, Kingston, Jamaica. pp. 182–192.

——— 1996. Hemispheric cooperation in scientific and energy policies. In Gayle, D., ed., Caribbean public policy: preparing for a changing world. Westview Press, Boulder, CO, USA.

Villarán de la Puente, F. 1989. Innovaciones tecnológicas en la pequeña industria: casos del sector metal-mecánico. Fundación Friedrich Ebert, Lima, Peru.

Vitta, P.B. 1990. Technology policy in sub-Saharan Africa: why the dream remains unfulfilled. World Development, 18(11), 1471–1480.

——— 1992a. Management of technology policy in sub-Saharan Africa: the policy researcher's burden. Journal of Asian and African Studies, 27(1/2), 32–40.

——— 1992b. Utility of research in sub-Saharan Africa: beyond the leap of faith. Science and Public Policy, 19(4), 221–228.

——— 1993. Short of target: why, in Africa, research rarely reaches use. Canadian Journal of Development Studies, 14(2), 245–260.

von Weizsacker, E.U.; Swaminathan, M.S.; Lemma, A., ed. 1983. New frontiers in technology application: integration of emerging and traditional technologies. Tycooly International Publishers, Dublin, Ireland.

Vrtacnik, M.; Cok, P.; Cizerle, A.; Dolnicar, D.; Glazar, S.; Olbina, R. 1992. Design of an expert system for water pollution determination/prevention. In Mann, C.K.; Ruth, S.R., ed., Expert systems in developing countries: practice and promise. Westview, Boulder, CO, USA. pp. 241–254.

Wahid, N.M. 1994. The Grameen Bank and poverty alleviation in Bangladesh: theory, evidence and limitations. American Journal of Economics and Sociology, 54(1), 1–13.

Waldrop, M.M. 1992. Complexity: the emerging science at the edge of order and chaos. Simon & Schuster, New York, NY, USA.

Walliser, B. 1977. Systèmes et modèles : introduction critique à l'analyse de systèmes. Éditions du Seuil, Paris, France.

Watanabe, S. 1993. Microelectronics and third-world industries. Macmillian, New York, NY, USA.

Weeramantry, C.G. 1990. Human rights and scientific and technological development. United Nations University Press, Tokyo, Japan.

——— 1993. The impact of technology on human rights: global case-study. United Nations University Press, Tokyo, Japan.

Wesley-Tanaskovic, I.; Tocatlian, J.; Roberts, K.H. 1994. Expanding access to science and technology: the role of information technologies. United Nations University Press, Tokyo, Japan.

Whitmore, et al. 1989. Foreign direct investment from the newly industrialized economies. Industry and Energy Department, World Bank, Washington, DC, USA. Working Paper Series, No. 22.

WHO (World Health Organization). 1983. Mass catering. WHO Regional Office for Europe, Copenhagen, Denmark.

——— 1985. Future use of new inaging technologies in developing countries. WHO, Geneva, Switzerland. 67 pp.

——— 1986. Health research strategy for health for all by the year 2000. Report of a subcommittee of the Advisory Committee on Health Research, WHO, Geneva, Switzerland. WHO/RPD/ACHR(HRS)/86.

———— 1989a. Health surveillance and management procedures for food-handling personnel: report of a WHO consultation. WHO, Geneva, Switzerland. Technical Report Series, No. 785. 47 pp.
———— 1989b. Safe food handling: a training guide for managers of food service establishments. WHO, Geneva, Switzerland.
———— 1993. Guidelines for cholera control. WHO, Geneva, Switzerland. 61 pp.
———— 1995. The use of essential drugs: model list of essential drugs (eighth list). Sixth report of the WHO Expert Committee. WHO, Geneva, Switzerland. Technical Report Series, No. 850. 138 pp.
WHO (World Health Organization); German Federal Health Office. 1994. Hygiene in mass catering: important rules. WHO, Geneva, Switzerland. Leaflet.
Williams Silveira, M.P., ed. 1985. Research and development: linkages to production in developing countries. Westview, Boulder, CO, USA.
Willoughby, K.W. 1990. Technology choice: a critique of the appropriate technology movement. Westview, Boulder, CO, USA.
Witter, M. 1994. Estimates of poverty in Jamaica: updating the poverty lines. United Nations Development Programme; Public Information Office of Jamaica, Kingston, Jamaica.
World Bank. 1989. Sub-Saharan Africa: from crisis to sustainable growth. World Bank, Washington, DC, USA.
———— 1990. World development report, 1990. World Bank, Washington, DC, USA. 260 pp.
———— 1992a. Development: the governance dimension. World Bank, Washington, DC, USA.
———— 1992b. World development report, 1992: environment and development. World Bank, Washington, DC, USA.
———— 1993a. Implementing the World Bank's strategy to reduce poverty: progress and challenges. World Bank, Washington, DC, USA.
———— 1993b. World development report, 1993: investing in health. Oxford University Press, Oxford, UK
———— 1994a. Jamaica: a strategy for growth and poverty reduction. World Bank, Washington, DC, USA. Country Economic Memorandum.
———— 1994b. World development report 1994: infrastructure for development. Oxford University Press, Oxford, UK.
WRI (World Resources Institute). 1992. World resources 1992–1993: a guide to the global environment, toward sustainable development. Oxford University Press, Oxford, UK.
———— 1993. World Resources Institute at a glance, 1993. Oxford University Press, Oxford, UK.
———— 1994. World resources 1994–95: guide to the global environment. Oxford University Press, Oxford, UK.

Wriston, W.B. 1992. The twilight of sovereignty. Charles Scribner & Sons, New York, NY, USA.

Yampolsky, S.L. 1994. Main directions to preserve and to develop the internal scientific and technological potential in Ukraine: vocational training in Ukraine. United Nations Conference on Trade and Development, Geneva, Switzerland. TECH/BASE/12. 6 pp.

Yiemene, G. 1994. Science and technology policy initiatives to address the basic needs of low income populations in Ethiopia. United Nations Conference on Trade and Development, Geneva, Switzerland. TECH/BASE/13. 20 pp.

Yost, R.; Itoga, S.; Li, Z.-Ch.; Colfer, C.; Amien, L.I.; Kilham, P.; Hanson, J. 1992. Expert systems for information transfer about soil and crop management in developing countries. In Mann, C.K.; Ruth, S.R., ed., Expert systems in developing countries: practice and promise. Westview, Boulder, CO, USA. pp. 115–126.